Second Edition

Family Ties & Aging

For my family and, especially, for Craig

The power of true, selfless, understanding, unconditional, and forgiving love can keep us whole and bind us together. To both give and receive such love is to experience the fullness of life.

—*CLB*

Second Edition

Family Ties & Aging

Ingrid Arnet Connidis

Department of Sociology, University of Western Ontario, Canada

PINE FORGE PRESS
An Imprint of SAGE Publications, Inc.
Los Angeles • London • New Delhi • Singapore

For information:

Pine Forge Press
An Imprint of SAGE Publications, Inc.
2455 Teller Road
Thousand Oaks, California 91320
E-mail: order@sagepub.com

SAGE Publications Ltd.
1 Oliver's Yard
55 City Road
London EC1Y 1SP
United Kingdom

SAGE Publications India Pvt. Ltd.
B 1/I 1 Mohan Cooperative
  Industrial Area
Mathura Road, New Delhi 110 044
India

SAGE Publications Asia-Pacific Pte. Ltd.
33 Pekin Street #02–01
Far East Square
Singapore 048763

Printed in the United States of America

Library of Congress Cataloging-in-Publication Data

Connidis, Ingrid Arnet, 1951-
Family ties and aging / Ingrid Arnet Connidis.—2nd ed.
      p. cm.
Includes bibliographical references and index.
ISBN 978-1-4129-5957-5 (pbk.)
    1. Older people—Family relationships—Canada. I. Title.

HQ1064.C38C66 2009
306.87084'6—dc22   2008036351

This book is printed on acid-free paper.

09   10   11   12   13   10 9 8 7 6 5 4 3 2 1

Associate Editor:	Deya Saoud
Editorial Assistant:	Nancy Scrofano
Production Editor:	Kristen Gibson
Copy Editor:	Marilyn Power Scott
Typesetter:	C&M Digitals (P) Ltd.
Proofreader:	Ellen Brink
Indexer:	Kathy Paparchontis
Cover Artist:	Ingrid Arnet Connidis
Cover Photographer:	Bob McFee
Cover Designer:	Candice Harman
Marketing Manager:	Jennifer Reed Bandando

Contents

Preface

When I read a book, I like to know something about the author, including how to pronounce his or her name if there is some doubt. "Ingrid" does not pose a problem but, over the years, I have heard many variations on "Connidis." To paraphrase some lyrics from the Gershwin brothers' song, "Let's Call the Whole Thing Off," "I say Con-NEE-dis."

One of the nice developments in scholarly writing over the past few years is openly recognizing the influence of an author's experience on his or her approach to a given subject. Although one may presume that a book such as this one has limited latitude for individual expression and bias, there is still room enough for authors to take quite different approaches—in the topics they choose to include, in the interpretation they give to mixed findings, and in the way they extend current knowledge to commentary about future directions and social action. So I offer some words about myself to allow you to judge how my experience might slant my views of family ties in middle and later life.

Although I am somewhat surprised by how resilient my views about aging and family relationships have been, there is no doubt that increasing age (I am now 57) and accumulated experience have shifted my standpoint. I am the oldest of seven children, five girls and two boys, as we still think of ourselves, even though it is some time since we could accurately be described as girls or boys. My parents are now in their 80s and grew up in other countries before coming to Canada. I am married to a very funny, intelligent, caring and talented man and, as I write, Craig and I have just had our first year of a mostly empty nest. We have four incredible children who span two generations. Our two older sons, Michael and Patrick, have expanded our lives with their families, our daughters-in-law, Nina and Nikki, and our grandchildren, Jackson and Troy, Duncan and Haley. Our son, Kai, is now a university graduate and living abroad, and our daughter, Nora, is in her second year of university. We have had a daughter, little Kari, die, an experience that stands as an enduring bond between us and a reminder of how valuable close family ties can be.

I have been fortunate by many standards to have such a strong family circle, and this may make me unduly positive about the possibilities of family ties. But if so, it is not because my family is a traditional one. The combined experiences of my extended family include single life, straight and gay partnerships, marriage, divorce, remarriage, having children and being childfree, step ties, being grandparents and great-grandparents, responding to special needs, dual-career couples, stay-at-home mothers and fathers, mutual caring in the face of illness, the loss of family members, and the addition of new ones. One benefit of a large family is the opportunity to have one's horizons and empathy expanded by close-at-hand experiences that are far more diverse than most of us can squeeze into our own lifetimes.

Professionally, I am a sociologist, and this leads me to focus more on the social than the psychological aspects of family ties and aging. When I trained as a sociologist, I took one course in the family that I didn't like very much. A product of its time, the course focused heavily on courtship and marriage. I didn't take a course on aging—there weren't any. Instead, my efforts as a graduate student concentrated on deviance and criminology, not the standard beginning to a career in aging or family. But I think it was a useful one, sensitizing me early to the atypical and how much it teaches us about all social life, raising fundamental questions about how we come to see some situations, actions, lifestyles, and people as ideal and others not, and how we define possibilities for various social groups on this basis. Realities and expectations about family life range widely due to gender, class, race, sexual orientation, and age. A fundamental challenge to exploring family ties and aging is to peel away assumptions about family life and to expose them as social creations, opening the door to many possible and equally acceptable ways for families to be created and recreated.

When I wrote the first edition of *Family Ties & Aging,* I noted that my purpose was to weave together the vast range of information we now have about the many facets of family relationships and aging into a critical, comprehensive and integrated whole. Since the first edition, research and theory in some areas has matured and expanded, making the challenge even greater to pull it together and to fairly represent the efforts of so many. Yet as I note at various points in the book, there are still areas where we need to know more in order to better understand the lives of real people in families. The intended audience for this book is all of those interested in the topic but particularly those who are learning more about family ties and aging as part of their education, research, or policy planning.

Chapter 1 provides a detailed overview of the book's approach and an expanded discussion of my theoretical orientation to studying family ties and aging. Throughout the book, I have also extended my previous coverage of groups and relationships that typically receive short shrift in commentaries about family life, to the extent that current research allows. I consider the ties of older persons to a partner (spouse or live-in, gay or straight), children, grandchildren, and siblings. Along the way, I explore the unique family situations of those who are single, childfree, divorced, and widowed and the implications of transitions such as divorce for other family relationships. Expanded discussions of sexuality, and alternatives for intimacy and intimate relationships, are included in this edition. Diversity in experience stemming from age, gender, sexual orientation, class, race and ethnicity is addressed in relation to each topic. In the final chapter, I discuss research and policy issues. How can our research be improved and how does it relate to social policy? What are the implications of social trends and globalization for aging and families? In this edition, I use the issue of elder mistreatment to demonstrate the links between concepts, research, practice and policy.

I hope that you read this book with questions in mind. May the book provide good answers to many of them, and may your unanswered questions be the ones that lead us to a better understanding of family ties and aging.

Acknowledgments

A second edition can only begin with thanks to those who used the first edition of *Family Ties & Aging*. My thanks also to the reviewers for your commentary on my proposal and some of the chapters for this edition; I appreciate your positive response and your helpful suggestions. The reviewers are: Lorraine T. Dorfman, University of Iowa, Cynthia Rife Hancock, University of North Carolina at Charlotte, Mary Hart, California University of Pennsylvania, Marilyn Helterline, SUNY College at Oneonta, Deborah Merrill, Clark University, Margaret M. Manoogian, Ohio University, Jean Pearson Scott, Texas Tech University, and Steve Wages, Abilene Christian University. Thanks also to my students for their feedback on the first edition. Deya Saoud at SAGE/Pine Forge Press has been a pleasure to work with as I made more extensive revisions than anticipated. Thank you very much for your patient support. My underestimation was thanks in part to the impressive maturation and expansion of theoretical approaches and research publications in the areas of aging and family. I am grateful to such an active community of researchers for their stimulating work. My thanks also to the copyediting skills of Marilyn Power Scott, once again a pleasure to work with, and to Kristen Gibson for overseeing the production of this edition.

My sincere thanks to Catherine Gordon; her assistance in collecting information and compiling available data on family ties was critical and so pleasantly and well done. Thank you to those from whom I have learned in my various research projects and whose words make ideas come alive. For financial support of those studies, thanks to the Social Sciences and Humanities Research Council of Canada and to the Ontario Mental Health Foundation.

I am fortunate to have a network of friends and colleagues who provide invaluable support and insight. My most sincere thanks to Lorraine Davies, Alexis Walker, Sarah Matthews, Julie McMullin, Anne Martin-Matthews, and Carolyn Rosenthal for their interest, concern and encouragement. A special note of deeply felt thanks to Donna Andreychuk for her warm friendship, her sense of perspective, and for continuing and deepening the camaraderie that began with Fred Harrison and the Tuesday Night Art Group.

And to my family, thank you for being the inspiring and dynamic people that you are. To my brother Michael and his partner Roy, special thanks for another nurturing stay with you. To my sister, Kristine, heartfelt thanks for your wisdom, thoughtfulness and understanding in our near nightly e-mail exchanges. To my older children, Michael and Patrick, thank you for being such steady and loving forces in my life and for bringing to our lives Nina and Nikki and our amazing grandchildren. To my younger children, Kai and Nora, thank you for being such bright light touchstones about what really matters and for your caring concern. And most of all, to my husband, Craig Boydell, there are not words strong enough; thank you for everything. I learn from you, I lean on you, I laugh with you, I love you. With your support, I can now leave my station.

PART I

Introduction and Overview

CHAPTER 1

Older Persons in a Family Context

My family has always been an essential part of my life, but the older you get, the more you feel . . . how much you need each other. As long as you are together, it is like a tree growing. . . . The longer the tree is there, the stronger the branches become and the more you are knit into one. So, the more you are together, the more you realize how important it is to be together and stay together.

—66-year-old married father of two

All of us share the experience of being family members and, whatever the nature of that experience, it is likely to be profound. For some, family life may be the idyllic safe haven from a heartless world; for others, early family traumas may set the stage for a lifetime of surviving harsh circumstances at the hands of loved ones. For most of us, family life falls somewhere between these two extremes. Although our focus in this book is the family lives of older persons, we must bear in mind that they have a history that goes back to childhood. Family ties in old age are the culmination of a lifetime of decisions made, roads taken and not taken, and changing times and social worlds.

Because older persons' family ties involve individuals from several generations, we look beyond the particular experiences and situations of older persons, to consider also how the lives of younger persons affect family relationships in older age. As a convention, older persons are considered to be aged 60 to 65 years or older, reflecting common practices of entitlement, such as pension and security benefits. We need not be quite that precise here, recognizing that family relationships may follow different trajectories depending on such facts as age at first marriage or birth of first child and upon variable social circumstances. For convenience, we shall assume that we are generally speaking of people aged 60 or more when we talk about older persons, realizing that there are substantial variations within this age group.

Families and Family Ties

Who do you think of as your family? Who considers you part of their family? Are there any older persons in your family? If so, who is in their family? When we think of families, we tend to concentrate on the nuclear family, that is, parents and their children living together in one home. Depending on our stage of life, this may refer to the family of orientation, comprising parents and siblings, or the family of procreation, consisting of spouse and children. Over time, the nuclear family model has become less applicable as more families break the traditional pattern through cohabitation, divorce, single parenthood, opting not to have children, and remarriage, for example. This model also downplays the significance of the single (never married) and the childless in family networks and minimizes the family relationships of those past the child-rearing stage—the middle-aged and elderly. As well, emphasis on the nuclear unit implicitly treats other arrangements as problematic or undesirable. Yet diverse familial arrangements reflect fundamental forms of diversity in society. Moreover, the non-nuclear family households that are common in later life are usually the outcome of expected life course transitions by family members, such as young adult children leaving home.

Because the life experiences of any age group are so closely tied to family life, examining the family ties of older individuals can improve our general understanding of later life. In this book, the focus is on familial relationships in older age rather than later-life families. This emphasis avoids some of the pitfalls of attempts to define a later-life family. For example, childless couples are often excluded from definitions that focus on the age and stage of children to define the family of later life. Trying to alleviate this problem by selecting a chronological age as the time when such couples become later-life families still excludes the never married. Yet both those who are childless and those who are single are active participants in family life as children, nieces, nephews, siblings, aunts, uncles and cousins. Our focus on family ties and aging emphasizes the fact that nearly all older persons remain family members and that the process of aging is associated with transitions in family relationships.

Definitions of family have both substantive and practical implications. At the substantive level is the need to recognize diversity by going beyond the nuclear family and beyond the household to include nonresident kin and those who are considered family by virtue of assumed obligations and the support that is extended and received (Scanzoni & Marsiglio, 1993). Practical implications may be most acutely felt when the state adopts definitions of family that either include or exclude particular individuals as family. Such applications can result in forcing someone to rely on an unreliable family member because he or she qualifies as the "closest" tie (legally or biologically) or having someone miss the opportunity for support from someone who acts as family but is not defined officially as family (e.g., a gay partner; Bould, 1993). Those with few "real" family members often consider their closest friends as family, a tie termed *fictive kin* by some (MacRae, 1992).

An essential fact about the family is that it does not take one fixed form (Cheal, 1993). Continuity is a central element of relationships in later life. Most relationships in older age are continuations of those begun earlier in life, and their nature is shaped by past patterns. Poor relationships will probably not become good ones simply because one reaches old age, and good ones are likely to remain that way. However, change also occurs. Some long-term relationships are lost, primarily through death, whereas others are gained, most notably through birth (grandchildren, great-grandchildren) and remarriage. Change in the nature of past relationships may also occur in response to other changes associated with aging. Widowhood may lead to a reorganization of family ties and more time spent with other family members. Retirement may alter the marital relationship, and health declines may lead to shifts in helping patterns and dependency. Change in the lives of other family members may also have profound effects. A child's divorce, for example, may alter dramatically the relationship between a grandmother and her grandchildren. Thus family life in older age is dynamic and involves both continuity and change.

The Place of Older People in Families of the Past and Present

Myths About the Past

Several myths about family life persist despite numerous studies over the years that do not support them (Haber, 2006; Hareven, 1991, 1996; Nett, 1993; Shanas, 1979). One predominant myth is that today's elderly are neglected or abandoned by their families, especially their children. The Golden Age myth assumes a better past for older people, based on assuming that three-generation households were typical in times gone by, that they signify better family relationships, and that the respect accorded older persons in the past can be equated with affection (Nydegger, 1983). What does historical research find? Earlier historical work showed that, contrary to popular belief, the typical 19th-century family household throughout the Western world, including the United States, Canada and Europe, was nuclear, with one generation of parents and their children (Darroch & Ornstein, 1984; Hareven, 1996; Nett, 1993). Much higher mortality rates and lower life expectancy across the life course made multiple generations living together a rarity. As young countries founded in their current form by immigrants, both the United States and Canada were even less likely to have multiple generations nearby. Thus only recently have multigenerational households in large numbers become a possibility.

More recent historical analysis shows the risk of over generalizing about the past as well as the present, a common outcome when the male middle-class experience is taken to represent all old people (Haber, 2006). Gender, class and fluctuating economic conditions are all tied to variations in living arrangements over time, including the prospect of co-residence. In days past, old men could remain head of the household until they died; old women often could not (Haber, 2006). Old women had a harder time than old men in maintaining their property and independent living if their spouses died. Thus the pattern of nuclear households was more common among old men than old women, as many old women had to find creative alternatives following the death of their husbands, including living with adult kin or moving into the city where they could run boarding homes.

Many have argued that a major reason for the shift toward living alone in old age has been the improved financial situation of older persons. However, research using U.S. census data indicates that, in the late 19th and early 20th centuries, co-residence was more likely among those with higher incomes, leading to the conclusion that "rising incomes cannot explain the decline of co-residence" (Ruggles, 1996:255). This association is consistent with two patterns of earlier times: older parents' power through land and property ownership and the common placement of impoverished older persons into poor houses, the only institutional alternative available to those families who could not afford to support an older parent. Again, further historical work shows varied experiences among old people in response to improved economic conditions. As income rose in the early 1900s, the middle-class pattern of having old family members live with their adult children shifted to independent living but only among those whose new wealth moved them out of the middle class (Haber, 2006). For those who moved from the working to middle class, a shift to co-residence with older family members was a marker of improved socioeconomic status. Thus improved economic conditions interacted with both class and gender to create different outcomes among old family members.

As well, then as now, co-residence of older parents and their children typically followed a lengthy period of independent living in nuclear households by both generations, rather than the continuation of three-generation households as a dominant family form (Hareven, 1996). When they did occur, three-generation households were a function either of inheritance laws and older parents' power through control over land or parents' dependence on their children after loss of a spouse. For example, in 1871, three-generation Canadian households were usually formed by a widowed parent moving in with a child and his or her family. When a child lived with older parents, it was more often sons than daughters who did so, "as one would expect in a society where control of property was largely vested in the male line" (Darroch & Ornstein, 1984:164). In New England, among parents whose children were born from 1920 to 1929, the typical pattern was close proximity to at least one child, with co-residence an outcome of a parent's widowhood and only after repeated attempts to assist the widowed parent's independent living (Hareven & Adams, 1996). The youngest daughter was most likely to care for an older parent.

Did taking an older parent into the home signal closer ties between an older parent and his or her (but usually her) children? No. At the turn of the century, publicly funded assistance for older people was either nonexistent or extremely limited, making three-generation households in many ways a forced choice for those elderly who could no longer function alone. Although living with children in old age might have been more probable, it did not necessarily reflect a happier or more desirable situation. Indeed, "All the children . . . who had taken care of aging parents in their own homes expressed a strong desire never to have to depend on their own children in their own old age. They considered living with their children the greatest obstacle to maintaining their independence" (Hareven & Adams, 1996:283). Current co-residence of parents and their adult children is discussed in Chapter 8.

Rising incomes over time have had the greatest impact on the poor elderly who now qualify for state-funded pensions and support. In both Norway and Sweden, as examples, declines in informal care and increases in formal support are due largely to the availability of state-supported alternatives, not the demise of the family (Daatland, 1990; Tedebrand, 1996). Similarly, solitary living among older persons is related to income; higher incomes among today's older persons account for more of them living alone, and among older persons, greater income increases the chances of solitary living (Kinsella, 1995; Wolf, 1990). Even widowed home-makers enjoy greater financial security than past generations, largely due to receiving publicly funded support (Gratton & Haber, 1993; Kinsella, 1995).

Although the elderly in times gone by appear to have received greater respect from younger family members and the community at large, such respect was based on economic power rather than either age itself or being more loved than the elderly of today (Nydegger, 1983). Indeed, when accumulated power among the elderly does occur, the result is typically intergenerational conflict and competition, not improved familial relations. The debate over intergenerational equity (see Chapter 14) in which the old are portrayed as getting too much from the government at the expense of the young is a current example of the price the old pay when they improve their economic situation. Attempts to find evidence of a "Golden Isle," a place in the world where the old are revered, also lead to the general conclusion that age alone is rarely a basis for preferred status in any culture (Nydegger, 1983).

Realities of the Present

Of course, discounting the assumptions that comprise the myth of a Golden Age does not establish that families of today provide better relationships or support for older adults. Nonetheless, the family has clearly not deserted its older members and continues to provide extensive support (Brubaker, 1990; Finch & Mason, 1993; Johnson, 1995; Wellman, 1990, 1992). The network of contact and exchange among nuclear households has resulted in the characterization of today's family as *modified extended* (Shanas, 1979). Family ties beyond the nuclear family household operate on a principle of revocable detachment wherein "dormant emotional ties can be mobilized when they are needed or desired" (George, 1980:79). Thus although the extended family does not typically live together, multiple generations are available to one another when needed, as Photo 1.1 reflects. The history of immigration and greater life expectancy means that there are now more families than ever with multiple generations in the United States and Canada.

Photo 1.1   Increased longevity means that more of today's older people are living to see their great-grandchildren.

Living longer also means lengthening the amount of time spent in particular familial relationships for today's old. Marriage and other intimate ties, relationships between parents and their children, between grandparents and grandchildren, and between siblings may all last longer. Parents can expect to know their children into their middle age, and increasing numbers of grandparents are living to see their grandchildren reach adulthood and become parents. When combined with less restrictive definitions of what constitutes family membership, living longer makes family relations more complex and could actually widen the net of family carers, despite times of lower fertility. These trends can only continue, however, if similar timing of key life transitions, such as age at marriage or birth of first child, continues over time. Last, speedier methods of communication (telephone, e-mail, instant messaging) and travel (car, air) enhance the opportunity for contact among family members. Overall, the near-universal provision of family care and support for older members in different cultures and historical periods indicates greater continuity than change in the responsibility family members assume for their elders.

The potential for conflict in families may be greater today, not because there is less love shared or because older family members are neglected, but rather because the demands and expectations on families "as a source of personal identity and satisfaction in life" (Laslett, 1978:478) are greater. These demands on family life often exceed the family's ability to meet them, creating a potential source of guilt and conflict. Contrary to popular belief, then, the importance of family has in some ways heightened, not diminished, but this creates additional strains within families. Regarding marriage, for example, Gillis (1996:151) argues that the increased expectations of marriage in which "the perfect couple now must be everything to one another—good providers, super sexual partners, best friends, stimulating companions" combine with longer life expectancies to make sustaining romance over the course of a marriage very difficult.

Conflict can be expected in other family ties, too. For example, the fact that parents and children share adulthood may increase the likelihood of counter opinions as older children behave more like peers than like children. At the same time, the greater likelihood of sharing more of life's transitions may enhance empathy between the generations. These possibilities underline the importance of exploring the *qualitative* aspects of older people's familial relationships and the need to consider the negative aspects of family life that may occur because of structural strains in the kinship system and in society. The coexistence of both positive and negative sentiments and the competing demands of familial relationships may be the basis for ambivalent inter- and intra-generational ties (Connidis & McMullin, 2002b; Lüscher & Pillemer, 1998; see Chapter 7).

Assessing Family Ties

Despite the fairly long-standing rejection of a Golden Age for families, the current hold of the family values debate illustrates just how attractive a myth this is. One can only speak meaningfully of the family's decline by assuming that there were better times. There is no question that both the ideals of family life and family life itself have *changed* over time (Gillis, 1996; Snell, 1996), but the monolithic treatment of "the family" as an institution in decline makes several questionable assumptions. First is the assumption that change signals decline. After dispelling the myth of idyllic family relations in the past, Snell (1996:4) concludes that "for both women and men in the past, old age was often a difficult time" but, he emphasizes, "this is not to argue that the nature of aging and of being old has not changed." Change is often discomfiting, leading us to favor old ways of doing things. This tendency raises the challenge to first identify the real ways in which family life has changed and then examine the consequences of any observed changes for *various family members*. As Atchley and Lawton (1997:187) observe about age-related deficits, "negative changes do not necessarily have negative consequences." More generally, changes in family life may reflect the resilience of this social institution rather than its decline (Amato, 2005).

The tendency to focus on the negative consequences of change is part of a larger phenomenon of looking at family life in relative terms. For example, when proposing that individuals should be considered active agents in their own destiny, Scanzoni and Marsiglio (1993:109) promote the view of family members as "persons struggling to create *better* lives for themselves and their families (italics added)." Although the general argument is sound, why better lives? Better than what? This orientation fits a dominant economic view of progress that rests on ongoing economic growth, but in terms of intergenerational comparisons, one should consider variations in the relative starting point of a previous generation's experience. One can understand the hope of parents during the Depression that their children's future would be brighter. But what of the generation that followed the post-World-War II economic boom of the 1950s? Is outstripping the prosperity of that generation necessary to establish that the subsequent generation has also had a good life? Most of us are not necessarily striving to shape our lives, including our ties with family members, in such relative terms. Instead, we might more accurately be said to be striving to create lives that we consider desirable, acceptable, satisfactory, good or fulfilling. Moving away from implicit relative treatments of family life can help us avoid some of the ideological pitfalls of many writings on family ties, including those on older persons.

A second problematic assumption embedded in much research on the family is that all members of a family share uniform experiences of family membership. Thus the impact of change is assessed in relation to "the family" rather than from the point of view of different family members. For example, rising divorce rates are often equated with familial decline. But does divorce have the same impact on all family members (husbands, wives, children, parents, grandparents, grandchildren)? The apparent success of marriage in earlier days, measured in terms of duration, often came at the expense of both the happiness and welfare of particular family members. Women were often financially dependent on their spouses and could not leave their marriages, either legally or practically, even in the face of harsh circumstances, such as being the victims of abusive partners. Did children in such marriages necessarily benefit from the lasting union of their parents? Another example is the questionable assumption that family members of a given generation have uniform experiences of social mobility. There may be considerable variation within a family regarding their socioeconomic circumstances relative to other members of the same generation and to the previous generation (see Chapter 12). Once again, comparisons across time require us to consider the impact of both continuity and change from the vantage point of different family members.

Views of the place of older persons in families have followed ironic twists and turns that correspond to general concerns regarding family life in North America. During the 1970s and early 1980s, serious attention was paid to the predominantly negative view of old age, including the portrayal of older family members as drains on family resources. Embedded in this concern was an empathetic stance toward meeting the needs of older persons, both within families and through social policy. This negative stereotype gave way to an equally inaccurate positive stereotype that focused on the virtues of old age, placing heavy emphasis on independence and the possibility of remaining youthful. Despite the good intentions of assuming that a more positive view would be the basis for greater inclusion of the older population, we find ourselves in a new century dealing with debates on intergenerational equity. In these debates, we see a return to a negative view of older persons as a serious drain on resources (see e.g., Guillemette, 2003; Jackson & Howe, 2003), "greedy geezers" who take far more than their share of the public purse at the expense of younger generations, particularly children (see Chapter 14). But this view can only be sustained by ignoring family dynamics and the significant contributions made by older persons to the younger generations of their families over a lifetime (Estes et al., 2003; Gee, 2000; Stone, 1998). At the same time, postmodern views of old age as a time of endless possibilities (Estes et al., 2003; Katz, 2005) reignite the positive stereotype of old age and minimize the inequality that results from current social arrangements. We have in a sense come full circle, with a competing focus on the positive and negative views of old age. Looking at aging in the context of family ties helps redress major inaccuracies in the broader public debate concerning an aging population, the place of older persons in social life, and related social policy.

Underlying Assumptions

This book does not aim to provide exhaustive coverage of theoretical developments about the family or about aging. I do make several underlying assumptions, however, and I favor some theoretical concepts and perspectives that frame my approach to family ties in later life. In this section, I will specify some starting assumptions, and then discuss my preferred theoretical approach. Concepts and theoretical frameworks that focus on specific elements of family life (e.g., caregiving) are addressed in the relevant subsequent chapters.

First, understanding the family ties of older persons requires examining relationships as entities in their own right. Family ties are not captured fully in an institutional arrangement referred to as *the family* or in statistical entities referred to as *households*. Most older persons do not live with most of their family members. The relationships that constitute family life have at least two points of view that may not be in complete accord. Thus one must strive for balance in understanding relationships between an older person and other family members by considering multiple vantage points. No party in a relationship only gives or only receives, although the contributions of the two at a given point in time may be imbalanced. Thus the issue of support is considered from the perspective of the givers and of the receivers, emphasizing the fact that older persons serve as both, operating within a system of family relationships (see Chapter 8). The broader context of a family network or system in which relationships are embedded is influenced in turn by a society's structural arrangements. Our society's tendency to organize family life on the basis of gender, for example, provides a fundamental parameter for family ties. Such parameters can be one basis for conflicting interests among family members and must be negotiated by the players involved.

Second, family membership should be defined broadly and not restricted to a traditional notion of what constitutes family. Although writing about a broad range of relationships is often made difficult by limited information on particular familial arrangements, it must nevertheless remain the goal. One can distinguish between formal and social families (Scanzoni & Marsiglio, 1993) to capture the difference between a narrow and broad view of family membership. Formal families are defined by such criteria as having a blood (biological parents and children) or legal (marriage, adoption) tie. This excludes many who develop social families that either cannot be formalized (e.g., marital unions between same-sex partners in most of the U.S.) or are not considered "real" family (e.g., friends who act as family in the eyes of the involved parties).

Defining families broadly also means a more inclusive treatment of family membership. In a typical family textbook, family life follows a trajectory starting with childhood, moving into early and middle adulthood, and, in some books, ending with old age. Along the way, certain groups tend to be dropped from the discussion. For instance, once the topic of marriage comes up, those who never marry tend to disappear, and once the subject of family formation arises, the childless are no longer part of the discussion. Yet those who remain single or do not have children, by choice or circumstance, remain family members. They may have active ties with parents, siblings, aunts or uncles, nieces or nephews, grandparents and so on. Looking at families broadly and in terms of relationships rather than as fixed groups enhances the likelihood of inclusiveness in the examination of family life. How we define families is critical to developing good theories about family relationships and their connection to social processes (Cheal, 2005).

Third, the patterns and arrangements of social life, what is commonly termed *social structure,* both encourage and constrain individual action, but they do not completely determine what individuals do. The fact that individuals in very similar circumstances can and do act in very different ways attests to the importance of individual agency, the ability to act on one's own behalf. At the same time, our position within the social structure will influence how much this is possible. A key challenge to appreciating how family relationships actually work is to understand their connection to the bigger social picture. Although none of us mindlessly follows a prescribed set of norms, none of us completely creates family life just as we would choose to have it. Instead, we work within the pressures exerted by social structure to negotiate as best we can what we consider to be a desirable family life. Key bases of social organization include gender, class, race and ethnicity, age, and sexual orientation (Arber et al., 2003; Calasanti & Slevin, 2001; Ginn & Arber, 1995; McMullin, 2004). Our negotiations of family life are influenced by our place in current structural arrangements, and the families of which we are a part will reflect the diversity that these structural arrangements create (Calasanti, 1996; Calasanti & Zajicek, 1993). To the extent that these change, we can expect that the nature of negotiating family ties will also change.

Fourth, the negotiation of family relationships takes place in the context of social structural arrangements that are imbued with cultural views of an ideal family and an ideal old age. Thus the meanings of family and of old age at both the cultural and individual levels are important facets of understanding how ties are both negotiated and evaluated by family members and by others of various ages (see Marshall et al., 1993). The ideals of family life (Gillis, 1996) and of a successful old age (Katz, 2005) may not be realized in practice, but they are typically the benchmark by which family life and aging are judged. Cultural ideals about family life and about aging change with time and intersect with each other. Shifts in the social desirability of old age as a time of relative dependency and disengagement or as a time of efforts to stay active and productive coincide with changing views about the place of older persons in families and of responsibilities toward older persons by younger family members and by society.

With these as my starting assumptions, there are a number of theoretical concepts and perspectives that are especially well suited to studying family ties and aging.

Theoretical Orientation

One of my favorite definitions of theoretical frameworks describes them as "ways of naming, ways of conceptually ordering our senses of the world. They are tools with which we decide what it is that we experience, why something is the way it is, and how it is that we might act or react to it" (Pfohl, 1985:9). In very few words, theory is aligned with the what, why, and how of social life and with ways of understanding and of acting on that understanding. Theory and practice are brought together rather than isolated as separate enterprises. In this section I outline my general theoretical orientation to family ties and aging. Other concepts and theoretical approaches that deal with specific aspects of aging and of family life can be incorporated within this perspective but reviewing all of them here is beyond the scope of this chapter.

Family life and aging enjoy long-standing public and policy interest. Although this has aided research in these areas, it has perhaps hindered theoretical development, as funding agencies have sought information (data) to meet immediate needs for building knowledge and developing policy. Discussions of theory suggest that the area of family has enjoyed more theoretical development than the area of aging (Cohler & Altergott, 1995). Nonetheless, researchers in both areas lament the data-rich and theory-poor character of their respective bodies of work (Bengtson et al., 2005; Estes et al., 2003; George, 1995; Katz, 2005), although such critiques may have a longer history in family studies (Dilworth-Anderson et al., 2005). Some claim convincingly that this critique no longer applies to theoretical development in aging (Bass, 2007), but a challenge to link theoretical thinking to research remains.

An interest in older persons and their family relationships brings into question traditional approaches to family life. Aging research has generated data that fill important gaps in the family literature, particularly concerning family ties that fall outside the nuclear household (Cohler & Altergott, 1995). In turn, family research that includes older persons works against the marginalization that occurs when the old are isolated for separate study. As well, researchers in the aging field can bring fresh insight to theoretical thinking about the family and vice versa. Thus there are benefits to bringing the two areas together and building on their respective strengths.

Being an outsider to a field frees the observer from the weight of history within a particular specialty; in a sense, one can think theoretically, unfettered by disciplinary or established approaches to the subject (Katz, 2005; Mann et al., 1997). In a more extreme version of this argument, Betty Friedan (2000 quoted in Ray, 2006:32), an influential feminist from the early 1960s, claimed that activists and serious journalists "have made as much or more of a contribution to social theory in America as formal academic social scientists. They aren't hampered by the old assumptions built into the jargon. They can cut to the cutting edge." Whoever the theorist—academic, activist, or journalist—research that is conducted on issues specific to either families, aging or their juxtaposition can inform broader theories of social life by addressing family and aging *processes* that can be applied to other social contexts (Turner, 2005).

There is some debate about whether theoretical approaches in family sociology have become more diverse and critical (Cheal, 1991) or whether they continue to be grounded in the functionalist perspective and its focus on stability and the maintenance of the status quo (Mann et al., 1997). Reflecting the influence of functionalist thought in North American sociology, approaches to both family and aging have their equivalents, and in both fields, functionalist approaches have been criticized severely. Of key concern is bias in favor of middle-class life, the importance of maintaining the status quo while ignoring the conflicting interests of different groups within society, the view of the individual as someone who follows norms rather than being an active agent in setting his or her course, and the failure to link societal or macro-level phenomena and individual or micro-level experience. Researchers of aging and of family have moved toward a more critical and interpretive approach to studying how social life works. This trend mitigates specifying or assuming a monolithic ideal family and encourages observing the lived reality of family life. Combining the two areas of family and aging by examining the family ties of older persons also moves us in this direction. But even though particular theories may have lost favor, their ideas often live on in social practice and policy. Thus we must be critical observers of the ideas that are embedded not only in theories but also in social institutional arrangements.

Much of the work in aging and in family research occurs outside the boundaries of particular disciplines—for example, in multidisciplinary units that focus on family studies, aging studies, gerontology and human development. There is some debate about whether this has helped or hurt theoretical development. Absence of a disciplinary home has often meant some lag time between the arrival of new discipline-based theories or perspectives and their application to either aging or family studies. At the same time, freedom from the constraints of discipline-based orthodoxies allows those working in aging, family and their intersection to selectively scavenge useful ideas from a variety of disciplines, regardless of whether they are currently in vogue within those disciplines (Katz, 2005). As well, researchers in aging and in family typically share a desire to consider how their findings and theories apply to policy concerns. Both theory and policy are interpretive enterprises (Estes et al., 2003) that require addressing the why and how of the findings generated by research (Bengtson et al., 2005). Specifying a theoretical perspective provides a crucial context for interpreting the observations that writers make about their fields, including mine about family ties and aging.

Theoretical development is an ongoing quest (Allen, 2005b), particularly in social scientific approaches to family and aging where we are attempting to observe and understand an evolving world of which we are a part. Our places in the structured social relations of age, gender, class, race and ethnicity create unique perspectives on social life and relationships and limit our ability to be value free in our research and in the theories that we create. If we begin with this awareness, we are more likely to be critical about who is and is not included in our theoretical thinking. As Pfohl (1994) argues,

> By directing attention to some things but not others, all theories politically empower (if only temporarily) certain viewpoints over others. . . . [W]e must be vigilant about the ways in which our own social positions both shape and are shaped by what we study. This demands a willingness to continually revise our theoretical viewpoints in accordance with what we learn and unlearn. (p. 9)

A profound example of the degree to which we rely upon conceptual frameworks for interpreting what we see—often unaware that we are doing so—is provided by Oliver Sacks's (1993) account of a man named Virgil, who, having lost his sight in early childhood, regained it 45 years later following surgery. We tend to think of sight as a sense that simply works on its own. Yet Virgil's experience, popularized in the movie, *At First Sight,* serves as a metaphor for the need to incorporate what we learn and unlearn into new viewpoints. When the bandages were removed from Virgil's eyes, he could not make sense of what he was seeing; the shapes and colors were meaningless and chaotic because he had not learned how to see them. Virgil was overwhelmed by the challenge of seeing, in much the same way that we struggle when our ideas or theories about social life are threatened by new ways of seeing (regarding family theories, see Bengtson et al., 2005).

The challenge to appreciate the influence of our own experience while trying to move beyond it draws me to ways of looking at family ties and aging that represent various groups in society, include the full range of family relationships that we negotiate over a lifetime, and relate our individual lives to the institutional settings in which macro-level forces play out in our lives. A framework that can meet these objectives of theoretical thinking requires three interconnected components: a life course perspective, a recursive and interactive multilevel framework, and a critical approach that includes a feminist perspective. Sociological ambivalence is a useful concept for bringing these orientations together in the study of family ties and aging (see Chapter 7). As a sociologist, I view the social arrangements that we take for granted as the way the world is—and sometimes turn into assumptions about the way the world should be—as social constructions; as our creations, we can also change them (Moen & Coltrane, 2005).

A Life Course Perspective

An older person's familial relationships are in substantial measure an outcome of decisions, actions and circumstances in younger years so that later-life relationships represent both continuity and change. Consequently, when striving to understand such issues as reciprocity in family relationships, one should take a long-term view of the exchanges that have occurred rather than focusing on one point in time (usually the present). The life course perspective links the experiences of later life to earlier life stages and of old family members to younger ones. Personal history or biography—a focus of life course research—puts current circumstances into context and improves our understanding of them. For example, research that examines marital history as opposed to current marital status deepens our appreciation for the link between relationships and loneliness (see Chapter 3).

The life course perspective enjoys unusual popularity in the social sciences in a variety of areas, including aging, family and health. Its evolution makes it critical to consider when particular critiques of the approach were launched because iterations of the approach over time have addressed some of them. A significant body of European work on the life course (Heinz, 2001; Marshall & Mueller, 2003) complements the orientation that dominates work in the United States and Canada. This review will focus on the central ideas of the life course perspective.

According to the life course perspective, aging is a biological, psychological and social process, starting at birth and ending at death. During this lifelong process, individuals make decisions and choices about the paths that they will take and are, therefore, active participants in building their biographies, reflecting the assumption of human agency (Elder & Johnson, 2003; Heinz, 2001). Individual experience is shaped by the historical context of variable social, political and economic conditions, creating unique influences for different age groups, an ever-changing milieu in which individual life courses are navigated within the constraints and opportunities of available options. This connection of individual agency with the larger social world is referred to as an *agency within structure* model (Settersten, 2003) and provides an important link between macro and micro levels of analysis in connecting larger social, political and economic forces (macro) and individual experience (micro) over time. A third meso level of analysis captures the social institutions or social spaces in which we live our lives, including the institutionalized arrangements of family lives. It is here that we experience directly the larger social forces of the macro level.

The four T's of the life course perspective are *trajectories, transitions, turning points* and *timing* (Elder & Johnson, 2003). Trajectories can be described as "long-term patterns of stability and change" (George, 2003:672) and refer to the long view of the life course and the sequences of various statuses that are occupied along the way. This includes statuses related to family relationships—for example, child, sibling, partner, aunt, parent and grandparent. There are multiple trajectories or pathways (Settersten, 2003), reflecting the various social domains or institutions (the meso level) in which we are engaged, including education, family and work. At any one time, we therefore occupy multiple statuses (child, parent, sibling, worker), creating a status configuration (Heinz, 2001). The life course can thus be described as a series of status configurations (Heinz, 2001), a succinct definition that captures movement across time in the multiple continuing and changing statuses that we occupy.

Transitions are the points along the life course trajectory when particular changes in situation occur (Elder & Johnson, 2003), for example, children leaving home, becoming a grandparent, and losing or gaining a partner. Transitions in combination with periods of relative stability are the building blocks of the life course trajectory. Turning points are dramatic transitions that mark "a substantial change in direction" (Elder & Johnson, 2003:55), a somewhat vague distinction that may explain the usual focus on transitions. Although the transition of becoming a grandparent or losing a partner would not seem to involve agency on behalf of the new grandparent or recently bereaved spouse, the negotiation of such transitions does involve agency as individuals figure out how to handle their new situations. Thus exercising agency applies to transitions across the life course trajectory, in terms both of paths taken or not taken and of how a particular chosen or imposed transition is negotiated.

In earlier formulations of the life course perspective, change typically emanated from the larger social world, leading to an implicit treatment of individuals as primarily reactive. For example, Elder's (1991) concepts of control cycles and situational imperatives propose a process in which social change prompts individual responses to regain control of a new situation, which can be seen as an adaptation response. The greater emphasis placed on human agency as a fundamental feature of social actors in subsequent work opened the door to considering the combined actions of individuals as a source of social change.

Time is another central concept of the life course perspective. One component of time, historical time, creates varying contexts in which different cohorts negotiate their life courses. Time also applies to expectations about when certain events or transitions should occur (timing) that serve as benchmarks for assessing transitions as on or off time and to the multiple time tables of different life course trajectories (Marshall & Mueller, 2003). For example, there is an age range during which transitions such as leaving home or committing to a partner or having a child or grandchild are expected. Those who follow such pathways at either younger or older ages are off time in relation to those social expectations. However, such expectations may change over time so that now, the typical age of making any of these transitions is older than it was for today's old people. In addition to the timing of transitions, there are cultural ideas about the appropriate sequencing of transitions (the order in which they should occur) and their expected duration (e.g., how long one should spend in school; Settersten & Mayer, 1997). To avoid an unduly normative undertone, these expectations are best thought of as shifting social and cultural constructions that are subject to change rather than as fixed imperatives that must be met in order for society to function (Hatch, 2000), an important distinction in the context of such debates as those over so-called family values.

Two other concepts add vitality to the life course perspective: the principles of life stage and linked lives. According to the life stage principle (Elder & Johnson, 2003; Marshall & Mueller, 2003), the impact of life transitions and events on personal biography is mediated by their timing and sequencing; both the age at which a transition or event is experienced and the place that the transition takes in the order of life course events alter its impact. For example, a shared historical time, such as the Depression or the Viet Nam War, varied in its effects on personal biographies for those who were young adults who had not yet had children when compared with somewhat older adults who were already parents. Consider this observation in relation to the current engagements in Iraq and Afghanistan.

The concept of linked lives emphasizes the interdependence of our lives with others and the reciprocal influences of connected lives (Elder, 1991; Elder & Johnson, 2003; Heinz, 2001), a significant asset when applying the life course perspective to family ties and aging. When the concept of linked lives is combined with our simultaneous engagement in multiple trajectories, the connection between our ties to family and our involvement in other spheres of social life, such as paid work, is highlighted. When considered in a multilevel model, there is also the potential for connecting our interpersonal experiences in families with larger macro-level processes. For example, the social capital of who you know, another form of linked lives, varies according to structured social relations so that some have more powerful connections than others.

In sum, the life course perspective has several strengths as an approach to studying family ties and aging. First, multiple levels of analysis are possible, encouraging the deliberate consideration of how individual experience (micro) is related to the arrangements of various social institutions, including family (meso), that are shaped by the larger social, economic and political forces of a particular historical time (macro). Studying the connections of family ties to aging is advanced by a life course approach because it highlights interdependence among "a changing society, dynamic family systems with complex webs of relationships, and individual life paths" (Hagestad, 2003:135). To the extent that traversing the life course is also placed in the context of age relations, there is a direct connection made between the experiences of individuals in families and their age status. Second, the life course perspective encompasses various facets of social life so that considering simultaneous involvement in family relationships and other social domains, such as work and retirement, is possible. Such links are important considerations when developing social policy. However, as a number of critics have noted, there are limits in the extent to which the life course approach has capitalized on these assets.

The life course perspective's widespread appeal underscores its potential weakness: limited theoretical development regarding how social life works. For example, through which mechanisms are constraints and opportunities produced and for whom? How are they negotiated in everyday life? An impressive number of concepts are explicated, but their connection and the assumptions made about each of them are not always clear. Does the emphasis on a normative life course captured in the concept of being on and off time reflect a functionalist or normative bias? These unanswered questions have led many to conclude that the life course perspective is not an integrated theory per se. Following Merton (1968), Elder himself describes the life course perspective as a theoretical orientation that establishes "a common framework to guide descriptive and explanatory research" (Elder & Johnson, 2003:54). This is not necessarily a problem because life course principles are useful as research guides, as context for interpreting findings, and as components of other theories (George, 2003). Thus, as Settersten (2006:15) suggests, the principles and concepts of the life course perspective are "probably most effectively used in conjunction with other social and behavioral paradigms." This makes it necessary to specify theoretical leanings beyond a preference for taking a life course approach to family ties and aging.

The life course perspective has theoretical roots in early work by Leonard Cain, a sociologist who drew attention to the significance of age status as a significant dimension of power relations (Cain, 2003; Marshall & Mueller, 2003). Cain avoided a static view of the life course by emphasizing process and argued against a deterministic view of identities as wholly shaped by institutional arrangements. I highlight these two points because they continue to haunt formulations of the life course perspective. In the first case, although the life course approach promotes studying historical context and the link between individual lives and the larger political, economic and social environment, it has often faltered in specifying the connection of the structured social relations of age, gender, class, race, ethnicity and sexual orientation to social institutions and to the everyday lives of individuals as they construct their life course. Consequently, the life course perspective has been faulted for focusing too much on the micro level of analysis in studies that concern the actions of individuals and the immediate factors that influence them (Estes et al., 2003; Hagestad & Dannefer, 2001; Marshall & Mueller, 2003).

Ironically, the critique that the life course perspective focuses too heavily on the micro level of analysis is in part due to the current emphasis on human agency (Hagestad & Dannefer, 2001). The irony rests in the fact that assuming human agency on behalf of social actors is key to avoiding an overly deterministic view of individual lives as ruled by social forces and policies. The assumption that all social actors exercise some degree of human agency—the capacity to act on their own behalf—is central to viewing the life course as an individual as well as social project; as individuals, we are active agents in constructing our biographies and family lives. Indeed, the key potential for dynamism in the life course perspective comes from the interplay of human agency on behalf of social actors, our interdependency with others (the concept of linked lives), and the constraints and opportunities created by structured social relations and key economic, political and social forces of a particular time.

A Critical Perspective

There is work on the life course, particularly by European scholars (Marshall & Mueller, 2003) that does consider the significance of the state and other macro-level factors for the construction of individual biographies. For example, Heinz (2001) discusses the need to include the experience of women in life course studies and emphasizes the gendered nature of linked lives that implicates men and women differently in the social domains of family and work. Such questioning of traditional approaches to the life course improves the model, enhancing its potential to link individual experience, institutionalized family relationships, and structured social relations, including those of age. In my view, this is central to formulating better theory and understanding and to developing social policies that combine individual and social responsibility for meeting the needs of various groups in society, including old persons. Such connections between theory and practice and between individual experience and social structure are central to a critical perspective. A critical perspective makes explicit some of the links that are hinted at in the life course approach and draws on the strengths of the modernist focus on social structure and of the postmodernist emphasis on narrative, personal meaning, individual choice and subjectivity (Baars et al., 2006).

A critical perspective combines the view that our social worlds are socially constructed with a reflexive perspective that values the subjective experience of individuals. A critical approach to aging makes explicit the influence of structural inequalities on everyday life *and* the unique interests of old people, including sources of meaning and fulfilment in later life (Estes et al., 2003). Thus at the same time that social arrangements related to age are seen to put old people at a relative disadvantage, older persons are also viewed as active agents in defining and creating their lives. However, because age relations intersect with other structured social relations, such as gender and class, there is substantial variation among old persons, including in their family situations.

The resurging interest in reflexivity is an important element of a critical approach because it is how human agency mediates the impact of social forces (Archer, 2007). Archer defines reflexivity "as a personal property of human subjects, which is prior to, relatively autonomous from and possesses causal efficacy in relation to structural or cultural properties" (15). We are not simply reactive; we take into account what is happening around us, and the actions that we take affect the social and cultural worlds in which we live. Archer argues that our conversations with ourselves "are the way in which we deliberate about ourselves in relation to the social situations that we confront . . . because that is the only way we can know or decide anything" (15). Through these internal conversations, we reflect on the social world and draw conclusions about how we will act in a particular situation. In the case of family life, this might concern a new situation, such as a parent's marriage, or it could involve an ongoing relationship.

A critical perspective connects structured social relations and macro-level forces, such as globalization, with individual action by viewing the institutional situations that we face as socially constructed and by viewing the action that we take as an outcome of a reflexive response to those situations. Our actions, in turn, may fit nicely with established ways of doing things and thereby help to reproduce them, or they may diverge from traditional practice. If enough individuals act in unexpected ways, they can produce change in institutional arrangements and in structured social relations (Katz, 2005). Rather than pitting agency against social structure, a critical perspective merges macro-level forces with social institutions at the meso level and interaction at the micro level in a reciprocal and recursive model (Estes et al., 2003). The interests of the individual are not necessarily represented by the status quo. A final ingredient of a critical perspective is to relate theoretical thinking to praxis in an effort not only to study the lives of older persons and their family relationships but also to facilitate their ability to make desired choices. One goal of this book is to consider whose interests and beliefs are best served by current family and age relations and to ask, how might current arrangements be changed to enhance the lives of older persons and their families?

Links to Other Perspectives

There are clear links between feminist theorizing and praxis and central rubrics of the critical perspective (Estes et al., 2003). "The personal is political" slogan coined by Friedan (1963) in an earlier wave of the feminist movement highlights the connection of everyday life to social structure and processes and of individual to social identities, underscoring the potential for change through individual action (Ray, 2006). The aim to be inclusive emphasizes the costs of marginalization, an experience of both old people and of particular familylike relationships. Variable interests of women and men based on age, class, race, ethnicity and sexuality exemplify the cross-cutting of various social relations and have been a challenge to both feminist theory and the feminist movement. Feminists were among the first to critically assess family life and the structured gender relations that permeate its institutionalized underpinnings. This critical gaze pulls back the façade of socially constructed family life to reveal some of its failings.

In the modernist tradition, feminist gerontology reveals the political and economic arrangements that fail to reward the reproductive labor that has dominated the lives of many older women and left substantial numbers of them with limited resources in old age (Powell, 2006). In the postmodernist tradition, feminist work on the body respects the physical significance of aging and its social and subjective consequences (Powell, 2006). These realities have consequences for negotiating family relationships in later life and are central to issues of intergenerational dependence and support. More recent feminist work on aging goes beyond a focus on women to explore gender relations (Allen & Walker, forthcoming; Arber et al., 2003; Connidis & Walker, forthcoming; Krekula, 2007), an important advance in understanding the multiple vantage points that characterize relationships, including those among family members.

A focus on gender relations extends discussions of inequality by considering the relative advantages and disadvantages of different groups of women and men in various social contexts, including family life. Work on masculinity now includes old men (e.g., Calasanti, 2003) and feminist gerontology's potential to include the experience of both old men and women as central to understanding gender relations is evident in recent writing on various topics including health, family relations, and sexuality and aging (Calasanti, 2004; Calasanti & Slevin, 2001; 2006). A multilevel life course perspective in which socially constructed relations of gender and age are seen to be embedded in social institutions and social interaction treats both gender and age as dimensions of power and provides the additional context of time (Hatch, 2000).

Although often aligned with macro-level theorizing, a critical perspective takes seriously individual-level concerns, including the meaning assigned to aging, personal identities, and their connection to family relations. A critical perspective has a point of view that is compatible with a range of theories that assume an ideology and power relations that favor some over others (e.g., political economy, conflict theory), in which individuals are social actors who negotiate the social world in their relationships with others (e.g., symbolic interactionism), and in which there is concern for emancipating the relatively powerless (e.g., feminist theory).

As we will see, involvement in family relationships is a core source of one's sense of self and place in the world. Age relations and normative views about family structure and about who carries which responsibilities create both opportunities and constraints for different types of family involvement. The emphasis on reflexively interpreting and negotiating social life, including ties to family and to transitions across the life course, is an essential ingredient of a critical perspective. Above all, the critical perspective challenges us to look below the surface, to question the taken for granted, and to ask which and whose ideas and beliefs are being met and to what purpose? These are especially important questions to ask about the fundamental processes of aging and age relations and about the social institution most central to our personal lives—family. In the chapters that follow, consider how these general assumptions and ideas apply to particular family relationships and to the more specific theoretical frameworks that have been designed to understand them.

Dimensions of Family Ties and Plan of the Book

Four dimensions of familial relationships in older age are discussed when we examine intimate ties, intergenerational relationships, and sibling ties in this book. First, the availability of kin is addressed in the next chapter through the presentation of data on the marital status and the number of children, grandchildren and siblings of older persons. Second, the extent of contact and interaction with particular available kin is discussed in the relevant chapter. Third, the quality of specific familial relationships in later life is explored. Fourth, the ties between older family members and various kin are examined as potential avenues for providing, receiving and exchanging support. In the final chapter, I discuss research and policy issues and use elder mistreatment as a case study to demonstrate the link between the questions that we ask, the ways that we answer them, and the implications for social policy.

The focus of this book is the United States and Canada. Although the culture, the structure, and the dynamics of family life of the two countries differ in important ways, in some areas, such as the relationships between adult children and their older parents, similar patterns are evident. Although the emphasis here is on research conducted in the United States and, to a lesser extent, in Canada, work from other countries is also included, providing some comparative context.

The emerging theoretical perspectives on aging and of family ties outlined in this chapter correspond with changes in research approaches. A primary shift is away from methodological turf wars and toward the greater use and acceptance of various research methods designed to study the processes and dynamics of relationships. Different research methodologies provide different views of the world and can be used to complement one another (Acock et al., 2005). Census data provide important baseline information regarding the parameters of family ties in later life. New statistical approaches allow for quantitative analysis that can explore relationships over time. More quantitative work is now related to theoretical frameworks, adding purpose to data collection that goes beyond gathering more facts. And a range of qualitative work is now enhancing our appreciation for multiple voices in families, for the influence of power on the internal dynamics of family life, and for the processes that link family life to the larger social world. The greater emphasis on reflexivity in theoretical thinking is now evident in research practices, including the use of reflexive personal narrative in which researchers analyze their own life stories to provide important insights about families (e.g., Allen, 2007a). The range of research methods used to study family ties and aging is represented in the work that is incorporated into this book.

As well, I refer to published and unpublished work from my own research throughout the book. This includes an early community study that involved interviews with a stratified random sample of 400 residents aged 65 and over (see Connidis, 1989a; Connidis & Davies, 1990). A second more qualitative study involves a convenience sample of 60 sibling dyads or 120 respondents ranging in age from 25 to 89 (see Connidis, 1992). In a third study, 678 persons aged 55 and over were part of a multistage quota sample and were interviewed in their homes (see Connidis & McMullin, 1993).

A fourth project is an intensive qualitative study of 10 three-generation families in which a total of 86 individuals ranging in age from 23 to 90 years participated through self-administered questionnaires and then follow-up personal interviews (see Connidis, 2003a, 2007). A fifth project mimics the fourth one but with the critical difference that at least one adult family member self-identified as gay or lesbian and that person was the initial contact. This study of three-generation families includes 49 individuals from 10 families, including 14 gay or lesbian adults, and respondents ranged in age from 22 to 88 years (see Connidis, 2005). From time to time, personal observations from subjects in these studies make the somewhat lifeless findings of research take on human dimensions. As you read each chapter, I encourage you to consider how your experiences and those of persons to whom you are close compare with the general conclusions drawn from research.

Thinking Ahead

There is now a fairly long-standing North American tradition of addressing the needs of families and of older persons through government policy. As researchers and experts in the area of family ties and aging, there is a responsibility to consider the implications of what we know for social policy. The final chapter of the book focuses on policy implications. As you read each chapter, consider the extent to which intervention by the state can improve conditions for older persons and their families. To aid in this consideration, be aware of the biases that are embedded in our current social arrangements and in your own way of thinking about individual versus social responsibility. To what extent do you think individuals and their immediate families should assume responsibility for their own welfare? And to what extent do you believe there is a social responsibility to ensure a reasonable quality of life for all citizens, including the old? This distinction between individual and social responsibility was made by C. Wright Mills (1959) some time ago, when he distinguished between approaching problems from a private troubles versus public issues perspective.

When we take a private troubles approach, we assume that individuals and those close to them should take care of themselves; when we take a public issues approach, we assume that there is some social responsibility for both creating and solving the challenges that citizens face. As we shall see, for many of the issues concerning family ties and aging, there are elements of both individual and social responsibility. The challenge is to find a balance between the two that recognizes the power of and limits to both individual and social action in creating a social world that benefits all citizens.

CHAPTER 2

The Availability of Family Ties in Later Life

Demographic Trends and Family Structure

In Chapter 1, I noted that structured social relations at the macro level, that is, our position in society due to our gender, age, class, race, ethnicity and sexual orientation, shape our personal experience. The structural features of families at the meso level of social institutions also create variable circumstances for individuals to negotiate in their relationships with one another. This chapter focuses on the demographic trends that shape family structure in terms of family size; the composition of a family, a generation, or a family subgroup, such as siblings, based on its members' combined attributes (e.g., gender, age and marital status); the number of surviving generations (the vertical dimension); and the size of each generation (the horizontal dimension; Dilworth-Anderson et al., 2005; Hagestad, 2003). The vertical dimension reflects the pattern of relative age differences between succeeding generations. In an age-condensed structure, one generation after the next has children at a young age, and the family is more vertical (more generations alive at the same time). In an age-gapped structure, one generation after the next has children at a relatively old age, resulting in fewer surviving generations. Family size—the horizontal dimension—reflects the fertility behavior of each generation.

Family structure can be used as a basis for studying variations among families at one point in time or across time. Much has been made of the vertical family structure of today, often referred to as the *beanpole family*, describing the increased number of surviving generations coupled with the smaller numbers in each generation. Fertility timing is crucial to the number of generations, and when succeeding cohorts delay the birth of their first child, coexisting survival of more than three or four generations decreases, as does the number of shared years between generations (Matthews &

Sun, 2006; see Chapter 1). Trends in partner formation (staying single, marrying, cohabiting, divorcing, remarrying, widowhood), fertility (timing and number of children) and mortality (life expectancy) all shape family structure.

Consider your own family network. What is your marital status? What about your parents? Do you have step parents? How many sisters and brothers do you have? Do you have a partner or expect to? What about children? Now think about old members of your family. Are they married, living with a partner, or on their own? Is this a long-term or recent situation? How many children do they have? Grandchildren? Siblings? This chapter considers continuity and change in availability of various family relationships across age groups and across time. Although having a particular family tie does not guarantee an active relationship with that relative, not having one certainly precludes it. Therefore, as a starting point, it is useful to consider the availability of various kin in later life as one parameter of family life.

Demographic and social trends set some boundaries to family life, but they do not portend a particular destiny for any age cohort (Connidis, 2002; Friedland & Summer, 1999). Both types of trends reflect how individuals have negotiated relationships with others in the context of current social arrangements and demands, including public policy. Demographic and social trends are at once a critical component of the social context in which family members negotiate their relationships and a product of their time. That is why we cannot simply apply trend data to our current way of doing things and assume that we have seen a complete picture of what lies ahead. For example, the social context of being married or cohabiting today is different from what it was in the 1950s. The information presented in this chapter is only one aspect of family ties in later life. Changes in the availability of one type of kin tie are likely to be met by adaptations in the way that other ones are negotiated. For example, if people have fewer children, they may negotiate more supportive ties with brothers and sisters. In later chapters, the nature of specific family ties in terms of their intensity (type and amount of contact), quality and supportiveness (the degree and direction of support exchange between older persons and particular family members), is examined. Combining knowledge of trends with that of the nature of different kin relationships and the social context in which they are negotiated helps us to anticipate continuity and change in future family forms and functions.

Over the past four to five decades, rates of marriage went down, cohabiting rates went up, divorce rates went up and then stabilized, and birth rates went down (Bianchi & Casper, 2005). Very recently, birth rates have increased slightly in the United States, and rates of staying single (neither marrying nor cohabiting) also went up among younger age cohorts. Throughout this time, life expectancy at birth has increased for both men and women, with an average life expectancy in 2005 of 80.3 years in Canada and 77.9 years in the United States. Women continue to live longer than men, but the margin of difference between them has decreased so that the 80.4 expected years of life for women is 5.2 years greater than that of men in the United States. Differences by race continue also: life expectancy for Blacks is 73.2 compared with 78.3 for Whites. Similar gender differences apply to both groups (National Center for Health Statistics, 2007).

In both the United States and Canada, the substantial proportion of the population which is foreign born is a significant source of diversity. In 2000, 10% of those aged 65 and over and 11% of the total U.S. population was foreign born (U.S. Census Bureau, 2004). In 2006, almost one fifth (19.8%) of Canadians were foreign born, the highest percentage in 75 years (Statistics Canada, 2007a). The foreign-born population is generally younger than the native born and, in the United States, has less education and lower income but with very substantial differences based on the region of birth (Larsen, 2004). For example, in 2002, those born in Asia were considerably more likely than the native born to be earning over $50,000, but the opposite was true of those born in Latin America, the Caribbean and Central America. These variations have consequences for the flow of support between generations.

Changes in couple relationships mean that more families contain couples, both straight and gay, who cohabit; more cohabiting couples and more unattached women have children; more families include step ties; more children live in other than nuclear families than live in them; and more grandparents raise grandchildren (Demo et al., 2005). Changes in fertility patterns mean smaller families among younger generations, change in the gender composition of families, later age of becoming grandparents and a greater age gap between one generation and the next. At the same time that we emphasize change, we must be cautious not to misrepresent it. For example, the rise in one-parent (usually one-mother) families receives considerable attention. Yet one-parent families are not new. What has changed is their composition; they are now typically the result of divorce rather than widowhood (Ambert, 2006) and, in growing numbers, births to unattached women. These shifting family structures have an important influence on family ties in later life, as we shall see in subsequent chapters.

How are these general trends reflected in the availability of particular family relationships across age groups and across time? We begin by looking at trends in marital status, number of children, and the availability of siblings and of grandchildren, and then examine the living arrangements of several age cohorts. In some cases, we consider racial and ethnic differences in the old population. Reliance on census data limits this discussion to particular racial and ethnic groups and to the sometimes puzzling definitions of ethnic versus racial group membership that are the focus of the U.S. census (McAdoo et al., 2005). For example, the 2005 U.S. Census includes Asians as a separate race, considers Hispanics an ethnic and a racial group, allows Filipinos to identify as Asian and Spanish in origin and provides no way of identifying oneself as Arab or Middle Eastern. A related issue is the impossibility of presenting national data based on sexual orientation despite estimates of there being about 2.8 million gay men and lesbians aged 65 years and over in the United States (Allen, 2005a).

We typically exercise choice in having partners and having children; we do not have direct control over the number of siblings or grandchildren that we have. Our focus here is on partners, children, siblings and grandchildren, but many older persons also have nieces, nephews and cousins, and substantial numbers of those in their 60s have parents, aunts and uncles as well. When considering the data that follow, step back now and again to consider how detailed information relates to the bigger picture; in essence, go back and forth between the forest and the trees, appreciating important variations (the trees) that occur within the general pattern (the forest).

The Availability of a Marital or Intimate Partner

As discussed further in the next chapter, a complete treatment of intimate couple relationships at any stage of the life course, including old age, must extend beyond marriage. Yet available data limit the extent to which alternative couple arrangements can be documented accurately. In this chapter, relying on census data means a focus on marital status but, as subsequent chapters illustrate, other than traditional marital ties are significant intimate bonds for both straight and gay adults. This said, the dominance of marriage as the primary socially and legally sanctioned intimate relationship of adulthood confers particular privileges and responsibilities that have consequences for family life in old age (see Chapter 3).

Marital status establishes a parameter of family life with both short- and long-term consequences for social networks, living arrangements and social support. Tables 2.1 and 2.2 present the distribution of the population by marital status at one point in time (2006). Remember that such cross-sectional data reflect current circumstances only. Regarding divorce, for example, they do not reflect the total number of individuals who have ever divorced but rather only those who are currently divorced.

In Table 2.1, we can see a similar distribution of marital status for 10-year age groups in the United States (2006) and Canada (2006) among those aged 45 and over, particularly in the likelihood of being married. The majority of all individuals aged 35 to 74 years are married. This continues to be true for men for all age groups, but for women only up to the age of 75 years. Among those aged 65 to 74, about three-quarters of the men are married but only 56% of the women are. By the ages of 75 to 84 years, just over 70% of men are still married, but only just over one-third of women have spouses. Among the oldest age group (85 and over), 60% of American and 54% of Canadian men have spouses but only 18% of American and 12% of Canadian women do so.

These gender differences in the likelihood of being married are due primarily to different widowhood rates. At the ages of 65 to 74, only 7% of the men are widowed, compared with one-quarter of women. This difference grows with age; for those aged 75 to 84, not quite 1 in 5 men is widowed, compared with half of the women. By the ages of 85 years and over, 1 in 3 men are widowed, compared with 3 of every 4 women. As can be seen in Table 2.2, these gender differences in the proportions that are married and widowed apply to all races in the United States and reflect the longer life expectancy of women than men and the cultural tradition of men marrying women younger than themselves. Although men are more likely than women to remarry once widowed, rates of remarriage for both widowed men and women are fairly low (see Chapter 6).

There are substantial differences by race in marital status distribution in the United States (see Table 2.2). Overall, Asian persons are the most likely to be married, followed by Whites, then Hispanics and then by Blacks. Thus, for example, among men aged 75 to 84 years, the percentage married is 80 for Asians, 73 for Whites,

TABLE 2.1 Percentage Distribution of Current Marital Status by Gender and Age: United States, 2006; Canada, 2006

	United States										Canada									
	Single		Married[a]		Separated[b]		Divorced		Widowed		Single		Married[a]		Separated[b]		Divorced		Widowed	
Age	Men	Women	Men	Women	Men	Women	Men	Women	Men	Women	Men	Women	Men	Women	Men	Women	Men	Women	Men	Women
25–34	46	34	48	56	2	3	4	7	0	0	63	51	34	43	2	3	2	3	0	0
35–44	21	15	65	66	2	4	11	14	0	1	32	24	57	60	4	5	7	10	0	1
45–54	12	10	69	66	3	3	15	17	1	3	19	14	63	62	4	5	13	15	1	3
55–64	7	6	76	64	2	2	13	18	2	10	10	8	71	64	4	3	14	16	2	9
65–74	4	4	77	56	4	4	10	12	7	26	6	6	75	57	3	2	9	10	7	25
75–84	3	3	72	37	1	1	6	7	18	52	6	6	70	35	2	1	5	5	17	52
85+	3	3	61	18	0	0	3	3	32	75	6	8	54	12	2	1	2	2	36	77

SOURCE: Data from U.S. Census Bureau (2006) and Statistics Canada, Census of Canada. 2006. Legal Marital Status (6), Common-law Status (3), Age Groups (17) and Sex (3) for the Population 15 Years and Over of Canada, Provinces, Territories, Census Divisions and Census Subdivisions, 2006 Census – 100% Data. Catalogue number 97-552-XCB2006007. Ottawa, ON: Statistics Canada.

NOTE: Row percentages do not add up to 100 because of rounding.

U.S. Bureau of the Census. 2006. *America's Families and Living Arrangements, Table A1: Marital Status of People 15 Years and Over, by Age, Sex, Personal Earnings, Race, and Hispanic Origin.* Retrieved from http://www.census.gov/population/www/socdemo/hh-fam/cps2006.html

a. The "married" category for the U.S. was derived from two separate categories: "married, spouse present" and "married, spouse not present." "Married, spouse present" includes individuals whose husband or wife was reported as a member of the household, even if temporarily absent on business trips, hospital visits, etc., whereas "married, spouse not present" included "people living apart because either the husband or wife was employed and living at a considerable distance from home, was serving away from home in the Armed Forces, had moved to another area, or had a different place of residence for any other reason except separation." U.S. Bureau Census, Current Population Survey (CPS)—Definitions and explanations (see http://www.census.gov/population/www/cps/cpsdef.html)

The "married" category includes common-law relationships for the United States but not for Canada. In Canada, common-law relationships are not counted in the legally married category but are dispersed throughout the other categories. In Canada, in 2006, the married category includes spouses in same-sex marriages.

b. The "separated" category includes married people with legal separations, those living apart with intentions of obtaining a divorce, and other people permanently or temporarily separated because of marital discord.

TABLE 2.2 Percentage Distribution of Current Marital Status by Gender, Age and Race: United States, 2006

Race and Age	Single Men	Single Women	Married[c] Men	Married[c] Women	Separated[d] Men	Separated[d] Women	Divorced Men	Divorced Women	Widowed Men	Widowed Women
White Only										
25–34	42	29	51	61	2	3	5	7	0	1
35–44	19	12	68	70	2	3	11	14	0	1
45–54	11	8	71	69	2	3	15	17	1	3
55–64	7	5	77	67	1	2	13	17	2	9
65–74	4	3	78	59	1	1	10	12	7	25
75–84	3	3	73	38	1	1	6	7	17	52
85+	3	3	63	18	0	0	2	4	31	75
Black Only										
25–34	64	58	29	30	3	6	4	6	0	0
35–44	35	33	47	39	4	8	13	19	1	2
45–54	22	24	53	42	8	7	16	21	1	5
55–64	10	14	61	39	7	8	18	23	4	16
65–74	8	8	59	33	7	4	15	16	11	38
75–84	6	6	53	19	4	2	8	11	29	61
85+	1	3	39	10	2	3	12	1	46	83
Hispanic Only										
25–34	42	28	53	62	2	5	3	5	0	0
35–44	22	13	67	66	3	6	8	13	0	2

Race and Age	Single		Married[c]		Separated[d]		Divorced		Widowed	
	Men	Women	Men	Women	Men	Women	Men	Women	Men	Women
45–54	11	10	72	62	5	7	12	17	1	4
55–64	11	8	67	56	4	6	13	18	4	11
65–74	4	5	75	50	4	4	10	13	7	28
75–84	5	5	70	33	2	3	7	9	16	51
85+	4	8	56	18	—	—	9	6	32	68
Asian Only										
25–34	55	32	44	64	1	1	1	3	—	—
35–44	17	11	77	82	1	2	5	5	—	0
45–54	9	8	82	77	1	2	7	9	1	4
55–64	4	8	85	70	3	2	7	11	1	9
65–74	2	4	87	59	2	3	4	10	5	24
75–84	2	5	80	40	2	1	1	7	14	46
85+	19	4	65	15	—	—	—	—	19	81

SOURCE: U.S. Census Bureau. 2006. *America's Families and Living Arrangements, Table A1: Marital Status of People 15 Years and Over, by Age, Sex, Personal Earnings, Race, and Hispanic Origin*. Retrieved from http://www.census.gov/population/www/socdemo/hh-fam/cps2006.html

NOTE: Row percentages do not add up to 100 because of rounding.

c. The "married" category was derived from two separate categories: "married, spouse present" and "married, spouse not present."

d. The "separated" category includes married people with legal separations, those living apart with intentions of obtaining a divorce, and other people permanently or temporarily separated because of marital discord.

70 for Hispanics, and 53 for Blacks. Corresponding figures for women in this age group are 40% of Asians, 38% of Whites, 33% of Hispanics, and 19% of Blacks. The distribution of widowed men aged 75 to 84 is 14% of Asians, 16% of Hispanics, 17% of Whites, and 29% of Blacks; for widowed women, it is 46% of Asians, 51% of Hispanics, 52% of Whites, and 61% of Blacks. Over the past 10 years, the propensity to be married and widowed has become much more similar between Whites and Hispanics (see Connidis, 2001). Differences in marital status set the stage for racial variations in living arrangements and support networks in old age.

For both men and women in the United States, the percentage of currently divorced individuals is in the double digits for those aged 35 to 74 years old, with slightly lower figures in Canada (Table 2.1). Only among 25–34 year olds, who are less likely to have been married in the first place, and those who are 75 years or over, is the percentage divorced in the single digits. As of 2006, about 1 in 10 Americans and Canadians aged 65 to 74 years were currently divorced. For men in this age group, being divorced is more common than being widowed; the opposite is true of women. When compared with those over the age of 65, a higher percentage of those aged 35 to 64 is divorced, indicating that more old individuals are likely to be divorced in the future.

With the exception of Blacks and Hispanics aged 85 years or more, for all races and ages, women are consistently more likely than men to be currently divorced, due largely to men's higher rates of remarriage (Table 2.2). However, there are some differences by race. Asians of all age groups have the smallest proportion of divorced individuals, with especially low numbers among Asian men. Among all age groups of 35 years or more, the highest proportion divorced occurs among Blacks, followed by Whites and then very closely by Hispanics. African American women aged 45 to 64 are most likely to be currently divorced; over one in five is in this situation.

The single constitute a relatively small proportion of older persons. Of those aged 65 to 74, 4% of Americans and 6% of Canadians never married (Table 2.1). The high percentage of single persons under the age of 35 represents in part later age at first marriage but may also indicate an increase in the proportion of single adults in the future. However, although not married, some of these single individuals may be in committed relationships that do not constitute legal marriage, including straight, gay and lesbian adults. Greater acceptance of alternative lifestyles has improved awareness and recognition of cohabiting and same-sex partnerships, and these relationships are discussed further in Chapters 4 and 6.

With the exception of the oldest (85 and over) age group, being single is most common among Black (8% of 65–74 year olds) and least common among Asian men and women (2% and 4% of 65–74 year olds; see Table 2.2). Whites and Hispanics fall between the two groups with similar percentages (3% to 5%) who are single. Generally, men are more likely than women to be single, but this pattern is reversed among Blacks aged 45 to 64 and among Blacks and Hispanics aged 85 or more.

What about trends in marital status over time among those aged 65 years and older (Table 2.3)? In the United States today, approximately 4% of older women and men are single, 74% of men and 44% of women are married, 13% of men and 42% of women are widowed, and 8% of men and 9% of women are divorced. Data on marital status by gender show that the distribution has remained fairly stable since 1971–1972 for this age group. However, there is some change over this 34-year period.

From the early 1980s in both the United States and Canada, the percentage of old married women rises steadily, with a corresponding decline in the percentage that is widowed. Among men, there is a slight decline in both the percentage married and widowed. This shift reflects longer life expectancy for both men and women and the more recent catch-up in male life expectancy. Although women still live longer than men, the shrinking difference in life expectancy increases shared survivorship.

The numbers remain small, but the most dramatic rate of change is the percentage of divorced individuals aged 65 and over, which has more than doubled since 1970 (Table 2.3). From 1995 on, the proportions of Canadian and American men and women who are divorced consistently equals or surpasses the proportions that are single. These trends indicate the growing acceptance of divorce as an option to a poor marriage among all age groups. The greater economic security of women, due to employment and to changes in social policy that ensure receipt of a share of a former spouse's social insurance benefits, may also facilitate being divorced and divorcing in older age (see Chapter 6). The latter is particularly significant in the lives of older women who have less financial security than men, but it depends on staying married for long enough (10 years) to qualify (Harrington et al., 2006).

There are variations in these trends over time among White, Black and Hispanic Americans aged 65 years and over (see Table 2.4). Because data regarding old Asian Americans are only available for 2000 and 2006, discussion of trends in their case is premature. Focusing first on the data for 2006, we see dramatic differences in marital status distribution among those aged 65 or more. For most groups, 3% to 4% are single, but among Black men and women, 7% are so. The percentage married varies greatly, ranging from 25% of Black women to 84% of Asian men. We would expect gender differences, but even within gender categories, we see significant variations: among old women, there is a range from 25% of Black women to 49% of Asian women married and a range from 56% of African men to 84% of Asian men married. White and Hispanic men and women fall between these extremes and have similar proportions married (46% and 42% of women, 75% and 72% of men, respectively). The lower percentage of married persons among old African Americans is reflected in higher percentages who are divorced or widowed and, among men, separated.

The percentage of single persons over 65 is relatively stable among White men since 1981 but has decreased slightly among White women for most years since 1972. The opposite is true for African American men and women for whom the percentage single has increased over time, with a slight drop among Black men between 2000 and 2006 so that they now share the highest percentage single (7%) with Black women. Hispanic men and especially women have more variable trends over time in the percentage single, possibly reflecting variations in migration patterns over time.

Despite declines in the percentage that are widowed among all groups, only old White women have experienced a consistent increase in the percentage that are married over time. Since 1981, Black and White men have actually experienced a decline in the percentage aged 65 and over who are married, as have Black women since 1991. Combining the percentages of divorced and separated old persons (these two groups were combined in the U.S. Census prior to 2000), we see steady increases among White and Black women and men over time and stabilizing percentages among old Hispanic men and women. Over time, Blacks have higher

TABLE 2.3 Percentage Distribution of Marital Status for Population Aged 65+, by Gender: United States, 1972–2006; Canada, 1971–2006

Marital Status and Gender	1972 U.S.	1981 U.S.	1991 U.S.	1995 U.S.	2000 U.S.	2006 U.S.	1971 Canada	1981 Canada	1991 Canada	1996 Canada	2001 Canada	2006 Canada
Never Married												
Men	5	4	4	4	4	4	11	9	7	7	6	6
Women	7	6	5	4	4	4	11	10	8	7	6	6
Married[e]												
Men	75	78	77	77	74	74	72	76	74	73	72	71
Women	35	37	41	42	43	44	39	40	40	41	41	42
Separated[f]												
Men					1	1					2	2
Women					1	1					2	2
Divorced												
Men	3	4	6	6	6	8	1	2	5	7	6	7
Women	4	4	6	7	7	9	1	2	5	6	6	7
Widowed												
Men	18	16	15	14	14	13	17	14	13	14	13	13
Women	56	54	48	47	45	42	49	49	47	47	45	43

SOURCE: Data from:

U.S. Bureau of the Census, *Current Population Reports* (Population Characteristics, Marital Status and Living Arrangements, March 1972, P-20 No. 242, Table 1; March 1981, P-20 No. 372, Table 1; March 1991 P-20 No. 461, Table 1; March 1995, P-20 No 491), *America's Families and Living Arrangements, Table A1: Martial Status of People 15 Years and Over, by Age, Sex, Personal Earnings, Race, and Hispanic Origin)* and Statistics Canada, *Census of Canada*, Canada Yearbook, 1975, Table 4.15, p. 167, Statistics Canada Catalogue 92-901, *Census of Canada*, 1981, Vol. 1, Table 4, Statistics Canada Catalogue 93-312, Census Canada, The Nation, *Census of Canada*, 2001, Catalogue 95F0407XCB2001004.

Statistics Canada. 2001. *Legal Marital Status (6), Age Groups (18A) and Sex (3) for Population, for Canada, Provinces, Territories, Census Metropolitan Areas 1 and Census Agglomerations, 2001 Census – 100% Data*. Ottawa: Statistics Canada, October 22, 2002. 2001 Census of Canada. Catalogue number 95F0407XCB2001004.

Statistics Canada, Census of Canada. 2006. Legal Marital Status (6), Common-law Status (3), Age Groups (17) and Sex (3) for the Population 15 Years and Over of Canada, Provinces, Territories, Census Divisions and Census Subdivisions, 2006 Census – 100% Data. Catalogue number 97-552-XCB2006007. Ottawa, ON: Statistics Canada.

U.S. Census Bureau. 2000. *America's Families and Living Arrangements, Table A1: Marital Status of People 15 Years and Over, by Age, Sex, Personal Earnings, Race, and Hispanic Origin*. Retrieved from http://www.census.gov/population/socdemo/hh-fam/p20-537/2000/tabA1.pdf

U.S. Census Bureau. 2006. *America's Families and Living Arrangements, Table A1: Marital Status of People 15 Years and Over, by Age, Sex, Personal Earnings, Race, and Hispanic Origin*. Retrieved from http://www.census.gov/population/www/socdemo/hh-fam/cps2006.html

NOTE: Row percentages do not add up to 100 because of rounding.

e. The "married" category for the U.S. was derived from two separate categories: "married, spouse present" and "married, spouse not present." The "married" category includes common-law relationships for the United States but not for Canada. In Canada, common-law relationships are not counted in the legally married category but are dispersed throughout the other categories. In Canada, in 2006, the married category includes spouses in same-sex marriages.

f. The "separated" category includes married people with legal separations, those living apart with intentions of obtaining a divorce, and other people permanently or temporarily separated because of marital discord.

TABLE 2.4   Percentage Distribution of Marital Status for Population Aged 65+, by Gender and Race: United States, 1972–2006

Marital Status, Race, and Gender	1972	1981	1991	1995	2000	2006
Never Married						
White Men	5	4	4	4	4	4
White Women	7	6	5	4	4	3
Black Men	4	5	5	7	9	7
Black Women	3	5	5	6	6	7
Hispanic Men	6	5	3	3	4	5
Hispanic Women	3	8	5	8	6	4
Asian Men					4	4
Asian Women					2	3
Married[g]						
White Men	77	79	78	78	75	75
White Women	36	37	42	44	44	46
Black Men	65	68	63	64	56	56
Black Women	30	29	31	29	27	25
Hispanic Men	63	71	78	70	70	72
Hispanic Women	30	38	42	39	41	42
Asian Men					83	84
Asian Women					50	49
Separated[h]						
White Men					1	1
White Women					1	1
Black Men					5	6
Black Women					4	3
Hispanic Men					3	3
Hispanic Women					3	3
Asian Men					3	2
Asian Women					1	2
Divorced						
White Men	2	4	5	6	6	8
White Women	3	4	6	6	7	9
Black Men	7	11	16	12	8	12
Black Women	8	10	13	13	9	13
Hispanic Men	7	10	8	13	8	9

Marital Status, Race, and Gender	1972	1981	1991	1995	2000	2006
Hispanic Women	8	6	11	14	11	11
Asian Men					1	3
Asian Women					2	8
Widowed						
White Men	17	15	14	13	14	13
White Women	55	54	48	47	44	42
Black Men	29	23	23	22	21	19
Black Women	65	60	55	56	55	52
Hispanic Men	29	19	14	18	15	12
Hispanic Women	65	50	45	44	39	39
Asian Men					9	9
Asian Women					45	36

SOURCE: U.S. Census Bureau. 2000, 2006.

g. The "married" category was derived from two separate categories: "married, spouse present" and "married, spouse not present."

h. The "separated" category includes married people with legal separations, those living apart with intentions of obtaining a divorce, and other people permanently or temporarily separated because of marital discord.

percentages of currently divorced or separated old people, followed by Hispanics and then Whites. The data discussed here concern current marital status; figures of those who have ever been divorced are higher (see Chapter 6).

Summarizing, the majority of men in old age have spouses, and the majority of women do not. This creates a very different perspective on later-life intimate relationships for men and women. Clearly, the qualitative dimensions of marriage are relevant to a greater proportion of older men than women. In turn, the issue of life alone following widowhood affects a majority of older women but only a minority of older men. When combined with the single and the divorced, the percentages and numbers of unattached old men and women are substantial, and the unique nature of their family ties requires separate attention. The steady increase in divorce rates over the past 40 years affects all ages, both directly, in terms of the elevated frequency of divorce at all stages of the life course, and indirectly, in terms of the repercussions of divorce in one generation for other generations (see Chapter 11). In combination with declines in widowhood, the profile of unattached old persons is changing. Significant variations in marital status by race also shape the relative significance of particular situations. For example, over two-fifths of old African American men, and three-quarters of old African American women are unattached, making the combined influence of race and gender an important contextual dimension to understanding intimate relationships in later life. Alternatives to marriage in later life are discussed in Chapter 6.

The Availability of Children

Although one can generally equate being single (never married) with childlessness in the older population, this is not true of the younger population. By 2006, 38.5% of all births in the United States were to unmarried mothers (CDC National Center for Health Statistics, 2007). Thus, being single can no longer stand as a proxy for no children, although the tabulation of births for ever-married women only in Canada until 1991 appeared to make this assumption. Total fertility (the total number of births per woman) has declined over several decades in the United States and Canada until a recent increase in both countries, particularly the United States. In comparison with other Western countries, the United States has a higher birth rate, attributed largely to higher fertility rates among African Americans and Mexican Hispanics (Swicegood & Morgan, 2002; Torrey & Haub, 2003) but also to earlier age of marriage and birth of first child in the United States (Statistics Canada, 2002a). As a consequence of ethnic or racial variations in birth rates in the United States, the racial makeup of the country is shifting, with a decrease in the percentage of all births to non-Hispanic White women (60% in 2002). An increase in what some have termed multipartnered fertility (Carlson & Furstenberg, 2006)—referring to having children with more than one partner—is also reshaping family forms, creating new situations for older persons to negotiate in their relationships with children and grandchildren.

The recent greater upswing in fertility in the United States than in Canada makes Canada's fertility rate more like that of Europe. As of 2006, Canada's total fertility rate was 1.54 compared with 2.1 in the United States (Population Reference Bureau [PRB], 2007; Statistics Canada, 2007b), a difference that slows down the aging of the U.S. population in comparison with Canada's. Increases in fertility in Canada and the United States during the 1990s also had different origins: In the United States it reflected higher fertility rates among young women, whereas in Canada it was a result of delayed childbearing, a shift that does not result in an increase in total number of births to one woman (Swicegood & Morgan, 2002). In the United States, a decrease in teen births from the late 1990s to early 2000s was met with an increase in 2006 (CDC National Center for Health Statistics, 2006, 2007); in Canada, women in their 30s continue to be the primary source of a slight increase in birth rates (Statistics Canada, 2007b). In the United States, higher fertility rates among women aged 35 and over were exceeded by women of the same age in earlier cohorts, especially those who bore the baby boom (CDC National Center for Health Statistics, 2001). The novelty of today's increased birth rates among older mothers is that they are more often the arrival of the first or second child rather that the fourth, fifth or sixth. Looking ahead, we will have a different picture of family size and fertility history between current and future cohorts of old people and between the United States and Canada.

Focusing on birth rates can provide a distorted picture because they do not portray family life as it is experienced. How does a total fertility rate of 1.54 or 2.1 translate into actual family size across the population? Data on number of children ever born to women who have completed their fertility give a better sense of what family life looks like over time because they reflect more closely family size from the perspective of mothers (number of children) and children (number of siblings). Table 2.5 presents estimates of the number of children ever born to women of different age groups in the

TABLE 2.5 Percentage Distribution of Number of Children Ever Born to Women Aged 45+ by Age Group: United States, 2005, Canada, 2001[i]

United States, 2005

Number of Children	45–49[i]	50–54	55–59	60–64	65–69	70–79[k]	80–84	85–89	90–94	95–99	100+
0	19	18	16	11	10	11	14	17	21	23	24
1	16	18	17	13	10	11	13	15	17	19	18
2	35	35	35	33	25	22	24	25	24	23	21
3	19	19	19	23	23	22	20	18	16	14	14
4	7	7	8	11	16	15	12	11	9	8	9
5+	4	4	5	9	18	19	17	14	13	13	14

SOURCE: Dye, Jane Lawler. 2005. *Fertility of American Women: June 2004*. Current Population Reports, P20-555. Washington, DC: U.S. Census Bureau, retrieved from http://www.census.gov/prod/2005pubs/p20-555.pdf

Canada, 2001

Number of Children	40–45	45–49	50–54	55–59	60–64	65–69	70–74	75–79	80 and up
0	22	20	18	14	13	14	14	16	21
1	18	19	16	11	10	10	8	12	12
2	39	39	39	36	28	20	20	19	21
3	16	16	19	22	22	18	20	17	17
4	5	5	6	11	13	16	17	14	12
5+	1	1	3	6	14	22	22	22	16

SOURCE: Statistics Canada. 2005. *General Social Survey of Canada, 2001. Cycle 15: Family History* (main file) [machine readable data file]. 6th edition. Ottawa, ON: Statistics Canada. 7/28/2005. Data are for all marital statuses.

i. The Canadian data are based on asking women of different ages about how many children they had (cross-sectional). The U.S. data asked women of the same age group (40–44) in different years how many children they had. U.S. data combine information from different sources to create the equivalent of cross-sectional data (see footnotes b and c). Both Canadian and U.S. data are for all marital statuses.

j. The U.S. data for the age categories 45–69 in 2005 are based on data for women 40–44 years old for the years 1980, 1985, 1990, 1995, and 2000 from Table 6 in Dye, 2005. The U.S. data for the age categories 70–79 and 80 and over in 2005 are based on data for women aged 55–64 from U.S. Census Bureau, 1990. Data are for all women.

k. The U.S. data for the age categories 70–79 and 80 and over in 2005 are based on data for women aged 55–64 from U.S. Census Bureau, 1990. Data are for all women.

United States (2005) and Canada (2001). U.S. data are based on the number of children born by the time women were aged 40 to 44 years, an age by which most but not all women have completed childbearing.

Similar trends among the younger end of the old age groups occur in the United States and Canada. Among American women aged 60 to 79 years in 2005, 89% had at least one child, and most had two or three; among Canadian women aged 55 to 74 years in 2001, 86% had at least one child, and most had two or three. In both countries, those aged 60 to 79—the mothers of the baby boom—are most likely of all age groups to have had four or more children. Although a current focus of concern is declining birth rates, in both countries the cohorts that are heading into old age or are in its earlier stages (ages 60 to 79 in the United States and 55 to 74 in Canada) have the lowest percentages of childless women. In both countries, the oldest (80 and over in the United States and 75 and over in Canada) and youngest (45 to 59 in the United States and 40 to 55 in Canada) age cohorts share higher rates of childlessness. For example, among American women aged 60 to 79 in 2005, the percentage of childless women is down to 11% compared with 21% or more of those aged 90 years or older and 19% of those aged 45 to 49 years. Data for American women aged 40 to 44 years in 2004 show significant differences by race, with a range from 14% childless among Hispanics, to 18% among Asians and 20% among non-Hispanic Whites and Blacks (PRB, 2007).

Looking across cohorts, an increasing percentage of women in both countries has had two children and a shrinking percentage three or more children. As the U.S. data show, the mothers of the baby boom stand out from previous and subsequent cohorts in their propensity to have had three or more children. When we compare the oldest (90 years and over) and youngest (45–59 years) cohorts, we see that childlessness in the old age group was offset to some degree by the higher proportion of women who had large families. These trends illustrate that declining birth rates among the younger cohorts when compared with baby boom mothers are a function of higher rates of childlessness and a shrinking proportion of the youngest women who have had three or more children. They also show interesting parallels in family size between the very old and women who are in their 40s and 50s.

The data reported here refer to children ever born and thus mask those cases where having no children or a small family is due to the death of children. The longer life expectancy of women makes them more likely than men to outlive at least one of their children, particularly among women who had their children at relatively young ages and among those who have sons. Speaking of her deceased daughter, a London, Ontario, widow of 92 notes the unexpected nature of such loss: "It never occurred to me that I would end my days without her. We were very, very close, and we had so much to do with the family." However, even taking this possibility into account, the vast majority of older Americans and Canadians have at least one living child.

There are clear parallels between the oldest segments of the current cohort of elderly persons—those who married and bore children in the Depression and post-Depression years—and the younger cohorts of today who are delaying both marriage and children. Compared to other time periods, both groups share low fertility, a similarity that is frequently overlooked in discussions about the future elderly. The parents of the baby boom represent the more novel case in having a *larger* pool of children from whom to receive support. Thus with respect to family size, the experience of many of today's oldest persons may be of particular relevance to those who are now of childbearing age, although the factors affecting childbearing decisions are quite different.

In sum, the majority of old men and women have at least one child, helping to offset the absence of a spouse among a majority of women. When data regarding marital status and number of children are combined, a significant minority of the oldest age groups have neither. In Canada (Connidis, 2002), 13% of women aged 55 to 64 years in 1991 had neither a spouse nor child; by the age of 75 and over, this number grew to 23%. For some of these women, siblings may be a particularly important tie in old age.

The Availability of Grandchildren

The current focus on grandparents as caregivers to grandchildren is evident in the lack of recent baseline data on number of grandchildren by age group in the United States. Of Americans aged 35 and over, 80% report being members of three-generation families, and 16% are in families of four generations (Szinovacz, 1998). The current interest in grandparents who are heavily involved in raising their grandchildren (see Chapter 10) may explain the greater availability of current data on that phenomenon than on the general patterns of grandparent and grandchild availability. Table 2.6 summarizes U.S. data for 1994 and Canadian data for 2001.

Among all Americans aged 65 and over and among Canadian women in that age group, about 80% have at least one grandchild. Among those 65 and over, there are racial, ethnic and gender differences in the likelihood of having grandchildren.

TABLE 2.6   Percentage Distribution of Those With Grandchildren by Age Group: United States, 1994; Canada, 2001

Percentage With Self-Defined Grandchildren	United States							Canada	
		Men			Women			Men	Women
	Total	Black	White	Hispanic	Black	White	Hispanic		
55–64	78	86	74	95	86	82	69	53	65
65–74	—	—	—	—	—	—	—	72	82
75+	—	—	—	—	—	—	—	78	78
65+	81	85	84	90	79	79	91	74	80

SOURCE: U.S. data are from Wave 2 (1994) of the National Survey of Families and Households (Sweet et al., as reported in Szinovacz, 1998, p. 43); Statistics Canada, 2003, Cat. No. 11-008.

Hispanic men and women are more likely than their Black and White counterparts to have grandchildren. In the Canadian case, more women than men report having grandchildren.

Among older persons who have children, the proportions with grandchildren are higher. Of older Canadian parents, 80% aged 55 to 64 years and over 90% of those aged 65 or older have grandchildren (Connidis, 2001). Similarly, among older Americans, 95% of those whose youngest child is at least 40 years old are grandparents (Szinovacz, 1998). In Canada, grandparents have an average of five grandchildren, and those now aged 75 and over have an average of slightly over six (Kemp, 2003). The smaller percentages of the 55- to 64-year-old group who report having grandchildren in the more recent Canadian data (Table 2.6) probably reflect the effect of delayed childbearing and increased childlessness in younger cohorts. Looked at from the vantage point of younger men and women aged 19 to 26 years, from 73% (Black) to 78% (White and Hispanic) have at least one living grandparent, and at least one in five have three living grandparents (Szinovacz, 1998). Thus, for a majority, ties to a grandparent extend into adulthood, and old age includes grandchildren.

The Availability of Siblings

Patterns of fertility also affect the availability of siblings. Families of orientation are the ones we come from and determine the number of siblings that we have. Families of procreation are the ones that we produce and determine the number of children that we have. A particular cohort will experience a simultaneous shortage of siblings and children only when the fertility rates of families of orientation and of procreation are low. As it happens, over the past 90 years, a small number of siblings (a small family of orientation) has been offset somewhat by a larger number of children (larger family of procreation). Thus, for example, the parents of the baby boom (born between 1922 and 1938) came from small families but produced large ones, and the baby boom (born between 1946 and 1964 in the United States and 1965 in Canada) came from large families but produced small ones.

The baby busters, born between 1966 and 1974, are the children of parents born during World War II (1939–1945; Statistics Canada, 2006; Swicegood & Morgan, 2002). They are a relatively small cohort, in part because they were born to a small cohort and in part because family size was smaller for this age group, resulting in a smaller network of siblings among baby busters. The cohort of the baby boomers' children—those born between 1975 and 1995—is larger than the baby bust cohort because their parents are a large cohort and because birth rates and resulting family size began to increase somewhat in the 1990s (primarily among the younger end of the baby boom). For these younger cohorts, both families of orientation and procreation are comparatively small.

Unfortunately, there are not recent detailed U.S. data available on number of siblings across time. A seven-country study that includes the United States, United Kingdom, Australia, Austria, Germany, Hungary and Italy reports that across all countries, over 85% of 50 year olds, 80% of 60 year olds and 75% of 70 year olds have at least one living sibling (Murphy, 2004). Reflecting gender differences in longevity, at the age of 70, over 60% have a sister compared with less than half who have a brother.

Recent Canadian data show that just over 80% of persons aged 75 and over have at least one living sibling, and over half have more (author calculations; Statistics Canada, 2002b). In older age categories, among those aged 55 to 64 years, only 3% have no living siblings, and 80% report having two or more. Among those 65 to 74 years old, 7% have no living siblings, and 75% have two or more brothers and sisters. A variety of earlier surveys in the United States also indicates the availability of siblings to most old persons (Cicirelli, 1995). Over 90% of Americans and Canadians aged 35 years or older have had siblings. Most continue to have surviving siblings into old age (Connidis, 2001).

Sibling ties are becoming more complex as more people grow up with brothers and sisters who do not share both biological parents. Thus, for example, although 11% of Canadians aged 25 to 34 years old in 2001 report having no full siblings, only 5% report not growing up with a sibling (author calculations, Statistics Canada, 2002b). An even smaller number reports not having a living sibling, suggesting that siblings have been acquired after leaving home. Among all age groups, there is a disparity between the proportions who report having no full siblings and who report growing up with no siblings, indicating that growing up with other than full siblings is not a recent phenomenon. However, the likelihood of having step and half siblings has increased over time. Among Canadians in 2001, 9% of people aged 75 and over had step, half, or adopted siblings compared with 22% of those aged 25 to 34 (author calculations, Statistics Canada, 2002b). This reflects changing patterns of family formation and heralds more complex sibling networks for older people in the future.

In sum, the majority of older persons have both inter- and intra-generational family members. Men are more likely than women to have partners, children and siblings, but women without partners are very likely to have either children, siblings or both. As well, African American men and women are less likely than other racial groups to have a partner in old age. In subsequent chapters, we explore the nature of these various family ties in later life and assess the extent to which the availability of particular ties translates into active family networks.

Living Arrangements in Later Life

The living arrangements of older persons are indicative of the availability of family ties, their continued involvement in family settings, and a trend toward living alone in the absence of a spouse. Only a relatively small proportion of all those aged 65 and over currently live in institutional care settings. Institutionalization is more likely among women than men, those with fewer children, the nonmarried, Whites and older seniors (Angel et al., 1992; Belgrave & Bradsher, 1994; Belgrave et al., 1993; Carrière & Pelletier, 1995). The lower institutionalization rates of Blacks when compared with Whites are offset somewhat by their greater reliance on paid home care and informal care but are also due to simply going without care

(Wallace et al., 1998; see Chapter 14). The presence of at least one daughter or sibling minimizes the chances of being placed in a nursing home (Freedman, 1996), providing a link between the availability of ties and their impact on social life in older age.

The living arrangements of older Americans and Canadians are shown in Table 2.7. The majority of those aged 65 and over lives with a family member, predominantly a spouse. Living with family was more common in the United States than in Canada until the mid-1990s and is the norm among older persons in both countries. However, there are substantial gender differences, with men much more likely to be in this situation than women: 78% of American and 81% of Canadian men lived with family members in 2006 but only 59% of American and 60% of Canadian women did so. These gender differences reflect primarily the higher widowhood rates among women.

The trend toward solitary living among older persons (see Chapter 1) has stabilized, and since the early 1990s, about one-fifth of old men and two-fifths of old women have lived alone (see Table 2.7). The fact that widowed women are more likely to live on their own if they did so for at least three months prior to the age of 60 (Bess, 1999) suggests that solo living will continue to increase among women because living alone at earlier stages of the life course is increasingly common.

Similar gender differences occur across racial and ethnic groups, but the living arrangements of older Black, White, Hispanic and Asian Americans vary (see Table 2.8). Among men, there are differences by race and ethnicity in the proportion who live with family members; in 2006, 69% of older Black men did so, compared with 78% of White, 80% of Hispanic and 90% of Asian men. Among women, Asian (77%) and Hispanic (73%) Americans have similar and markedly higher levels of living with family members than do Whites (59%) and African Americans (57%).

The aggregate data presented here mask additional differences. For example, White persons aged 60 and over are far more likely to be living with a spouse only, whereas Asian, Black, Hispanic and Native American persons are far more likely to be living with other kin only (Himes et al., 1996). Being foreign versus native born also increases the likelihood of living with families rather than alone in later life (Current Population Reports, 2002). There are also differences in three-generation co-residence. In Canada, although a fairly small proportion (3%) of all households fit this pattern, the numbers are increasing, and nearly half of all three-generation families are headed by immigrants, particularly Asians (Che-Alford & Hamm, 1999). Clearly, ethnicity and race are important short-term and long-term factors in the living arrangements of older persons (see Chapter 14).

When adult children and their older parents do live together, the usual assumption is that the parents are living with their children and that, if there is an issue of dependency, it is the older generation who depends on the younger one. Co-residence, however, also represents the dependence, sometimes temporary, of adult children (see Chapter 8). Canadian data show that, in the case of three-generation households, co-residence provides support for those of all ages who have activity limitations, not just the old (Che-Alford & Hamm, 1999).

As we saw in Chapter 1, living alone is often preferred by older persons as a way of maintaining independence, and receiving help from formal services may be preferred to getting help from children (Daatland, 1990). The situation of a 77-year-old Canadian woman is typical of many healthy old women. She is described as "too busy to get lonely, with bowling, yard chores, work at a local school, and duties at the . . . war brides association and is well able to take care of herself" (Walton, 2002:A6). Her daughter would like her to move in with her but she says, "I don't think I should. . . . They have their own lives. I would rather go into a seniors place or something where there are people my own age" (Walton, 2002:A6). Economic resources (are they sufficient to sustain independent living?), health (is one healthy enough to live on one's own?) and the availability of kin, particularly children and a spouse (Zsembik, 1996), are influential factors in living alone, and they are differentially distributed across the older population.

Generally, extreme limits in the ability to function independently and being in poor health make living alone less likely (Waite & Hughes, 1999; Wolf, 1990). The considerable racial rift in economic circumstances encourages the more fluid and collective sense of households and resource flow in Black families, and unattached Black women are more likely to head a multiperson household in older age (Olson, 2003). In turn, White women are more likely to both live alone and to be non-head members of multiperson households (see also Peek et al., 1997). Similarly, the chances of living in care institutions are lower among older Blacks and Hispanics than among Whites (Angel et al., 1992; Belgrave & Bradsher, 1994; Belgrave et al., 1993). The contrasting contexts and dynamics of family life among Black and White women over a lifetime go beyond the impact of differential resources alone. Yet the significance of serious economic disadvantage and racism must not be minimized, including their role in fostering supportive kinship networks among African Americans (Belgrave et al., 1993; see Chapter 14).

Last, a broader issue of living arrangements is migration. Patterns of migration among the elderly have significant implications for their welfare and for public policy (see Chapter 14). Older persons may concentrate in particular localities for three major reasons: accumulation, where older residents are left behind in communities that younger residents leave in order to find more prosperous locations; recomposition, when older persons migrate to an area that younger persons are leaving; and congregation, in which case older migrants outnumber younger migrants but persons of all ages are moving in (Morrison, 1990). Typically, congregation involves relatively well-off older persons seeking to improve their situation by moving to a desirable location, such as Arizona. In contrast, accumulation usually occurs in economically disadvantaged communities, for example, the Mississippi delta, leaving older persons with fewer resources to fend for themselves. The poorer economy of these regions also limits the ability to offer locally supported community support to older residents. The accumulation that results from aging in place while younger persons migrate, a trend evident in both the United States and Canada, requires mechanisms for the redistribution of wealth by higher levels of government (Moore & Rosenberg, 1997).

Geographic location also reflects ethnic and racial differences and changing immigration patterns. Currently, ethnic and racial minorities comprise 16% of the population aged 65 and over, and one-third of the total U.S. population (Olson, 2003); by 2050 half of the American population will be of African, Asian or Latin origin (Angel & Angel, 2006). In addition to the age grading of ethnic and racial

TABLE 2.7 Percentage Distribution of the Population Aged 65+, by Type of Living Arrangement and Gender: United States, 1972–2006; Canada, 1971–2006

| | Family | | | Nonfamily | | | |
| | Primary[a] | | Secondary[b] | Primary Individual Living Alone[c] | | Living With Others[d] | Collective Dwelling[e] |
	U.S.	Canada	Canada	U.S.	Canada	Canada	Canada
1972 U.S., 1971 Canada							
All Men	84	67	3	16	11	16	4
All Women	60	41	2	40	24	28	5
1981 U.S. and Canada	Families			Householder			
All Men	85	72	—	15	13	8	5
All Women	57	42	—	43	32	15	8
1991 U.S. and Canada	Families			Householder			
All Men	83	78	2	17	15	4	—
All Women	57	49	6	43	38	6	—
1995 U.S., 1996 Canada	Families			Householder			
All Men	81	81	—	19	16	3	—
All Women	57	52	—	43	38	10	—
2000 U.S., 2001 Canada	Families			Householder			
All Men	79	81	—	20	17	2	9
All Women	58	60	—	42	38	2	5

	Family			Nonfamily			
	Primary[a]		Secondary[b]	Primary Individual Living Alone[c]		Living With Others[d]	Collective Dwelling[e]
	U.S.	Canada	Canada	U.S.	Canada	Canada	Canada
2006 US, 2006 Canada	Families			Householder			
All Men	78	81	1	22	17	2	—
All Women	59	60	1	41	37	1	—

SOURCE: Saluter, 1992, 1996; Statistics Canada, 1973, 1982, 1992, 1996, 2006; U.S. Census Bureau, 1972, 1981, 2006.

Statistics Canada, 2006. Senior Women in Social and Aboriginal Statistical Division *Women in Canada: A Gendered Based Statistical Report* (5th ed., pp. 265–290). Ottawa, ON: Statistics Canada. Catalogue Number 85-583-XIE

Statistics Canada. Census of Canada, 2006. Table 97-553-XCB2006018: Household Living Arrangements (11), Age Groups (20) and Sex (3) for the Population in Private Households of Canada, Provinces, Territories, Census Metropolitan Areas and Census Agglomerations, 2006 Census—20% Sample Data. [machine readable data file]. Ottawa, ON: Statistics Canada. 6/9/2007

U.S. Census Bureau. 2000. *America's Families and Living Arrangements, Table A2 Family Status and Household Relationships of People 15 Years and Over, by Marital Status, Age, Sex, Race, and Hispanic Origin.* Retrieved from http://www.census.gov/population/socdemo/hh-fam/p20-537/2000/tabA1.pdf

U.S. Census Bureau. 2006. *America's Families and Living Arrangements, Table A1: Marital Status of People 15 Years and Over, by Age, Sex, Personal Earnings, Race, and Hispanic Origin.* Retrieved from http://www.census.gov/population/www/socdemo/hh-fam/cps2006.html

a. Living Arrangement: Census Families are groups of two or more persons residing together and related by blood, marriage or adoption. Primary Families include the head of a household.

b. Individuals with Secondary Family living arrangements are living with relatives who are not considered primary family.

c. Primary Individuals are household heads with no relatives in the household; they are included as "householder" from 1981 on.

d. Includes lodgers and noncensus family members (e.g., adult siblings).

e. Primarily institutional settings; excluded in1991.

TABLE 2.8 Percentage Distribution of the Population Aged 65+, by Type of Living Arrangement, Gender and Race: United States, 2006

2006	Families	Nonfamily
All Men	78	22
White Men	78	22
Black Men	69	31
Hispanic Men	80	20
Asian Men	90	10
All Women	59	41
White Women	59	41
Black Women	57	43
Hispanic Women	73	27
Asian Women	77	23

SOURCE: U.S. Census Bureau, 2006.

diversity, concentrated settlement patterns in the United States and Canada already mean regional variation in the extent of such diversity for both countries. For example, although about half of the states in the United States are predominantly White, about half of all Latinos live in California and Texas, 60% of all African Americans live in only 10 states, and just over half of all Asian Americans or Pacific Islanders live in 10 western states (Cauce, 2005). The impact of membership in a particular race or ethnic group is also variable, based on immigration history and generational status.

Summary and Conclusion to Part I

In Chapter 1, you saw that older family members of the past did not enjoy a particularly advantaged position in our society. Today, more old people are able to maintain chosen independence due to improved social security measures. However, welfare policies are under threat, and there are important variations among old people due to the structured social relations of gender, class, race and ethnicity. Understanding family life in old age requires going beyond definitions of family as the traditional nuclear household and recognizing the family lives of single, childless, gay and lesbian older persons as siblings, children, aunts and uncles, partners, parents and grandparents. A multilevel theoretical framework that combines a life course perspective with critical and feminist approaches emphasizes that family relationships are negotiated over time in the context of a given family and of the larger society. Family members may have quite different views of how their families work. As particular family ties are examined, consider the ways in which the challenges of family life and of aging can be considered private troubles or public issues.

In Chapter 2, some broad parameters of family life were established by looking at trends in the availability of various family members in later life. These data show that most old people have children, grandchildren and siblings. Nonetheless, there are significant variations in the availability of family ties, depending on gender, age, race and ethnicity. For example, most old men have a spouse, whereas most old women do not. These variations interact with class to create unique challenges in old age. Consider the situation of old Black women who are also much more likely to be poor than their White counterparts (Olson, 2003).

The trends in family ties and living arrangements discussed in Chapter 2, along with other social trends that are discussed in subsequent chapters (e.g., the increase in cohabitation rates; see Chapter 6), add up to a changing population and to changing family structures. Our focus on the older population sometimes conceals shifts that are occurring in the younger population. But such shifts affect the old along with the young, even when they are not the direct experience of today's old. The population is becoming less and less dominated by Whites over time but much more so among younger than older cohorts (Angel & Angel, 2006). As well, a substantial portion of the changing behavior regarding partnering and parenting applies primarily to younger cohorts. The combination of higher birth rates among non-White than White younger women, the increase in births to unmarried women, the rise in cohabitation rather than marriage, and the delay of the birth of the first child will reshape the racial and ethnic composition of the population as well as the dynamics of family life (Demo et al., 2005; Teachman et al., 2000).

These factors are highlighted in subsequent chapters about the central family ties of older people. Each chapter begins with a discussion of contact with the family member in question before examining support exchanges and qualitative dimensions of the relationship.

PART II

Intimate Ties

CHAPTER 3

Intimate Ties in Later Life

The term pure relationship *. . . refers to a situation where a social relation is entered into for its own sake, for what can be derived by each person from a sustained association with another; and which is continued only in so far as it is thought by both parties to deliver enough satisfactions for each individual to stay within it. Love used to be tied to sexuality, for most of the sexually "normal" population, through marriage; but now the two are connected more and more via the pure relationship.*

—Giddens (1992:58)

Defining Intimate Ties

Are you involved in an intimate relationship? Despite the debate in academic circles about what constitutes an intimate tie, my guess is that you have a pretty good idea of what I mean when I ask you this question. I expect that you are not thinking about your parents or siblings or children. Although all of our family ties are characterized by some form of intimacy, even something as basic as sharing a bathroom or knowing one another's personal habits, they do not all fit the label of an intimate relationship. Whether or not you are currently in an intimate relationship, you probably can list some of its defining features.

Scholarly definitions of intimate relationships often include five relational components: commitment, deep feelings and expressions of caring and compassion, thinking about another and sharing values and goals, physical intimacy ranging from close proximity to sexuality, and interdependence (Blieszner & de Vries, 2001;

Moss & Schwebel, 1993). Despite differences among intimate ties and within the same relationship over time (Brehm, 1992), intimate relationships are *expected* to be intense, committed, emotional, caring, mutual and sexual. When they are not, they are considered at least unusual and often problematic. Sexual involvement sets intimate relationships apart from other family ties; they are the only relationships that hold the socially approved potential for sexual intimacy. This view of intimate ties parallels what Huyck (2001) refers to as romantic relationships. Unlike other family ties, we usually choose our intimate partners.

Do relationships have to be sexually active in order to be considered intimate? Not necessarily. A relationship may qualify as intimate based either on *assumptions* of sexual intimacy as a hallmark of institutionalized relationships, such as marriage, or on the *presence* of sexual intimacy in the case of noninstitutionalized relationships. In our society, sexual interdependence is typically a restricted exchange involving two persons (a dyad); a third party is not a legitimate alternative to either player (Scanzoni & Marsiglio, 1993). Even outside marriage, serial relationships are socially sanctioned to a far greater degree than are multiple partners, reflecting the restricted exchange associated with sexual relationships.

When other intrinsic exchanges are added to sexual interdependence, the resulting relationship is described as erotic friendship and as a sexually bonded primary relationship (Scanzoni & Marsiglio, 1993). We might as readily use Giddens's term, *pure relationship*, to describe such ties. For our discussion here, intimate ties include pure relationships and those ties that are formalized by marriage. In some ways, to qualify as intimate ties, pure relationships have a greater burden of proof (the presence of sexual relations) than do marriages (where sexual relations may or may not occur). At the same time, however, the institution of marriage carries with it a heavy burden of obligation to provide mutual support. At the very least, intimate ties as discussed here parallel Huyck's (1995:181) view of "marital-like partnerships" as presuming "potential sexual sharing." Although other familial ties as well as friendship may offer emotional intimacy, they are characteristically different from these intimate ties and cannot serve as full substitutes for them.

Traditionally, this chapter could have been titled "marriage in later life," or something like it, and been accepted as covering the intimate relationships of older persons. Now, such a focus is too exclusive. Even though marriage represents the intimate relationship of their lives for many older persons, this is not true of all old people and will be less common in the future. A range of romantic relationships is possible in later life: marriage, remarriage, same-sex partnerships, opposite-sex cohabitation with sexual sharing, living apart together (committed relationships with sexual sharing and different households), affairs, abandoned relationships, absent relationships (through death or illness), and unrequited relationships (Huyck, 2001). For our purposes, we will focus on the first five (marriage, remarriage, same-sex partnerships, opposite-sex cohabitation with sexual sharing, and living apart together with sexual sharing). However, relationships that have been abandoned, are absent through death, or are unrequited may meet needs for intimacy even though they do not occur in real time (Connidis, 2006). Affairs are a unique category and generally challenge fundamental assumptions about commitment.

More recent work is starting to address long-term same-sex partnerships and intimate heterosexual ties outside of marriage, particularly by researchers in Europe and the United Kingdom. Nonetheless, marriage remains the central focus of research on intimate ties in later life, making awareness of serious gaps in research and an appreciation for the broader context of intimate ties crucial. For example, as we know from Chapter 2, the majority of older women are not married. To discuss only marital ties excludes other intimate relationships that some of these women may have. As well, discussions of single persons tend to assume that there are no intimate relations occurring when, in fact, some of these persons may be gay or lesbian and some, whether gay or straight, may have ongoing intimate ties. Our failure to ask about this side of life in old age makes it unlikely that we will discover much about it. But it is intimacy, not marriage per se, which is important to well-being and health (Traupmann & Hatfield, 1981). Therefore, we need to better understand the intimate relationships of older married *and* unmarried individuals.

How do our social arrangements help or hinder the prospects of having different types of intimate relationships flourish at varying points in the life course? Reflecting current age relations, we tend to view change, particularly in the realm of sexuality and intimate relationships, as the purview of young people (Connidis, 2006). The experience of old people is assumed to be stable and, implicitly, stale—certainly not where new things are happening. Yet the young old, those aged 65 to 74 years, are described by some as important actors in creating new ways of engaging in intimate relationships (Borell & Ghazanfareeon Karlsson, 2003). Among today's old people, changes over time in gender relations, sexuality and monogamy have set an important context for the negotiation of intimate relationships over their life course.

More egalitarian gender relations and the greater openness to and variety of sexual expression, including its separation from marriage, go hand in hand. Younger cohorts experience the result of these changes; older cohorts have lived the transitions that created them. Despite ageist views that align innovation with youth, greater longevity may be one reason that we are now more receptive to putting into action shifting views of gender and sexuality. An older society is not necessarily a more conservative one; instead, aging is often associated with greater tolerance among older persons (Danigelis et al., 2007). The longer we live, the more change is a constant feature of our lives and a lifetime commitment a much longer reality. As well, more time in a stage of life that is not dominated by paid work can redefine gender relations in intimate partnerships.

In sum, intimate relationships are characterized by continuity and change. Most people continue to marry, and most of those who do not marry form other types of intimate relationships. There is also a long history to the types of intimate partnerships that we now consider new, including living with a gay or lesbian partner and engaging in a long-term liaison that is not sanctioned by marriage. What has changed is the numbers of people who engage in these options and their openness about doing so. Despite the considerable change that we witness regarding intimate relationships, however, the significance of marital status and the power of marriage as an institution cannot be denied.

The Significance of Marital Status

Marital status is a central facet of family structure and is related to a variety of outcomes, including living arrangements, loneliness, psychological and material well-being, and health. The impact of marital status stems in part from the macro-level structured social relations that pervade family life: gender, age, sexual orientation, race, ethnicity and class. The historically patriarchal institution of marriage bestows privileges and assumes obligations differentially, depending upon gendered power relations (Arber, 2004). As a social institution, marriage extends rewards that are not available to other intimate relationships (Wilmoth & Koso, 2002). Growing flexibility in such practices as offering work-based benefits to partners other than a spouse dilutes the impact of being married somewhat, but this rarely applies to today's old people. Marital status, along with household composition and other family situations, also shapes life chances (Hatch, 2000). The intersection of structured social relations with one another and with family circumstances creates a dynamic variety of outcomes based on occupying a particular marital status.

Having a wife or partner reinforces masculinity among older men, and partnership status is crucial to material well-being and social relationships, but in different ways for men and women (Arber, Davidson, et al., 2003). Men benefit more than women from the relationship skills and investments of their partners, putting unattached men at risk of social isolation in old age (Arber, Price, et al., 2003). Older women rely greatly on their partners for economic security, putting unattached old women at particular risk of poverty (Arber, Price, et al., 2003; Price & Ginn, 2003; Street & Connidis, 2001). The intersection of gender with marital status is more complicated than this, however. Research in the United Kingdom (Arber, 2004; Arber, Price, et al., 2003) indicates that divorced and never-married men are especially prone to social isolation and also to poverty. Among old women, social connections are strong, regardless of marital status. Although widowed and especially divorced old women experience dramatic material disadvantage, women who never married are generally financially secure, as are married women. Thus the different life course contexts of today's old men and women alter the impact of a particular situation, such as being single or married.

Marital status is also related to health, both psychological and physiological. The married enjoy higher well-being than the unmarried (George, 2006). Although earlier work suggests that being married enhances happiness more than does cohabiting (Stack & Eshleman, 1998), the fact that greater gender equality enhances the longevity of cohabiting relationships (Sprecher & Regan, 2000) makes cohabitation a desirable option for egalitarian women and men. As well, older couples who cohabit enjoy improvements to their well-being that parallel the impact of being married (Brown et al., 2005).

Among the unmarried, the never married report higher levels of life satisfaction and well-being than do the widowed, divorced and separated (Cotten, 1999; Stack & Eshleman, 1998). Living alone after being widowed may matter more than marital status itself for well-being in old age when compared with earlier life

Photo 3.1   Special occasions, such as weddings, bring family members together, including those who are widowed.

stages (George, 2006). Although the single elderly have a smaller network of immediate family because they have always been spouseless and, with very few exceptions, childless, they more often live with someone else than do their previously married peers (Stull & Scarisbrick-Hauser, 1989). Among the never married who do live alone, solo living is more often a long-established lifestyle than is the case for the widowed. Special occasions, such as weddings, provide opportunities for those who have lost a partner to be part of their larger family networks, as illustrated in Photo 3.1.

The lower morale of the widowed compared to the single indicates the greater negative impact of desolation (feeling forsaken and lonely) than isolation (being on one's own; Gubrium, 1974). Loneliness is also greater among the unmarried who have had previous relationships than among those who have not (Peters & Liefbroer, 1997), indicating the greater impact of losing a partner than simply not having one.

Black married women are less satisfied with their marriages than White women, and Black men and women report less harmonious marriages than do White Americans (Broman, 1993). The less-rewarding marriages of African Americans are due in part to their lower levels of spousal support and financial satisfaction. Nonetheless, although African American older women show more depressive symptoms than White women, being married means better well-being for both White and Black women (Cochran et al., 1999). As is true of heterosexuals, a committed monogamous relationship increases life satisfaction among gay and lesbian older persons. Gay men with such intimate ties are less lonely and depressed and happier than those who are unattached (Brown et al., 1997). Loneliness among heterosexuals is also offset by having a partner but more so for men than for women (Peters & Liefbroer, 1997).

Overall, regardless of age, married persons are the healthiest, followed by single, widowed, divorced and separated persons (Verbrugge, 1979). Cohabitation tends to mimic the positive effects of marriage on health. However, important variations appear if age and living arrangement are considered. The relationship of marriage to health is partly due to the selection process in which the healthy are more likely to marry and the unhealthy to stay single or fail to remain married (Verbrugge, 1979). Marriage also has protective effects over the life course (Moen & Chermack, 2005). Being married promotes better health because a partner encourages healthy behavior and provides support when ill (Schone & Weinick, 1998; Umberson, 1992a). Living with someone else and having greater economic security, especially for women, are additional reasons that marriage enhances health (Hahn, 1993; Waite, 1995; Zick & Smith, 1991). Marriage reduces the need to rely on formal services, a common measure of illness or health decline, and is the basis for a broader range of assumed and actual informal support, especially among older men (Connidis & McMullin, 1994; Moen & Chermack, 2005). The better health of the never married than the previously married suggests again that desolation is more stressful than simply being unmarried. Indeed, some research indicates that marital status variations in subjective health reflect the strains of divorce and widowhood rather than the gains of being married (Williams & Umberson, 2004).

Clearly, marital status is a critical context of social life. The preceding discussion illustrates the necessity to distinguish among various forms of being unmarried (widowed, divorced, separated and single) and the gendered impact of marital status. Just as important is the need to consider marital history and variations in marital quality. Most research focuses on current marital status, but this masks major life course differences among older persons of the same status. Being married once or three times, or being divorced after one long marriage or after three short ones, constitute significantly different life course trajectories and consequent outcomes in later life. For example, work in the Netherlands (Peters & Liefbroer, 1997) shows that the more relationship breakups one has experienced, the lonelier one feels, regardless of current marital status. Time does tend to heal, and loneliness (Peters & Liefbroer, 1997) and declines in subjective health (Williams & Umberson, 2004) abate as the time lapse grows since a breakup. Variations in marital quality also make a difference. Although being in a relationship generally enhances well-being, being in an unhappy one does not, in which case being alone is a better alternative (Ross, 1995).

A life course approach to marital history takes into account the sequencing or ordering of marital transitions, the movement in and out of marital statuses themselves, and the duration or length of time spent in a particular marital status (Dupre & Meadows, 2007). Data over a 50-year period for men and women born between 1931 and 1941 show that marital status sequencing, transitions, and duration contribute to health across time but in different ways according to gender. Among women, age at first marriage, marriage duration, and the number of divorces over time are key contributors to health. Early marriage and more divorces increase the risk of a serious health condition, but the benefits of marriage duration to health also offset the negative impact of divorces on women's health later in life. Among men, the length of time spent married and the number of times widowed appear to be key; the longer men are married, the less likely they are to become ill as they age. However, marriage duration does not diminish the negative impact of widowhood transitions on men's health.

Similarly, wealth in middle age is associated with marital history, not marital status alone, and the impact is shaped by gender. Among 51- to 61-year-old men and women, marital dissolution means less accumulated economic wealth, especially when it is due to divorce rather than widowhood, occurs more than once, and is not followed by remarriage (Wilmoth & Koso, 2002). When compared with men, women's wealth is more negatively affected by staying single (counter to work on older cohorts in which women's career aspirations and marriage were not compatible with getting married), divorcing, and separating from a second marriage. On the other hand, men and women share the financial benefits of remarriage. Marital history is also related to mortality; being married over an extended period reduces the risk of mortality for both men and women, and remarrying lessens the mortality risk of marital dissolution for all but divorced men (Brockmann & Klein, 2004). Finally, stage in the life course alters the impact of transitions in marital status on subjective health. Remarriage early in life improves subjective health but, among those aged 70 years or more, marrying again makes it *less* likely that men and, especially, women view their health as very good or excellent (Williams & Umberson, 2004). The significance of marital history and its timing reflect the value of applying the life course perspective to intimate relationships.

We now turn to consider an aspect of later life that is, to date, profoundly affected by marital status: sexuality.

Sexuality and Aging

Sexuality . . . is now a means of forging connections with others on the basis of intimacy, no longer grounded in an immutable kinship order sustained across the generations.

—Giddens (1992:175)

Although much of the research on sexuality and aging focuses more on the mechanics of sex than feelings about it, it does clarify some misconceptions about aging and sexual activity. *Ageism* is now a familiar concept. One longstanding example of ageist attitudes is the view of older persons as asexual adults who are not and should not be interested in sex. Fortunately, this view has softened among all age groups, and today, older persons are more open to discussing and engaging in sexual activity (Hooyman & Kiyak, 1999). The incredible media attention paid to impotence and sex-enhancing drugs, such as Viagra, has brought the issue of aging and sex into the open, even though relatively few men actually use the drug (American Association of Retired Persons, 1999a).

Historically, a major reason for linking sex with marriage was to ensure that reproduction occurred within marriage (Sprey, 1972). Generally, reproduction does not apply to sexual activity later in life (unless it involves an older man and a much younger woman), potentially weakening the concern of confining sex to marriage in later life (Connidis, 2006). Unlike heterosexual ties, gay and lesbian sexual relationships have not been associated with reproduction at any age (Giddens, 1992). Thus, as barriers to sexual activity outside marriage are broken down, gay and lesbian relationships could prove instructive about the nature of sex in later life for everyone. The intersecting influence of sexual orientation and differential access to the institution of marriage is evident in the contrasting sexual pathways of straight and gay men:

> Like the opposite poles of a compass, the possibility and impossibility of marriage . . . [propel] heterosexual men into career trajectories characterized by a reduction in sexual partners and the gradual, if imperfect, adoption of monogamous norms and dyadic commitment and, conversely, [drive] homosexual men into sexual career trajectories characterized by increasing sexual exploration, dyadic innovation, and a reevaluation of the meaning and value of monogamy. Yet, these contrasting structural positions aside, both sets of men articulate shared ambivalences around structured life paths that permit the satisfaction of some desires while frustrating or precluding altogether the realization of others. (Green, 2006:164)

The structured social relation of sexual orientation creates unequal access to the right to marry, creating ambivalence for both groups of men by curtailing agency in the choices to honor monogamy and sexual freedom.

Over the past few decades, a new set of sex rules has evolved as people of all ages try out alternatives to marriage, such as cohabiting, same-sex partnerships, and living apart together (Connidis, 2006). The separation of sex from marriage raises the issue of monogamy. When many of today's older persons were children or teenagers, monogamy had already come to mean sexual exclusiveness within a relationship, not only one person for a lifetime as was true in earlier times (Folsom, 1937). Despite more equal relations of gender and sexual orientation, monogamy remains a pivotal assumption of committed intimate relationships (Waite & Joyner, 2001). Discourse and research on a variety of intimate relationships often returns to monogamous sex as either essential to commitment or as the greatest challenge to forging new forms of relationships. Drugs like Viagra that promote male sexual functioning lead older wives to fear their husband's infidelity (Potts et al., 2003), cohabiting couples to worry about their partners' commitment to monogamy (Treas & Giesen, 2000), and gay partners to keep secret their sexual encounters with others (Worth et al., 2002). At the same time that there is greater openness to alternative intimate ties, marriage continues to be valued (Thornton & Young-DeMarco, 2001).

Assuming that old people hold traditional views of marriage and sex ignores the reality of their early years (Connidis, 2006). Writing in 1937, Folsom (1937:720) observed, "Persons already married and dissatisfied with their sex life are stimulated by the surrounding ideology to demand supplementary relationships, which under the traditional culture, they would have regarded as unthinkable." During World War II (1939–1945), the number of babies born outside of marriage in the United States shot up, especially in the last two years of the war (Leder, 2006). This most obvious sign of sexual activity did not apply only to single women; women in their 20s and 30s married to overseas servicemen also had a high rate of births that did not involve their husbands. During this time, despite rules to the contrary, the armed forces also provided a venue where lesbian relationships flourished. Considering intimate relationships among today's older persons reveals how aging and age relations cut across views of gender, sex and monogamy, illustrating both continuity and change in attitudes and behavior.

Two shortcomings of the limited research on sexuality in old age have distorted our understanding of this topic (Hooyman & Kiyak, 1999). First, attention has often focused on the frequency of heterosexual intercourse to assess the significance of sex to older persons' lives. This approach excludes discussion about the quality and meaning of sex and excludes gay and lesbian sexual relations altogether. Among heterosexuals, declines in intercourse alone need not signal a decline in either the interest older persons have in sexual relations or in the importance of sex to their intimate relationships. Sexuality is a far broader concept than sexual intercourse, and touching, caressing, holding hands and kissing are important forms of sexual expression in older age (Neugebauer-Visano, 1995).

Second, most research on sexual activity is cross-sectional so that the activity of one age group is compared with the activity of other age groups. Such a comparison shows that older persons engage in sexual intercourse less often than other groups but cannot tell us about changes in sexual activity over time. Research that does address sexual activity over the life course finds that our practices as younger adults are carried into old age; those who are active in younger years remain that way in old age, given the opportunity (Hooyman & Kiyak, 1999). As well, older people who are more sexually active are more satisfied with their sex lives (Matthias et al., 1997), and their view of themselves and their competence is bolstered by sexual activity (Marsiglio & Donnelly, 1991). Thus sexuality remains a significant component of intimate relationships in later life.

Research on sexuality and aging reported by AARP (1999a), in an article titled "Great Sex: What's Age Got to Do With It?," updates our understanding of later-life sex and identifies important issues on this topic among heterosexuals. The AARP study is based on mail surveys completed by 1,384 adults aged 45 and older in 1999. Two-thirds of the men and almost 60% of the women believed that a good sexual relationship is an important contributor to their quality of life. Among men and women with sexual partners, 60% of those aged 45 to 59 had sexual intercourse once a week or more, and one quarter of those aged 75 and over did so. More than 75% of this group had sex once a month or more.

Specifying that we are talking about people with partners is an important qualifier, as information on this group alone masks several gaps among older persons. There is a *partner gap* that is related to age and gender. As we know from Chapter 2, men are far more likely than women to have partners, particularly spouses. Because being married is overwhelmingly the most significant predictor of sexual activity among heterosexual women (Matthias et al., 1997), differences in marital status are important to our understanding of gender variations in sexual activity. Indeed, among those who are married, there are no gender differences in sexual activity (Marsiglio & Donnelly, 1991).

Sexual invisibility is an experience often reported by older women, who have mixed views about it. Those who would like to be noticed find this a drawback of aging. One group that is especially prone to experiencing invisibility is lesbian women (Auger, 1995). The combination of being old, women, and lesbian makes them a particularly marginal group, of limited interest to mainstream culture and research. Many remain in the closet, fearful of coming out to others, including children and grandchildren. But for some, older age provides some license to explore their sexuality:

> When [my daughter] told me that she was gay I thought about it quite a lot. I have also loved women, liked them better than men. Now, I just wish that there was someone I could meet so that I could have a lesbian relationship. I have given it a lot of thought and I am ready for that thrill. No one cares about little old ladies of 70 anyway, so I should be able to get away with it until I die. (Woman in her 70s; Auger, 1995:109)

For some women, such as well-known feminist Gloria Steinem, the invisibility of old age is a welcome relief from a lifetime of attention. At 65, in an interview with Claudia Dreifus, she observed,

> The sexual response of men you're not attracted to can be awful . . . [Invisibility] is a complaint many older people have, but it's not a problem for me. While most women have had too little visibility in their lives, I've had an overdose of it. (AARP, 1999b)

Mixed responses are also evident in letters to advice columnists from women whose partners are taking sex performance drugs, such as Viagra. Although many are delighted that their spouses can engage in desired sexual activity once again, some feel cheated of the relief from sexual obligations that impotence provided. This disparity is evident in research as well, with some women happy to anticipate sex for life and others bemoaning their partner's resurging ability to have intercourse (Potts et al., 2003; Vares et al., 2007; see Chapter 4).

The AARP (1999a) study also reports *gender and age gaps* in views on sexual activity. Sexual activity is considered a more important dimension of life quality by men than by women, and its significance declines somewhat with age. However, these differences are likely to reflect in part the acceptance of limited opportunity by women (the absence of a partner or health limitations) and a focus on other sources of satisfaction in later life rather than innate differences between men and women or a feature of aging itself.

Last, a *generation gap* regarding appropriate sexual activity makes it probable that future cohorts of older persons will more freely engage in sexual relations outside of marriage. As well, the acceptance by young and middle-aged adults of sexual activity that extends beyond intercourse (AARP, 1999a; Giddens, 1992) will make declines in male performance (e.g., erectile dysfunction) less central to satisfactory sex for future older persons. Aging itself may improve sexual satisfaction, as some evidence suggests that men and women become more similar in their sexual preferences as they age (AARP, 1999a, 1999c), once the transition through midlife menopause and viropause (the male parallel to menopause, also called andropause) is complete. Other conditions also converge to potentially enhance sexual satisfaction after 50: more free time, no fear of pregnancy, no children at home, and enjoying sex beyond "the Act" (AARP, 1999c).

In sum, aging brings with it a decline in sexual activity, but for those with partners, a history of an active sex life is carried into older age. Sexual activity remains important to older persons of all sexual orientations, but access to a partner can prove difficult, especially for women. Studies of sexuality and aging must pay more attention to alternative ways of sexual expression, the fundamental significance of intimate bodily contact, and the meaning of sexual intimacy to older persons. Broader conceptions of sexuality highlight the benefits of intimate ties, the challenges of not having a partner, and the failure of formal responses to care to accommodate this important dimension of later life. Even those married couples who have private rooms in institutional settings find that expressing their sexuality is constrained. An 88-year-old husband observes, "We just get started, and it takes longer to start these days, when they come in here. It is so embarrassing. We don't feel we are able to have a normal life or a complete marriage any longer" (Neugebauer-Visano, 1995:25). In subsequent chapters we consider sexuality further in the context of particular partnerships and in their absence.

CHAPTER 4

Intimate Partnerships

Interdependence in
Long-Term Intimate Partnerships

In a close relationship there is high interdependence and intense activity and interaction between partners (Kelley, 1981: 279). Interdependence varies based on its extent, the balance of dependence between partners (equal versus unequal), whether partners' interests are shared or in conflict, and the degree of individual versus joint action (Kelley, 1981). How do life transitions that often occur in older age affect these dimensions of long-term intimate partnerships? Some changes may increase interdependence and contribute to a closer relationship; others may disrupt prior patterns of interdependence and undermine closeness between partners. Because the four properties of interdependence vary among couples, so too does interdependence in their relationships.

The dialectic of personal growth and physiological decline that comes with aging is at the heart of close relationships (Allen & Walker, 2006) and is associated with greater interdependence in the marital relationship. Most married persons aged 50 and over maintain considerable reciprocity in support exchanges with their spouses (Depner & Ingersoll-Dayton, 1985). In part because social contacts and leisure activities decline in older age, the companionship and communication provided by a partner take on heightened importance as sources of satisfaction. A shortage of shared interests threatens gratifying interaction between spouses. Research in the Netherlands finds that companionate interdependence grows later in life, as the time spent together in leisure activities increases, following a decline in the middle years (Kalmijn & Bernasco, 2001).

Interdependence in the marital tie is shaped by culture and by circumstance. For example, Japanese couples are much more likely to emphasize complementary mutual dependence on one another's gender-based roles than are White Americans, who focus more on equity in later-life marriage (Ingersoll-Dayton et al., 1996). African American couples are also highly interdependent, but in their case, both partners develop parallel skills so that they can substitute for one another when needed, an innovative response to the more frequent necessity to have both partners in the labor force. There is less exclusive reliance on spouses in African American and Latino families, however; in both cases, a broader caregiving network places less primacy on the spouse as the source of care (Yarry et al., 2007).

Whether straight or gay, partners who value independence are less satisfied with their relationships than are couples who value interdependence (Julien et al., 1999; Kurdek, 1992). Because transitions associated with older age may increase the need for interdependence and decrease the emphasis on gender among heterosexual couples, aging may actually enhance intimate ties. We now turn to a closer examination of marriage, the marital status most common among today's older persons for most of their lives. Because this currently means a focus on heterosexual couples, long-term gay and lesbian relationships are discussed in the following section. In Chapter 6, other types of intimate relationships are discussed.

Marriage in Later Life

> There is an intrinsic and inescapable conflict in marriage. Human beings want incompatible things . . . They want excitement and adventure. They also want safety and security. These desiderata are difficult to combine in one relationship. Without a commitment, one has freedom but not security; with a commitment, one has security but little freedom.
>
> —Bernard (1972: 89)

In the foregoing quote, Bernard captures the ambivalence of marital ties. Yet much research on marriage across the life course looks at marriage in binary terms, such as good or bad, satisfying or unsatisfying, enhancing or limiting. This curtails our capacity to capture the realities of married life. Marriage can be both satisfying and unsatisfying, rewarding and stifling, and looking at the coexisting positives and negatives of being married allows for a more nuanced and realistic understanding of what happens in marriages over time (Carroll et al., 2005; Fincham & Bradbury, 2005). Are there shifts in what couples experience as good and bad about being married over time? Answering this question involves both the mixed sentiments or psychological ambivalence of marriage and the sociological ambivalence that results from the contradictions embedded in marital relationships, such as those based on gender.

Most men and women who have a partner in old age are married. Current interest in divorce, cohabitation, living apart together, and other issues of change have displaced attention to long-term marriage. Studies of previous cohorts of long-term married couples are instructive, but we are left wondering whether the story of what keeps couples together and happy remains the same. The focus on love as the centerpiece of marriage has endured for generations now (Connidis, 2006). Over 70 years ago, Groves (1934:412) concluded that marriage "is chiefly an adventure in affection. . . . The love-craving of modern men and women is making marriage success harder to achieve. . . . Marriage success is difficult in the modern world because marriage means so much." The view of marriage as primarily concerned with companionship, love, and intimacy (Praeger, 2000) and as a way of securing love (Skolnick, 1998) still holds. Among individuals married 17 years or more, the top-ranked factor for keeping their marriages together is love (Previti & Amato, 2003).

Marital Satisfaction Across the Life Course

Those who are more satisfied and happy with their marriages enjoy better mental health and well-being (Quirouette & Gold, 1995). Persistent marital strain is more detrimental than divorce to mental health, ongoing conflict between spouses concerning daily roles may lead to depression (Keith & Schafer, 1985), and a poor marriage may also threaten physical health (Umberson & Williams, 2005). These findings underscore the need to attend to the qualitative dimension of marriage as well as the impact of marital status. Looking at marital satisfaction over time reflects a life course focus on trajectories that takes into account the impact of particular transitions, such as having children, on the long-term dynamics of a relationship, in this case, marriage (Umberson et al., 2005).

Traditionally, research on changes in a couple's marital satisfaction over time focused on the impact of the family life cycle, typically employing the eight stages of family life, or variations on them, initially proposed by Duvall (1967). This model uses age of the oldest child to determine the stages of the family cycle. Couples who are childless following seven years of marriage are often excluded, and only individuals or couples whose marriages remain intact tend to be included. This makes generalizations to all married couples problematic. As well, the historical reliance on a cross-sectional design (comparing the marital satisfaction of different age groups at one point in time) means that observed differences may occur because the younger age groups include unhappy couples who eventually divorce, whereas the later stages include only those couples whose marriages have survived. Also, those who have been married for a long time may be more likely to report being satisfied with their marriages to justify having stayed married for so long.

Based on such work, the conventional wisdom for years was that marriages follow a curvilinear pattern in which marital satisfaction starts out relatively high, decreases for a time until children are launched, and then increases in the later stages, after children have left home (Lupri & Frideres, 1981; Vaillant & Vaillant, 1993). Are the observed improvements in marital satisfaction in the later stages of the life course real? Age-related changes in the criteria of assessment may help account for apparent gains in marital satisfaction in later life. As an 80-year-old woman in one of my studies observed, one becomes "a little easier with people, a little less critical perhaps, as you get older. You can see your own faults and perhaps you are a little more tolerant with other people's faults." When long-term marital partners reflect on their marriages, they observe the standard curvilinear pattern with a dip in satisfaction during the child-rearing or midlife years of marriage (Vaillant & Vaillant, 1993). When the same individuals report on the current state of their marriages at different points in time, marital satisfaction is remarkably stable over the middle and later years. The latter prospective accounts are favored as "truer" accounts of what "really" happened, but perhaps it is only with the advantage of hindsight that one can judge the relative merits of a marriage over time.

Developments in longitudinal analysis have improved our study of marriage over time. Glenn (1998) suggests that observations of change in marital satisfaction are actually a function of cohort effects—differences among cohorts in marital stability and quality rather than differences over time in the course of all marriages. Rather than following a curvilinear pattern, marital success, gauged in terms of staying together and of assessing an intact marriage as very happy, tends to experience quite a dramatic downturn in the first two decades and a slower downturn thereafter. Indeed, among parents, after an earlier decline, marital love and satisfaction tend to plateau at the 20-year mark while marital conflict is fairly stable over the second decade of marriage (Whiteman et al., 2007). There is no evidence of an upturn in marital quality in the later years of long-term marriages (Glenn, 1998) and some evidence of declines over time among those aged 55 and over (VanLaningham et al., 2001). Thus, the apparent improvement in marriages over time is a function of relying on cross-sectional designs that fail in part because they do not take into account divorce and its increase over succeeding cohorts.

Recent research (Whiteman et al., 2007) shows declines in marital love and marital satisfaction and a slight increase in marital conflict when children hit puberty, typically at about the 14th to 17th year of marriage. Children appear to be central to the assessment of a marriage among parents, and childless spouses tend to be happier and more satisfied with their marriages than parents (Lupri & Frideres, 1981), a pattern that is magnified among more recent cohorts (Twenge et al., 2003). Couples without children spend more leisure time together than do married couples with children living at home (Kalmijn & Bernasco, 2001), suggesting one reason that marital satisfaction is higher among them. Also, children are seen as a primary barrier to leaving a marriage among those who have been married for 17 years or more (Previti & Amato, 2003), which may lead some parents to stay together even when they are not happy with their marriages.

Indeed, although aging softens the edges of relationships with parents, children and best friends, growing old together does not have the same impact on the sentiments of long-term couples; instead, they become more apt to see their mates as too demanding and irritating with the passage of time (Akiyama et al., 2003). Older Black couples experience more marital conflict than older White couples (Carr, 2004a). Over the life course, both men and women experience increased marital strain, but after the age of 30, women experience higher levels of strain than men do (Umberson, et al., 2005; Umberson & Williams, 2005). The impact of such changes is compounded by the fact that negative marital quality (dissatisfaction, conflict) has a greater impact on personal well-being than does positive marital quality (satisfaction, love, harmony) as marriages last longer (Proulx et al., 2007). Among those with marriages characterized by unhappiness and conflict, barring divorce, the prognosis is further deterioration in the marital relationship as they enter old age.

On balance, older couples appear to be more satisfied with their marriages than their middle-aged and younger counterparts, but they are not happier with their marriages than they were when they were younger (Umberson et al., 2005). Nonetheless, today's older men and women in long-term marriages tend to enjoy relatively high levels of marital satisfaction (Lauer et al., 1995; Umberson et al., 2005). The fact that the vast majority of couples whose children refill the empty nest are very satisfied with their marriages suggests that long-term marriages develop their own resiliency, making couples able to handle unexpected trajectories in the life plans of other family members (Mitchell & Gee, 1996).

The Nature of Long-Term Unions

A qualitative study of marriages that endured for 50 years or more (Dickson, 1995) reveals three types of long-term marriage: connected couples who are very close, intimate and mutually dependent; functional separate couples who are happy, caring and satisfied with their marriages but also enjoy their own activities and independence; and dysfunctional separate couples who are distant and dissatisfied with their marriages. Thus, even among long-term married couples, there is disparity in degrees of marital contentment and satisfaction, as well as in what makes a marriage rewarding

Do long-term marriages have qualities that are different from their shorter-term counterparts? Qualities that enhance long-term marriage are love; mutual trust, respect and support; loyalty and fidelity; mutual give and take; similar philosophy on life; shared fun and sense of humor; shared interests; enjoying one another's company; mutual interest in their children; and, especially among American couples, corresponding religious beliefs (Lauer et al., 1995; Sharlin et al., 2000). Commitment to one's partner, not just to the principle of marriage, differentiates happy from unhappy marriages (Lauer et al., 1995). Sexual orientation does not create differences among long-term couples (together for 30 years or more) in which factors enhance relationship satisfaction (Mackey et al., 2004). Straight, lesbian and gay couples are more satisfied with their relationships when there is psychological intimacy, meaning open and honest communication with a partner, and minimal conflict. As marriages and committed relationships endure over time, they require ongoing negotiation in response to changing times and situations; marriages are in motion as spouses perpetually engage in "doing marriage" (Van den Troost, 2005: 273).

The two most commonly listed trouble spots in longer marriages are having different values and philosophies of life and lack of mutual interests (Sporakowski & Hughston, 1978). These dimensions of marriage tend to be relatively enduring, indicating an incompatibility between spouses that is unlikely to surface for the first time in older age. Therefore, the continuity of the marital relationship must be highlighted, for it is rare that an unhappy marriage becomes a happy one in old age. Concerns about the future of a long-term marriage include financial security, especially among older couples, and shared views of sexual fulfillment (Sharlin et al., 2000).

As we have seen, gender relations play out in long-term marriages; older men are more satisfied with marriage than older women. Although both men and women enjoy health benefits when marriages are good, the greater marital quality reported by men than women means a greater net health benefit of marriage to men than women (Umberson & Williams, 2005). Are there reasons for the greater marital satisfaction of men and for differing priorities in marriage by gender? Women, particularly older women whose marriages are more traditional, are more emotionally responsive to their partner (Quirouette & Gold, 1995). Both husbands and wives agree that when marriages or phases of them are inequitable, it is the men who gain and the women who lose (Peterson, 1995). Indeed, old women but not men are more satisfied with their marriages when decision-making powers are equal (Kulik, 2002). Yet men but not women are happier with their later-life marriages when they hold more egalitarian views (Kaufman & Taniguchi, 2006). Perhaps more egalitarian attitudes among men make them more accepting of the greater similarity between partners in their social situation that comes with aging, such as both being out of the labor force.

Women generally have a more extensive network of close relationships than men (Moen & Chermack, 2005). Although men and women have similar numbers of primary relatives, men restrict confidant status primarily to their wives, whereas women include all primary relatives along with close friends among their confidants (Depner & Ingersoll-Dayton, 1985; see also Connidis & Davies, 1990, 1992). There also tends to be greater closeness between female kin (e.g., mothers and daughters and between sisters) than between other gender combinations (see Chapters 7 and 11). Women's broader array of potential confidants provides a basis for comparison that may sometimes favor other relatives or friends over their spouses, leading women to judge their marriages more harshly than men do (Depner & Ingersoll-Dayton, 1985). With fewer alternatives, men may place a higher value on the spousal relationship.

Much of the effort to assess whether marriages are good rests on individual satisfaction. Critics suggest that signs of a good marriage should include such individual attributes as sacrifice and loyalty, as well as the positive impact of marital well-being on families, the community, and society (Carroll et al., 2005). This multilevel approach is in keeping with the theoretical framework outlined in Chapter 1, but the challenge is to take a *critical* multilevel approach. Because marriage is permeated by structured social relations, the contributions that marriage can make to the well-being of families, communities and society are unevenly made by particular family members. The current imbalanced focus on individual satisfaction is a counter to previous imbalances in which the interests of some groups of individuals, notably women but also gay and lesbian adults, were sacrificed in the name of assumed family, community and societal interests.

We now take a further look at the unique features of long-term unions. The personal stories of long-married couples indicate that a key contributor to marital success is mutual support of one another's independence and pursuit of separate interests (Thomas, 2005). Given how gender relations have changed over time, such support is likely to have required adjustment on behalf of one or both spouses, as was true for former President Jimmy Carter and his wife Rosalynn. Both agree that Jimmy Carter's earlier male chauvinism gradually gave way to a shared view that "a good marriage allows each partner to have some breathing room" (Thomas, 2005: 3). At the same time, other transitions that come with aging may create shared needs and heighten interdependence, transforming gender relations in late-life marriages.

Sexuality in Long-Term Marriages

A unique feature of marriage and similar intimate ties is the emotional closeness that comes from sexual sharing that need not include intercourse (Ade-Ridder, 1990). Among straight, lesbian and gay long-term couples in one study, sexual relations declined but remained important (Mackey et al., 2004). Over time, the nature of love and sexuality in marriage changes, as erotic love gives way to friendship-based love by middle age (Grote & Frieze 1998 in Hendrick & Hendrick, 2000), and passionate love and sexual activity decline as couples get old (Sprecher & Regan, 2000). Sexual intimacy continues to be important in long-term marriages, and among sexually active couples, greater sexual interest and activity are related to happier marriages (Ade-Ridder, 1990).

Sexuality in late-life marriage involves the ongoing negotiation of intersecting age and gender relations. Husbands and wives agree that sex is critical to marital happiness at the same time that they vary in sexual desire (husbands being more interested than wives) and experience sex as conflict-ridden terrain in their relationship (Elliott & Umberson, 2008). Both men and women are subject to age-related views of what constitutes physical and sexual appeal as well as virility (Connidis, 2006). Feminist approaches tend to ignore this reality for men, but they do underscore the different realities of men and women and the power relations of negotiating sex in marital relationships. However, even feminist perspectives tend to pay limited attention to the unique experiences of old men or women, including their sexuality (Vares et al., 2007). Research on middle-aged men and women shows the earlier onset of aging's negative impact on the sexual activity of women than of men, suggesting the intersection of ageism and sexism, but it does not delve into couple relationships (Carpentier et al., 2006).

The focus on intercourse that results from the marketing of male sex-enhancing drugs reinforces traditional heterosexual sex in which the male is dominant and the female submissive (Potts et al., 2003). A husband's independent use of Viagra or similar medications may enhance his attempts to exercise agency regarding sexual performance at the expense of his wife's power to have her preferences heard. At the same time, such medical interventions can help to preserve a couple's loving sexual relationship when a husband's health problems have interfered with sexual performance (Jacoby, 2005). As well, when men's sexual performance diminishes, the renegotiation of sexual relations that follows leads some couples to engage in new forms of intimacy that improve their relationship and sexual satisfaction (Vares et al., 2007).

Race and class relations also influence sexuality in later life. Among White, Asian, African Americans and Hispanics, White Americans are most likely to believe that sexual activity should be confined to marriage, and Asian and White Americans are more likely to see sex as less important to older people (AARP, 2005 reported in Skultety, 2007). Living arrangements also make a difference. Despite improved conditions, institutional environments tend to limit opportunities for sexual intimacy, as does co-residing with an adult child (Skultety, 2007).

The medicalization of sexuality in old age through hormone replacement therapy for women and sexual performance enhancing drugs for men reinforces the cultural emphasis on youth and freezes masculinity and femininity in time and in hormones (Marshall & Katz, 2006). Equating sexual success in later life with the performance and preferences of much younger ages risks making old couples feel inadequate sexually and fails to highlight real advantages of being older (see Davis, 1980; Katz, 2005; Katz & Marshall, 2003; Potts et al., 2003: 711). When in her 70s, Heilbrun (1997) argued for new ways of defining adventure in old age that did not hold old persons to the same cultural equation of yearning with sex that is promoted for the young, and not necessarily to their advantage either.

Older persons typically describe their sexual partners (usually spouses) as their best friends and as kind and gentle, reflecting qualitative dimensions of the sexually active relationship (AARP, 1999a). The fact that the cessation of sexual activity, usually due to the husband's inability to perform, is not related to lower marital quality (Ade-Ridder, 1990) shows that couples find alternative ways of providing sexual intimacy and happiness to one another (Vares et al., 2007). Indeed, having a good relationship is important to more old people (9 out of 10) than is a good sexual relationship (67% of men and 57% of women; AARP, 1999a).

For some couples, the passage of time actually improves sexual relations. A 68-year-old man says,

> My wife and I have been married for 40 years and I have never looked back. She's the light of my life, and as sexy as ever . . . our sex life is better now than when we first got married. (Neugebauer-Visano, 1995: 21)

One reason for this is suggested by a 70-year-old wife's observation: "I find it easier to talk about my [sexual] needs in my old age." Similarly, a husband, aged 69, says, "After a while you feel comfortable enough to ask your partner to do things that you only dream about doing, without being shy about it" (Neugebauer-Visano, 1995: 21). The importance of building trust and comfort over time raises the question of causal order. Although it may be that sexual activity enhances marriage, the reverse may also apply, namely, that the quality of a relationship is important to a good sex life, particularly in older age (AARP, 1999a).

Gay and Lesbian Partnerships

In August 1999, *Maclean's Magazine* (Canada's equivalent to *Time* or *Newsweek*) ran a cover story titled, "Sex and Marriage: Can passion survive kids, careers and the vagaries of aging?" (August 9). In a subsequent issue (Letter to the editor, August 23, 1999:4), a reader wrote from New York City,

> You may not realize how cool it was to feature a gay couple among the pairs profiled in your "Sex and Marriage" cover story. Even better, the two men received no special treatment; they were integrated matter-of-factly into the piece. As a reader, I value that kind of fairness.

The extent to which gay and lesbian relationships are "integrated matter-of-factly" into discussions of intimate ties is a measure not only of fairness but also of our progress toward truly respecting and accepting diversity. Despite recent attention to same-sex marriage, giving special attention to these relationships remains necessary because there is less known about them and because we must emphasize the importance of including them. Much greater public and political awareness of issues related to sexual orientation is reflected in a growing body of related research, despite the ongoing backdrop of antigay discrimination (Patterson, 2008). Photo 4.1 gives a glimpse of the richness of extended family ties for some same-sex partners.

Over the past decade, a number of countries have recognized the right of same-sex couples to marry. Canada is one of these countries; the United States, generally, is not (see Chapter 14). The road to approving same-sex marriage in Canada was a

Photo 4.1   Gay couples are key players in family networks as uncles, brothers, and sons.

rocky one, and once passed, there was the threat of repeal when the government changed hands from the Liberals to the Conservatives. However, that failed, and since 2005, same-sex couples may and do marry legally in Canada. Indeed, a number of American couples have come to Canada to marry. In the United States, Massachusetts issues marriage licenses to same-sex couples; Connecticut and Vermont allow same-sex civil unions; California allows domestic partnerships; and Hawaii, Maine and New Jersey grant some marriagelike rights to unmarried couples (Allen, 2007b). At the time of writing, California voters failed to uphold same-sex marriage, and Connecticut has instituted it. Increased recognition of same-sex couples is in part attributable to research that documents their parallels with opposite-sex couples, making it hard to justify discrimination against same-sex unions (Peplau & Fingerhut, 2007; see Chapter 14 on research and policy). Yet the ongoing stigma of being other than straight leads some same-sex couples who are not out to claim single status as a cover for being gay or lesbian (Koropeckyj-Cox, 2005).

Because the right to marry (where it exists) is so new, we do not know whether it will make a difference to the nature of long-term same-sex unions. For those who marry, it makes an immediate difference to be recognized as legal next-of-kin and to be socially legitimized as a couple (Hull, 2005; Pinello, 2006). Reflecting the multilevel approach discussed in Chapter 1, legislation about who has the right to marry is a manifestation of socially structured relations of sexual orientation and underscores the link between the state at the macro level (Cohler, 2006), the institution of family at the meso level, and individual experience in families at the micro level (see Chapter 1). The strong cultural hold of marriage as an institution and an appreciation for its social standing is evident in the high percentages of gay and lesbian individuals who favor legalizing same-sex marriage (Hull, 2005) and in the dreams of marriage held by gay and straight adults when they were young (Green, 2006). A gay man in his 30s remembers that as a child and adolescent, "I wanted to have a beautiful wife, and have six to eight children. It was very important to me" (Green, 2006: 168). At the same time, a strong contingent of gay, lesbian and straight people question the patriarchal foundations of marriage (Diamond, 2006; Hull, 2005).

The ongoing issue of gay rights and a focus on homosexual identity and the coming-out process result in very little research on same-sex *relationships,* particularly those in later life (O'Brien & Goldberg, 2000). In jurisdictions that do not recognize same-sex marriage, coexisting claims of same-sex couples to be treated as committed partners with legal definitions that do not support them create socially structured ambivalence in the family relationships of gay or lesbian couples (Connidis, 2003b). Recent attempts to legalize same-sex marriage create a picture of gay and lesbian partners attempting to catch up with their heterosexual counterparts. Yet as Giddens (1992: 15) argues, "Gay women and men have preceded most heterosexuals in developing relationships . . . For they had to 'get along' without traditionally established frameworks of marriage, in conditions of relative equality between partners." Engaging in an intimate relationship that lacks a supportive social definition creates ambivalence and forces same-sex partners to self-consciously negotiate a shared personal meaning of what it means to be in a committed relationship. Thus, rather than assume that heterosexual relationships are the ideal to which homosexual partnerships should aspire, we can extend our understanding of how to create intimate relationships by understanding more about gay and lesbian unions.

The general invisibility of the old in our society is heightened for those who are old and gay or lesbian (Grossman, 1997; Lee, 1989). Even more invisible are bisexual older persons, in part because bisexuals are not embraced by the gay or straight communities. Another reason that bisexuality remains an underexplored topic in the context of partnerships is that its practice does not meet social expectations of a long-term committed relationship, monogamy, and serial rather than simultaneous relationships (Dworkin, 2006; Hunter, 2005). The greater openness to alternative sexual identities and to sexuality itself as a fluid concept has yet to translate into a body of research about the intimate partnerships of those engaged in relationships that are also defined more fluidly. The focus of this section is on gay and lesbian couples, in part because of the scant research on bisexual partners and in part because, although a limiting simplification, it permits comparisons based on one conceptual distinction: whether intimate ties are with the same or opposite sex (Connidis, 2003b).

Research to date has relied heavily on small and unrepresentative samples of gay and lesbian persons. This is especially true of research on older persons who faced far greater stigma due to their sexual orientation than is true today and are thus more difficult to locate for study. As Patterson (2008) notes, life course studies of sexual orientation are aimed at a moving target because historical time is particularly salient to the experience of gay and lesbian couples. The likelihood of having public same-sex relationships varies greatly among cohorts because of major changes in historical time and because of the age at which these changes were experienced by each cohort, two central life course principles (Cohler, 2006; see Chapter 1). Unlike younger and middle-aged adults, one study finds that older gays and lesbians who conceal their sexual orientation at work and are not very involved with the gay community are *more* satisfied with life (Adelman, 1991). For some older persons at least, concealment of a homosexual orientation appears to have been an effective strategy for managing stigma. But this contributes to their invisibility. The fact that younger cohorts tend to adjust better to a gay or lesbian identity when they disclose their orientation and are visibly involved in the gay community reflects an important generational shift (Adelman, 1991). Improving attitudes toward homosexuality have also increased openness about being gay among older men (Brown et al., 1997).

Some argue that managing the stigma of homosexuality leaves older gay persons better equipped for dealing with aging (Friend, 1996), but this conclusion may reflect the experience of relatively affluent and active gay and lesbian research participants (Ehrenberg, 1997). For many older persons, occupying two stigmatized statuses—being gay or lesbian and being old—may make older age *more* of a challenge (Bergling, 2004; Grossman, 1997). The fact that many old people are not open about being gay or lesbian suggests that their sexual orientation has not served to bolster their ability to deal with stigma. A 95-year-old lesbian emphasizes her own incredulity about staying closeted for a lifetime: " . . . all my life, literally . . . I haven't talked about it . . . It's amazing, really, that all my life . . . I've never discussed it" (Clunis et al., 2005, cited in Thompson Jr., 2006). Even some members of groups such as Senior Action in a Gay Environment (SAGE) are not out, sometimes in order to protect their current relationships with wives and children (Hunter, 2005).

Clearly, staying in the closet impedes forming long-term relationships with a same-sex partner. Coming out tends to be more difficult for members of ethnic minorities (Hunter, 2005; Manalansan, 1996) and, among gay men at least, for members of the working class (Chapple et al., 1998). Religious beliefs and cultural traditions of filial responsibility make acceptance of gay or lesbian identity more difficult among African and Asian American parents (Hunter, 2005). Conversely, Native American culture views sexual orientation as one of multiple forms of difference that are not the basis for exclusion. These differences influence both the probability of forming long-term same-sex ties and the success of such partnerships when they are formed, because concealing a gay or lesbian identity and negative reactions from family members produce strained relationships (Peplau et al., 1996). Ethnicity and class are shared with other members of one's family but typically, being gay or lesbian is not (Fullmer, 1995), heightening the potential for isolation, not only from mainstream society but also from family.

Gay and lesbian individuals are not either open or closed about their sexual orientation. Instead, choices are made about safe audiences so that some are out to everyone, some are out to friends but not family, some are out to friends and family but not at work, and so on (Bergling, 2004). This variation occurs within couples as well; the difference that family acceptance can make to the well-being of gay or lesbian partners is evident in Pat's reflections on her 32-year relationship with Betty:

> Betty's mother and sister . . . for a long time they could not accept Betty's lesbianism. There was a period of estrangement from Betty's family after her mother and sister read a letter that I had sent to her. . . . When it came down to her disappearing from their lives altogether or accepting her, they grudgingly accepted her lifestyle . . . I think that Betty was never really comfortable with herself as a lesbian. (Whipple, 2006: 46)

The issue of disclosure is unique to gay and lesbian couples and is one reason that new typologies of long-term relationships other than those of heterosexual marriage are needed (Cruikshank, 1991). A major cohort difference is the substantial number of old gay and lesbian persons who were once (or still are) in heterosexual marriages (Herdt & de Vries, 2004; Whipple, 2006). The words of a participant in a study of 44 middle- and upper-class older lesbians about her decision to marry illustrate the combined impact of dominant societal expectations and personal agency:

> In those days that's what you did, got married. It was assumed that you would get married. And so you did. But truly speaking, I wouldn't have gotten married had I not wanted to. I was in love with this man. I cared a lot for him. He filled a lot of needs for me emotionally at the time, till I grew up. Once you grow up, you know. (Claassen, 2005: 53)

For substantial numbers of old gay and lesbian persons, coming out earlier in life was not seen as an option, in part because they had married (Hunter, 2005). A 67-year-old gay man recalls,

> By the time you started seeing the parades and this explosion of homosexuality in the public consciousness, I was already a married man with small children. It wasn't like I didn't love my wife either. I loved her very much, and our kids. After she passed away, I even considered getting remarried . . . since a straight life was all I knew. (Bergling, 2004: 170)

Among gays and lesbians who are now in old age, marriage represented the obvious route of adulthood and, for some, it was seen as the only way to have children (Claassen, 2005). Coming out in unions that turn out to be mixed-orientation marriages presents dramatic challenges to both partners (Buxton, 2006). The gay or lesbian member is likely to be ahead of their straight partner in coming to terms with their sexual orientation and its consequences. Meanwhile, the heterosexual partner goes through a period of questioning his or her sexuality, marriage and future. Partners in mixed-orientation marriages often love one another very much and are likely to explore ways to stay married. Three years postdisclosure, however, only about one-sixth of these couples is still married (Buxton, 2006).

On balance, although the vast majority of gays and lesbians favor being in couple relationships and most would marry if legally able to do so, fewer are actually in such partnerships (Diamond, 2006). Among previously married gay and lesbian middle-aged and older couples, ties to a same-sex partner are as durable as ties between opposite-sex couples and, for many, their current relationships have lasted longer than their previous straight marriages (Claassen, 2005). From 28% to 60% of gay men and 44% to 80% of lesbians are estimated to be part of a live-in couple relationship at any one time (O'Brien & Goldberg, 2000; Peplau & Fingerhut, 2007). Higher numbers are in steady romantic relationships (Garnets & Peplau, 2006; Wierzalis et al., 2006). Although these numbers are substantially lower than the proportion of heterosexuals who are married, they are impressive given that the institutionalized support of marriage is missing. They also suggest that aging may bring an increased desire to maintain a long-term monogamous partnership:

> When you get older you need more stability in your life. I've had my flings— I know what it is like to love other women, but I want to be settled down and get on with what's left of our lives together, so that when either one of us is gone the other will have wonderful memories to look back on. (58-year-old lesbian; Auger, 1995:111)

Similarly, a gay man of 65 says,

> I've been with Ryan for 10 years and I've never been happier . . . We were made for each other. I only wish we had met sooner. It would have saved me some heartache . . . Love improves with age and I think our sex life has improved too. (Neugebauer-Visano, 1995:24)

What type of attachments do gay and lesbian older persons form, and how do they compare with heterosexual partnerships? Same-sex and opposite-sex couples use the same criteria for assessing the quality of their relationships, have comparable perceptions of the quality of and satisfaction with their relationships (Diamond, 2006; Julien et al., 1999; Kurdek, 1998), fall in love in parallel ways, experience similar levels of intimacy (Julien et al., 1999) and relationship dynamics (Kurdek, 1994, 2006), and derive stability in their relationships from similar sources (Diamond, 2006). Affection, dependability, shared interests and similar religious beliefs are valued by all types of couples (Peplau & Fingerhut, 2007). Comparisons of straight couples with two groups of committed lesbian and gay couples, one in an official civil union and one not, reveal striking similarities among them (Balsam et al., 2008; Roisman et al., 2008), including parallel levels of relationship satisfaction and methods of handling conflict (see also Hunter, 2005). Long-term relationships between gay and lesbian partners offer support, acceptance, a shared history and memories, and their quality does not differ from that of heterosexual bonds (Fullmer, 1995; Peplau & Fingerhut, 2007; see also Berger, 1996).

Mirroring comparisons of married and cohabiting opposite-sex couples, among same-sex couples with an average age in their 40s, couples in official civil unions are more likely to stay together than those who are not in civil unions (Balsam et al., 2008). None the less, the unique situation of gay and lesbian couples fosters the use of unique measures to secure stable relationships, including finding gay-friendly locations to live, work and socialize (Diamond, 2006). In the absence of legal marriage, other markers signify commitment to a relationship, including buying a house together, making binding legal agreements, and having children (Porche & Pervin, 2008). Heterosexual couples appear to be more committed to monogamy in both principle and practice than is true of same-sex partners, especially gay couples, who are more likely to engage in extrarelationship sex (Schwartz & Rutter, 1998) or to be polyamorous, meaning that they have more than one partner (Bettinger, 2006). The vast majority of lesbians in civil-union relationships, however, are committed to monogamy (Garnets & Peplau, 2006).

Gender cuts across sexual orientation in gay and lesbian relationships, and the pervasive cultural view of masculinity and femininity is reproduced in all intimate relationships (Kimmel, 2000). In the case of gay or lesbian couples, two men or two women negotiate ties with one another, a contradiction in structured social relations that can create ambivalence in their ties with straight family members (Connell, 1995; Connidis, 2003b). Hunter (2005) uses the term *sex/gender* to capture the intersection of sexual orientation and gender in the lives of women who make the transition from sexually active heterosexual marriage to a subsequent attraction to women. Shared gender is the basis for more egalitarian relationships (Connell, 1995; Kimmel, 2000; Weeks et al., 2001). Most partners in the majority of gay and lesbian relationships are or were in the labor force (Peplau & Fingerhut, 2007) and tend not to engage in a gendered division of labor based on so-called masculine and feminine tasks (Rothblum, 2006; Walter, 2003; Whipple, 2006). But the combination of gender and sexual orientation also creates important differences in the intimate partnerships of gays and lesbians (Fletcher, 2002). Lesbians tend to favor what is termed a feminized version of love and to prefer monogamous partnerships, while gay men do not (Claassen, 2005; Huston & Schwartz, 1995). They also appear to work together more harmoniously than either gay or opposite-sex couples (Roisman et al., 2008). Lesbian couples appear to be more positive about and satisfied with their relationships than gay couples are (Kurdek, 2003).

Despite shared gender, power differentials apply to gay and lesbian as well as straight couples (Carrington, 1999; Weeks et al., 2001). Less powerful partners rely more heavily on withdrawal and appeasement, more powerful partners on bargaining and bullying, in their relationships with one another (Peplau & Fingerhut, 2007). Among gay couples, the one who makes more money and is more attractive tends to have more power; among lesbian couples, the partner engaged in fewer hours of paid work does more of the housework, and a woman who is a biological mother has power over her partner because she provides access to children (Huston & Schwartz, 1995). Gay and lesbian couples also hold differing views of how their relationships challenge the conventional structure of straight partnerships (Weeks et al., 2001). Lesbians view their more egalitarian relationships as a challenge to the traditional division of household labor; gay men see their partnerships as a challenge to the less expressive and communicative masculinity of straight men. The relationship between women in same-sex partnerships is described as particularly intense and emotionally satisfying (Walter, 2003; Whipple, 2006).

Although both gay and lesbian couples report more autonomy than opposite-sex couples (Kurdek, 1998), gay couples tend to maintain greater independence from each other, whereas lesbian couples are more inclined to merge their identities and to equate sex and love (Fullmer, 1995). Despite these differences, some lesbians are vocal critics of monogamy as a patriarchal form of control, and aging leads gay men to be more involved in committed relationships that, for a growing minority, include monogamy (Huston & Schwartz, 1995).

In the context of gay and lesbian networks, a long-term intimate tie and a family-like network of primarily gay friends, sometimes referred to as fictive kin or chosen families, are central to attaining effective social support (Brown et al., 1997; Fullmer, 1995). Like straight couples, life satisfaction is higher among same-sex couples who are happy and communicate well (Lee, 1990). In some cases, homosexuality may be the basis for estrangement from one's family of orientation (parents and siblings) as well as a partner's family, and only a small minority of old same-sex couples has children (Kurdek, 2004). The fact that the support offered to straight couples by family members, especially parents and in-laws, enhances the marital success of longer-term marriages (Bryant & Conger, 1999) underscores the challenge to gay and lesbian partnerships that lack such support.

The extent of sexual activity among older gays and lesbians is unclear, largely due to the reliance on unrepresentative samples. Generally, gays and lesbians engage in more episodic sex (gay men more so) and have more serial monogamous relationships than straight persons do (Giddens, 1992). As is true among heterosexuals, the level of sexual activity declines with age. In a small sample of gay men ($n = 87$; Pope & Schulz, 1990), more than four-fifths of men aged 50 and over reported that they continue to engage in sexual activity, with two-fifths of those aged 60 and over stating that they have sex once per week. Gay couples have sex more often than do lesbian partners, but sexual activity is the norm for both, with its frequency declining over time (Peplau & Fingerhut, 2007; Schwartz & Rutter, 1998). With increasing age, the number of partners with whom gay men are active declines, with the majority restricting their activity to one person (Berger, 1996). As is true of opposite-sex couples, satisfaction with their sex lives is strongly related to overall relationship satisfaction among same-sex couples (Diamond, 2006; Garnets & Peplau, 2006).

Like straight women, old lesbians are subject to the cultural emphasis on youth and also engage in cosmetic methods of concealing the effects of aging (Slevin, 2006). The premium placed on youth in gay culture can make the aging experience difficult for old gay men as well (Bergling, 2004; Wierzalis et al., 2006). The relative shortage of peers and potential rejection by younger gay men puts old gay men at risk of isolation and shifts greater attention to emotional rather than sexual intimacy.

Finally, recent research on the impact of civil unions gives a glimpse into the future family ties of gay and lesbian couples. Comparisons of lesbian women who are and are not in legal civil unions and straight married women show that married women have more contact with and feel more supported by their families of origin, but lesbians in a civil union are closer to their families of origin than lesbians who are not in such a union (Rothblum, 2006). Similarly, married men have greater contact with their original families than do gay men, but gay men in civil unions have more contact with their families of origin than do gay men who are not in civil unions. These findings suggest the potential of legalized unions to enhance the relationships of gay and lesbian adults with other family members.

The Impact of Life Transitions on Intimate Ties

Retirement and declining health are two major age-related transitions that affect intimate partnerships later in life. To date, most related work has focused on married couples, especially research on the effects of retirement, and research on how life transitions affect same-sex relationships remains sparse.

Retirement

Retirement age in both Canada and the United States has declined over time with a slight rise among men in the past few years. On average, retirement occurs around the age of 62, making the initial transition one of early old age. Variations in the circumstances that lead to retirement and in available resources at the beginning of retirement mean different starting points among retirees. The growing reality of older displaced workers who lose their jobs due to company closures or work layoffs is an important facet of work history that changes the face of retirement. A life course perspective encourages a consideration of the impact that different work trajectories are likely to have on relationships in retirement. Among those who retire because they could not find work, marital relationships already may have undergone strain during a time of unsuccessful job-seeking (McMullin & Berger, 2006). In a gendered world that assumes the greater significance of paid work to men than to women, a husband may face strong pressure from his wife to get work, as in the case of this 57-year-old displaced worker:

My wife is the same as other wives, she cannot just accept that this man is idle, doing nothing; no earning . . . and, you know when a man is doing nothing then he's not in a good mood. He cannot be a happy man. And all of these are something that makes a family life difficult. (McMullin & Berger, 2006: 216)

This attitude also makes it tough for older women to compete for jobs; ageism and sexism combine to make them less desirable candidates and to devalue their assumed need for work. In both cases, a history of seeking employment unsuccessfully or taking on inferior jobs is brought to the experience of marriage in retirement.

Hegemonic views of masculinity and femininity that dominated the life course of today's old set different contexts for men and women in retirement. Traditional views of masculinity rest heavily on performing well in paid work and in tasks requiring physical strength. When these sources of masculinity are undermined, they trigger change in power relations between couples (Meadows & Davidson, 2006). Men who enjoyed being good providers or doing the more physically demanding household chores, such as gardening, suffer a sense of loss when they are no longer able to keep up what they see as their side of the couple relationship. Engaging in the domestic labor that was typically their wife's domain is further reminder for such men of their diminished masculinity. Indeed, men who are especially dependent upon their relationships with their wives tend to delay retirement, possibly in a bid to maintain their status in their marriages (Szinovacz & DeViney, 2000).

Although retirement is usually treated as an individual decision, plans to retire are heavily influenced by one's spouse (Henkens, 1999; Smith & Moen, 1998). Gay, lesbian and straight couples plan for and experience retirement in parallel ways, but lesbian couples are less financially ready for retirement (Mock, 2002). This suggests that the intersection of gender and sexual orientation leaves a pair of women in poorer economic circumstances, despite the fact that both partners in lesbian relationships are typically in the labor force.

The gendered arrangements of marriage are evident in two opposite trends: the later age of retirement among married than unmarried men and the earlier retirement of married than unmarried women (Morgan, 1992). In similar fashion, remarried widows are more likely to retire and remarried widowers less likely to retire than those of other marital statuses (Szinovacz & DeViney, 2000). This difference is partly a matter of economics—married men and unmarried women need their incomes more than their respective counterparts—and partly due to the desire of married women to retire at the same time as their generally older husbands. Men are more likely to make their wife's entitlement to social security a factor in deciding to retire, whereas women are more responsive to their husband's income in their choice to retire (Szinovacz & DeViney, 2000). As well, those couples who have happy marriages and enjoy spending time together may retire earlier than couples who are less happily married. These gender differences in retirement age are one reason that women have a shorter paid work career than men, weakening their economic situation in old age.

What is the impact of retirement on a couple's relationship? The effect of retirement on the gendered division of labor and, in turn, on marital quality has several facets: equity in the actual division of labor (who is doing how much of what), perceptions of its fairness, and the attitudes held toward the traditional division of labor. Retirement of one or both partners has the potential to change the division of household labor between partners, given the increased common ground of old men and women as gendered activities, such as parenting and paid work, decline and their social worlds become more similar. These shifts do not necessarily mean that men and women lose gender in any sense in old age; rather, they are in more similar circumstances. Is the potential for greater gender flexibility that these gender-associated changes suggest realized in retirement?

Despite the dramatic rise of women's labor force participation throughout Canada and the United States, the division of labor in the home is slow to change. Women of all ages take on more of the responsibility for housekeeping, kinship and child care, whether or not they work outside the home. Men and women tend to remain involved primarily in gender-linked tasks over the course of long-term marriages (Ward, 1993). Women are more engaged in traditionally feminine tasks, such as cooking, laundry and housekeeping, whereas men focus more on traditionally masculine tasks, such as taking out the garbage, household repairs, and cutting the lawn. Consistent with old men's attempts to maintain dominant conceptions of masculinity (Meadows & Davidson, 2006), the most typical change in their household duties postretirement is an increase in the masculine tasks they perform (Askham, 1995). Retired men do perform more traditionally feminine tasks than do employed men, however (Dorfman, 1992; Vinick & Ekerdt, 1992), and the more egalitarian relationships of younger couples will make this more likely in the future.

The employment status and patterns of wives influence the household labor of husbands. Retired husbands of women either in the labor force or with a longer work history do more housework than their counterparts (Szinovacz, 2000). These efforts are curtailed when their wives retire. With children no longer living at home, older spouses carry a more balanced share of *all* responsibilities in running the household, even when they follow a traditional division of labor. In this sense, aging and retirement can be said to contribute to more egalitarian ties even when little real change occurs in sharing the household responsibilities that remain.

Much of the research on retirement adjustment concerns the male retiree and assumes that wives are full-time homemakers. Recent information on couples with retired husbands and working wives or with both spouses retired from the labor force indicates that patterns established before retirement are critical determinants of its impact on marriage. Couples who continue to share recreational interests begun earlier in their marriage tend to deepen their relationships (Henkens, 1999). If spouses spend little time together and develop few mutual interests over the course of their marriage, more time together following retirement may be unsettling to their marriage. Because working-class couples are more likely to have divergent interests (Kelley, 1981), they may have more difficulty in adjusting to the husbands' retirement.

Retirement demands more of spouses than a simple increase in the amount of time spent together. In the absence of coworkers and a job, the bolstering of self-esteem and the maintenance of a positive self-image occur primarily within the marital dyad, particularly for older men (Ade-Ridder & Brubaker, 1983). Without a positive sense of self-worth, spouses of either gender are inclined to act as either so-called doormats or aggressors intolerant of any discordant views (Medley, 1977). This creates considerable potential for friction in postretirement marriages if changed needs are not met by the spouses (more often the wives). Older homemakers are more likely to report disadvantages of their spouses' retirement than are their retired husbands (Keating & Cole, 1980). Their main concerns are shrinking personal freedom, too much time together, and too many demands on their time. The increased dependence of retired men on their wives for companionship, a sense of usefulness, and self-affirmation may instill a level of interdependence between spouses that either enhances their relationship or creates an imbalance that threatens it. The fact that assessments of marriage in the retirement years tend to be good suggests that the net effect of the retired males' increased dependence is a more equitable balance in dependency between husband and wife.

The rise in dual-career couples raises interest in the equity of marital relationships at various life stages. Some conclude that equity in the areas of food preparation, housekeeping, being the provider and companionship contributes to marital satisfaction among long-term spouses (Keith et al., 1995). Others find that equity only affects perceptions of marital quality if it affects perceived spousal support. Among women in their 50s to 70s, especially those who are employed, unequal sharing of household labor leads to dissatisfaction with spousal support, which leads in turn to lower assessments of marital quality (Pina & Bengtson, 1995; see also Suitor, 1991).

Perceptions of fairness rather than equity itself may be key to a marriage's success. Among older couples, perceived fairness of household labor, but not the number of hours engaged in housework itself, enhances marital happiness among women (Szinovacz, 1996; Ward, 1993). This apparent contradiction suggests the importance of views about marriage and gender. Although couples in which the husband is retired and the wife employed appear to have lower marital satisfaction, this is primarily true among couples who hold traditional views of gender responsibilities (Szinovacz, 1996). In turn, traditional couples are highly satisfied with their marriages when the wife is retired and the husband is still in the labor force.

The well-being of husbands and wives in retirement responds variably to the synchronicity of a couple's retirement and shared activities (Szinovacz & Davey, 2004). Retired men whose wives continue their paid work are more likely to display depressive symptoms than men whose wives have not been in the labor force and men whose wives retire at the same time. Recently retired men benefit from their wives' subsequent retirement *if* it means sharing joint activities, but this is a short-term impact. Meanwhile, recently retired women have lower well-being if their husbands are already retired (Szinovacz & Davey, 2004). This may be because wives feel pressured to retire by their usually older husbands. The impact of power imbalances applies to both men and women; in either case, retirement satisfaction suffers when the still-employed spouse had more say in decisions prior to the other spouse's retirement (Szinovacz & Davey, 2005). With more couples in the labor force, the need to anticipate retirement as a joint project is clear.

Central to the impact of retirement on marriage is the issue of health. Although retirement rarely leads to poor health, declining health of either partner can lead to retirement. Men are at greater risk of retiring when their wives are in poor health (Szinovacz & DeViney, 2000), but the balance of research suggests that, following a lifetime of caring behavior, women are even more likely to leave the work force when their husbands are ill (Dentinger & Clarkberg, 2002). However, men who stay in the labor force rather than retire in response to their wife's poor health may be doing so out of necessity as the primary income earner. Men in this situation are less satisfied with their work, indicating a tension between being in the workforce and having wives at home who are ill. A change in health status of either spouse may have the most profound effect of all on the nature of marriage in later life.

The Impact of Declining Health

> How do you take care of yourself when the person you love is dying? I would go back and forth between wanting to be with her every minute possible and wanting to run away. There were days that I wanted to escape from her neediness and other days that I did not want to leave her side, afraid to lose any moment we could have together. (Midlife lesbian partner; Whipple, 2006: 50)

As the foregoing quote reveals, caring for an ill partner, especially in the case of terminal illness, is a profound experience. Reflecting the available literature, more of the discussion in this chapter focuses on the marital dyad, but our observations are likely to apply to all long-term intimate relationships. The health of one's spouse is related to both marital and life satisfaction. Among older married persons, good health enhances happiness (Crompton & Kemeny, 1999) and in turn, a good marriage is good for one's mental and physical health. Over time, older couples acquire experience in adapting to such age-related changes as hearing loss, a situation that challenges prior relationship patterns but is generally met with new efforts at better communication and balancing dependency with autonomy (Yorgason et al., 2007). Such adaptations may provide a foundation for responding to more threatening health conditions.

The need to care for a spouse has practical implications, such as making adjustments at work or leaving paid employment, along with its impact on a long-term relationship and the well-being of each of its partners (Carpenter & Mak, 2007). Just as discussions of paid and unpaid employment emphasize that both are work, recent treatment of caregiving emphasizes that it is also work. Caregiving has two essential components distinguished as *caring for* and *caring about* (Calasanti & Slevin, 2001). Caring for refers to looking after someone's needs, and caring about captures the affective dimension of emotional attachment and concern for someone. Both are critical dimensions of caring, but typically, when we think about assuming care for a spouse, our focus is on caring for, because caring about is already assumed as a feature of marriage. The pivotal transition lies in having to look after a partner's needs, but continuing to care about a spouse is reflected in studies that consider the emotional costs of caring for a spouse.

Given the greater likelihood that men will be married in later life, the experience of caring for a spouse is, consequently, much more likely for women. Demographics alone ensure that more older women than men will both care for an ill spouse and rely on someone other than a spouse to care for them should help be needed. Thus one must not deduce that women are turning to daughters and others for care because they have been neglected by their husbands. That said, the expectation to provide care is greater for women than for men (Allen et al., 1999; Thompson, 1993), and married women are more likely than married men to serve as primary caregivers to their spouses. The gender relations of caregiving are reflected in a usual research focus on the types of support and feelings about them that are typical of women's traditional experience (Calasanti & Slevin, 2001; Matthews, 2002b). In an unusual reversal, it is the experience of White, middle-class women that becomes the standard against which others are measured (Walker, 1992). The result is a limited understanding of the full range of caring that occurs in relationships, including marriage, and the ways in which intersecting age, gender, class and race relations may alter what that range looks like. Bear this in mind as we review findings about men's and women's experiences in response to their partners' health decline and need for care.

Interdependence and Gender in Caregiving Relationships

Framing discussions of caring requires a careful balance between appreciating the respective positions of the person being cared for and the person or persons providing care, and at the same time appreciating their engagement in relationships with one another. Much of the research on caregiving tends to emphasize the former, the situation of being cared for or of providing care, with a consequent focus on the implications for one partner in the relationship. Thus, as we have just seen, the burden, stress, health costs, and, less often, benefits of caring for the caregiver receive primary attention.

Looking at caring in the context of marriage and long-term intimate relationships draws attention to the relational quality of caring. Remembering that these relationships within families reflect broader societal and cultural views of knowledge and of structured social relations also underscores the relational nature of caring. In Western society, the dominant medical model defines aging and age-related health changes as decline, the dominant view of the state is that caring is a family matter (Biggs & Powell, 2001; Dunham & Canon, 2008), and structured social relations produce a gendered pattern of caring. Cultural variations that emanate from other countries or from traditions of particular ethnic and racial groups create variations within the dominant culture regarding expectations for spousal caring (Yarry et al., 2007). African Americans more often assess their caregiving situations positively and rely more on religion to provide a positive outlook than is true among European American caregivers (Yarry et al., 2007). Such differences reflect a long tradition and the life course experience of old African Americans to strongly favor family and community support over institutional alternatives (Ball et al., 2005; see Chapter 14). The illness of one partner may be the basis for a couple's symbiotic interdependence (Depner & Ingersoll-Dayton, 1985), but severe illness and disability can create imbalanced dependence between partners that can lead in turn to rifts between them.

Although the expectations may vary, both members of a couple are constrained by the caregiving relationship because it is imbued with expectations about giving and receiving care (Dunham & Cannon, 2008). Although the helping spouse may derive satisfaction from behaving altruistically and performing roles previously assumed by the ill spouse, difficulties in mastering new skills may arise and create frustration (Kelley, 1981). Similarly, the care recipient often experiences ambivalent feelings as the help provided by a spouse is both a positive reflection of the marital relationship and an ongoing reminder of the need for help (Rose & Bruce, 1995). Both partners experience the altered nature of their relationship deeply and meet its challenges in part through using "a rhetoric of coping" (e.g., "in sickness and in health," "you have to laugh;" Rose & Bruce, 1995: 124) and a restrained expression of loss.

Gender-based distinctions between heterosexual partners tend to extend into advanced old age (Wilson, 1995). However, when a partner becomes ill, such distinctions and a couple's interdependence may be altered dramatically. Examinations of shifting dependence usually focus on the increased dependency of the person receiving care. However, providing care can also create dependency, as the caregiver withdraws from other activities to meet a partner's needs (Calasanti, 2006). Similarly, the dependency brought on by ill health is usually assumed to decrease the relative power of the ill partner. Then again, the partner providing care may also lose power in the relationship, in part by becoming subject to the needs of the ill spouse: Being the ill person does not always mean being the most dependent partner in an intimate relationship, nor does being the care provider guarantee having the most power. Indeed, other factors, such as gender, may be more important in determining power balances. For example, women who look after their spouses often feel unable to have visitors in their homes for fear of upsetting their husbands (Rose & Bruce, 1995).

For both husbands and wives, greater emotional closeness makes naming a spouse as the primary source of care more likely (Allen et al., 1999). The nature of marriage prior to the onset of illness is critical to developing a good caring relationship. Close partnerships lay a foundation for successful caring, whereas a poor marriage increases the risk that illness will result in negative physical and psychological consequences for both spouses (Allen et al., 1999). The common practice of women to retire in order to care for their spouses may also affect marital quality. Women in this situation appear to find their husbands more critical and demanding of them than do wives who are not caring for their partners (Dentinger & Clarkberg, 2002). The nature of marital relationships also mediates the impact of health declines and disability. Disagreement between spouses increases the negative psychological impact of disability (Bookwala & Franks, 2005), and the need for a partner's care can expose problems in a couple's relationship. Shared views of what needs to be done enhance satisfaction in marriages that involve caregiving (Carpenter & Mak, 2007). Older couples in shorter-term marriages find the adjustment to one partner's dependency more difficult (Rose & Bruce, 1995), in part because they have had less time to accumulate a history of problem-solving strategies. Length of marriage heightens mutual positive sentiments between spouses where one partner is caring for the other (Chappell & Kuehne, 1998). In turn, such shared sentiments enhance well-being for both partners.

Advanced old age (aged 75 and over) is associated with far less concern about domestic power as both men and women focus more on day-to-day survival (Wilson, 1995). The growing dependency due to the illness or disability of one or both partners is met with an "over-riding desire for independence" that "erodes previously gender-determined allocations of tasks, even before the demands of extreme dependency leave little choice other than to do what needs doing or to accept separation and institutionalization" (Rose & Bruce, 1995: 120). This suggests that the illness of one of the partners leads older couples toward the interdependent ideal of marriage with its emphasis on care, commitment, mutual nurturing and encouragement, and the acknowledgement by both partners of their need for each other (Thompson, 1993). The failing health of one partner does heighten closeness among long-term couples, especially when the wife is ill, because this situation fosters more nurturing by the husband (Ingersoll-Dayton et al., 1996).

Generally, caregiving spouses are less healthy than spouses who are not caring for a partner (Wallsten, 2000). Nonetheless, the majority of spouses express positive sentiments about their marital relationship, although women who care for their husbands are much more likely to express negative sentiments about their partners than are husbands who care for their wives (Chappell & Kuehne, 1998; Wallsten, 2000). Women also experience greater burden and health strain than do men when providing care to their spouses (Calasanti & Slevin, 2001; Yee & Schulz, 2000). Comparisons of husbands and wives who care for their spouses with husbands and wives who do not, show that the greater psychological costs of caring experienced by wives are a function of caregiving itself and not an artifact of general gender differences (Rose-Rego et al., 1998). What might account for such variations?

The psychological toll of caregiving is reduced by having a larger helping network (Smerglia & Deimling, 1997). Among the married, women are more likely than men to be the sole care provider to their spouses and to provide both more hours and more types of help to them (Allen, 1994; Stoller & Cutler, 1992). When cared for by spouses, women more often face unmet needs in the area of household maintenance than do men, but needs for personal care appear to be equally well met (Allen, 1994). Among very ill women, the deficit in help with household tasks is made up for by other helpers, but this is not true among married women who are less ill. When unable to function independently, married women are more likely than married men to receive simultaneous support from a child, sibling, friend, or formal service provider (Barrett & Lynch, 1999). Thus the larger social networks negotiated by women are helpful in terms of additional support when a married woman is herself ill, but it does not translate into additional assistance in caring for an ill spouse. Conversely, married men receive more help from others in providing assistance to their spouses. This is consistent with a gendered view of helping in which women are assumed to be more adept at providing care on their own.

Another reason for the greater burden of spousal caregiving for women may be that, for women, particularly mothers, caregiving is the resumption of an activity recently (or never) relinquished, whereas for men, it is often newly acquired (Fitting et al., 1986). An extreme example from my research is a mother of nine who raised two grandchildren, provided concurrent care for her mother and father-in-law until they died, and was then faced with caring for her husband as he died of cancer. Another widowed mother with five sons tells her story:

> After [my sons] grew up, I had my ill husband to look after for seven years . . . I couldn't get out. I was always there . . . The only chance that I had of getting out was when the boys (sons) would come to look after him . . . I guess the easiest time that I had was after he died.

Last, women and men do caregiving differently in terms of how much they treat it as emotion work. Men's treatment of caring as a job with associated tasks contrasts with women's greater focus on the emotional side of the caring relationship and on reaching standards of what they consider good care, a difference that should not be confused with how much a spouse cares about his or her partner (Calasanti, 2006). Men appear to more effectively separate their feelings from the task at hand. Women also face particular difficulties in the physical demands of caring for partners with dementia (who are often also larger than their wives) due to their own health problems and limited physical strength.

The presence of an established gender script is not enough to simplify caring for a spouse in old age. The complicated implications of gendered family relations are recognized by both men and women who provide care. A qualitative study of old Portuguese men who look after their partners emphasizes the ambivalent situation that caregiving creates; its reflection of socially constructed views of gender makes the negotiation of masculinity a significant element of caring for spouses among old men (Ribeiro et al., 2007). These men maintain masculinity in their daily lives as caregivers by employing three interconnected strategies: extending the definition of what constitutes manliness and being a man, emphasizing the identity of being a husband with responsibilities to care for a wife, and retaining power by staying in charge. Similarly, qualitative work in the United States (Calasanti & King, 2007) finds that men caring for partners (with dementia) take approaches to care work that reflect gender relations and dominant views of masculinity. These include exerting force, focusing on tasks, blocking emotions, minimizing disruption, engaging in distracting activities, and self-medication.

Dementia: A Unique Caregiving Relationship

Those looking after spouses with dementia, including Alzheimer's disease, are at heightened risk of threats to their own mental and physical health because they invest more time in caregiving than do those helping someone with other health problems (Hooker et al., 1998; Ory et al., 1999). Caring for an elder with dementia is made more difficult by the severity of the dementia, including memory and behavioral problems, rather than the level of physical burden (Kramer, 1997; Williams, 2005). Yet both wives and husbands increase their tolerance for dealing with these problems over time (Johnson, 1985; Kramer, 1997).

Qualitative work on men and women who are caring for spouses with dementia finds that they provide similar levels of care, including personal care, and that they share seeing care as part of marital commitment (Calasanti, 2006). Thus a wife caring for her husband says, "I love him, and I am married to him. I think it's my duty to take care of him," and a husband caring for his wife says, "This is my wife and I love this lady so I am going to give her the best that I can" (Calasanti, 2006: 274).

Spouses caring for a demented family member, however, experience more strain when their financial resources are limited (Williams, 2005), a significant component of class relations that is not evenly distributed by race. Whether African American or White, men and women caring for a demented partner give the same types of care to their spouses, but African Americans who provide care for demented spouses or parents are more inclined to see positive sides to caring *and* to experience a greater emotional cost when the care recipient has more memory and behavioral problems (Miller & Kaufman, 1996).

The view of caregiving as women's work and women's stronger belief that looking after a demented spouse is emotional work (Miller & Kaufman, 1996) help account for gender differences in the distress created by this unique caring situation. Men also may experience greater social reward in successfully caring for their spouses in substantial measure because they emerge as Mr. Wonderfuls for fulfilling a role that is usually the purview of women (Rose & Bruce, 1995). The need to assert claims to a masculine identity is also satisfied in part through positive social recognition of the caregiving role among old men (Ribeiro et al., 2007). Conversely, precisely because caring is considered normal and natural for women, caring for a husband is not as effective a diversion from grieving his partial loss to dementia.

The potential for violence is a unique feature of dementia and other illnesses (e.g., strokes) that impair cognitive functioning. This leaves women more likely than men to be frightened by actual or possible violent outbursts because of their relative inability to defend themselves, heightening the extent to which caring controls their lives (Rose & Bruce, 1995).

In the case of dementia, it is difficult to speak meaningfully of the impact of illness on the quality of marriage because, in its advanced stages, the situation resembles having lost a spouse. This feeling makes adjustment to the caregiving role particularly hard. Because the spouse is alive, mourning seems inappropriate, but severe impairment limits the spouse's ability to satisfy the needs of the caregiver, including companionship. Describing older couples in their study, Rose and Bruce (1995: 118–19) emphasize the significance of emotional work in this adaptation: "Emotional labour on one's own feelings was a large part of the invisible work carried out by carer and cared for as they struggled to survive disabilities and illnesses that were laying siege to their quality of life." Despite being captive to their illnesses, partners with dementia continue to exert power in their relationship through the demands that they make and their resistance to help that is offered (Dunham & Cannon, 2008).

Given the intensity of spousal relationships, the increase in negative interactions that commonly comes with dementia and the greater impact of negative than positive interaction on psychological well-being (Akiyama et al., 2003; Newman et al., 2005; Rook & Zettell, 2005), looking after a spouse with dementia is a particularly demanding situation. Yet even in such times, the history of a long marriage allows a bright side to emerge, as one husband observes about caring for his wife:

> That has been something of a surprise to me to realize that I have not experienced the disease in negative terms only. Perhaps the reason lies in the way our marriage is structured. Even before, I used to look after all the practical things, to do all the planning and arranging, although my wife did do all the "women's chores." Now that her memory has failed and she no longer knows how to use the washing machine or make coffee or cook, that's no problem. I'm the one who does these things. (Kirsi et al., 2000: 158).

Contradictory demands created by gender relations and experienced by men and women are but one source of ambivalence in the unique challenges of caregiving relationships in which one partner has dementia. In a study of women caring for partners or parents with dementia, a number of them explain providing care by noting gender knowledge—the assumption that women are better carers and that women have the responsibility to care—at the same time that they are disappointed and resentful that men in their families are often key decision makers about care but not hands-on caregivers (Dunham & Cannon, 2008). The ambivalence of caring for a family member, including a partner, with dementia stems from the contradictory demands of trying simultaneously to maintain the cared-for person's dignity and control over the situation and to balance feelings of anger and guilt with acceptance (Dunham & Cannon, 2008). A qualitative study of women caring for husbands with dementia describes the women as *married widows* who negotiate a web of contradictions that include the simultaneous presence and absence of their husbands, the certainty and uncertainty about their husbands' lucidity, being both open and closed in communication with their husbands, and the disparity between their past and present circumstances (Baxter et al., 2002). These contradictions do not exist at the level of mixed emotions only. The expectations of family care by governments that limit social welfare expenditures, the gendered construction of obligations to care, and the range of available resources stemming from class, race, and gender relations combine to create structured contradictions that individuals must negotiate in their relationships when a partner is in need of care.

Caregiving Among Same-Sex Couples

Age-related declines in health and a consequent need for social services may force the issue of disclosure for older gay and lesbian individuals, leading either to coming out more publicly in older age or to isolating themselves from needed support (Heaphy & Yip, 2006; Hunter, 2005; Richard & Brown, 2006). Health problems may also be the basis for public questioning of a long-term partner's right to serve as a care provider or guardian, including challenges by other family members (Brotman et al., 2007). Health care settings that do not respect gay or lesbian relationships (Brotman et al., 2003; Claes & Moore, 2001; Cohler, 2006) may mean the heartbreak of being mistreated as either the patient or partner when help is sought. This creates unique challenges to same-sex relationships that are not posed by poor health among heterosexual, particularly married, couples. A midlife teacher who was not out at work recalls caring for her terminally ill partner:

> Having to keep this to myself was impossible. So through my daily tears I had to say something. I announced that my sister was dying. Now I could keep my job as an educator and get support from my colleagues. It was acceptable to have a dying sister, not a dying partner. (Whipple, 2006: 66)

Problems of isolation are especially strong among those who are not out. This isolation and concerns about discriminatory treatment by health service staff make caring for old gay or lesbian partners or family members a heavier individual responsibility for care providers (Brotman et al., 2007).

Caregiving among same-sex couples has received sparse research attention, but HIV and AIDS have been a key impetus for conducting such research, particularly among gay men. Examinations of older gay couples tend to include those who are 50 years or older rather than the conventional cutoff of 60 or 65 years. Caregiving in the context of HIV/AIDS is unique because of the relatively young age of AIDS sufferers, the stigma associated with the illness, and the marginal status of same-sex relationships (Ory et al., 1998). A gay person caring for a partner with HIV or AIDS is likely to share with his partner associated risk factors and either the illness itself or survival guilt for not being ill (Brennan & Moore, 1994; Walter, 2003). These factors combine to create a difficult caregiving context for gay men with HIV/AIDS. However, like their straight peers, gay persons are most likely to receive care from partners (Brennan & Moore, 1994). Others are engaged in providing care to gay persons with HIV/AIDS, but because of the sufferers' younger age, sexual orientation, and usual childless status, parents are the family members most likely to be key caregivers (Mullan, 1998). Testament to the improvement of medications for managing HIV/AIDS and of greater openness about being a gay couple is the fact that grief counselors are dealing with an ever-aging clientele of gay partners (Bergling, 2004).

Gay partnerships that involve caregiving fundamentally transform the gendered nature of caring that predominates among heterosexual couples (Mullan, 1998). Relatively young and isolated from family, gay caregivers are more likely to seek support from friends in the gay community than from family and to rank support received from gay peers as most helpful and support from family members as least helpful (Mullan, 1998). However, the stigma of HIV/AIDS, particularly high in minority populations, leads some couples to keep the diagnosis secret, limiting their ability to reach out to others for help (Brennan & Moore, 1994; Brown & Sankar, 1998). Among African Americans, the influence of religious institutions that have publicly denounced homosexuality reinforces the stigma of AIDS and further undermines the support received from family members (Brown & Sankar, 1998). For some gay persons, however, the illness serves as a catalyst for contact and a renegotiated relationship with previously estranged members of their partners' families (Brennan & Moore, 1994). Growing acceptance of same-sex unions should help to relieve the isolation and outsider status of gay and lesbian persons caring for partners.

Summary

In sum, long-term marriages and relationships are characterized by interdependence. Based on available research, similar factors contribute to satisfying and happy relationships in middle and old age, whether conventional marriage or long-term committed relationships between same-sex couples. Although recent work indicates that long-term intimate relationships do not become closer due to the passage of time, today's older couples tend to be quite satisfied and happy with their relationships. Sexual orientation, gender, race and class shape the negotiation of intimate relationships over time. Although certain forms of sexual activity may decline with age, sexual expression remains an important component of long-term relationships.

The transitions to retirement and to caregiving relationships in response to illness or disability heighten the interdependence of older spouses and partners. Both partners must make considerable adaptations, and unique challenges face men and women as they negotiate retirement and the caregiving relationship. The spouse of an older person who suffers major mental impairment due to dementia or stroke faces a particularly challenging situation—he or she confronts the loss of the spouse while having to care for him or her, often for many years. Even in this situation, however, caregiving should not be treated solely in negative terms.

Our examination of spousal caregiving indicates the significance of a relationship's history and quality and of gender relations to understanding support in later-life intimate ties. The models of support that have dominated research on caregiving in later life (see Chapter 8) emphasize assumed features of particular relationships and fail to consider how gender structures family ties so that they are characteristically different for women and men (Allen et al., 1999). Even in old age, when health losses by one or both partners require greater interdependence, family life continues to be organized around gender.

Caring for a spouse may heighten interdependence in a marriage, but it often leads to isolation of the couple as well (Johnson, 1985). The comments of a 67-year-old childless woman from one of my studies exemplify how her husband's illness has cut them both off from the outside world:

> My husband is very possessive since he nearly died. I have got to be here. He had been very sick . . . and I have been very afraid since then. He nearly died. I have the feeling that he is very afraid. He doesn't like to be alone. So I try to understand, but it does not make me feel good. Like, if I say that I am going to go to the shopping mall, he says, "Oh no." I am not free.

Should illness be followed by death, extreme interdependence can prove debilitating to the surviving spouse, as commitment to the caregiving role may have deprived the surviving spouse of ongoing contact with others. Once again, the gendered nature of social relations is critical as it creates variations in the impact of one's own and one's partner's health on contact with others. Regardless of their own health status and that of their spouses, older married women maintain high contact with other social network members. Conversely, the health of married men is irrelevant to the amount of contact they have with others, provided that their wife is healthy (Crompton & Kemeny, 1999). However healthy they may be, married men suffer a notable drop in social contact if their spouses are ill. This situation reflects the greater emphasis on network development and maintenance among women than men, a difference with important implications following the loss of a spouse (see Chapter 6).

CHAPTER 5

Being Single in Later Life

I will, by choosing to live a free single life, be helping to raise the status of singlehood. In doing this, I will be strengthening rather than weakening marriage, for when we truly have the option not to marry, marriage will be seen as a free choice rather than one demanded by a pairing society. . . . Being self-aware, autonomous, free, self-fulfilled, and whole . . . comes from being ourselves. (Edwards & Hoover, 1974: 217)

The term *single* refers to the never married, in contrast to the *unmarried* who are widowed, divorced or separated. Unfortunately, much research does not make this distinction and instead, includes single, divorced, separated and widowed persons in one category, often labeled *unmarried* or *unattached*. Yet there are significant differences in the experience of occupying these various civil or marital statuses and the partner histories that they partially represent. At the same time, restricting the category of single to those who have been called seriously single because they have chosen and are committed to remaining single (Williams & Nida, 2005) excludes the experience of those who stay single for other reasons. This chapter's focus is those persons who expect to be always or forever (ever) single.

Portrayals of Being Single

Images of being single have changed over time. The large number of baby boomers born from the mid-1940s to mid-1960s initially combined with the availability of birth control and the women's movement to increase sexual activity among single persons (Schwartz & Rutter, 1998). For the first time, the opportunity for sex outside of marriage was considered acceptable for both men and women, although still more so for men, lending an attractive aura to being a single person. As the front-runners of the baby boom reached adulthood, however, the women experienced a demographic squeeze, there being more of them than of slightly older men of desirable age for marrying. This situation was the basis for extensive media attention in the 1980s. For example, in June 1986, *Newsweek*'s cover story was titled "Too Late for Prince Charming?" and reported that well-educated women of 35 had only a 5% change of marrying. This news was described as "traumatic" and as confirming the widely held view that women with high-paying jobs could not have husbands too. The actual impact of the demographic squeeze was both overstated and dramatized. In fact, the appeal of marriage to women was waning somewhat, and men were finding it more difficult to find jobs, a major impediment to marrying (Siegel, 1995). Nonetheless, the flurry generated by this report and others like it demonstrated how highly valued the state of marriage remained.

And remains. By 1991, the situation reversed, and the number of eligible American men outnumbered single women (Faludi, 1991), a result of the smaller cohort following the baby boom. This left the men at the end of the baby boom to compete for mates from a smaller pool of women roughly two years younger than themselves. At the beginning of the new century, this trend was the one featured in the headlines. "The Man Glut," cried one newspaper (McLaren, 2000)—"Two Boys for Every Girl. Remember when they said a single woman was as likely to be attacked by terrorists as find a husband? Well, now the demographic tables have turned." In the future, the tables will no doubt turn again, and the focus will probably still be on the odds of marrying rather than exploring single life. However, recent media treatment of being single has had a more positive spin in both Canada (*Maclean's Magazine*, May 8, 2000, p. 37: "I Am Single—More Canadians than ever before are choosing to live alone—and liking it.") and the United States (*Time*, August 28, 2000, p. 37: "Flying Solo—More women are deciding that marriage is not inevitable, that they can lead a fulfilling life as a single.").

In our society, remaining single occurs in the context of a cultural ideology that favors marriage and stigmatizes being single (Byrne & Carr, 2005; DePaula & Morris, 2005). Some argue that the stigma attached to being single is a form of prejudice and discrimination termed *singlism* (DePaula & Morris, 2005). Evidence offered in support of singlism includes favorable views about the assumed positive characteristics of married versus single people; less access to employee benefits and to loans, especially among women; fewer tax breaks; and the inability to bequest benefits and social security because only spouses or children are potential beneficiaries. Among a sample of persons aged 25 to 74 years, single persons are more likely than married ones to observe being treated poorly interpersonally, but they do not differ in reports of institutional discrimination (Byrne & Carr, 2005). Casting single persons as "victims who have defaulted to singlehood" (Byrne & Carr, 2005: 89) or defining statements of fact as "single strain," such as it being harder to have desired intimacy when one is single (Pudrovska et al., 2006) misrepresent single life and further the negative stereotype of this civil status. Attempting to appreciate the challenges of negotiating a single life in a promarriage culture requires hearing the voices of those who are single.

Singles fall in the one civil or marital status category that is defined by what people are not: they are not married (DePaula & Morris, 2005). We tend to focus far more on transitions from one civil status to another, including the move from single to unsingle or married, than on transitions within a marital status category. Moving from temporary to stable singlehood, however, is a significant transition. Family structure in the form of civil status is permeable; one can change one's marital status at all stages of the life course, including deciding to get married after a long life of being single (DePaula & Morris, 2005). Indeed, three-quarters of a small sample of single women aged 40 and over, an age by which lifelong singlehood is often assumed, would still consider getting married, primarily for companionship but also with an eye to financial security and friendship (McDill et al., 2006). It is not surprising, then, to find being single described as an unfinished tale (Baumbusch, 2004).

The ambiguity of single status leads some to treat being single and being married as part of a continuum in which one may move from one state to another, reflecting the new reality that being single does not necessarily mean having no romantic involvements and being married does not guarantee remaining so (Trimberger, 2005). This fluid view of marital status is also encouraged in order to avoid defending either being single or being married by knocking the alternative. Some question whether there is value to using the term *single* at all to refer to those who do not marry, given its uncertainty as a permanent status and its inclusion of quite variable experiences (Clark & Graham, 2005). This logic, however, could be applied to delineating any groups, as our discussion in Chapter 1 regarding the intersection of structured social relations and resulting within-group heterogeneity emphasized. As well, anticipating or actually being a lifelong single involves significant transitions in identity.

Examining the experiences of older persons informs us about their present circumstances and how they have negotiated their family lives as single persons, providing us with a glimpse into the future for younger persons who do not marry. In this chapter, we examine trends in remaining single, the transition and pathways to being permanently single, and living life as a single person, including how being single affects social networks and well-being.

Trends in Staying Single

Among persons aged 65 and over, the proportion that are single has remained fairly stable, at about 5% (see Chapter 2). Because the proportion of the population that is old has increased significantly, so too have the absolute numbers of single elders (Rook & Zettel, 2005). As we have seen, there are notable differences by race, with Asian Americans least likely to be single, African Americans most likely to be single, and Hispanics and Whites falling in between. The substantially higher proportion of single persons in the younger cohorts reflects, in part, delays in marriage and a preference for alternative relationships, but it also suggests an increase in the likelihood of remaining single, particularly for Black Americans.

The trends that underlie increased rates of staying single among younger age groups reflect the interplay of social change and demographic shifts. In all age groups, educated women are a readily identifiable group with elevated rates of remaining single (Barrett, 1999; Doudna & McBride, 1981). The greater economic independence of women and a decline in the stigma associated with being single in general, and being a single parent in particular, are likely to sustain increased rates of singlehood, especially among women (Siegel, 1995). The higher probability of being single among African Americans may result in less stigma attached to being single, making less of a difference between those who do and do not get married (Barrett, 1999; Pudrovska et al., 2006). Sheer numbers alone are not enough to explain this difference, however. Both identity and experience are more profoundly affected by race, gender or class, for example, than by one's marital status (Koropeckyj-Cox, 2005). For those who occupy positions of relative privilege, the significance of occupying a particular marital status may be greater (Kaiser & Kashy, 2005). The intersection of race and class relations shapes the experience of being single in later life. At the same time that race affects access to material resources, the growing middle class of African Americans continues to live a different reality from their White counterparts (Collins, 2000).

Today's older singles are unique, in part because they usually have neither children nor spousal kin in their family network, unlike those who are widowed or divorced. As we saw in Chapter 2, we can no longer assume that staying single means not having children. For all cohorts but especially younger ones, the increased separation of sex from marriage (see Chapter 3) changes the implications of being single for involvement in intimate relationships and for our view of being single. For example, celibacy carries its own stigma (Trimberger, 2005) and is often assumed to go hand-in-hand with being single, especially among today's old women. Straight, gay and lesbian middle-aged and older singles all note that being single raises questions about their sexual orientation (Koropeckyj-Cox, 2005).

To date, the cross-cutting of gender with being single has received more attention than other structured relations (Barrett, 1999), in part because old women are more often the focus of research on singles than are old men. Years ago, Jessie Bernard (1972) described never-married women as the crème de la crème and never-married old men as the bottom of the barrel. Objective indicators like income, health, social networks, and well-being substantiated such a characterization. But this was based on a cohort in which career aspirations among women often precluded marriage, leading well-educated and accomplished women to be a substantial portion of the single population. As well, unique world events like the Great Depression thwarted prospects for marriage among women who otherwise had good prospects. Meanwhile, men who could not carry the responsibility of providing a household income on their own were less desirable partners in the marriage market.

Fast forward a few cohorts, and we see that women with careers can and do marry, and some of them marry men who would have a hard time being the sole income earners. These changes in who stays single alter the connection between being single and health, income, and well-being. Indeed, among middle-aged Americans, never-married men are better off financially than never-married women (Wilmoth & Koso, 2002). This said, when we focus on marital status comparisons of those who are currently old (see Chapter 3), we see that the observations of earlier times continue to apply: older single men are not as healthy, financially well off, socially integrated or content as older single women.

Some argue that when demographic shifts lead to a sex ratio favoring women, as was the case for those born at the end of the baby boom, the probability of major social change, such as the women's movement, escalates (Doudna & McBride, 1981). As unmarried, educated women sought to find a place for themselves outside the traditional family unit, attempts to change socially structured barriers to their progress occurred in areas such as the labor force. In turn, a sex ratio of more marriageable-age men than women tends to encourage conservatism as men engage in more traditional courting rituals (e.g., an evening out dining rather than drinking), as their focus on getting married is heightened (McLaren, 2000: R6).

Among older women, commitments to family, particularly parents (O'Brien, 1991), and the pursuit of higher education and a career were key reasons for staying single. The reflections of well-educated, single (mostly never-married) mothers with an average age of 41 years suggest additional reasons for staying single (Siegel, 1995). On balance, single mothers have a less positive view of men than do married mothers. They often hold a very idealistic view of marriage, but their experience of disappointing ties with their fathers, their parents' poor marriages, and their preference to be in control and avoid compromise steer them away from marriage. For others, having children as a single woman is a matter of timing; the biological clock ticks faster in relation to childbearing than to marrying, and having a child does not preclude the desire to also eventually marry (Trimberger, 2005).

The Transition to Singlehood

Like those who remain childless (see Chapter 9), being single may be a function of both choice and circumstance (Baumbusch, 2004; McDill et al., 2006; Sharp & Ganong, 2007; Trimberger, 2005). Some singles view staying single as the exercise of agency; being single is a preferred choice over getting married. For others, being single is the outcome of circumstances and other life course choices, including not meeting the right person, focusing on a career, or the demands of a particular time, such as the Depression. Over time, those whose singlehood was unintended often come to see the virtues of their situation, as in the case of this older woman:

> I was born in 1924, so by the time I was in high school the war had broken out. . . . I guess it's just the way things work out whether you marry—whether you meet someone. I think too, in my generation you had a lot of ideas about the perfect mate, and as I got older I just thank my lucky stars. I wouldn't have lasted you know. (Baumbusch, 2004:111).

In addition to being voluntary or involuntary, being single may be a temporary or stable (permanent) state (Stein, 1981). Combining these two dimensions creates four categories of single persons. Voluntary and temporary singles include those who are postponing marriage but are not opposed to the idea of marriage.

Involuntary and temporary singles would like to find a partner but have yet to do so. Voluntarily stable singles are those who choose to be single and oppose the idea of marriage—what some term seriously single (Williams & Nida, 2005). Also included in this group are those whose religious commitments include celibacy. Involuntarily stable single persons wanted to marry but have not found mates and accept being single as their probable life state. Older singles are likely to be stable singles, but when does this change in identity occur?

To date, little is known about the transition from temporary to stable singlehood because staying single is not typically treated as a life transition (Davies, 2003). Unlike childlessness (especially for women), there is not a clear line of demarcation between a time when changing one's status is possible and a time when it is not. Unlike marrying, divorcing or being widowed, there is neither a ceremony nor another party involved. In our culture, most adults expect to marry, and when this does not happen, a transition from defining oneself as someone who will marry to someone who is permanently single often occurs. When they are about 30 (Gordon, 1994) or more recently, 36 (Kaiser & Kashy, 2005), an age by which many have married, those who have not may start to consider their current status in relation to their expectation to marry.

In her qualitative study of middle-class, childless, single persons aged 40 to 57, Davies (2003) reports that most of the men and women do experience a transition to becoming single. Yet even though they do not anticipate getting married, they remain open to the possibility of an intimate relationship. At this point in their lives, these middle-aged singles are comfortable with being single and highlight its perceived advantages. For some women, in part because of the association of singlehood with childlessness, the initial redefinition of oneself as single may be experienced as a crisis, but eventually most women appear to experience this transition positively (Peterson, 1982). Some suggest that men do not go through an equivalent transition and instead, experience singlehood fairly uniformly over the life course (Waehler, 1996).

The transition to defining oneself as single occurs in a cultural life course context of expecting transitions to occur at particular ages. A birthday is often a key event, although the particular age that marks singlehood varies considerably (Davies, 2003). Seeing oneself as single is also negotiated in the context of gendered social relations. Middle-aged women view buying their own houses as a marker of considering oneself permanently single:

> I always thought you got married, you bought a house. Well, I bought a house and I'm not married. . . . I've laid down roots. . . . You're sort of saying, "Okay, this is it." And it makes you feel more settled. (Davies, 2003:348)

The dissolution of a serious relationship or engagement, instigated by either party, also precedes defining oneself as single.

Circumstances of a given time and family may lead some individuals to drift into, rather than choose, staying single. For example, obligations to their families of orientation (parents and siblings) took precedence over personal aspirations related to education, work and marriage among single women of advanced age and various class backgrounds two decades ago (Allen & Pickett, 1987; O'Brien, 1991). In the words of one woman,

My parents were my whole life. . . . [My mother] was quite bad [ill] when I was
in high school, and that probably contributed some to the fact that I didn't go
on. . . . They were basically years when I was just sort of stuck with my mother,
and I didn't have too many young friends. (Allen & Pickett, 1987:523)

Hitting marriageable age in the 1920s and 1930s, a time when the heavy emphasis
placed on the familial obligations of women was reinforced by the Depression, fundamentally shaped the prospects of marriage for a number of women of this cohort.
For some, it was delayed; for others it was postponed forever. Such circumstances are
key to understanding why "[n]one of the women claimed to have made a conscious
decision not to marry. Nor did marriage appear to have been an important goal in
any of their lives" (O'Brien, 1991: 309). Thus although staying single was not chosen,
it was not actively resisted either, a reflection of the strongly entrenched familistic
ideology of the time (Allen, 1989; Allen & Pickett, 1987). Like all women of their day,
these single women were honoring their family responsibilities. Consequently, they
paralleled their married counterparts as involved family members; they simply
engaged in an alternative family career (Allen, 1989; Allen & Pickett, 1987).

When staying single is the outcome of such circumstances, should it be viewed
as voluntary or involuntary? Middle-aged respondents often view being single as a
result of a lifetime of choices and decisions, even when there was never a deliberate
choice to be single (Davies, 2003). Similarly, older women who assigned priority to
caring for their parents did not necessarily choose to stay single. The dichotomy
between being voluntarily and involuntarily single is limiting in assuming that only
those who choose to stay single act with agency in their lives. No doubt, some single individuals may have been captives of circumstance, but others stay single as an
indirect consequence of other choices (Trimberger, 2005). Thus the dimension of
voluntary versus involuntary singlehood is probably best conceived of as two continua rather than a dichotomy, reflecting varying degrees of both circumstance and
choice in staying single. For single women, intersecting gender relations and expectations based on marital status constrain options when parents need care (Byrne &
Carr, 2005), but choices are also made that result in remaining single.

Just as women of marriageable age in the Depression did not resist staying single, one might argue that women of marriageable age in the subsequent cohort did
not resist marriage. The very high marriage rates of the postwar 1940s and early
1950s were one reason for the baby boom. Both situations speak to the impact of
major events (the Great Depression, World War II and its aftermath) and their timing in the life course (being of marriageable and childbearing ages) on individual
outcomes and cohort differences in views and experiences of being single.

The Lives of Older Single Persons

For today's older population, being single typically means being childless. The very
strong proscription against having children outside of marriage made childlessness
a usual result of remaining single. Even though older single women may not express
regret about being single, some are sorry not to have had children (O'Brien, 1991;

Trimberger, 2005). For others, staying single served as a cover for not wanting to have children and legitimated being childless (Trimberger, 2005). With time, even those who wanted to have children tend to focus on their current situations and social networks. The weakening association between being single and being childless is evident in more births among all unmarried women, including the ever single (Trimberger, 2005; see Chapters 2 and 3). This trend is especially strong among African American and Hispanic women. Having children in turn affects the kinds of ties that single persons negotiate with other family members. As we examine the social networks of today's older single persons, consider how changes in family form are likely to affect intergenerational relationships and the future family and friendship ties of single persons.

For most single women, not marrying means working in the labor force, an activity often viewed as an important accomplishment (McDill et al., 2006). The cross-cutting of gender relations with the period in time when today's old single men and women were at the life stage of starting jobs and possibly marrying created a different set of choices and realities for them than is true for subsequent cohorts. Older single women of today were in a unique situation when compared with their married peers because, in their day, getting married often required leaving the workforce. Thus work was both a cause and outcome of remaining single; for some, the desire to have careers meant not marrying; for others, not marrying meant finding work (O'Brien, 1991). Their longer and more continuous work careers pay off in old age when single women enjoy more stable and secure financial circumstances than do widowed, divorced and separated women (McDonald, 1997). One woman notes the relative advantage of a lifetime of paid work:

> I think that when you are a single woman, when you have worked and you retire, you are a lot more aggressive about life. . . . [W]omen who stayed home, they have done a wonderful job bringing up their kids and staying home, but then when their husband passes away some of them are out to sea. (Baumbusch, 2004:114)

Historically, older single women have had both more education and higher incomes than single men (Buunk & van Driel, 1989), but the extent of these differences has diminished over time (Davies, 1995; Seccombe & Ishii-Kuntz, 1994). Shifting gender relations and the related ideal of being able to combine a career with an egalitarian marriage may present a particular challenge to the assessment of being single among women (Trimberger, 2005). Although today's old women may view a satisfying career as the gain of staying single, for younger single women, the possibility of combining marriage and paid work may mean that a career is no longer perceived as a unique reward of staying single.

The single are often assumed to be, by definition, isolated and have been typed by some as lifelong isolates (Gubrium, 1975), in part because their overall contact with others is lower than is true for the married and widowed. One must consider different forms of social involvement to better appreciate the impact of being single on social networks. Older single persons do appear to be less socially involved than both their married and previously married peers, and contact with relatives, friends, and neighbors declines with age among single persons but increases among the ever married (Barrett, 1999). Among adults aged 35 to 64 years, single persons spend less time with their relatives than do their married peers (Seccombe & Ishii-Kuntz, 1994), and older (Barrett, 1999) and middle-aged (Marks, 1996) singles are less likely to report having a confidant than are ever-married seniors. Yet a study of 24 women aged 40 years or more finds that these ever-single women see themselves as part of a supportive network of family, friends and community involvements, with more time available to invest in others (McDill et al., 2006).

There are important differences in social involvement within the single population. Regarding gender, single women maintain a relatively large network of siblings and their families, friends and neighbors; see family and friends more often; and receive far more familial support than do single men (Barrett, 1999; Mugford & Kendig, 1986). Among middle-aged singles, a similar pattern emerges, with single women in far greater contact with relatives from whom they receive more emotional support than do single men (Seccombe & Ishii-Kuntz, 1994). Higher education levels also enhance levels of interaction and socioemotional support among older single persons (Barrett, 1999).

What do we know about the family ties of older single persons? Older single women continue very strong attachments with surviving family members and describe their childhood relationships with parents and brothers and sisters very positively (O'Brien, 1991). The single tend to maintain especially close ties with siblings, nieces and nephews when compared with either married people with children or childless, widowed individuals (Rubinstein et al., 1991; see Chapters 12 and 13). A lifetime of less competition from other relationships (no spouse) permits single individuals to maintain sibling relationships more effectively than those who marry.

Older single persons invest more heavily in friendships than their married, divorced and widowed peers. More friends and greater contact with them (Seccombe & Ishi-Kuntz, 1994) make friends an important source of intimacy and continuity in the lives of single persons. Friends often take the place of family and provide enduring, trusting and supportive ties in later life. There are important gender differences, however, with older single men more likely to receive help from friends, whereas older single women are more likely to be helped by family members, including children (Barrett & Lynch, 1999). Older single women generally favor basing their friendships on "voluntary mutuality" rather than dependency and thus do not tend to view friends as potential caregivers in old age (Rubinstein et al., 1991). Both older single men and women are more likely than married persons to rely on paid help for assistance with daily activities, a difference that may reflect a long-term pattern among the single of relying on such help as a way of maintaining independence (Connidis & McMullin, 1994).

Very old singles have a higher rate of co-residency than the divorced and widowed, largely because living with someone who is unrelated or with siblings, cousins, aunts or uncles is more common among the single (Stull & Scarisbrick-Hauser, 1989). For many single elders who live alone, solitary living is a transition that occurred in mid to later life, following the death of a parent, sibling or other person with whom they lived (Rubinstein et al., 1991). A 68-year-old woman in one of my studies did not worry about her future until her mother died six years prior to retirement:

I lived with my mother till . . . [s]he died when she was 91. It was lovely living together. When she was with me, I didn't think much about retirement because I was thinking about her. But after she died, I started thinking about it. I was anxious about where I would live and if I'd have enough money.

Thus it cannot be assumed that living alone in older age is a familiar and well-established tradition for all single persons. More recent research finds that the next cohort of widowed and divorced old people is more likely than single persons to live with someone (Pudrovska et al., 2006). This may reflect the growing trend of adult children to remain in the parental home longer or to return again after leaving (see Chapter 8).

Clearly, single older persons, particularly women, negotiate relationships with a range of family ties and friends. What is unclear is whether the absence of a romantic relationship that is both exclusive and voluntary makes a difference to the lives of older single persons (Clark & Graham, 2005). Friendships are voluntary but not exclusive, and some family ties, such as between a mother and child, are often exclusive but not voluntary. Among older adults, having a spouse or romantic partner lowers emotional loneliness (Green et al., 2001), highlighting the need to pay more attention to the intimate involvements of single persons and to explore whether single persons negotiate their relationships with friends and family ties so that they mimic the contributions of good romantic relationships.

The issue of exclusivity may create ambivalence in single persons' relationships with other family members who have partners. The exclusivity and accepted priority of commitment to a spouse and to children put these relationships at the apex of a triangular hierarchy of ties, below which fall commitments to other relations and to friends (Clark & Graham, 2005). In such a social hierarchy of relationships, a single person may be very committed to a relationship, for example to a married sibling, but at the same time feel limited in the extent to which this relationship can be called upon for support. Yet a unique feature of being single in mid and later life is the greater opportunity to choose whom to care for and about and the parameters of close relationships (Byrne & Carr, 2005).

In sum, older single persons experience greater continuity in their lives than is true of other unmarried groups. Single persons are less likely to experience changes in residence in older age, having typically made such transitions in midlife. Instead, a sizeable portion of single persons reach old age with an established pattern of living, either alone or with others. As well, most single persons are not isolates and maintain quite active ties with relatives and, particularly, friends.

The Subjective Experience of Being Single

One would think that choosing to be single would create a happier state than involuntary singlehood, but as yet, there is no research on the subject. Perhaps by the time one has been single for 60 years or more, the reason for being single matters little. Those who see being single as desirable are less lonely in old age (Dykstra, 1995) indicating the significance of one's view of being single on subjective feelings. When reviewing studies about being single, pay close attention to the samples used. Some research uses samples of younger singles who still hope to marry (Sharp & Ganong, 2007), a group that is likely to have quite different views of being single than those who either choose to be single or who have led long lives as single persons.

The implicit view of being single as avoiding desolation minimizes the attachment that single persons have to their closest friends or relatives and the impact on their lives of losing these individuals. Although the necessity to forge "uncharted territory" may make single persons more adaptable than their ever-married peers (Stein, 1981), the depth of their attachments and the extent of their loss when significant persons in their lives die or move away are substantial (Trimberger, 2005). Rather than assume that single persons are somehow impervious to desolation because they have no spouses to lose, one might ask instead about the impact of being single on their well-being.

Research generally shows that the always single are less satisfied than their married peers (Barrett, 1999). More research with large samples is needed to appreciate the vantage point of middle-aged and old persons, however, given that married women appear to be no more satisfied than single ones except during the life stage when many marry (DePaulo & Morris, 2005). The strains of being on their own are felt more strongly by the widowed and divorced than by the single (Pudrovska et al., 2006), and more generally, being single has advantages over being divorced or widowed, a sign of the costs of relationship dissolution rather than the benefits of marriage (Rook & Zettel, 2005; re older women, Williams & Umberson, 2004). A perceived advantage of being single in a qualitative study of older women is knowing how to be alone and look after oneself (Baumbusch, 2004). This extends to single women assuming that they are better off than women who must adjust to losing a partner.

More people agree that single women than single men can live a "fully satisfying life without getting married" (Koropeckyj-Cox, 2005:92). Single women are more satisfied than are single men. Yet single women report more hassles in their networks than do single men, possibly reflecting the greater likelihood that, as single women, there are high expectations about the help they will offer other family members, especially parents and siblings (Barrett, 1999). Among single women, psychological well-being is related to age; older single women are better off than younger single women and than older single men (Davies, 1995). Parallel observations apply to middle-aged persons: Single women in their early 50s do not differ from married women in distress levels, but single men experience greater distress than their married peers (Marks, 1996). On the other hand, single men and women do not fare as well as their married counterparts in terms of self-acceptance, environmental mastery, positive relations with others, a sense of purpose in life, and personal autonomy and growth. These differences at middle age may reflect cohort differences. Alternatively, they may mark a transitional phase to being permanently single and later become the more positive views reported by older single persons, particularly women.

There are racial differences as well, with single White persons more satisfied with life than single non-White persons, even though non-Whites report fewer hassles from network members by virtue of being single (Barrett, 1999). Within racial groups, gender acts in opposite directions (Pudrovska et al., 2006). Old White women experience more strain from being single than do old White men, but old

Black women experience less strain than single Black men. Race and gender also intersect so that White old women experience more strain as a result of being single than do Black old women (Pudrovska et al., 2006). There are not parallel race differences among old single men.

Like most situations, being single has advantages and disadvantages. Among women in middle and old age, being alone, being in control, being free to engage in chosen activities and pursuits, independence and freedom are assets of being single (Baumbusch, 2004; Gordon, 1994; McDill et al., 2006). Independence extends to being able to choose one's company due to a smaller network of obligatory family ties and to being able to choose one's activities without consulting with a spouse (Baumbusch, 2004). Costs of staying single include the need to ensure social contact, loneliness, the expense of single living, feeling peripheral in a couple-oriented society, and the stigma of being single (Gordon, 1994). Lack of companionship extends to the basic human desire for touch, as noted by an old woman who schedules regular massages "because I think I just needed to have someone touch me and be loving and kind and touch me" (Baumbusch, 2004: 115). The combination of viewing being alone as an advantage and loneliness as a disadvantage of being single suggests that being single creates the risk of emotional but not social isolation (see Weiss, 1973), an interpretation supported by the active social ties with family and friends noted earlier.

When reflecting on their lives, older single women (aged 80 and over) express no regret about having met familial obligations to parents and siblings or about remaining single, but some regret not having children (Allen, 1989; O'Brien, 1991). When asked directly whether they felt any regret about never marrying, a small majority of single men and women said they did (Rubinstein, 1987). At the same time, only a minority believed that life after 65 is more difficult for those who never marry. The greater loneliness of single than married persons (Dykstra, 1995; Rubinstein, 1987) underscores one of the losses of never marrying. In turn, however, the greater loneliness of formerly married compared to single persons illustrates the adaptation to single life made by most single individuals by the time they reach older age. As well, loneliness is offset by support from friends (Dykstra, 1995), a reward for the greater involvement of single persons in friendship ties. The relative adaptability of single individuals may be due in part to the stability created through a lifetime of work. When compared with older widows, single retirees "felt better about themselves . . . , friendlier toward others . . . , and more in control of their own lives" (Norris, 1980:142).

Being Gay and Lesbian
Singles in Middle and Later Life

The dilemma of trying to characterize the experience of being single given its heterogeneity is captured in the quite different contexts of being single based on sexual orientation. When attention is paid to the intimate ties of older gay and lesbian persons, the usual focus is on same-sex relationships (Connidis, 2006). This focus ignores the comparatively high proportion of gay men and substantial number of lesbians who are single (de Vries, 2006; Hostetler, 2004). Lack of clarity regarding identification based on sexual orientation together with unclear and heterosexist definitions of single make it especially difficult to calculate the number of gay and lesbian ever-single older persons (de Vries, 2007).

Like straight individuals, gay and lesbian adults place a premium on being attached rather than single, as indicated by a majority of gay men in one study who disagree with the statement, "I prefer being single" (Bergling, 2004). Age makes a difference, however, with those aged 30 to 39 least likely to agree and those aged 60 or over (30%) most likely to agree. Such age differences reflect in part the impact of being at a specific life stage at a given point in history that is central to the life course perspective. For example, different realities characterized the lives of lesbians who were born in the adjacent cohorts of 1917 to 1929 and 1930 to 1939 and who now would be in their 80s to mid 90s versus their late 60s and 70s (Claassen, 2005). The older cohort was born into the optimism of the 20s that ended with the Great Depression of 1929 to 1939 and a period in which marriage was expected and lesbians were viewed as neurotic. The younger cohort experienced World War II in their childhood, came of age during the post-war period when women who had replaced men in the labor force were expected to return home and raise children, and homosexuals were among the targets of witch hunts during the anti-communist McCarthy era in the United States.

Age relations cross-cut gender and sexual orientation and produce special challenges for middle-aged and old gays and lesbians (Connidis, 2006). The high premium placed on youth among singles creates unique pressures on aging gay men and lesbians. Compounding the emphasis on youth is the relative shortage of possible gay or lesbian partners that places limits on age segregation (Cohler, 2004). Although gay men are more likely than lesbians to be single (see Chapter 4), relationship stability is more tenuous among lesbians than among straight couples (Hostetler, 2004). Age relations in gay and lesbian communities create a particular disadvantage for their old members because, when compared with straight persons, the negative impact of aging on prospects for intimacy is less likely to be protected by being in long-term relationships, particularly marriage.

When compared with old straight men, old gay men are much more likely to live alone and to be without the usual family supports of straight men (National Gay and Lesbian Task Force, 2000). This leads some of them to create informal group homes in which gay men offer support to one another. As we shall see in subsequent chapters, gay and lesbian men and women are involved in other family relationships. Learning more about how older people negotiate single life regardless of sexual orientation is likely to improve our understanding of family ties and of the unique situations of gay, lesbian and straight singles.

Options for Intimate Relationships for Older Singles

Being single does not necessarily mean the absence of intimate ties. Unfortunately, however, little is known about the intimate involvements of older single persons, partly due to our tendency to make traditional assumptions about intimacy in older age; one is either married or celibate. As well, when these topics are explored, the activities of the previously married tend to receive more attention than those of the ever single. Thus dating and cohabitation tend not to be viewed as the ongoing arrangements of single persons but rather as the followup to marital dissolution (see Chapter 6). This orientation also limits examinations of same-sex relationships that have not been legally sanctioned. Because most studies on dating and cohabiting concern younger people, their findings are generally irrelevant to the experience of older persons. We need more information about the extent to which these phenomena occur, more attempts at understanding why they occur, and more research on their unique features in later life.

Summary

In sum, older single people, particularly women, appear to negotiate involved familial and friendship ties and successful work careers over the course of their lives, offsetting the lost potential advantages of marrying. They define single life as "normal" and derive satisfaction from sources other than family life. But they also remain active family members, extending their responsibilities for and attachments to their family of origin into adulthood. As well, they actively negotiate ties to friends over the life course, with some friends serving familylike roles in their lives. Although most single persons do not feel lonely, they are more likely to do so than are their married counterparts, and old single men are at risk of being socially isolated. They also receive less emotional, social, and instrumental support from family than do the married, primarily because they do not have spouses or children, in most cases. A better understanding of single life's realities helps to normalize staying single and may encourage more people to marry for the right reasons rather than as a way of escaping the stigma of being single (Trimberger, 2005).

On balance, research to date indicates the need to reconceptualize single life in order to avoid implicitly accepting marriage as the exclusive intimate relationship of adult life. The significant place of single persons in family networks and the crucial support that they provide to various family members must also be recognized. We need to know more about the romantic attachments of single persons in older age, an area that we are more likely to explore as acceptance of sexuality in later life grows.

CHAPTER 6

Transitions in Intimate Relationships

Losses and Opportunities

Old age is often associated with loss, and paramount among these losses is the death of a spouse or long-term partner. Even after such fundamental losses, there are opportunities for intimacy in later life. As is true of all life stages, those in middle and later life vary in their responses to loss and their views of desirable alternatives for intimacy. This chapter explores usual responses to losing a spouse or long-term partner through death or relationship dissolution and then explores remarriage, cohabitation, living apart together (LAT) relationships, dating, and sexual intimacy in middle and old age.

Widowhood

Today's older persons are far more likely to experience widowhood than divorce, and this is especially true for women (see Chapter 2). Widowhood in older age is a transition for most and a status already acquired earlier in life for others.

A feminist life course approach encourages a more complete view of widowhood, taking us beyond an unduly negative view of older widowed women (Chambers, 2005). Incorporating a critical perspective more explicitly includes the experience of men and the cross-cutting of age and gender relations with those of class, sexual orientation, race and ethnicity (see Chapter 1). This combined orientation links the impact of a partner's death on individuals to socially structured practices regarding marital status, gender and age (Chambers, 2005). A partner's death also occurs in the context of prior life experience and includes both short-term bereavement and longer-term widowhood. The patriarchal values embedded in gender relations have consequences for men and women as they approach life without their long-term partners.

The Transition to Widowhood

Much of our understanding of becoming and being widowed comes from qualitative research in which in-depth interviews and narratives reveal the process and dynamics of this major life transition.

> Widowhood is a different way of life. My husband was frail for several years and needed a lot of attention and care. I had to give up so many things that I was doing before and lost so much contact with so many of my friends. After his death it was difficult for me to pick up the pieces. . . . I was 80 when my husband died. . . . I had a friend who lost her husband when she was young and she had a tiny boy. I remember so well her saying to me, "After my husband died I made up my mind that I was not going to sit around and mope all the time because if I did, I would lose all my friends." You know, I never forgot that. That's what I thought when my husband died. I wasn't going to sit around and mope all the time. It wasn't going to do him any good and it certainly wasn't going to do me any good.
>
> —Widow, aged 92

As was the case for this widow, caregiving often precedes widowhood in later life for both men and women (Wells & Kendig, 1997). Because women remain much more likely than men to be widowed, widowhood is often considered a women's issue, and much of what we know about widowhood is based on their experiences (Martin-Matthews, 1999; Williams et al., 2006).

Reflecting our emphasis on gender relations, when possible, we will examine the unique experiences of men *and* women who have made this transition. Losing a spouse is linked to gendered marital relations in which today's old women are likely to have depended on their husbands for financial support and today's old men are likely to have depended on their wives for emotional support, homemaking skills and links to a larger social network (Carr, 2004b). Thus, gender variations in the response to widowhood reflect socially structured gender relations that are reproduced in traditional marriage. Apparently individual responses to being widowed are linked to the nature of the lost relationship and the broader institutional and structural arrangements in which it was embedded.

The initial stage of widowhood, bereavement, lasts for roughly two to four years. During this time, individuals undergo a period of grieving and mourning characterized initially by profound psychological disorganization (Martin Matthews, 1991). The popularity of a timetable of stages of grief masks the fact that grieving is variable, both in terms of how long it lasts and how severely it is felt. The process of grief and mourning includes shock, intense pain, grief work, and, once ready to rebuild one's life as a widow or widower, reality testing (Heinemann & Evans, 1990). Joan Didion (2005) describes the year after her husband's death as one of magical thinking during which she felt invisible and understood only by others who were in the same situation. A granddaughter's words capture the initial response of her widowed grandfather:

> [My grandparents] had been married for more than sixty years, raised three children together, sometimes fought bitterly, and were inseparable to the end. During the long time that my grandmother was dying, my grandfather . . . didn't hide any of his sorrow or hope from the rest of us. His need for her was raw. Almost to the moment of her death he was adamant that she would get well and on the day of her funeral he refused to join the rest of the family for dinner . . . at a local restaurant. "I was married to her for a long time," he said. "I have a lot to think about." (D'Erasmo, 2004:62–63)

The raw emotions that dominate the initial stages of grief coexist with quite positive feelings of joy, happiness and relief and eventually give way to emotion management that involves feeling numb, willful self-control, faith, distracting oneself through activity or passivity, and sharing feelings with others (Lopata, 1996). Over time, the dead spouse is incorporated into the surviving partner's life through images of heaven, hallucinations, memories, rituals and conversation. Daily functioning may then change as a result of less commitment to previous activities, including work and social encounters, and to declines in health. Eventually, relationships with other persons are altered, becoming either more close or distant, and the bereaved make the initial adjustment to life without a partner.

The comments of an 84-year-old widow in one of my studies exemplify several dimensions of grief as she moved on with her life:

> My husband was suffering so much that I eventually got the idea that it wasn't fair to want him to go on doing that. Nevertheless, for about a year, I was absolutely numb. Everywhere I turned, I ran into things that I missed.
>
> However, I have a strong nature. I made up my mind that I couldn't do that, that it wasn't fair to my daughter and it wasn't fair to myself. The last words that my husband said to me were, "Now don't sit down and brood. Make all you can out of the rest of your life." And I have done so. There isn't a day in my life that I don't think about him. But it has developed now into just happy thoughts of the times that we had.

The caregiving experience that often precedes the death of a spouse has implications for the transition to widowhood. Caring for a departed spouse allows some widowed persons to anticipate their loss and to feel some relief in their death (Hansson & Stroebe, 2007). Yet widowed persons who were caregivers continue to feel guilty and depressed, to have sleeping problems, and to report elevated levels of strain (Carpenter & Mak, 2007; Wells & Kendig, 1997). Even the quasi widowhood experienced by those whose spouses are institutionalized (Ross et al., 1997) does not necessarily leave older persons better prepared emotionally for widowhood.

The ambivalence that comes from wishing for a spouse's death as relief from suffering at the same time as wishing for the partner to survive (Kestin van den Hoonaard, 2001) underscores the complex of emotions and demands that extended caregiving for a spouse can trigger.

These findings reflect the mixed results concerning whether adjusting to sudden death or death following a long illness is more difficult. Didion's (2005) response to her husband's sudden death was wonder at how life can change in an instant, making it difficult to absorb that her husband had died. Yet despite the greater shock of sudden death, in the short term, greater anxiety occurs among surviving spouses who cared for partners whose death was expected and slow (Carr & Utz, 2004).

Gendered responses to sudden versus anticipated death also occur. Some research finds that men yearn for their deceased wives more if their deaths were prolonged; women yearn for their deceased husbands more if their deaths were sudden (Carr & Utz, 2004). For widowers, however, taking care of spouses provides an opportunity to learn homemaking skills and competence that facilitate adjustment once their wives die, an opportunity that the shock of sudden death does not allow (Moore & Stratton, 2002). Among widows (Kestin van den Hoonaard, 2001) more than widowers (Moore & Stratton, 2002), lengthy illness provides an opportunity to talk about the dying partner's death and the future life of the surviving spouse. Once widowed, these exchanges are enmeshed with the experience of being widowed more than of being married; a husband's expressed views of her future are part of a widow's present. On balance, anticipating widowhood through the illness of a spouse tends to make adapting to losing one's partner easier (Martin Matthews, 1991).

The life course perspective's emphasis on the greater ease of adapting to transitions that occur at the expected age (on time) is supported by the finding that losing a spouse in later life softens the loss, regardless of whether or not the loss is sudden (Lopata, 1996). There is more variability in the reactions among old than among younger persons (Hansson & Stroebe, 2007), however, and, some conclude that bereavement is no easier at younger or older ages (Hatch, 2000). The unexpectedness of off-time widowhood at younger ages is offset in extreme old age by a smaller support network and poorer health (Martin Matthews, 1991). A cost of being widowed on time, that is, in older age, is the reduced opportunity for finding a new partner, new job or new social network (Wu & Schimmele, 2007). Thus widowhood has age-related consequences that make it different but not uniformly easier or more difficult to be widowed at a particular age.

Class also shapes the widowhood experience. Widowhood is more clearly and positively defined in working-class than in middle-class and upper-class cultures, thus easing the process of bereavement for working-class women (Walker et al., 1977). The family-based social network typical of the working class is also helpful in the initial stages of bereavement and is generally the primary coping resource of older adults who lose loved ones (Hansson & Stroebe, 2007).

Generally, six months after losing their spouses, women's self-esteem is enhanced, men's self-esteem is lowered, and women experience more personal growth than do men (Carr, 2004b). These outcomes are moderated by features of the marital relationship so that men who depended on their late wives' homemaking skills more often suffer a decline in self-esteem once widowed. Assuming responsibility for emotional needs in the case of widowers, and of home maintenance and finances in the case of widows, enhances self-esteem and personal growth once widowed. Marital quality also influences the response to widowhood. Those who had warm and interdependent relationships yearn more for their lost partners; those whose relationships were characterized by conflict and strain yearn less (Carr & Utz, 2004). In more extreme cases, a very painful marriage makes widowhood feel like a relief, a situation that should be less likely in the future, as younger couples turn to divorce more readily than today's older persons did (Martin-Matthews, 1999).

Lengthy and serious illnesses may affect the quality of marital relationships and, consequently, the transition to widowhood. For old widowers whose spouses were ill for a long time, decreased sexual activity, separate bedrooms, and different routines often came to characterize their marriages and foreshadowed life as widowed persons (Moore & Stratton, 2002). Seeing someone through dementia also alters the quality of the marital relationship so that a partner's death feels like a relief, as described by an old widower: "When she died, I felt relieved for her. Before that, as a person, she had left me" (Moore & Stratton, 2002:37). Whatever the preceding circumstances, the first night alone at home following the death of a partner marks a dramatic and challenging life transition (Kestin van den Hoonaard, 2001; Moore & Stratton, 2002).

The focus of many widows on surviving and prevailing as they take charge of their lives and become more independent over time suggests that adapting to widowhood represents a transformation rather than a recovery (Martin-Matthews, 1999). An 83-year-old woman, widowed for 14 years, observes, "I became more independent, a lot more my own person. You have to, to be on your own without your husband's help. . . . It makes you a stronger person" (Martin Matthews, 1991:28). For some widows and widowers, the passage of time heightens rather than diminishes grief (Lopata, 1996) and leads to personal changes judged to be negative (Martin Matthews, 1991), but these responses are not typical (Hansson & Stroebe, 2007; Moore & Stratton, 2002).

The Impact of Widowhood on Objective Conditions

What are the longer-term consequences of widowhood? Widowhood is associated with an elevated risk of morbidity and mortality, especially among those who are widowed more than once (Zhang, 2006) and among Whites married to Whites when compared with Blacks married to Blacks (Elwert & Christakis, 2006). These differences reflect the significance of marital history rather than marital status alone (see Chapter 3) and the impact of different marital cultures and contexts among White versus Black couples that have a historical backdrop of structured race relations.

Gender relations that led many of today's old women to rely on their husbands' earnings are reflected in the relative impoverishment of the current cohort of older women following widowhood (Martin-Matthews, 1999), an experience that men typically do not share if their wives die. The financial hardship of widowhood in older age is intractable for many without the support of family and the state, particularly among those groups such as Black and Hispanic widows who experience very high rates of poverty (Angel et al., 2003; Angel et al., 2007). A majority of Canadian widows depend on government pensions as their key source of income, and the poorest among them are older, less educated, retired from lower-prestige occupations, less prepared for retirement, and more likely to have retired to care for a family member (McDonald, 1997). Similarly, in the United States, unmarried women rely more heavily on Social Security as an income source than either unmarried men or married couples (National Economic Council, 1998).

To date, employment does not guarantee economic security among retired widows, largely because the meshing of work histories and family careers has resulted in intermittent employment in jobs with no or paltry pension benefits (Street & Connidis, 2001). Changes in family form make state-based support more precarious, as growing numbers of women, especially African American women, reach old age without the requisite 10 years of marriage needed to qualify for either spousal or widow benefits (Harrington Meyer et al., 2006). Among Mexican Americans, widows report fewer resources, more financial strain, and greater openness to accepting welfare than their male counterparts (Angel et al., 2003). Some older widows also have limited experience with managing money and making financial decisions. Even among those who are relatively well off, the immediate paperwork and financial arrangements that follow their husbands' deaths, the individual responsibility for making decisions about money and investments, the need to rely on others for financial advice, and the fear of having their vulnerability exploited combine to make financial issues a challenge of widowhood (Kestin van den Hoonaard, 2001).

One outcome of widowhood for some is residential mobility. Although widows and widowers remain in their residences for an average of 15 years, the probability of moving peaks during the first year of widowhood (Chevan, 1995). Good health and higher incomes decrease this probability. Among widows, home ownership is associated with having more close friends in the neighborhood, due largely to length of residency (Bess, 1999). Living alone is more common among widows and widowers and raises unique concerns among older persons with health problems. As one 78-year-old widower observes, "At this stage of the game, I think one of the biggest things that concerns me is health; when you have health problems at this stage, and you have no one here, you're pretty dead in the water if you need help" (Moore & Stratton, 2002:115). In the longer run, being widowed alters living arrangements by increasing the chances of being placed in a nursing home or similar long-term care institution (Lopata, 1996; Wolinsky & Johnson, 1992).

The socially constructed gender relations that limit the financial security of widows have a parallel effect on the social networks of widowers (Blieszner, 1993). Women generally and widows in particular have a more extensive and diverse network of support from family and friends than do their male peers (Antonucci, 1990; Barrett & Lynch, 1999; Bengtson et al., 1996). Widowed men are less likely than married men and than women of all marital statuses to feel needed and appreciated and to have someone to accompany them when engaging in activities outside the home (Connidis & McMullin, 1994). At the same time, widows face challenges in trying to fit into a couple-oriented world and in negotiating support from their friends in the wake of losing their husband (Kestin van den Hoonaard, 2001).

The loss of a wife's homemaking and interpersonal skills requires a major adjustment of most widowed men. Although the traditional skills of a wife tend to be socially undervalued, they are fundamental to daily life (Thompson & Walker, 1989). Thus acquiring the ability to prepare meals and keep dishes, clothes and home clean—or finding someone else to do these tasks—is essential following a wife's death. Older widowed men more readily acquire such skills, however, than older widows acquire such traditionally male tasks as driving a car or house and yard upkeep (Kendig, 1986; O'Bryant, 1991). Widowers make claims to masculinity by labeling themselves as bachelors rather than widowers and by linking their culinary efforts to those of professional male chefs and defining cooking as necessary rather than enjoyable (Davidson et al., 2003; Kestin van den Hoonaard, 2007). Widows enjoy mastering new skills, such as learning to drive, making household repairs, and using home entertainment equipment (Kestin van den Hoonaard, 2001), without the apparent need to claim femininity as a result of doing so.

Children, especially daughters, are the central individuals in the family network of widowed men and women (Kestin van den Hoonaard, 2001; Moore & Statton, 2002), and contact with them is higher among the widowed than the married (Barrett & Lynch, 1999; Martin Matthews, 1991; see Chapters 7 and 8). This relationship represents considerable familial stability for widowed parents, particularly in the initial stages of bereavement when contact with children is very helpful. Widowed men and women are more likely than their married counterparts to confide in at least one child (Connidis & Davies, 1992), indicating that both the quality and extent of interaction with children increase when widowed. Mothers engage in more reciprocal relationships with their children than do fathers following the death of their partners (Carr & Utz, 2004). Children are more inclined to offer instrumental support and financial advice to their widowed mothers than widowed fathers, and mothers are more inclined than fathers to offer emotional support to their children following the shared respective loss of their husbands and fathers.

Widows also work to maintain reciprocity in their relationships with children by offering to babysit or cook meals and to maintain balance by resisting their children's help when it becomes overprotective and by limiting their own expectations for support (Kestin van den Hoonaard, 2001). Gender differences should not diminish the value of family to widowers, however. Research from the United Kingdom finds that widowed men tend to socialize more at home, primarily with family, and to depend more heavily on their children than old men of other marital statuses (Davidson et al., 2003). They also enjoy a special tie with their grandchildren. There can be too much of a good thing; if support comes only from children, the benefits of filial support are diminished (Martin-Matthews, 1999).

Widowhood also may prompt more involved ties with siblings, especially between widows and their sisters (Martin Matthews, 1991; see Chapters 12 and 13). For those whose relationships with siblings change following widowhood, most observe greater emotional closeness, improved ties, and more frequent and supportive contact (Connidis, 1992). Qualitative research suggests that widowers have close relationships with brothers and sisters, and as peers, siblings may encourage involvement with others outside the family, including potential mates (Moore & Stratton, 2002). The benefits of sibling contact are also evident among rural widows for whom sibling contact staves off loneliness (Dugan & Kivett, 1994). Among childless widows, siblings compose a larger portion of the confidant network than is true of childless wives (Connidis & Davies, 1990). Although widowed persons receive more help from siblings than do married persons (Barrett & Lynch, 1999), siblings tend to be important socioemotional ties rather than sources of instrumental help (Connidis, 1994b).

Friends emerge as important network members in widowhood (Lopata, 1996; Martin Matthews, 1991). Both widowers and widows are more likely than the married to consider a friend both a confidant and a companion, and friends occupy a larger portion of these networks among widowed persons (Connidis & Davies, 1990, 1992). Widows tend to have more friends than do widowers and are more likely to confide in them (Connidis & Davies, 1992; Martin Matthews, 1991). Having friends and neighbors reduces loneliness and worry among widowed women (Lee, Willetts et al., 1998), illustrating the benefits of maintaining and establishing personal relationships beyond family. The value of friends for support after losing a spouse is noted by an 83-year-old widow:

> I think it's very important that people have friends who can help you at that time [of becoming widowed], because your children can't. And I realized they couldn't help because they're dealing with their own feelings. If I hadn't had all these kind friends, I would have been much worse off than I was. (Walter, 2003:72–73)

Men also benefit from a greater sense of personal fulfillment as widowers when there is more support from an active social network (Carr, 2004b). The relative scarcity of fellow widowers and of late-life male friendships in general (Moore & Stratton, 2002), however, leaves men more isolated than women and may partially explain their higher remarriage rates.

The greater reliance of working-class persons on a homogeneous network focused on relatives puts the working-class widow at greater risk of isolation if her children do not live nearby (Walker et al., 1977). A family-based network can also be counterproductive when the widow is ready to establish a new way of life with new activities and people. The more dispersed networks and higher education of middle-class widows put them at a relative advantage for making this transition (Lopata, 1996). Yet widowhood is more disruptive among the more highly educated women of the middle and upper classes because their relationships with their husbands were typically more interdependent.

In sum, the gendered experience of widowhood mirrors the gendered relations of our society. Women experience greater economic hardship and men greater isolation on the loss of spouses. The fact that the older widows who are best able to self-sufficiently perform male- and female-associated tasks spent the most years in the labor force (O'Bryant, 1991) suggests the benefits of changing social structural arrangements in the areas of family and work. The greater involvement of today's younger women in the labor force and younger fathers in the lives of their children may have long-term benefits for their social networks in old age. This has been a gradual shift, and the extent of its impact remains to be seen. The cumulative negative effects of working in jobs that do not include pension benefits, that are part time, and that are intermittent and of earlier divorce and prior widowhood on the financial security of married and widowed persons do not bode well for upcoming cohorts of women.

The Subjective Impact of Widowhood

An initial reaction to widowhood is a sense of lost identity (Kestin van den Hoonaard, 2001). Particular triggers, like having to fill out marital status on a form, or being introduced as someone's widow, or the sudden self-realization of being a widow, start the process of acquiring a personal and social identity as a widow (Kestin van den Hoonaard, 2001)—the move from becoming to being a widow (Martin Matthews, 1991). This process is described by an old widower: "I have to recreate my life, have to recreate my thinking" (Moore & Stratton, 2002:87).

As the earlier discussion of marital status and its effects showed, widowed persons have lower levels of psychological well-being than the married (see Chapter 3). One of the longer-lasting consequences of widowhood is elevated levels of loneliness (Dugan & Kivett, 1994; Moore & Stratton, 2002). On balance, men appear to experience greater psychological suffering than women when their spouses die (Lopata, 1996; Martin Matthews, 1991). Both men and women tend to underestimate their chances of being widowed (Holden & Kuo, 1996), but women are more inclined to expect widowhood and to imagine how they would handle it, a process referred to as *anticipatory socialization*, which aids adjustment (Martin Matthews, 1991). Among men, the expectation that they would be the first to go by virtue of being men is one element of the unexpected that widowers must negotiate (Moore & Stratton, 2002). Men typically spend a shorter time than women in the widowed state, and psychological well-being does improve with time (Lee, Willetts et al., 1998). Yet even when length of widowhood is considered, widowed men remain significantly more depressed than widowed women. This difference may be because the higher rates of remarriage among men are selective, leaving a pool of widowers who are particularly depressed (Lee, Willetts et al., 1998).

Gender differences in objective conditions are directly related to variations in life satisfaction (Stevens, 1995). When compared with widows, widowers enjoy less financial stress, more education, fewer somatic symptoms, and more frequently have new intimate relationships, all factors that typically enhance life satisfaction. The one relative advantage for widows is more regular contact with friends. Yet when all of these factors are taken into account, widows are still more satisfied than widowers (Stevens, 1995). Women's virtuosity in nurturing a range of relationships (see Chambers, 2005; Dykstra, 1990) clearly has benefits when meeting the challenges of widowhood.

Chambers' (2005) feminist life course exploration of widowed lives in the United Kingdom puts the various responses to losing a spouse in the context of individual, social, and cultural contexts over a lifetime. Her qualitative study of widows aged 55 and over and widowed for at least five years identifies three groups: those who emphasize loneliness and despair, those who get on with their lives, and those who experience widowhood as a transition. The first and smallest group of widows combines feeling lonely with a loss of confidence, a sense of someone missing, confusion, feeling different, limited pleasure in life, and a bleak view of the future. A larger group that got on with their lives accepts the inevitable, holds on to good memories, has few regrets, enjoys being alone, deals with financial and health challenges, feels validated by others, keeps busy, and faces the future one day at a time. The largest group experiences widowhood as a transition, parallel to Martin Matthews's (1991) description of the long-term negotiation of widowhood as a transformation. These widows, though sorry to have lost their husbands, experience new self-awareness, making themselves a priority for the first time, freedom, new relationships, interdependence with others, new interests and opportunities, and an optimistic forward-looking stance toward the future.

The three dominant narratives of widowhood are fluid so that women may alternate their view of being widowed even though one of the narratives dominates (Chambers, 2005). Thus even those who see widowhood as positively transformative sometimes lapse into a focus on widowhood as lonely and bleak. Also, these subjective accounts of being widowed shape the impact of objective circumstances, cautioning us against treating similar conditions as similar in their effects. For example, one widow for whom widowhood is a time of loneliness and despair views poor health as an impediment to being socially engaged; other widows who either get on with their lives or experience widowhood as a transition view poor health as a challenge to be surmounted. The response to being widowed is shaped by a life course of experience, a history of making and turning to friends, high self-esteem, and a positive view of one's capacity to deal with change that feeds a positive response to being widowed.

The Death of a Same-Sex Partner

How does the experience of widowhood compare with losing a long-term same-sex partner? Marital status is a basis for distributing privilege (see Chapter 3), so that those who lose a spouse have their loss legitimated and their grief recognized. In contrast, both opposite-sex and same-sex partners who were not married often experience disenfranchised grief (Doka, 2002a; Walter, 2003); as official outsiders to family networks, their right to grieve goes unacknowledged even though the bereavement process is similar (Shernoff, 1998). Because homosexual unions are generally not recognized as marriage, sympathetic allowances in the work place and among acquaintances are fewer, professional support services are limited, and financial difficulties may follow the loss of a partner (Doka, 2002a; Whipple, 2006). Family members, particularly those of the deceased partner, may not be supportive, sometimes to the point of intervening in funeral and subsequent arrangements or discounting the relationship entirely (Fullmer, 1995; Peplau et al., 1996). Estrangement from other potential sources of support, such as religious institutions, may heighten the sense of loss that follows a partner's passing (Fullmer, 1995).

Sadly, the disenfranchisement of gay and lesbian family members may extend to their exclusion following the deaths of others, as the following experience relayed by a clergy person illustrates:

> There was a family in my parish . . . who had a son, Chris, who was gay. The . . . father was clearly very uncomfortable about his son's friends—especially his lover, Sean—mixing with . . . extended family. . . . I suggested he tell his family and friends that the visitation was on Monday night and tell his son's friends to come on Tuesday. Monday night his mother (Chris's grandmother) seemed annoyed. "I cannot believe," she told her son, "that Sean's not here—they were lovers, you know." It turned out that the two would visit her often. (Doka, 2002b:142)

This account reminds us not to assume that it is the old members of a family who are most likely to be offended by new situations. Such exclusion motivates gay and lesbian persons to create their own funeral rituals (Whipple, 2006).

Death due to AIDS adds additional stresses to losing a partner, most commonly among gay men, because of the stigma associated with the illness, the fact that death often occurs at younger ages, and, in some cases, survivor guilt (Doka, 2002c; Peplau et al., 1996; Shernoff, 1998; Walter, 2003). As well, the loss of an intimate partner often occurs in the context of multiple losses due to AIDS within a closely knit community (Mullan, 1998). As the treatment protocols for HIV/AIDS continue to improve, and as more gay and lesbian adults form open, long-term relationships, their experience of losing partners later in life will become a more common public occurrence. In the words of a lesbian widow, "As the rest of the world begins to understand our love as something more than a sexual attraction that can be satisfied by any one-night stand, but rather as fully committed and lovingly intimate relationships, they may also come to recognize the extent of our grief, the depth of our loss" (Whipple, 2006:6).

The intersection of gender with sexual orientation is part of identity negotiation over time, as lesbians and gay men negotiate being women and men as well as lesbian and gay in their relationships and after they are gone. This can mean both additional challenges and unique advantages. As an example of the latter, when compared with straight women following widowhood, the more egalitarian relationships of lesbian couples mean that lesbian widows typically do not have to learn new skills previously performed by their partners (Walter, 2003; Whipple, 2006).

Despite the significant differences based on sexual orientation, a qualitative study of persons 1 to 16 years past the time of losing their gay, lesbian, or straight long-term partners reminds us of the common human experience of such loss, regardless of marital status or sexual orientation (Walter, 2003). A frequent experience after losing a partner is the ambivalence of simultaneously wanting to hang on to the lost partner's memory *and* wanting to avoid the painful feelings of losing a partner that such memories might trigger. The shift from "we" to "I" that characterizes acquiring a widowed identity occurs among lesbian widows as well (Whipple, 2006). On the second anniversary of the death of her 31-year partner, Pat reflected,

This was a critical time for me to review our life together and to find myself outside of our relationship. . . . Because I was brought up to put my personal desires secondary to those of my mate, our relationship worked well for Betty. Essentially it worked for me as well, at least until I no longer had a mate. Then I had to learn a new way of living. (Whipple, 2006:152- 53)

There are also signs of change evident in findings that lesbian women who are out about their sexuality and their relationships do receive family support after a partner dies (Whipple, 2006). However, for those who are not out, there is the further isolation that comes from ignorance of what the relationship meant to them or the decision to come out.

In sum, the initial loss of a long-term partner or spouse is an intensely personal period of bereavement. The link between negative objective outcomes, such as financial setbacks and reduced social involvement, and the subjective feelings of widowed persons means that there is the potential for social policy intervention (see Chapter 14). Many of the consequences of widowhood reflect socially constructed relations of gender and sexual orientation in the social domains of work and family. Changing these relations is fundamental to ameliorating core problems faced by those whose long-term partners die.

Divorce

As the figures in Chapter 2 showed, a relatively small proportion of today's older persons—7% of Canadians and 8% to 9% of Americans—is divorced. The risk of divorce is greatest in the first few years of marriage, and younger persons account for the majority of all divorces (Hiedemann et al., 1998). Those who divorce in middle age, however, are less likely than those who divorce at younger ages to remarry, resulting in growing numbers of individuals who will reach old age unattached due to divorce (Wu & Penning, 1997).

The current risk of divorce by the 30th wedding anniversary for all marriages is 44% for Americans and 38% for Canadians (Ambert, 2005; Schoen & Canudas-Romo, 2006). These figures include redivorces for one or both spouses, making the risk of divorce for first marriages lower. The percentage of divorces that are redivorces is 16% in Canada and 33% in the United States. Marriages that ended in divorce in recent years lasted an average of 14 years in Canada and 11 years in the United States.

U.S. divorce rates peaked in 1990 and have stabilized since that time (Schoen & Canudas-Romo, 2006), in part because increased cohabitation decreases the opportunity to officially divorce. Less stabilization has occurred among Black than White women, and the more common practice of separating but not formally divorcing among African Americans means that divorce data underestimate marital disruption among them (Sweeney & Phillips, 2004). The greater dissimilarity in attitudes between spouses among African American than non-African-American couples (Clarkwest, 2007) and the socially created racial barriers to economic success that create marital financial conflicts for inner-city Black men aged 65 and over (Barker et al., 1998) help to account for their higher risk of divorce.

More people are entering and will enter old age with marital histories that include one or more divorces. Because divorce usually occurs at younger ages than is true for widowhood, the experience of divorce in later life more often concerns the long-term consequences of long-ago events and relationships. Older divorced persons are a particularly diverse group, based on when they divorced (Ambert, 2005). In this chapter, we focus on the subjective and objective consequences of divorce and relationship dissolution for older persons. Unfortunately, we must often extrapolate from data regarding younger couples. In Chapter 11, we consider the impact on intergenerational relations of both a parent's and an adult child's divorce.

The Transition From Marriage to Divorce: The Subjective Impact

Divorce is a process, not a discrete event, that begins during the marriage and ends years after the divorce papers are signed (Amato, 2007). Including the separated in discussions of divorce, especially concerning older persons, is essential to accurately assessing the extent of marital breakup and the process of adjustment that follows. Although separated persons may not divorce, all divorced persons were once separated, and separation marks a significant phase in the emotional and physical break with a partner. As well, among older individuals there may be fewer incentives to actually divorce (e.g., no other marriage prospects), even when the separation is considered a permanent rather than a temporary arrangement.

Unlike widowhood, divorce often means a profound loss not only in the present but also of the marriage's past (Katz, 2006). The circumstances of divorce may prompt a revision of a marriage's history as spouses question what they thought it had been. Also, unlike widowhood, divorce is considered a choice by at least one partner, potentially revocable, and possibly the 'fault' of one party, in which case a critical eye rather than sympathetic ear may follow (Froschl, 2006). The first year of separation is marked by feelings of ambivalence that combine a sense of longing with a feeling of relief, regardless of which spouse triggered the separation (Cherlin, 1992). For most separated persons, the heightened anxiety, periodic depression, and personal disorganization typical of this period are followed by several years of reorganization during which a new identity and lifestyle are negotiated (Cherlin, 1992).

Most older divorced men and women went through this transition earlier in their lives. For older women, the transition to divorce often meant making another key transition from being a homemaker to being a paid worker (Connidis, 2003a). On balance, women appear to experience greater psychological distress than men following divorce and to feel more lonely, angry, sleepless, guilty and anxious (Sev'er, 1992). Some of this variation may simply reflect gendered responses in how and when distress manifests itself. Men tend to react later and sometimes more severely in the form of higher rates of suicide, accidents, and psychiatric care. Divorce has a cumulative effect so that those who have divorced two or more times have higher depression scores than those who have divorced once (Kurdek, 1991).

Although both men and women aged 50 and over tend to see their lives after divorce as either the same as or better than life during the year before separation, women are more likely than men to note improvement in their social life and overall happiness and in being a parent (Hammond & Muller, 1992). Two to three years after a divorce, men are more likely than women to feel friendly toward and pre-occupied by their ex-spouses and to have lower well-being (Masheter, 1991). Such responses are shaped by the nature of the marriage before divorce (Amato, 2007). Research on couples of various ages who divorced in the early 1990s finds that those who suffered through very difficult marriages due to alcoholism, violence, or con-stant conflict experience relief, improved well-being and happiness after divorce. Those who were moderately content and thought they could do better than their current marriages are often disappointed and experience a decline in well-being following divorce. Thus, when a poor marriage prompts divorce, greater happiness is likely to ensue; when a weak commitment to marriage is the motivator, divorce dampens happiness (Amato & Hohmann-Marriott, 2007).

Race also has an impact on subjective responses to divorce. Blacks adjust better and feel less stigmatized by divorce than Whites four years after separation (Kitson et al., 1989), and Black women experience less strain than White women following divorce (Pudrovska et al., 2006).

The Objective Situation of Older Divorced Persons

As we saw in Chapter 3, divorced persons do not compare favorably with mar-ried adults in various measures of health and well-being (Amato, 2000). There is some evidence that middle-aged women are vulnerable to the health threats of emotional distress and socioeconomic status that accompany divorce (Zhang & Hayward, 2006). With regard to psychological well-being, however, parents with young children living at home experience greater declines than do older persons following divorce (Williams & Dunne-Bryant, 2006).

Referring to divorce as economic suicide for women captures the dramatic financial consequences that a marital breakup can have (Dailey, 2006). Although both men and women feel a sense of relative deprivation (Holden & Kuo, 1996), the financial impact of divorce is far greater for women (Sev'er, 1992). Two key factors that characterize the lives of today's older persons account for this difference: fol-lowing divorce, men are more likely to be in the labor force and in better-paying jobs and women to have custody of children. Even for those women in the labor force, interrupted employment, primarily to engage in family responsibilities, low-ers earnings and benefits in old age (Daily, 2006; Street & Connidis, 2001). Despite advances in education and employment, women continue to suffer major economic costs of divorce (Sayer, 2006).

Men also suffer a financial hit when they divorce, but this is primarily true for the economically disadvantaged (Sayer, 2006). For men, divorcing later rather than earlier in life has greater economic consequences because they can no longer make significant financial gains in the work world to compensate for the expenses of dis-solving a marriage (Keith, 1985). For both men and women, the financial setback of divorce carries over into the preretirement years, even following remarriage (Holden & Kuo, 1996). This helps account for the fact that divorced women in their 50s are more likely to work and to expect to retire later than their widowed and married peers (Morgan, 1992). Reduced financial circumstances following divorce, particularly among women, heighten the challenge of living alone. The increasing numbers of women who will be reaching old age after many years of being divorced and its attendant socioeconomic consequences is a significant social issue. Persistent poverty is most likely among female-headed households, especially Black female-headed households (Cherlin, 1992), a reflection of the greater economic costs of divorcing among Black than White men and women (Sayer, 2006).

Recent research suggests that the relative earnings of husbands and wives are influential regarding marital stability. Women are generally more likely to initiate divorce (Sweeney, 2002), but among couples with an average age in the mid-30s, those couples in which spouses make similar economic contributions to the household are more likely to divorce, and divorce is as likely to be initiated by the husband as by the wife (Rogers, 2004). Equal dependence appears to make both members of the couple confident that they can each survive on their own. These findings suggest some protective effects on marriage of a traditional division of paid labor, but research in the Netherlands finds that such effects only hold when wives hold traditional gender values (Kalmijn et al., 2004). As well, among dual-income couples, when wives perceive inequality in household labor, divorce is more likely to follow (Frisco & Williams, 2003). These findings suggest that, although economically egalitarian marriages are more likely to end in divorce, marriages in which nonegalitarian economic and household arrangements persist appear to protect marriage only when partners hold values in support of them. Traditional arrangements will not keep partners together when women are committed to egalitarian relationships.

In the period immediately following separation, both younger (under 50) and older (50 and over) men and, more so, women rely on multiple sources of emotional support, particularly parents, siblings, friends and children (Hammond & Muller, 1992). Among parents divorced after at least 19 years of marriage, mothers rank their children as their most supportive tie during the early stages of divorce, whereas fathers rank their friends and parents above their children (Wright & Maxwell, 1991). Ongoing, supportive ties with former in-laws following divorce are unusual despite widespread normative support for them (Finch & Mason, 1990). Generally, older persons rely less on others for emotional support following separation than do younger men and women.

Divorce erodes the support network, especially ties with married friends, more than widowhood does, in part because the role of kin and friends is ambiguous, and the normative expectations for self and others are less clear and uniform (Brubaker, 1990; Martin Matthews, 1991). Nonetheless, the likelihood of receiving help from friends is greater among the divorced than the married (Barrett & Lynch, 1999). Although the social networks of divorced older women remain sizable, they are also homogeneous and are characterized by a tendency to rely on one close friend to satisfy most needs for emotional support (Gibson & Mugford, 1986).

Although women are improving their economic independence, some argue that "in old age, as family relationships based on marriage and parenthood grow in importance, it is males who are at risk" (Goldscheider, 1990:531). Currently, divorced men receive considerably less support from their grown-up children than do divorced women (Barrett & Lynch, 1999), and old, divorced men have less involved and more strained relationships with their adult children and grand-children than do married and widowed men (Davidson et al., 2003). This relative social isolation of divorced men reflects a customary lack of involvement with their young children following a divorce earlier in life and could be lowered if men became more directly involved with their children (see Chapter 11). Ongoing disparities in paid work and family involvement will make it some time before men and women share enough common experience in the labor force and at home to have dramatic effects on support networks and economic security among older divorced persons (Lampard & Peggs, 2007; McDonald, 1997).

"Divorce . . . ends a marriage, not a relationship" (Doka, 2002c:156), distin-guishing it from widowhood. The far reach of a former spouse is indicated by the grief that some feel years later upon the death of their ex-spouse (Doka, 2002c). Such grief is more likely among those who do not resolve the initial loss of the rela-tionship through divorce. Among older persons today, especially women, their future depended so much on marriage that when marriage did not work out, the pressures of independence and single motherhood could be the basis for a lifetime of strain and regret (Connidis, 2003a). The greater acceptance and frequency of divorce may improve the ability of older persons to successfully negotiate divorce in the future.

In sum, the stress of divorce manifests itself in different ways for men and women. The greater initial personal trauma experienced by women motivates them to make greater changes in their lives, which, in the longer run, appear to leave them better adapted and more content in later life. However, one dilemma of comparing long-term divorced men and women rests on the fact that remarriage rates are higher among men. Thus there is a greater selection effect among men than women, potentially distorting the results of comparisons between men and women beyond the initial stages of separation.

Dissolution of Same-Sex Relationships

There are fewer barriers to dissolving relationships among same-sex couples in the absence of legal and religious foundations for marriage or impediments to breaking up, along with the less supportive stance of families toward same-sex than toward opposite-sex unions (Kurdek, 1998). Despite this, the likelihood of breaking up over an 18-month period among longer-term couples (10 years or more) is very similar for straight, gay, and lesbian couples (Peplau et al., 1996). Unfortunately, the long-term effects of dissolving same-sex partnerships have received scant attention. One might expect, however, some parallels to the impact of divorce.

The benefits of marriage extend to divorce; those who are unable to marry legally do not enjoy the attendant protections of divorce (Allen, 2007a, 2007b). This is a serious concern for long-term gay and lesbian partners who, for example, find themselves denied access to nonbiological children by the biological parent and without recourse to the courts to resolve the situation. The isolation created by not having the loss of the partner relationship acknowledged—another case of disen-franchised grief (Martin, 2002)—is multiplied by also not having one's parental relationship with a child recognized (see Chapter 11).

The absence of legal marriage for same-sex couples has paradoxical consequences: At the same time that partners are not bound together in a bad relationship, they are also not encouraged to work out difficulties by the barrier to easy separation created by marriage (Peplau & Fingerhut, 2007). Cultural heterosexism and fewer successful role models also create special challenges to the survival of same-sex relationships (Hunter, 2005). Generally, however, both the reasons for separation (desire for independence, differences in interests and in attitudes about sex, partner problems, including affairs) and its consequences (feelings of loneliness, anger, guilt, and confusion coupled with relief, happiness, and independence) are similar for same-sex and opposite-sex partners (Peplau et al., 1996).

The following words of a 62-year-old woman about her lesbian partner could as readily have been spoken by a woman about her husband:

> When D said she wanted out of the relationship, to be with a younger woman, I was really devastated. I knew that things hadn't been going all that well for a while, but I really thought that after 22 years we would stay together forever. . . . I can't imagine who would want me now or where the hell I would ever meet anyone. (Auger, 1995:110–111)

There are two key differences between the dissolution of same-sex versus straight relationships, however. First, same-sex couples experience the complexity of being gay or lesbian in a heterosexist society as a reason for breaking up (Peplau et al., 1996), a factor that is irrelevant to heterosexual couples. Second, gay and lesbian couples may be more likely than straight couples to renegotiate their relationships with ex-partners as friendships, possibly in part because they share and invest in a smaller and more closely knit community of chosen families (Diamond, 2006). An older gay respondent observed, "My sister has gone through three husbands and I have gone through three lovers. The difference is that I have remained good friends with all of my ex-lovers" (Berger, 1996:155).

There is much to be learned about the dissolution of same-sex marriages. The introduction of civil unions in some states and marriage in two of them (see Chapter 14) raises the question of their impact on relationships and their dissolution. In Vermont in 2003, 85% of those who obtained civil unions there came from elsewhere (Diamond, 2006), and some have since discovered that they must return in order to dissolve the union.

Options for Intimate Relationships and Intimacy in Middle and Later Life

Staying single or losing a partner does not necessarily mean not having an intimate partner, either presently or in the past. As we saw in Chapter 5, middle-aged and old single persons have a range of reasons for not marrying, including having other types of partners. Cohabiting, living apart together (LAT), or having a series of intimate relationships without committing to one partner challenge the concept of *ever single* as meaning any more than not getting married. Taking us full circle in the issue of how to define and label singles (see Chapter 5), middle-aged and old persons who are involved in romantic relationships tend to view themselves as unmarried rather than as single (Koropeckyj-Cox, 2005).

Because old men are more likely to be married and to benefit from being married, it is old women who are more likely to be the catalysts for creative alternatives to marriage (Connidis, 2006). Less confined by the demands of being good wives and mothers, old women may be especially open to new ways of doing things.

Remarriage

Since the 1970s, remarriage following divorce and widowhood has declined (Cherlin, 1992; Goldscheider, 1990; Lee Willetts et al., 1998; Uhlenberg et al., 1990), and cohabiting following divorce has increased (Ambert, 2005; Cherlin, 1992). Among couples with one previously married partner, remarried couples are more likely than cohabiting couples to be White and to have higher incomes (Wineberg & McCarthy, 1998). Following widowhood, men are about five times more likely than women to remarry (Lee Willetts et al., 1998), partly because more unattached women than men result from women living longer and marrying older men. Generally, remarriage is more common following divorce than widowhood, largely because divorce usually occurs at a younger age than widowhood. About three-quarters of men and women in the United States remarry following divorce (Cherlin, 1992), with lower rates of remarriage among Hispanic and especially Black Americans (Bramlett & Mosher, 2001; Cherlin, 1992).

At the younger ages when divorce usually occurs, socioeconomic status affects the chances of remarriage for divorced women but not divorced men. High socioeconomic status discourages remarriage among women aged 25 at the time of divorce but makes remarrying more likely among those divorced at age 45 (Sweeney, 1997). Similarly, women with a university education are more likely than high school graduates to remarry (Sweeney, 2002). These findings suggest that women who remain divorced as they enter old age are particularly prone to face financial difficulty and that, although women's greater economic independence may threaten marital stability, it does not lead to a negative attitude toward marriage itself.

If remarriage does occur in old age, it is more likely after widowhood than after divorce, but both widows and widowers express reluctance to remarry (Kestin van den Hoonaard, 2001; Moore and Stratton, 2002). Men are more inclined to remarry in old age, but increasing age makes remarriage less desirable and likely for men and women, and most old people do not remarry and prefer not to remarry (Carr 2004b; Davidson, 2004; Mahay & Lewin, 2007; Stevens, 2004; Uhlenberg et al., 1990; Wu, 1995). The lower inclination to remarry in old age is explained by objective limitations (scarcity of older men, poorer health, reduced mobility, poorer finances), the absence of incentives common to younger ages (being pregnant, wanting children, proving adulthood, conformity to life cycle timing), a short future (making it harder to justify the necessary changes brought about by marriage), and the social pressure to protect one's estate (Talbott, 1998; Treas & Van Hilst, 1976). Losing a former spouse's pension and the perceived threat to children's inheritance are unique financial impediments to remarriage later in life (Moore & Stratton, 2004).

Among men and women in advanced old age who have formed new relationships, women do not want to marry, whereas widowed men typically do (Wilson, 1995). Past experience with marriage influences attitudes about remarrying. Among widows aged 61 to 85, those whose previous marriages were particularly good or bad were least interested in remarrying, whereas those whose marriages were generally positive but flawed were most open to considering remarriage (Talbott, 1998). Many older widows, most of whom had very traditional marriages, are reluctant to give up their independence, to return to taking care of a man, and to risk losing another partner (Davidson, 2001, 2004; Heinemann & Evans, 1990). For example, a 66-year-old widow in one of my studies says she would not remarry because

I am enjoying my freedom too much now. I brought up my children, and I looked after my husband to the best of my ability. I cared for my parents until they died, and it was a joy and I liked it, but I am enjoying the freedom now of not having to account to anybody for what I do.

An 81-year-old widow is even more direct:

I wouldn't get married again for all the tea in China. . . . Oh no . . . I am set in my ways, and I wouldn't want a young fellow running around all the time, and I wouldn't want an old man with one foot in the grave either. Then stop and think that you would have to wash for them, you would have to iron, you would have to have meals to suit them. Now, if I feel like eating, I eat, and if I feel like going out, I go out.

A qualitative study of widowers indicates that old men are aware of being a liability when they have health problems or disabilities; said a 100-year-old man, "What would I have to offer a woman—two years of taking care of me, and then I would die?" (Moore & Stratton, 2002:137). There are also women who miss the companionship of a man and assume that any woman who claims that she is not interested in remarrying must be lying (Talbott, 1998). This is, however, still the minority view among today's older women.

Among those who do remarry, marriage occurs far more quickly after widowhood in later life than at earlier ages (Lopata, 1996). When remarried couples aged 30 to 45 years are compared with remarried couples aged 60 to 75 years, women in both age groups are equally satisfied with life, but the older men are more satisfied with life than are the younger men (Bograd & Spilka 1996). This difference may be due to the fact that remarriage more often follows divorce for the younger group and widowhood for the older one, situations that we have seen create quite different life course outcomes for men's social networks and ties to children.

Remarriage in later life is negotiated in the context of a lifetime of accumulated experience that is quite different from the circumstances of a first marriage. In a qualitative study of women aged 55 to 90 years (Hurd Clarke, 2005), those who remarried happily later in life often negotiated power, resources and household responsibilities with their husbands more effectively, resulting in more balanced marriages than the first time around. A number of women who had poor first marriages describe their current marriage as the one that they wish they had had all along; those who had been happily married before find that their present marriage meets their changing needs in old age. Describing her first and second marriages, a 90-year-old woman reflects,

> Second marriages are different . . . For one thing, you're mature. You're much older and sex is never a driving force in a second marriage . . . We did things together . . . It was a very pleasant interlude in my life and it was for him, too. (Hurd Clarke, 2005:35)

Other differences are noted by remarried widowers in the Netherlands who observe that partners in a second marriage have "a whole life behind them" at the same time that they "know it can never last long. If I live to be 80, then we have 10 years together. If I make it to 85, we'll have 15 years. . . . It's a totally different relationship" (Stevens, 2004:55).

Although discussions of family networks in older age often focus on losses, remarriage is a potential basis for enhancing one's kin network. Over time, remarriage can form the foundation for close family ties (see Chapter 11), as in the case of a 71-year-old man in my community study:

> I hear a lot of people around my age being lonely. Well, I don't know what it is to be lonely really. I have two sons and their families and my daughter. I have eight grandchildren . . . We also have five great-grandchildren. I was married twice. I was married very young and then that marriage broke up, and my present wife and I have been married 31 years. Mary is the present wife's daughter and the other two are my first wife's sons. We see the boys frequently, and I am very happy that they are fond of my present wife, so we get along very well . . . We are a very close family.

Repartnering Among Unattached Gays and Lesbians

One outcome of exclusion from mainstream life among gays and lesbians, especially for younger cohorts, is investment in building strong, familylike communities (Walter, 2003). Such communities create supportive networks for negotiating new relationships following the loss of a partner and foster a different response from that in straight relationships. Among lesbian widows in a small qualitative study, for example, talking about their deceased partners with new lovers and receiving support rather than jealous insecurity in return is common (Whipple, 2006). This is attributed to the general inclusion of ex-lovers, whether through death or relationship dissolution, in lesbian and gay communities. The inclusion of ex-lovers and reference to past relationships potentially enhances continuity in community involvement and ongoing friendships among those who find new partners.

Some argue that middle-aged and older lesbians have unique advantages for finding sexual partners, should they want to, because they do not experience the decline in their pool of possible partners that straight women do, and they do not experience the same threat of younger competitors that straight women and gay men do (Garnets & Peplau, 2006).

Staying sexually active is considered an important part of healthy sexual identities and satisfying relationships among gay men (Wierzalis et al., 2006). But like their straight peers, those who lose long-term partners may not be interested in finding new ones. A man of 72 comments on losing his partner:

> It was very hard. My gay retirement group and my friends helped me get through it. I'm not over him. I wouldn't want to be over him. I don't look at other people, I'm not remotely interested in another relationship. Nobody could come up to his standards. (Bergling, 2004:182)

Given that legal marriage is generally not an option for other than heterosexual unions in the United States, the concept of remarriage does not apply. In many respects, this makes gays and lesbians leaders in negotiating arrangements that are experienced as relatively novel among straight couples and individuals.

In sum, a relatively small percentage of today's older individuals either marry in later life or enter old age remarried, but these numbers are growing in the wake of elevated divorce. A lifetime of experience influences decisions about remarriage, including accumulated ties to other family members, particularly children; the quality of previous marriages; gendered experiences of caring for a spouse; and financial circumstances. There is still much that is unknown about remarriage in later life and its impact on other family relationships. The increase in divorce has changed the dynamic of remarriage because now more remarriages follow divorce rather than widowhood. (In Chapter 11, the impact of divorce and remarriage of either older parents or their adult children on relationships between parents and their children and between grandparents and grandchildren is explored.) We now turn to consider alternatives other than remarriage for intimate relationships in later life.

Cohabitation

Much of the research on cohabitation focuses on its incidence, its stability when compared with marriage, and younger populations. By the turn of this century, one million persons, comprising 4% of the U.S. population over the age of 50, were cohabiting (Brown et al., 2006). Mixed findings regarding cohabitation and its success are in part due to the variety of motivations for and types of cohabiting unions. The relatively monolithic cultural view of marriage does not guarantee that everyone will experience it in the same way, but it does enhance sharing a common view of an ideal marriage. Despite changes in practice, the symbolic importance of marriage remains high (Cherlin, 2004). In the case of cohabitation, there are multiple ideal types that provide an important context for gauging research on cohabitation and its merits for different age groups and in comparison with other union statuses, particularly marriage.

Six ideal types of cohabitation are these: (1) marginal, in which a cultural proscription against cohabitation prevails; (2) cohabitation as a prelude to marriage, in which cohabitation is a testing ground; (3) cohabitation as a stage in the marriage

process, in which living together is a normalized step toward marriage; (4) cohabitation as an alternative to being single, in which living together is preferred to living
apart among young people who want to postpone forming a family; (5) cohabitation
as an alternative to marriage, in which case cohabiting is preferred over marriage but
the intent to form a family is parallel; and (6) cohabitation as indistinguishable from
marriage in which case couples are indifferent to marriage because cohabitation is a
culturally acceptable alternative with parallel privileges (Heuveline & Timberlake,
2004). As cohabiting becomes a more normative arrangement that approximates
marriage, it appears to become more stable. For example, in areas of Canada where
cohabiting is more normative, such as Quebec, stability of cohabiting relationships
has increased over time (Ambert, 2005; Le Bourdais et al., 2004).

These ideal types of cohabitation are useful for placing the cohabiting patterns
of a particular country in context and for establishing an appropriate basis for comparison with marriage. In the United States, cohabiting as an alternative to being
single prevails but with some evidence of an increase in cohabitation as a prelude
to or stage of marriage (Heuveline & Timberlake, 2004). For these types, expecting
cohabitation to mimic marriage is questionable. Only when cohabitation is entered
into with expectations similar to those of marriage does comparing their respective
outcomes as stable unions make sense.

A striking feature about these ideal types of cohabitation is their focus on
younger couples and family formation. Yet they can also be useful for better understanding old people and their entry into cohabiting relationships. In the absence of
family formation as an objective, cohabiting among older couples can be seen as
both an alternative to being single (but without the intent to form a family later)
and as an alternative to a second or subsequent marriage. Among old couples,
cohabiting is rarely a prelude to marriage or a stage in the marriage process, as it is
entered into for its own sake rather than as a trial period for getting married
(Chevan, 1996). Instead, cohabitation is more likely to follow than lead to marriage.
Comparisons of younger with older (over the age of 50) persons in cohabiting
unions confirm that older persons are more likely to see their unions as an alternative to marriage and younger persons as its precursor (King & Scott, 2005).

In the United States, 90% of cohabiting adults over the age of 50 were previously
married (Brown et al., 2006). Most of these persons have children and may be concerned about the implications of remarriage for their children's inheritance. In this
context, cohabiting rather than remarrying is a method of protecting, not threatening, the well-being of their children. The disconnection between couple and
family formation among old couples also creates some freedom from social censure
regarding cohabiting later in life. Already marginalized due to age relations, the
marginality of cohabiting is less of a social concern regarding older than younger
couples because dependent children are not involved. This age-based context for
understanding cohabitation is echoed by a race-based context in which cohabitation is more often a prelude to marriage among Whites and more often a substitute
for Blacks and Hispanics (Phillips & Sweeney, 2005).

Older men are more likely than women to cohabit, as are the very poor, the young-
old, those who have divorced or separated (a number that we know is also growing),
and residents of the Sunbelt states, where a seniors subculture free of outside (family)

influence is more likely to have emerged than anywhere else in the United States (Chevan,1996). Comparisons of remarried, cohabiting, and unattached middle-aged and older (over the age of 50 years) persons indicate a greater impact of union status on the lives of women than men (Brown et al., 2006). Women who cohabit have lower incomes than remarried women, are no more likely than unpartnered women to own their homes, and are more likely than both groups to be employed full time. In combination, these findings indicate the greater economic disadvantage of cohabiting women, but being employed full time may also indicate the greater egalitarianism of cohabiting relationships.

Indeed, the gender inequality of marriage makes cohabitation an attractive option for many women (Cunningham & Antill, 1995). Differences in gender relations in the two union types are evident in findings about what leads them to succeed. When married couples engage in a more traditional, specialized division of labor, risk of divorce is diminished (Brines & Joyner, 1999). For cohabiting couples, however, equal employment and earnings between partners lowers the risk of relationship dissolution; inequality, particularly in favor of the woman, increases the risk of breaking up. The perceived value of being in a union is often greater among older than younger men, creating a more equal footing between men and women who choose to cohabit later in life (Ambert, 2005). Comparisons of older with younger adults confirm the significance of age to understanding cohabiting relationships. Older cohabiting couples report higher levels of fairness and relationship quality and fewer disagreements, heated arguments, and concerns about their relationships' future than do younger ones (King & Scott, 2005). With respect to marital status, cohabiting and married middle-aged and old women share similar levels of well-being (Brown et al., 2005).

In sum, gender, age, class and race relations combine to create different contexts of cohabitation across the life course. In old age, with a history of intimate relationships and family formation behind them, cohabitation offers a more egalitarian relationship than marriage and better protects the interests of adult children. Cohabitation also provides a financial cushion for those with less economic security, particularly women, through the sharing of expenses and appears to have a positive impact on well-being. In the context of more egalitarian gender relations, cohabitation may be more accurately viewed as an adaptive alternative to marriage than as an indicator of a declining commitment to intimate relationships (Connidis, 2006).

Living Apart Together

LAT is an alternative intimate relationship in which both members of the couple continue to live in their one-person households and intermittently share their households with one another (de Jong Gierveld, 2004a). This option is increasingly popular in Europe and Scandinavia (Borell & Ghazanfareeon Karlsson, 2003; Ghazanfareeon Karlsson & Borell, 2004; de Jong Gierveld 2004b; Moore & Stratton 2004; Stevens 2004). A consensual union, living apart together has features that resemble marriage and cohabitation. Couples who live apart together have a long-term commitment to one another, publicly acknowledge their love for each other, are publicly known as a couple, and are sexually active (Stevens, 2004). Like the pure relationship described by Giddens, living apart together focuses primarily on the emotional bond between the couple and "depends fundamentally on the mutual satisfaction generic to the relationship, rather than on structural bonds" (Borell & Ghazanfareeon Karlsson, 2003:59). In the absence of clear rules, couples who live apart together negotiate the boundaries and understandings of their relationship, balancing intimacy with autonomy and companionship with independence (Davidson & Fennell, 2004).

As with cohabitation, LAT relationships reflect the impact of intersecting age, gender and class relations, as well as the life course perspective's emphasis on life stage. In comparisons of different age and marital status groups, living apart together is especially appealing to old persons and those with previous long-term relationships (de Jong Gierveld, 2004a, 2004b). In a study in the Netherlands, when compared with previously married persons who were younger than 55 when their last relationship ended (due to death or divorce), those who were 55 years or older were three times more likely to be in a LAT relationship (de Jong Gierveld, 2004a). In addition to appealing to older persons who have marriages and children behind them (life stage), LAT is a class-based option available to those who can maintain two households.

Gender relations are also behind the unique appeal of LAT relationships among older women. Living apart together allows women to escape the gendered expectations of marital relations in which they have more responsibility for cooking, housework and caring (Borell & Ghazanfareeon Karlsson, 2003). A separate household ensures desired boundaries around the relationship and enhances the often new-found independence. A 63-year-old Dutch woman in a LAT relationship observes, "I'm very happy with him but I don't want him here all the time. Then I'd lose the freedom I have now." (Stevens 2004:53). Living apart together is an established couple form among same-sex partners and leads to underestimating the extent of committed same-sex relationships (de Vries, 2007).

Both men and women note the potential risks to health of advanced old age and the challenge that it would present to a partner who is also old. Said one man in a LAT relationship, "At our age it's impossible to care for a sick partner" (de Jong Gierveld, 2004b:101). Living apart together is an effective way of negotiating an intimate tie that also limits the untenable demands that declining health may impose on a partner. Age relations and life stage also apply to those who are parents. Even more than cohabitation, which can come to be defined as a legally binding relationship that makes a long-term partner a beneficiary, living apart together is seen to protect children's inheritance (de Jong Gierveld, 2004b).

As is true of those who cohabit, LAT relationships also come to an end through death or dissolution. At the age of 89, Ida lost a partner with whom she had lived apart together for 12 years. She says,

> You feel like you've lost a part of yourself. You feel like you've lost quite a bit. And the older you are, the more you feel you've lost because you're not as active. He called me every morning and every night, to see if I was all right and to let me know he was all right. . . . You do think about your good times . . . but you think about how they're gone and not coming back. Gone for good. And then you think, when you're ninety years old, what companionship are you going to have now? (Walter, 2003:105–106)

Ida's comments raise the question of how one finds intimacy in old age in the absence of an intimate relationship and the particular challenges of doing so as a woman in advanced old age.

Dating and Steady Companions

For lack of a better word, we will use the term *dating* to refer to going out with or seeing someone. Growing numbers of old persons and internet matchmaking services have drawn more media attention to romance in later life, but there is not much research on this topic. Gender and age relations combine to shape the dating experience (Connidis, 2006). For both men and women, the likelihood of dating declines with age (Bulcroft & Bulcroft, 1991). Among women and men who do date once a month or more, almost half describe themselves as being involved in steady dating. The timeless experience of meeting and falling in love are evident in the comments of a 75-year-old man:

> We met five years ago at a single's dance. I saw her across the room. I thought she was the most perfect creature, extremely lovely to look at. I could tell that she found me attractive as well. When our eyes met, we both knew it was destiny. (Neugebauer-Visano, 1995:22)

The ongoing significance of sexual attraction also shines through in a 72-year-old woman's observations: "My love and I are very attracted to each other. Oh definitely, he is very handsome and distinguished looking. He does it to me" (Neugebauer-Visano, 1995:22).

Despite these similarities among age groups, like cohabitation and living apart together, dating is not part of a mate selection process for older persons (Chevan, 1996). For daters aged 40 to 69 years, the main incentive by far for dating is to have someone to talk to and do things with, and those in their 60s are both happier and more hesitant about getting married than the younger daters (Fisher & Montenegro, 2003). These differences suggest the *greater* significance of dating in old age as a source of intimacy in its own right.

Men are far more likely to report dating later in life (Carr, 2004c), in part due to the greater availability of suitable partners for men, given women's longer lives and men's involvement with younger women. Among unattached Americans aged 40 to 69 years, one-third has an exclusive dating relationship, two-fifths have not had a date in a year (Fisher & Montenegro, 2003), and over one-third of those in their 50s have "not been kissed or hugged in the last six months" (Mahoney 2003:2).

Trepidation about dating and intimacy among those who have been out of the dating scene is shared by younger and older persons, men and women. Some older widowers comment on the usual challenges of dating someone, such as avoiding hurt feelings and not wanting to get too involved too fast (Moore & Stratton, 2002). Women and men in their 50s share a dislike for dates who have a lot of baggage or who want to get too serious too quickly (Fisher & Montenegro 2003). Some older widowers describe entering the dating game as "akin to an hour on the rack" and "my worst nightmare" (Moore & Stratton, 2002:145). Possible intimacy is also intimidating. Baby boomers "find getting naked in front of someone new a difficult transition" (Mahoney, 2003:2). Neither men nor women escape the negative views of aging bodies in an ageist society that holds up youthful ideals of masculinity and femininity as the standards against which people of all ages are measured (Calasanti & Slevin, 2001).

Some older persons prefer platonic relationships with people of the opposite sex, described in research in the Netherlands as *steady companions* (Stevens, 2004). Such relationships involve shared affection and mutual helping but do not extend to being defined as couples. These arrangements are more likely to be favored by women; older men in such relationships may prefer more involvement, as was the case for this 72-year-old man: "I'm alone every night. That's not easy. I'm quite healthy and capable of living intimately with a woman. But, I don't get a chance" (Stevens, 2004:58). Nonetheless, having a steady companion is as good as having a consummate partnership for staving off loneliness.

Sexual Intimacy Among the Unattached in Later Life

A challenge in discussing opportunities for sexual activity among unattached older persons is striking a balance between avoiding ageist assumptions that characterize old people as asexual and avoiding being part of the claim that old age is great as long as it is just like being young (Connidis, 2006). The pressure to perform that is captured in the proliferation of male sex-enhancing drugs and to look forever young that is captured in the relentless hawking of cosmetics and cosmetic surgery, especially to women, now carries into old age (Calasanti & Slevin, 2001; Gott & Hinchliff, 2003). Optimistically, this may signal greater equalization in age relations. Cynically, it may simply mean going after an aging market. In either case, a focus on never-ending performance and youth reproduces particular views of masculinity and femininity that are embedded in current gender relations and extends them into old age. At the same time, viewing old unattached individuals as sexless beings was described years ago as "unfair and oppressive" (Felstein, 1970:123).

As I mentioned in Chapters 3 and 4, today's old people did not necessarily associate sex only with marriage when they were young. Research from earlier times shows that among those who are now in their 70s, 80s and 90s, almost a quarter of women had had sex with someone who they did not eventually marry, and over half of unattached White men in their 20s had had sex with "a nice girl" (Hohman & Schaffner, 1947:503). However, old women face limited opportunity for sexual activity due to a shortage of men available to them, old or young. One study reports that among those aged 70 or more, older married men are two and a half times more likely than unmarried men (31%) to be sexually active, but married women are 11 times more likely than unmarried women (5%) to engage in sexual activity (Matthias et al., 1997). Among those who do not have regular sexual partners, less than 1% of women and 6% of men aged 60 and over have intercourse once a week or more (AARP, 1999c). In a sample aged 70 and over, 31% of men and 3% of women had had sexual relations in the past month (Matthias et al., 1997). These studies focus on specific forms of sexual activity and do not address how activity compares with desire for sexual encounters.

A growing clientele of middle-aged and old people for online matchmaking and dating services suggests a more open interest in sexual activity in later life. A very public example of a woman in pursuit of a sexual partner is Jane Juska (2003). Referring to herself as a round-heeled woman, an old-fashioned term for a prostitute, Juska (2003:20) details her search for sexual partners, initiated by a want ad which stated, "Before I turn 67—next March—I would like to have sex with a man I like." After sorting through responses to her ad, a number of trysts followed. As exhilarating and satisfying as these liaisons proved to be, Juska (2003:272) asks, "Once you've had a lot of sex with a man you like, how do you stop wanting him?" Her query addresses the connections among sex, love, and commitment and, for women, the particular challenge of separating them.

Although gender relations put more pressure on women than men of all ages to associate sex with commitment, aging and the experience of a long-term relationship may make both men and women reluctant to engage in sex outside a committed relationship. Some older widows and widowers continue to associate sex with marriage (Kestin van den Hoonaard, 2001; Moore & Stratton 2004). This is one reason that the merits of nonsexual companionship should not be underrated. Some widows enjoy the physical contact of dancing while out with a man (Kestin van den Hoonaard, 2001), and some widowers enjoy the companionship of steady dating without sex because they do not feel sexually attracted to other women, they are impotent, or they feel too old for a more involved relationship (Moore & Stratton, 2002). With changing sexual mores a part of their cultural and social landscape, older persons may discover new ways of finding and enjoying sexual fulfillment, as in the case of a 77-year-old widow who discovered the pleasures of a sex aid (Gott & Hinchliff, 2003). Her discovery reminds us to move beyond counts of sexual intercourse as a measure of sex in later life and to consider the broad range of sexually satisfying activities available at all ages. We should also appreciate that very fulfilling lives can be led without being sexually active.

Summary and Conclusion to Part II

Intimate relationships are important across the life course. The need and desire for intimacy, including sexual relations, continue into old age, but venues and methods for its expression may change. A more inclusive view of intimate relationships encourages us to consider the intimate ties of older people outside as well as within marriage. In an ideal world, a more inclusive view of intimate relationships would be supported in law and social custom, enhancing the prospects for intimacy by increasing the range of venues available for its realization (Geller, 2001).

Long-term couples, whether married or cohabiting, whether gay or straight, tend to derive considerable satisfaction from their relationships. Interdependence between partners is heightened in later years as a consequence of being together more of the time, sharing household tasks (primarily along traditional lines in the case of married couples), and the declining health of one or both partners. Such symbiosis permits older couples to live independently.

Providing care to an ill spouse for a long time can lead to isolation of both partners. This may leave a newly widowed person poorly prepared for dealing with life alone. Nonetheless, most old persons make the transition to widowhood successfully. Although widowhood is more common among women, it has repercussions for both men and women. Men are less likely to experience some of the objective losses, such as income, that are a consequence of widowhood for many women. However, subjective losses seem to be greater for men, in large part because of their more exclusive reliance on spouses for intimacy and sharing confidences. Women tend to turn to other family ties following widowhood, whereas men are more inclined to turn to another mate.

Although a relatively small proportion of older individuals have ever divorced, the numbers are increasing, and growing numbers are either reaching old age having divorced earlier in their lives or are divorcing later in life. Both men and women, but women much more so, experience financial costs to divorcing. Women in particular tend to discover advantages to being alone, including increased self-worth and newly gained independence. As in the case of widowhood, following divorce, women more typically seek and receive support from family and friends, whereas men more often find support through remarriage. Divorced older men appear to be more isolated than other men and than women of all marital status groups.

Relatively small numbers of old people remarry, but remarriage among today's older persons is generally successful. Remarriage rates among all age groups have declined over the past two decades, largely because cohabitation is more common. For some older persons, cohabitation and living apart together provide good options for those who both want a partner and value independence. The more egalitarian arrangements of both alternatives are particularly appealing to women. Cohabitation and living apart together are both seen as methods of protecting children's inheritance. The ongoing advantage in life expectancy for women reduces the availability of opposite-sex relationships of all kinds for women. Women are also less interested than men in finding a committed relationship.

Recent research indicates the continuing significance of sexual intimacy in old age. We need to learn more about the intimate ties of those who are unattached, especially given that sexual relations are no longer seen as the exclusive domain of marriage.

Contrary to common conceptions, older single persons, particularly women, are not isolated. Although their social networks are smaller, this is due to having fewer kin. Single women tend to cultivate lifelong friendships that complement their smaller family networks. They also develop closer attachments to some of their own kin, especially siblings and their families (see Chapter 9 on childlessness and Chapters 12 and 13 on siblings). Nonetheless, the single rely more on formal support services than the married and the widowed with children. As is true of the widowed and divorced, single women are more satisfied than single men. The consistency of these differences indicates the propensity of men to depend on spouses, whereas women develop broader familial networks. These proclivities by gender are also evident in intergenerational ties, the subject of the next five chapters.

PART III

Intergenerational Relations

CHAPTER 7

Exploring Intergenerational Relations

The most central intergenerational ties for most old persons are those with their adult children and with their grandchildren, as reflected in Photo 7.1. To reflect the reality of parent-child ties during most if not all of a parent's old age, we first look at general features of this relationship before exploring the extensive support that older parents and their adult children exchange (Chapter 8). I take a comparative approach to exploring the significance of children in older age by considering the situation of childless older persons (Chapter 9). The ties between grandparents and grandchildren and the mediating role of the middle generation are then discussed (Chapter 10). Two issues of growing significance to these relationships—changing gender relations and higher divorce rates—are considered throughout this section (see Chapter 11 for divorce). Related policy concerns are addressed in the book's final chapter.

Increased longevity means that most of us will spend more of our lifetimes in many family relationships, including intergenerational ties between parents and children and between grandparents and grandchildren. As we saw in Chapter 2, declining birth rates have led to the verticalization of family structure: the number of family members in each generation except the oldest (due to longevity) has decreased, whereas the number of generations has increased. For a time, families of four and more generations were expected to become common, but this possibility has been offset by older ages at first marriage and at birth of the first child among younger cohorts. Parent-child and grandparent-grandchild ties must be negotiated and renegotiated to meet transitions and changing circumstances across the life course, especially now that more individuals have a longer stretch of overlapping lives with their parents, children and grandchildren. At the same time, there will be aspects of continuity in relationships over time.

Photo 7.1   Intergenerational ties between parents and children and between grandparents and grandchildren last longer due to greater life expectancy.

Some argue that the greater diversity and expansion of families through divorce, cohabitation and remarriage are the basis for a new family structure, which they term a *latent kin matrix* (Riley & Riley, 1996). This matrix is defined as "a latent web of continually shifting linkages that provides the potential for activating and intensifying close kin relationships as they are needed" (Riley & Riley, 1996:287). Reminiscent of the modified extended family model (see Chapter 1), the latent matrix places greater emphasis on the voluntary relationships between former in-laws and stepfamily members. The authors speculate that this new family type will make the parent-child tie less focal by providing "a wide choice of kinship bonds" that will "transcend" age-based conflicts (Riley & Riley, 1996:290). Implicit in this argument are two important assertions: that the adult child-parent relationship is losing its significance in the overall network of family ties and that the net effect of divorce, cohabitation and remarriage is the enhancement of kin networks. Let us consider these points in light of current evidence about the relationships between generations and about the impact of life transitions, including divorce and remarriage, on these relationships.

Perspectives on Intergenerational Relations

Exploring intergenerational relations lends itself to the life course perspective (Silverstein, 2004). Interest in how relationships between parents and children are negotiated over time necessarily considers aging as a lifelong process; the inter-dependence of linked family lives; the broader cultural, economic and political environments that shape generational experiences and relations; the significance of biography, family history and historical time; and the ongoing exercise of agency as individuals work out their relationships within the constraints of social arrangements. These life course tenets, in combination with a critical perspective, indicate the dynamism that underlies intergenerational ties, as members of differ-ent historical contexts share family time in varying ways across the life course. A case study of three generations shows the impact of changing social conditions on the negotiation of work-family balance across generations and of the experiences one has as a child on one's own attitudes toward parenting (Connidis, 2004). Across generations, parents perceive their parenting styles as offering more free-dom and openness to their children than their parents offered them. However, continuity is also evident as gender pervades intergenerational relations across time. As well, multiple voices indicate disparate views of shared situations *within* families, due in part to occupying different locations in class relations over time. This internal variety is often lost when we focus on broad trends across families.

For some time, two approaches dominated the study of intergenerational rela-tions, especially those between parents and children: one focused on solidarity and the other on problems (Lüscher & Pillemer, 1998; Marshall, Cook et al., 1993). More recently, the concept of ambivalence has been applied to intergenerational ties as a way of establishing the coexistence of solidarity and conflict in these rela-tionships and of linking the negotiation of family ties to structured social relations (Connidis & McMullin, 2002a, 2002b; Lüscher & Pillemer, 1998). These perspec-tives are briefly reviewed as a backdrop to our discussion of parent-child and grandparent-grandchild relations.

An approach to intergenerational relations that emphasizes problems and con-flicts in families is evident in much of the caregiving literature and in terms such as *caregiver burden.* This approach focuses on the problems created for children, and sometimes, parents, when children care for their older parents (Marshall, Matthews et al., 1993). Although some have termed this a conflict perspective (Lüscher & Pillemer, 1998), in fact, most of this work does not deal directly with conflict beyond the level of interpersonal relations. In Chapter 8, conceptual approaches that focus more specifically on caregiving are presented.

The intergenerational-solidarity perspective focuses on the extent of solidarity or strength of intergenerational bonds between parents and children (Bengtson & Schrader, 1982). Solidarity has six analytic dimensions: (a) associational—type and frequency of interaction and activities, (b) structural—factors such as geographic distance that influence the extent of interaction, (c) functional—exchange of assis-tance and support, especially instrumental help, (d) affectional—sentiments and feelings, (e) consensual—agreement between generations on opinions and values, and (f) normative—the extent to which family members share expectations of family life (Silverstein & Bengtson, 1997). These are important factors for intergen-erational relationships, but the value added by referring to these dimensions of family life as solidarity is unclear.

The solidarity concepts and studies that use them indicate the multidimensional nature of intergenerational relations. An ongoing concern about the solidarity perspective, however, is its tendency to minimize family diversity and to treat problematic or conflicting features of intergenerational relationships as simply the absence of solidarity (Connidis & McMullin, 2002a, 2002b; Marshall, Matthews et al., 1993). One consequence is that conclusions drawn from analyses applying this approach are somewhat proscriptive, with either implicit or explicit recommendations on how families can better reach the ideal of solidarity.

More recent applications of solidarity have tried to incorporate notions of paradox and conflict in family ties (Bengtson et al., 2002). Explorations of conflict within the solidarity concept have been primarily at the level of interpersonal relations—asking parents and children about their differences, disagreements, and disappointments with each other (Clarke et al., 1999). These attempts to incorporate conflict provide useful information about different types of families, but the normative assumptions of solidarity place limits on examining structured social relations as a root to understanding intergenerational relationships (see Connidis & McMullin, 2002b). Most likely to be ignored are the conflict and contradictions that are embedded in social structure and social institutions, such as gender relations in the colliding worlds of paid work and family life.

Applying the concept of ambivalence is a recent development in the study of intergenerational relations. Initial formulations used ambivalence to address the coexistence of solidarity and conflict, rather than emphasizing one or the other as the overriding feature of intergenerational relationships (Lüscher & Pillemer, 1998). Intergenerational ambivalence refers to contradictions in parent-child ties, and these contradictions apply at both the psychological (primarily subjective) and sociological (institutional resources and requirements) levels. Debate over the concept of ambivalence has prompted more sophisticated theorizing and research about intergenerational relations. A concern with both psychological and sociological ambivalence reflects the link of this concept to both critical and symbolic interactionist perspectives and the connection between individual agency, the negotiation of family ties, and structured social relations (Connidis & McMullin, 2000a, 2000b; Curran, 2002; Lüscher, 2004; Lüscher & Pillemer, 1998; Pillemer & Lüscher, 2004).

A primary feature of ambivalence is the movement away from dualistic thinking about intergenerational relations as good or bad, smooth functioning or conflicting (Pillemer & Lüscher, 2004) toward a focus on the complexities of relationships that stem from the inherent contradictions of social life. Psychological ambivalence refers to the contradictions that people feel, the mixture of positive and negative sentiments or emotions about their family relationships. The study of intergenerational relations must also address how social structural forces create contradictions and conflicts that are made manifest in the social interactions of family life and must be worked out in family members' encounters with one another, that is, sociological ambivalence (Connidis & McMullin, 2002b). A significant component of the ambivalence concept is its connection with change: The continual negotiation of ambivalence may either reproduce established ways of doing things when they are repeated or initiate social change if enough individuals negotiate relationships in new ways. Awareness and transparency of negotiating contradictions in family relationships is most likely during periods of transition or in nonconventional relationships (Connidis, 2003b).

The concept of sociological ambivalence seeks to make explicit the connections of family life to the macro world of structured social relations and the micro level of individual action as family members attempt to exercise agency when negotiating their relationships with one another. Age relations are central to intergenerational ties, but our interactions with adult children, aging parents, grandchildren and grandparents are also shaped by entrenched ways of relating by gender (including sexuality), class, race and ethnicity. We have seen the cross-cutting of these various structured social relations in our exploration of intimate ties and will continue to consider their influence on intergenerational relations.

In the 1960s and 1970s when intergenerational confrontation and the admonition not to trust anyone over 30 seemed to threaten the stability of society, the reassurance of research documenting intergenerational solidarity within families was a welcome contribution to our understanding of family relations. But solidarity within families does not assure solidarity outside them, and establishing degrees of solidarity or conflict within families does not explain how they came to be that way or show their connection to the pervasive dynamics of unequal social relations. Intergenerational family relations are an exception to the usual age segregation that occurs in other institutions (Allen & Walker, 2006; Hagestad & Uhlenberg, 2005). They also serve as a conduit for learning about historical generations through the shared personal memories of family members (Attias-Donfut & Wolff, 2005). Intergenerational family relationships lead people to experience past events and social change personally because they are conveyed as real-life stories (Connidis, 2004). Nonetheless, negotiating intergenerational ties involves confronting dominant age relations outside the family circle.

The concept of sociological ambivalence is a mechanism for encouraging theoretical thinking and research activity that addresses how what happens within families and between generations relates to what happens outside them. As individuals and as family members, we do not negotiate our relationships in isolation from the rest of the world. Instead, our relationships are negotiated in the context of the contradictions created by structured social relations. Sociological ambivalence, therefore, is conceptually prior to either solidarity or conflict and cannot be subsumed within the concept of solidarity (Lüscher, 2002). As long as structured social relations characterized by inequality and contradiction persist, so too will the challenge of negotiating ambivalence in relationships. The extent of this challenge varies, given our different positions in the various sets of structured social relations (Connidis & McMullin, 2002b).

The concept of ambivalence does not assume that relationships are characterized by the presence of mixed emotions and contradiction at all times. Rather, all relationships, to varying degrees, involve negotiating the ongoing undercurrent of ambivalence that results from the contradictions of structured social relations. Parallels are found in the concept of relational dialectics, in which those engaged in intergenerational relationships are "continually managing opposing interdependent forces that stand in dialectical association with each other" (Fisher & Miller-Day, 2006:9). At a specific point in time, our relationships may be running smoothly, riddled with conflict, estranged, or dominated by the contradictions of mixed emotions and incompatible demands. Identifying the conditions that create solidarity, conflict or ambivalence as the dominating feature of family relationships at a particular point in time and for particular groups is pivotal to understanding the dynamics and processes of family life.

Because ambivalence can apply to individuals, to relationships, to social institutions and to societies, researchers must ensure that their measures are appropriate to the level of analysis being explored (Lettke & Klein, 2004). Neither relational nor sociological ambivalence can be captured in a measure of mixed feelings, and qualitative studies are often best for exploring ambivalence in relationships (Katz et al., 2005). The conceptual construct of sociological ambivalence encourages us to consider the reciprocal links between what happens within families and the social world outside them, sensitizing our interpretations of findings about family relationships (Willson et al., 2003). Thus, ambivalence is a conceptual complement to the critical, feminist and life course perspectives (see Chapter 1) that inform the study of family ties and aging.

Intergenerational Ties of Older Gay and Lesbian Persons

Before we turn to parent-child relations, a word about the intergenerational ties of older gay and lesbian individuals. First, referring to gay families is no more appropriate than referring to straight families, given that identity as gay or straight is an individual, not a familial characteristic (see Stacey, 1998). Rather, one might speak more accurately of the families of gay or straight individuals. With regard to intergenerational relations involving gay or lesbian persons, the most common topic is the coming-out process. As mentioned in Chapter 4, many of today's old gay and lesbian adults did not come out until they were themselves in mid and late life, and some are still not out. Among younger generations, coming out is more often a process of late adolescence or early adulthood and thus involves the response of relatively young parents. Young adult children who confront coming out must deal with the ongoing social stigma of their sexual orientations as part of the context in which they negotiate their identity with their parents. The desire to share their identity with their parents while knowing of the potentially negative attitudes that their parents may hold about it makes coming out an ambivalent situation.

Coming out as gay or lesbian usually results in disappointment on behalf of parents, for some because it is assumed to deny their future as grandparents (Cohler, 2004). Same-sex couples and nonbiological parents (and their families) negotiate a socially created ambivalent situation when attempts to act like family are not backed by the legal status of spouse or parent (Connidis, 2003b; Skinner & Kohler, 2002; re consequences following loss of a partner, see Chapter 6). Producing a grandchild, however, especially as the biological parent, can assist the negotiation of ambivalence between a gay or lesbian adult and his or her parents (Hequembourg & Farrell, 2001).

To date, there is little exploration of intergenerational ties involving older gay or lesbian parents, partly because of a reluctance to acknowledge the families of gay and lesbian individuals and partly because the impediments to family formation result in relatively few openly gay and lesbian persons having children. The estimates of 1 to 5 million lesbian mothers and 1 to 3 million gay fathers in the United States and of 6 to 14 million children having gay or lesbian parents (Patterson, 1996) indicate the uncertainty of statistics about gays and lesbians (Allen, 2005a).

The need for generativity has been proposed as one explanation for the frequent age disparity between men involved in gay relationships, a difference that is not observed among older lesbians who more commonly have children (Ehrenberg, 1997). There are several routes to parenthood for gay and lesbian individuals paralleling those of heterosexuals (O'Brien & Goldberg, 2000). Lesbian mothers and gay fathers may have children from former marriages, a possibility that is more likely among older gays and lesbians who may have passed as straight by marrying. Older gay and lesbian parents who have not come out may fear being rejected by their adult children or grandchildren should they do so (Quam & Whitford, 1992). Most divorced and separated gay fathers, like heterosexual ones, do not have custody of their children (O'Brien & Goldberg, 2000). Lesbian mothers are less likely than straight mothers to maintain child custody (Patterson, 1996), reflecting a tendency to stigmatize lesbian mothers (Causey & Duran-Aydintug, 1997).

Gay and lesbian couples differ from straight couples because there is never more than one partner who is biologically linked to their child (O'Brien & Goldberg, 2000). Like some heterosexual couples, however, gay and lesbian persons may elect to become parents through stepparenting, adoption, or by means other than standard heterosexual reproduction. Thus far, the research that has delved into the ties of gay or lesbian parents with their children has focused, understandably, on policy issues (see Chapter 14) and on younger children. For example, recent research explores the relatively recent separation of being gay from being childless and the turning points that lead gay men to consider having or to actually have children (Berkowitz & Marsiglio, 2007). Qualitative research on becoming mothers among lesbian couples suggests that biological motherhood sometimes creates challenges to maintaining an egalitarian relationship, a parallel to the experiences of straight women (Goldberg & Perry-Jenkins, 2007).

The reverberating ambivalence of negotiating sexual identity in a heterosexist society is evident among adult children of gay, lesbian or bisexual parents. First, the parents vary in whether and when they are out to their children, and then the children go through a process of deciding whether to come out about their parents (Goldberg, 2007). Both situations mimic the process of coming out on one's own behalf. Some children are not out about their parents, some come out selectively, and some view coming out about their parents as a method of educating others or screening out those who will not be receptive. Children often suspect their parents' sexual orientation, as was the case for this 67-year-old father who did not come out until he was 60:

> After I decided to come out I called them [his children] together, ready to drop this bomb on them. My daughter never even blinked. She said, 'good for you, Daddy, it's about time.' It seemed like they always knew, which makes me wonder what my wife thought. (Bergling, 2004:170)

Not all responses are as positive, particularly when grandchildren are involved and adult children are concerned about having a parent stay in their home with a same-sex partner (Weeks et al., 2001).

In the meantime, there is a dearth of research about the ties of adult children with their gay fathers or lesbian mothers or about the ties of older parents with their adult gay and lesbian children. One qualitative study of lesbians finds a range of ties to older parents, with more on good terms than bad and with no apparent difference between ties with older mothers or fathers (Claassen, 2005). The relative silence about parenting and grandparenting among old gay and lesbian persons appears to be echoed in informal gay networks in which those with children or grandchildren are quiet about them out of concern for their peers who do not have family (Kristiansen, 2004).

Older Parents and Their Adult Children

> *I can sit and listen to my children talking and feel pride in them because I see the way that they have grown inside. I see the characters that they have developed and things like this. It makes me feel good inside. And I think to myself, I was apart of all that, you know. They have been instrumental in building up my character, too, because many many things happened to them, as they do to all families.*
>
> —66-year-old mother of five

Like all relationships, parent-child ties include at least two vantage points, that of the older parent and that of the adult child, which often differ from each other. When considering research results, pay attention to the source of information: is it a parent's or a child's perspective? To date, research has paid more attention to the adult child's perspective and to ties involving mothers and daughters, reflecting both the age and gender distribution of family researchers.

Contact Between Older Parents and Adult Children

As we saw in Chapter 2, the majority of older persons (ranging from about 80% to 90% among those aged 65 or more) are parents. Although a current concern is declining birth rates, recall that today's older population includes the parents of the baby boom. How does the general availability of children translate into accessibility and contact?

Most old parents have at least one child living close by, reflecting the preference of parents and children not to live far from one another. Among parents who do not live with a child, about three-quarters reside within a 35-minute drive of their nearest child, and half have a second child within this radius (Lin & Rogerson, 1995). One-quarter have a child less than one mile away. Factors associated with greater proximity to the nearest child are family size (the more children a parent *and* a child have, the closer the nearest child lives), health of the parent (healthier parents are more geographically distant), age of the parent (parents over 80 live nearer by), age of child (increasing age increases geographic distance from parents), a parent's socioeconomic status (SES; higher SES means greater geographic distance), and parent or parents' marital status (married parents live nearer to the most proximate child than do divorced or separated parents; the most proximate combination is widowed mothers and their daughters; Lin & Rogerson, 1995).

The fact that the very old (80 and over) live nearer to their children reflects the growing expectation with age that older parents will move closer to adult children if they need support (Silverstein & Angelleli, 1998). Such moves have been described as reunions, with ambivalent feelings of both wanting to be there and fearing what it will be like (Moss & Moss, 1992). Both parent and child must renegotiate their relationship, setting boundaries and attempting to create a good balance between autonomy and dependency so that they may enjoy their renewed proximity.

Most parents see their children on a regular basis, with as many as 80% of older parents reporting weekly contact with at least one of their children (Chappell, 1992). Although greater distance limits personal contact, proximity has no impact on the quality of parent-child ties (Rossi & Rossi, 1990; Waite & Harrison, 1992). Distant children are in contact with their parents through infrequent overnight visits, telephone conversations and letter writing (DeWit et al., 1988). More recently, cell phones, e-mail and instant messaging have served as means of staying in touch with older parents and grandparents.

Quality of contact with children is more significant than its frequency for older parents' well-being (Koropeckyj-Cox, 2002), so we must attend to the nature of contact and not just its frequency. Older age groups report similar levels of positive interaction but fewer negative interactions with their children when compared with younger age groups (Akiyama et al., 2003). Less overall contact at older ages is associated with fewer negative interactions. Negative encounters with children have a more powerful impact on lowering parents' well-being than positive ones have on raising it (Krause & Rook, 2003). Thus the amount of contact with children itself does not stand as a good indicator of relationship quality.

A different pattern emerges from the adult child's perspective. The frequency of negative interactions with mothers and fathers decreases as one moves from younger to older age groups, until a turning point at ages 49 to 53 years regarding interaction with fathers, and at ages 64 to 68 years for interaction with mothers, when negative interactions go up slightly with age (Akiyama et al., 2003). The increase in negative interactions concerns quite old parents, especially mothers, and may be a reflection of their declining capacities and increased need for support (see Rook, 2003). At earlier stages in the life course, forming partnerships lowers younger adult children's contact with their parents, but having children increases it (Bucx et al., 2008). The arrival of children may trigger transitional marital problems as couples negotiate the ambivalent situation of welcome support from and too much involvement of their parents or parents-in-law (Beaton et al., 2003).

Generally, the social networks of the working class are composed to a greater extent of family members, including children, siblings and their families, aunts, uncles and cousins (Nett, 1993). Thus working-class older parents see their children more often than do their middle-class peers, a tendency that is compounded by their greater geographic proximity (Greenwell & Bengtson, 1997).

Getting together in person is often arranged by older parents, who take the view that their failure to oversee such contact would mean seeing less of their children (Eisenhandler, 1992). Typically, this situation is seen as reasonable, given that their children have less time and flexibility in their daily lives. Yet qualitative research reveals the ambivalence that results when old parents would like to see more of their children but accept that it is limited by their children's successful and busy lives (Peters et al., 2006).

The Nature of Parent-Child Ties in Later Life

> You never cease being a parent, you know. Now my daughter is married, she has a home of her own and a husband to take care of her and a family to look after, but when she is out on the road in the winter time and the roads are icy, I worry about her just as much as I did when she was a child coming home, you see. We have become friends. . . . But she is also my daughter.
>
> —76-year-old widow

What are parent-child ties like once parents are older and their children adults? Older men often act as family heads, whereas older women play the roles of kinkeeper and comforter (Rosenthal, 1985, 1987). The kinkeeper serves to keep family members in touch with each other; the comforter provides emotional support and advice. Thus older parents serve a cohesive function in the family, drawing members of different generations together as part of an extended family network.

A range of studies documents ways in which parents have a lasting impact on their adult children Sons and daughters who observed their parents engage in nonstereotypical gender ways and who heard progressive attitudes toward gender relations in adolescence grow up to be adults who share in domestic labor (Cunningham, 2001). Parents have similar influences on their children's educational and occupational goals and on their values across both the baby boom and

Generation X generations (Putney & Bengtson, 2003). Mothers' preferences for their children's age at marriage, completed education, labor force involvement, and family size are reflected in the eventual behavior of their children, and their views about timing of the first child are more influential than the child's own preference (Barber, 2000). Constructive parenting also is passed from parents to children (Chen & Kaplan, 2001). These and many other studies on intergenerational transmission (see Chapter 11 for related studies on divorce) indicate the long-term impact of parents on their adult children.

There are several common themes regarding the nature of parenting in older age, despite the diversity of family types at this stage of life. Among middle-aged parents of children 21 to 44 years of age, the two most common hopes and dreams for children are their happiness and educational achievement, followed by career success, having happy families, personal fulfillment, and being good and healthy persons (Ryff et al., 1994). These priorities on behalf of children are shared by mothers and fathers and indicate a parental focus on the successful launching and independence of their adult children. When they are met, old parents feel more positive (Pillemer, 2004) and are less likely to hold conflicted feelings about their children (Pillemer & Suitor, 2002).

The value placed on independence carries on into old age, when parents in their 70s value their children's maturity and have a corresponding concern for having their own independence respected by their children (Eisenhandler, 1992). Older parents are most likely to view their ties to children positively if they are in good health, active in their own interests, and independent. The continuing significance of independence for old parents is evident in observations from qualitative research that conflict and tension in relationships with children is most likely to erupt over the issue of parental autonomy (Katz et al., 2005). As well, parents' contradictory feelings about their children are lower when their children rate them as important in their social network and when their children are more invested in their own marriages (Fingerman et al., 2006). Not being depended upon by children in combination with feeling valued by them minimizes contradictory feelings about children among older parents.

A lifelong tendency for parents to be more invested in their children's lives than children are in their parents' lives continues into old age (Fingerman, 2000). Yet although appreciating that they may continue to be important in their children's lives, on balance, being a parent is not considered central to one's identity in old age for mothers or fathers, as it was earlier in their lives (Eisenhandler, 1992). The more hands-off approach to parenting in later life is evident in the comments of one older mother:

> My responsibility is to be there should the children need me . . . you know, just to be in the background. To be sort of an anchor. That is all. Not to be *in* their lives, you know, just to be on the peripheral edges. (Goodman & Rubinstein, 1996:307)

Older parents whose children are busy with careers and families accept this, often proudly, as a stage in their lives and do not want to interfere (Peters et al., 2006). One father observes,

My attitude is, I don't want to impose on them. They have their own lives. They have their own things to do. And I don't want to ask them to do things for us that would interfere with things they want or have to do. (Peters et al., 2006:546)

Parents also express concern about the toll that being so busy may be taking on their children's lives. Like a father who worries about his daughter's combined career and family responsibilities, they typically "wouldn't say a word" (Peters et al., 2006:545) about such concerns. These tendencies to be hands-off are magnified in very old age, when parents in their late 80s and beyond no longer try to exert influence over their children and continue to value as much independence as they can maintain (Johnson & Barer, 1997). Their older children, in turn, have fewer competing commitments, leading to more relaxed support from child to parent.

Affectionate ties between parents and children drop when children are adolescents, peak when they are in their 20s, and then drop slightly before leveling off during their 30s to levels similar to those when children were 10 years old (Rossi & Rossi, 1990). From the vantage point of older parents, children are key confidants, dominating the confiding networks of mothers and fathers when children are geographically proximate (Connidis & Davies, 1990). Although the majority of parents consider at least one child to be a confidant, previously married parents are more likely than married parents to do so (Connidis & Davies, 1992). Confiding between parent and child is typically reciprocal, with both parties seeking and giving advice and reassurance (Wenger & Jerome, 1999). These findings suggest close bonds between parents and children in later life, reflecting the growing egalitarianism of this tie with time. On the other hand, children do not typically serve as companions to older parents when they are engaged in activities outside the home (Connidis & Davies, 1990, 1992), and for older parents, spending time with friends has a more positive effect on well-being than does spending time with children (Pinquart & Sorensen, 2000).

Gender plays out in the bonds between parents and children. Generally, adult children feel closer to their mothers than to their fathers. In one study, nearly 75% of children reported feeling "very close" to their mothers, whereas 60% felt this close to their fathers (Silverstein & Bengtson, 1997). In turn, when compared with fathers, mothers perceive stronger ties to their children (Lynott & Roberts, 1997). On balance, mothers report closer ties to both sons and daughters than do fathers, daughters report closer ties to both fathers and mothers than do sons, and daughters and mothers are closer to one another than any other parent-child combination (Rossi & Rossi, 1990). Gender differences in parent-child ties are also indicated in studies of ambivalent feelings. As reported by adult children, mixed feelings are more likely in mother-daughter ties (Willson et al., 2003), and when reports of both parents and adult children are compared, mothers and adult children have similar ambivalence scores; fathers and children do not (Fingerman et al., 2006). Mothers and daughters who are not close to one another tend never to have been so, reflecting the significance of a relationship's history. So too does the association between adult children's reports of mixed emotions regarding their parents when they did not get along well earlier in life (Willson et al., 2003).

Shifting gender relations and the greater involvement of many fathers in their children's lives may alter these results. More attention to fathers at younger ages helps to redress the substantial gap in research about their place in families (e.g., Marsiglio et al., 2005). Gender relations are usually seen to privilege men, but they also have their costs for men. Older fathers of today led working lives that separated them from their families and limited opportunities for investing in their relationships with children. More of today's fathers can engage more actively in family life, creating prospects for more involved intergenerational ties as they age.

Older parents have two abiding concerns: leaving a fair will and resolving problematic relationships, either between themselves and a child or between their children (Eisenhandler, 1992). Parents consider having children get along a hallmark of good parenting, and they typically follow the principle of leaving their children equal shares in a will (Finch & Mason, 2000). Based on their own descriptions of parenthood in later life, older mothers and fathers are described as *emeritus parents* engaged in paradoxically closely distant or distantly close relationships with their children (Eisenhandler, 1992). This view is reflected in the comments of a 67-year-old woman in one of my studies:

> You would think that children are enough fulfillment but actually they are not, because they are little people on their own, and they are going to grow up and they are gone. And they have their own little circle, their own little world, and you are not really part of it. You love them and they love you, but that is another unit, you know.

These observations describe common experiences of being parents in later life, but intergenerational ties vary across families. A qualitative study of mother-daughter relationships over time finds two types of mother-daughter ties: connected and enmeshed (Miller-Day, 2004, cited in Fisher & Miller-Day, 2006). Connected ties are more in keeping with the move toward independence and a hands-off approach of aging mothers. Enmeshed mother-daughter ties are inflexible and stable over time, and mothers perceive change in their daughters' lives as threats to their relationships. These two types of ties represent different ways of negotiating the dialectical tension between being open and closed in relationships and between maintaining stability and welcoming change.

In another study, five types of relationships between parents and adult children are created, based on children's assessments of emotional closeness and similarity of opinions (affinity), geographic proximity and contact (opportunity), and the giving or receipt of instrumental support (functional exchange; Silverstein & Bengtson, 1997). Tight-knit intergenerational ties are characterized by high levels of affinity, opportunity for contact, and instrumental exchange. Sociable parent-child ties share high levels of emotional and physical closeness and contact but do not involve much instrumental exchange. The difference between these two family types could simply be differing needs for support, a factor that is not included in this study. Obligatory relations involve high levels of opportunity and support exchange but are lower on affinity. Conversely, intimate but distant intergenerational ties are strong emotionally but low on physical contact and functional exchange. Last, detached relationships are cases where parents and children are not engaged on any dimension. The most common intergenerational types, overall, are tight-knit and sociable. However, when examined separately for mothers and fathers, ties with mothers are more likely than those with fathers to be tight knit (31% vs. 20%), whereas ties with fathers are more likely than those with mothers to be detached (17% vs. 7%).

These family types provide an example of the diversity of intergenerational relationships, but they do not capture the meaning or experience of being either a parent or child in any of these situations. Is it any better or worse to be in one type than another? Each may have advantages for particular circumstances or at particular times in the relationship between parent and child. For example, with increasing age, children are generally more likely to have relationships with their parents that are sociable or detached rather than tight knit (Silverstein & Bengtson, 1997). Although we tend to think of tight-knit ties as preferable, moving from a tight-knit to sociable or detached tie over time may reflect greater independence and reduced responsibility for each generation. Indeed, from the older person's point of view, intense involvement with children often has had undesirable catalysts, such as their own changed needs, a crisis in the life of a child, or the eruption of unresolved conflict (Eisenhandler, 1992).

Research in the Netherlands (van Gaalen & Dykstra, 2006) incorporates measures of contact; emotional, financial, and instrumental support; and conflicts over material and personal issues in a typology of relationships between adult children and older parents. Five types emerge: harmonious relationships, with high contact and emotional support; obligatory relationships, with high contact and moderate exchanges of support and more conflict than in harmonious ties; ambivalent ties, with high contact, high level of support exchanges, and high levels of conflict; affective ties characterized by emotional exchange, some conflict on personal issues, and limited contact and instrumental exchange; and discordant, with low contact, support exchange, and some conflict over material issues but high conflict over personal issues. As in the U.S. study by Silverstein and Bengtson, (1997), relationships with mothers are more likely to be harmonious. Adult sons and fathers are more inclined toward obligatory ties than are adult daughters and mothers.

The inclusion of conflict in the Netherlands study (van Gaalen & Dykstra, 2006) reveals that those who engage in extensive support exchanges also are more prone to conflict, indicating ambivalent rather than cohesive relationships, as Silverstein and Bengtson (1997) suggest. As well, those who exchange the least support are not simply detached; their relationships are characterized by discord. The Netherlands study also addresses the implications of relationship type by testing its connection to relationship quality. Harmonious relationships receive the most positive rating, followed in order by ties that are ambivalent, affective or obligatory, and—dramatically lower—discordant. These findings underscore the error of assuming that the presence of conflict necessarily means a poor relationship or that extensive exchange marks a good one.

A study of parent and child viewpoints on intergenerational ties finds that two-thirds of both parents (average age of 62) and children (average age of 39) observe differences, disagreements or disappointments with each other regarding communication and interaction, habits and lifestyle choices, child-rearing practices, work orientation, and politics and religion (Clarke et al., 1999). These disagreements and differences do not necessarily translate into conflict and often reflect ongoing concern for one another. For example, a father worries about his daughter's failure to save for a rainy day, a daughter wishes her mother would support her choice to cohabit and not have children, and a son notes that his parents "have the money to do whatever they want, but yet they deprive themselves of things they can well afford" (Clarke et al., 1999:266). One reason that disagreements and differences in opinion do not necessarily become open conflict is a tendency for parents not to offer unsolicited advice, a situation that creates ambivalence when parents would like to say something but feel they must bite their tongues (Peters et al., 2006). Withdrawing from active parenting later in life involves leaving children to their own devices, in part as a way of protecting relationships with them.

Variations in parent-child ties occur within families. Parents distinguish among their children in terms of how positive or ambivalent their relationships are (Peters et al., 2006). Studies of favoritism also show within-family differences, with many mothers favoring some children over others either emotionally or in support exchanges (Suitor & Pillemer, 2006; Suitor, Pillemer et al., 2006). Adult children tend to report more favoritism than do their older parents (Suitor, Sechrist et al., 2006). Eighty-four percent of children believe that their mother is emotionally closer to one of her children, compared with 68% of mothers who report that they are. In a case study of one of my multigenerational families, all mid-life participants agreed that their mothers favored one of their sibling group. This was not problematic for their ties with one another, but the ambivalence of being treated differently in the face of expected equal treatment by parents created tensions in ties with their mothers for some of the siblings. This observation corresponds with greater ambivalence in the form of contradictory feelings in the vertical ties between parents and children than in the horizontal ties between siblings (Fingerman et al., 2004).

For those whose parents or children are married, intergenerational in-law ties add another dimension to parent-child relationships. Adult children are more likely to have mixed feelings about in-laws than about their own parents (Merrill, 2007; Willson et al., 2003). Among parents, a better relationship with a child-in-law improves relations with children and grandchildren; conversely, contact with and closeness to children is threatened by poor ties with children-in-law (Peters et al., 2006). In her qualitative study of mother-in-law and daughter-in-law relationships, Merrill (2007) documents a range of experiences and an array of relationship types, including tight knit, distant but positive, obligatory, estranged, cordial, and conflicted but affectionate. The most common type is tight knit, with mothers-in-law more inclined than daughters-in-law to describe their relationships this way. The next most common choice among daughters-in-law is estranged, but among mothers-in-law it is cordial.

Like all close ties, those between parents and children typically involve tensions and ambivalence that may lead to conflict or be successfully negotiated. Positive relationships characterized by emotional support (feeling cared for, loved and listened to) mean less psychological distress for parents and children; more negative relationships (critical and demanding) heighten distress (Umberson, 1992b). Unfortunately, the negative side of the parent-child relationship has a more powerful effect than the positive on levels of distress for both parties.

Our understanding suffers from a lack of research on the ties between fathers and sons, fathers and daughters, and mothers and sons in middle and later life. Recent research comparing two cohorts of middle-aged and old fathers suggests more contact between fathers and their adult children in current than previous cohorts (Taylor et al., 2006). Ideally, future research will tap aspects of relationships that apply across the gendered experiences of men and women to better reveal the unique relationships of various gender dyads of older parents and adult children. Understanding the reality of parent-child ties and their impact requires moving beyond the idealized emphasis on harmony to analyzing their power dynamics (Pyke, 1999).

CHAPTER 8

Support Exchanges Between Older Parents and Their Children

The lengthening of parent-child ties means that both generations will go through numerous life transitions that are likely to have an impact on their relationship with one another. Children leaving the parental home, changes in a child's or parent's marital and parental status, and the declining health of a parent are typical age-related experiences that occur in the mid and later life of parents. In this chapter we explore what happens to ties between parents and their children when such shifts occur. We begin by considering theoretical perspectives on support exchanges in later life. The consequences for parent-child ties of divorce in either generation are discussed in Chapter 11.

Perspectives on Support Exchanges

Obligation, duty and responsibility ... are commitments developed by real people not abstract principles associated with particular relationships.

—Finch (1989:181)

Support is usually distinguished as formal versus informal. *Formal support* refers to the help provided by agencies, services, professionals and workers whose jobs are to supply particular forms of assistance. *Informal support* refers to various forms of help, ranging from emotional support to hands-on nursing care, that are provided by people that we know, primarily family, friends, and neighbors. The term *intergenerational family transfers* emphasizes the array of aid that generations provide one another, including money and in-kind goods, time committed to the labor of helping, and space in the form of housing (Silverstein, 2006). Too often, informal and formal sources of support are treated as alternatives when, in practice, at all ages, we receive support from both informal and formal sources (see Chapter 14). Even among Canadians over the age of 65 who receive help due to long-term health problems, 42% are assisted by informal sources (family, friends and neighbors), 34% by formal sources (paid employees, volunteers, and government and nongovernment organizations), and 24% by a combination of informal and formal sources (Statistics Canada, 2002a).

Living alone and having no living children—both more likely for women—make formal support more probable in the face of health problems (Statistics Canada, 2002a). For both men and women, getting older means getting less support from informal sources only (Cranswick, 2003). Among men, however, informal support outranks either formal support or a mix of formal and informal support for all age groups; for women aged 85 and over, a mix of formal and informal support is most common, followed by informal support. Over time, more care has shifted from formal and institutional sources to community-based and informal sources (Cranswick, 2003; Ward-Griffin & Marshall, 2003).

Moving more formal services out of institutional settings and into the community creates a highly enmeshed situation of informal and formal support when home care workers offer services in the client's home (Martin-Matthews, 2007). The juxtaposition of strangers and the intimate setting of one's home, of competing claims to control and cooperation in the home setting, and of public and private domains is a prime example of socially created ambivalence that must be negotiated by family and professionals. The focus of this chapter is the vast majority of support provided to older persons—over 80%—that comes from family members (Merrill, 1997). But in the real world, the private sphere of families and the public sphere of formal support are not so neatly separated, and the blurring of boundaries includes viewing home care workers as friends and like family as well as employees (Martin-Matthews, 2007). The overlapping of informal and formal care is particularly dramatic for care workers, mostly women, who provide informal care to a family member and formal care to clients (Ward-Griffin, 2008; see Chapter 14).

Four models of social support have dominated discussions and examinations of the help provided to older persons by family members. The *hierarchical-compensatory* model (Cantor, 1979) assumes that older persons have a hierarchy of favored relationships from whom all forms of support are sought. A spouse and children are at the top of the list, but if they are not available, substitutes can be found from lower on the list. These substitutes compensate for the preferred but unavailable ties. The assumption is that those without spouses or children or both are missing a fundamental source of all kinds of help. The *task-specificity* model (Litwak, 1985) focuses on tasks rather than particular relationships and posits that certain forms of aid are best provided by ties with complementary features. Thus for example, help that requires proximity is best provided by a neighbor. This suggests the importance of diversity in social networks.

Two other models offer a more varied and dynamic conception of informal support networks. The *functional-specificity of relationships* model (Simons, 1984) is more flexible in taking the view that a particular relationship, for example, that with a sister, can be negotiated in different ways. For some people, a sister may be a very important source of support, whereas for others she is not. Thus in a particular person's life, a relationship may serve one or many functions, and particular functions are not tied to specific relationships. Diversity is an important dimension of social networks, not because given relationships specialize in the same task for all persons but because the same relationships are negotiated in different ways. The *convoy* model (Antonucci & Akiyama, 1995) adds a dynamic view of social support. A convoy is a network of persons to whom an individual is connected by the giving or receiving of support. As we move through life, the convoy changes as the nature of social exchanges shifts or as members join or leave the convoy. Thus different ties may be significant, not only for different groups of individuals but also for the same individual at different points in the life course.

The hierarchical-compensatory and task-specificity models have fairly fixed notions of support networks, minimizing variability in the ways that ties to family, friends and other individuals can be negotiated over time and in different circumstances. In these models, emphasizing normative assumptions about particular familial bonds also fails to incorporate gender as an organizing feature of social life (Allen et al., 1999). The conventional view of family embedded in the hierarchical-compensatory model favors the traditional nuclear family (spouse and children) as the primary relationships in the lives of all adults. By definition, this excludes those without spouses or children and views their networks as inadequate (Connidis, 1994b). For these reasons, a combination of the functional-specificity and convoy models is a superior perspective for understanding the dynamic negotiation of varied informal support in later life.

An optimal way to understand social support within families is to combine the influence of culture, social structure, family history, and individual preferences as central to negotiated commitments (Finch, 1989). These factors are embedded in the concept of *legitimate excuses*, which refers to socially accepted reasons for avoiding obligations to help in particular situations (Finch, 1989). For example, a married father in the labor force could argue effectively that his prior claims as father, husband and worker excuse him from the responsibility of caring for his mother, especially given that his sister is a married homemaker and thus more available to help. The gendered nature of social life in general and of family life in particular means that such an excuse would carry the additional weight of different gender claims in the assumed responsibility to care.

The imbalanced focus on help provided by children, caregiver burden, the sandwich generation, and women in the middle creates the impression that all older people need help and downplays their role as helpers in old age. Yet help flowing from parent to child is an ongoing component of parent-child relationships in old age (Stone et al., 1998), making the focus on support *exchange* essential. Exchange includes assumptions of reciprocity (Gouldner, 1967), and reciprocity or balance in a relationship enhances life satisfaction for adults of all ages (Antonucci et al., 1990). Receiving either more or less than one's share in an exchange undermines well-being.

Reciprocity is at the root of filial responsibility, reflected in the view that a primary reason children should look after their parents is because their parents looked after them when they were young (Dwyer, Lee, and Jankowski, 1994).

Almost two-thirds of older parents in my study of 400 community-dwelling persons aged 65 or more both give and receive support in a variety of areas. Just over one-fifth give some assistance but receive none, and 15% receive some assistance but give none. These parents also judge their exchanges with children as fair: 95% of them believe that their children give them about the right amount of help, and 92% believe that they in turn give their children the right amount of help.

Nonetheless, there are limits in the extent to which the relationship between parent and child can ever be truly balanced. "Children have an irredeemable obligation toward parents. Nothing they do can ever make up for the initial parental gift" of life and nurturing (Berman, 1987:25). In turn, older parents experience irreplaceable loss. Although they may engage in new activities and make new friends in old age, they are unable to replace people and times that went before (Berman, 1987). Both parents and children may thus feel unable to offer as much to each other as they feel they owe (children) or would like to give (parents). The essential tension between the irredeemable obligation of children and the irreplaceable losses of parents cannot be resolved in daily interaction and is an ongoing source of ambivalence.

Life course transitions that involve shifting needs for support and consequent changes in exchange patterns reveal and often heighten ambivalence in intergenerational relations (Connidis & McMullin, 2002b). Adult children report higher levels of ambivalence in the form of contradictory feelings when their parents face health problems (Fingerman et al., 2006; Willson et al., 2003), indicating the challenges faced when life transitions require the conscious renegotiation of intergenerational relationships. These contradictory feelings coincide with structural arrangements that create sociological ambivalence, for example, in the case of colliding demands between paid work and family responsibilities, particularly among daughters.

Cultural expectations to honor responsibilities toward parents are mediated by structured social relations based on gender, class, ethnicity and race. The history of relationships within a family also helps determine who will assume what obligation to support a family member (Finch, 1989). Negotiating support for any family member, including a parent or adult child, involves a dynamic interplay of the interests and concerns of all those who could be implicated in providing that support. Even those who appear to be uninvolved are likely to have negotiated that position through claims to acceptable competing and overriding responsibilities as legitimate excuses for not offering support.

Child Support to Older Parents

When she was small, our daughter depended on us for decisions, for help from us in so many ways. Now, I find that the roles are somewhat reversed. She is much younger [than we], and she is out in the world more, and I think we tend to lean on her a little. We try not to, but there are times when I feel that we do. She is just like the Rock of Gibraltar.

—Married mother, 77 years old

The most likely providers of family support to older persons are spouses and, in their absence, children. Over a third of older persons who require daily help receive it from a child (Aldous, 1994). Children provide a broad range of help, from emotional support to extensive, long-term, hands-on nursing care. Some of the support that is termed *caregiving* is viewed more accurately as the usual stuff of close relationships, a difference captured in the distinction between caring for and caring about a family member (Martin-Matthews, 2000a). For example, when is emotional support a form of caregiving and when is it an ongoing feature of a family tie? Individuals caring for old family members tend to view the care that they provide as an extension of their ongoing relationships with those persons until others define what they do as caregiving (O'Connor, 2006).

Variability in the samples and research methods used to study caregiving may underlie apparently contradictory results in the research literature. Some samples include children who are in or out of the labor force, whereas others include labor force participants only. Some address a range of living situations, whereas others study co-resident parents and their caregiving children. Older parents vary in the amount of support they require, a factor which some studies consider and others do not. Most studies are cross-sectional, examining caring at one point in time. This snapshot view fails to capture the dynamics of the caregiving process, including the ebb and flow of involvement by different family members over time. This problem is heightened by focusing on a primary caregiver, the person identified as being most responsible for care. This misses the negotiation of support over time, when children may take turns according to the shifting needs of parents and their variable ability to help.

Finally, a gender bias in research that favors the kinds of support more traditionally offered by women heightens their apparent dominance as caregivers and effectively minimizes the support provided by sons (Matthews, 2002b). When coupled with the assumption that more so-called feminine forms of support are better for parents (Matthews & Heidorn, 1998), the efforts of sons and of less traditional daughters are treated implicitly as inferior and suspect. Consider these caveats as we explore the help that children give to their parents.

Pathways to Caring

The possibility that a child will provide care to an older parent is heightened if the parent is a mother, is not married, has few children, and is in greater need of help (Bengtson et al., 2000; Ikkink et al., 1999; Lang & Schütze, 2002; Sims-Gould & Martin-Matthews, 2007). Daughters are more likely than sons to provide care to parents and to provide more of it. Among *employed* persons caring for a parent, most caregivers are married (Sims-Gould & Martin-Matthews, 2007). Employed women are more likely than employed men to be primary caregivers, and employed women and men are equally likely to be helpers, not primary caregivers. Adult children rarely provide support to parents without direct or assistive support from others, particularly spouses, sisters, sisters-in-law, brothers, brothers-in-law, and their own children (Sims-Gould & Martin-Matthews, 2007). Thus although many studies focus on primary caregivers, care is usually delivered within a larger family network (see Chapter 13).

Race also affects care dynamics, with African American carers more likely to be children, and White carers more likely to be spouses (Connell & Gibson, 1997; Stommel et al., 1998). This helps account for the fact that White primary caregivers more often provide care on their own, whereas Black primary caregivers receive more support from others (Stommel et al., 1998). African American and Hispanic couples are generally more engaged in supporting parents and parents-in-law than are White couples, and Black sons-in-law are more supportive of their wives' caring efforts than are White sons-in-law (Shuey & Hardy, 2003). Older African Americans get more help from their families in co-resident situations (Peek et al., 2000), and intergenerational help exchanges occur in a broader network of supportive family ties in which elders are equals (Becker et al., 2003).

Black elders are less likely to be institutionalized despite being in poorer health and receiving less care from relatives (Belgrave & Bradsher, 1994). However, as reported by caregivers, African Americans tend to provide more hours of support and to be caring for older persons who have more health limitations (Bowman et al., 1998). When health and wealth are taken into account, Black and White adult children are more inclined to help their parents financially and Hispanic children less so (Wong et al., 1999). Filipino Americans also view economic support to parents as a priority (Becker et al., 2003). On balance, Black adult children are most willing to sacrifice meeting their own needs to provide financial aid to their parents.

The apparent strength of family ties among non-White groups may create a false impression of needs being met. Several reasons may account for unmet needs, including the greater need for personal support among Hispanics than among Black and White elders; the poorer health of Hispanics and Blacks than Whites; and the poorer access to alternative sources of help, given their poorer financial situation (Zajicek et al., 2006). When all sources of informal support are considered (relatives and unpaid nonrelatives), Black elders actually receive less assistance than their White counterparts (Norgard & Rodgers, 1997). Although the informal networks of older Blacks are more likely to include someone other than spouses, children, or children-in-law, they are no larger than those of older Whites (Burton et al., 1995). Thus the availability of family to older non-White persons must not detract from the need to improve accessibility to other forms of support.

Characteristics of families are also important determinants of caring. Families that manage conflict positively, engage in compromise, and work hard at conflict resolution tend to give far more help to older members with Alzheimer's (Lieberman & Fisher, 1999). Families in which decision-making authority is granted to one family member, with input from others, give more aid to elders than do more democratic families. However, families who have a high level of agreement between spouses and their children regarding the behavior of a co-resident older person experience less stress and depression and greater satisfaction and mastery as a result of caregiving (Pruchno et al., 1997a). Understanding these kinds of family dynamics is essential to understanding how the caring work of families gets done.

The sexual orientation of old parents or adult children creates novel circumstances for care from adult children. Among old lesbians, about 45% are parents, primarily through a former heterosexual marriage (Claassen, 2005). Some of today's old lesbians cannot necessarily assume that their children will be there for them because their children have rejected them or are distanced from them because of their sexual orientation (Claassen, 2005). Among those children who do care for an old gay or lesbian parent, respecting the privacy of their parent's sexual identity and fearing discriminatory treatment pose a particular challenge when trying to serve as an advocate (Brotman et al., 2007).

Among adult children who are gay or lesbian, providing extensive medical care to a family member, including a co-resident parent, is more likely when lesbian and gay couples have been together for a long time (Carrington, 1999). The greater emotional closeness to mothers evident in the tendency for young adult children to disclose their sexual orientation to their mothers over their fathers (D'Augelli et al., 1998; Savin-Williams, 1998) combine with the longer lives of women to make support from adult gay and lesbian children to their old mothers more likely (Connidis, 2003b; see, e.g., Raphael & Meyer, 2000). For some, however, staying in the closet continues even when extensive support is being offered to a parent. One study suggests that lesbian caregivers are older, less educated, and more often in couples than lesbians who do not provide care to their parents; gay carers also appear to be older and are more likely to be unemployed than gays who do not provide care (Hunter, 2005).

The widely held view that children should help their parents is not unconditional (Finch & Mason, 1991), and norms of filial responsibility begin to decline in midlife, a time when one's vantage point moves away from thinking about being the provider of care to an older parent and toward thinking about receiving care from adult children (Gans & Silverstein, 2006). Children who subscribe most strongly to norms of filial commitment also give their parents more help (Ikkink et al., 1999), although a stronger sense of obligation appears to have a greater impact on the amount of help given by sons than by daughters (Silverstein et al., 1995). Filial norms are more strongly felt among women than men (Gans & Silverstein, 2006), and non-White and Black caregivers have stronger cultural traditions of commitment to filial support than do Whites (Connell & Gibson, 1997; Dilworth-Anderson, Brummett et al., 2005).

Children's support of older persons is enhanced by emotionally close bonds. Daughters are more engaged in help exchanges with their mothers when their relationships are characterized by greater intimacy (Schwarz, 2006), and help from sons and daughters to mothers is more extensive in closer relationships (Bengtson et al., 2000). Nonetheless, previous conflict between children and their parents does not stop current support exchanges (Parrott & Bengtson, 1999). Among daughters, obligation dominates affection as a motive for assistance with activities of daily living but not for more general forms of social support (Merrill, 1997).

Qualitative research reveals family dynamics in several pathways to caring (Merrill, 1997). Some children are selected as the caregiver de facto, meaning that no one else was available or perceived to be adequate to the task. Others become primary helpers following family meetings, usually held in response to major changes in circumstances. After such gatherings, one child usually emerges as the caregiver after others offer legitimate excuses (Finch, 1989) to justify their inability to serve as caregiver. However, some siblings decide to share care equally (see Chapter 13). A third scenario, most common among working-class families, is for caregivers to be chosen by their parents, who express their preference on the assumption that the elected child is willing and able (Merrill, 1997). Other qualitative research finds that parents are generally reluctant to ask their children for help, however, preferring to find alternatives, including hiring someone (Peters et al., 2006). Some children report that the caregiving situation just happened, evolving over time as situations shifted and the need for support intensified (Merrill, 1997).

When asked which child they think would be most likely to provide support if it were needed, mothers are most likely to identify the child to whom they feel closest, a daughter, and the child who has provided help in the past (Pillemer & Suitor, 2006). Hypothetically at least, gender, family history and emotional attachment override pragmatic factors, such as proximity, in a mother's choice. Reflecting the life course implications of early experience and gender relations, a mother's, but not father's, willingness to ask her children for help later in life is affected by relationship patterns with her children during their adolescence and early adulthood (Schooler et al., 2007). Mothers who were more responsive to their children earlier in life are more likely to ask for personal help, and mothers who were both more responsive and less dominant are more willing to ask for financial assistance.

When parents' need for support grows, their adult children confront the mixed feelings of wanting to help and observing a parent's decline and the structural contradictions of meeting the demands of other midlife responsibilities, such as paid work and possibly children, at the same time that parental needs for support are escalating (Lang, 2004). Adult children identify multiple sources of ambivalence in their anticipation of providing parental care, some concerning the personal ambivalence that comes from opposing feelings and some concerning structural ambivalence that comes from contradictions in available courses of action, such as in-home and institutional care (Lorenz-Meyer, 2004). Although multiple sources of ambivalence can stymie decision making, dealing with them also has transformative outcomes. Gender relations are central to the ambivalence created by current social arrangements regarding both work and family.

Gender and Caring for Parents

One response to population aging has been a heightened concern about the sandwiched generation, those caught in the middle of caring for both their older parents (more often a mother) and their young children. Looking ahead, when the baby boomers reach old age, there will be fewer children to look after old parents due to declining birth rates, and delayed partnering and parenting will make overlapping parent and child care responsibilities more likely (Williams, 2004). But currently, the experience of caring for dependent parents and children simultaneously is not typical (Martin Matthews & Rosenthal, 1993). Indeed, recent commentary on the sandwiched generation of women suggests that this is another instance of overselling population aging (Martin-Matthews, 2000b; Rosenthal, 2000).

In Canada, although about a third of women in their late 40s are in the structural position of having an older parent, dependent children, and a job, the highest percentage of any age group who were actually combining work and children with helping a parent once a month or more (women aged 50 to 59) was only 7% (Rosenthal et al., 1996; for the UK, see Evandrou & Glaser, 2004). In the United States, 9 to 13% of households with telephones and someone aged 30 to 60 involve working, sandwiched couples, defined as people with children aged 18 or under living at home who are caregivers to older parents (Neal & Hammer, 2007).

The numbers sandwiched between generations at one point in time are low, but among older women with a surviving parent, one-third of those aged 60 to 75 provides parental care (Himes, 1994), and among women aged 45 to 49 who have a living parent, 50% will probably become a caregiver to that parent at some point in the future. Although women trying to meet these competing responsibilities have a formidable task at hand, overstated and alarming claims that large numbers of stressed-out employees need support while caregiving may scare off work-based initiatives to support workers (Martin-Matthews, 2000b). As well, there are both rewards and costs to caring for parents, and having multiple commitments itself does not necessarily add to the stress of caring (Penning, 1998).

When parents are well, sons and daughters are equally active in supporting them (Ikkink et al., 1999) and do not differ in their expression of filial obligation, in their stated emphasis on equality and fairness in sharing responsibility (Finch & Mason, 1991), or in their reported ability to provide support to parents following hospitalization (Wolfson et al., 1993). In practice, daughters are more likely than sons to care for parents and to provide a wider range of help under an array of circumstances (Dwyer & Seccombe, 1991). Sons are especially unlikely to be engaged in body work (Twiggs, 2004), the hands-on personal care, or caring in the intimate home spaces of a mother's bedroom or bathroom (Martin-Matthews, 2007). Even the possibility of a parental preference to receive care from a child of the same gender does not erase gender differences. Sons are more inclined to help fathers than mothers and daughters are more likely to help mothers than fathers, but daughters are still more likely than sons to help both mothers and fathers (Lee et al., 1993). Support provided to both self-sufficient and dependent old mothers by daughters is an extension of long-established patterns of helping between generations of women (Walker & Pratt, 1991).

The lower level of help provided by sons may be compensated for considerably by the greater involvement of daughters-in-law than sons-in-law in hands-on assistance. Even when sons are primary caregivers, direct personal care may shift to the son's wife (Merrill, 1997). Couples are more responsive to the needs of the wife's than the husband's parents (Shuey & Hardy, 2003), reflecting the fact that women help their parents more than their in-laws, but men do not (Lee et al., 2003). These findings suggest that some of the ambivalence in the intergenerational tie between mothers- and daughters-in-law (Turner et al., 2006) may be the daughter-in-law's overriding commitment to her own parents.

A German study of middle-aged children and old parents reveals that a parent's need for care alters parent-child relationships by increasing one-way support to parents and reducing reciprocity. Daughters are more likely than sons to be engaged in relationship patterns that involve support to parents. Among daughters, gender of the parent prompts different relationship patterns—strained altruism with mothers and resilient giving with fathers, highlighting the significance of gender as a feature of relationships, not individuals.

A significant issue related to gender and caring is labor force participation, discussed shortly.

Sons Who Care

Although daughters tend to give more support, especially hands-on care, sons help their parents more in areas that are traditionally masculine and important in their own right, particularly financial support and home and yard maintenance (Martin-Matthews, 2007). Employment history is one reason that men are less engaged than women in caring for parents, but gender differences remain even among employed men and women. Characteristics of men's families, particularly the women in their lives, shape men's involvement in caregiving. Wives and daughters draw men into caring for others, including parents and parents-in-law, but having sisters tends to relieve them of this responsibility (Gerstel & Gallagher, 2001). Sons who act as primary caregivers are likely to be only children, to have no sisters or to have sisters living far away from the parent, and to be working-class (Martin Matthews & Campbell, 1995).

The gender bias of research suggests that parents who must "make do" with sons as caregivers are at risk of receiving inferior aid (see also Chapter 13). Yet when sons take on primary caregiving responsibilities, their commitment is as stable as that of daughters, and the patterns of involvement become quite similar for sons and daughters (Martin Matthews & Campbell, 1995; Stoller, 1990). Sons in families with no daughters negotiate directly with parents rather than with siblings and work hard to foster their parents' independence, an approach that may be preferable to the more traditional hands-on style of daughters (Matthews & Heidorn, 1998; Matthews, 2002a). Although women may be more involved than men with caring for parents, qualitative research on sons who care for their parents shows that sons provide a broad range of help, including personal care, as needed (Harris, 1998).

Like daughters, sons vary in the support that they give, in part based on circumstances such as their parents' health and marital status. Sons looking after a parent with dementia take four key approaches to caring (Harris, 1998). The dutiful son has an intense sense of duty toward his parents, which motivates him to help. The son who goes the extra mile usually has one or both parents living with him, and his efforts mimic those of a spouse. Sons who are strategic planners are emotionally involved in the management strategies used to ensure that care is provided personally and by others. Last, the son who shares care works with a parent or siblings (or both) as equal team players. These caregiving sons receive emotional support from their wives but do not expect them to care for their parents. Filial responsibility is met in a nurturing and loving manner, in varying ways.

Labor Force Participation and Caring: Work–Life Balance

Unless noted otherwise, this section refers to employed adult children. Men and women who combine paid work, care for parents, and parenthood are as satisfied with life as employed parents who do not have all three responsibilities, but they have higher stress levels and are less satisfied with work-family balance (Williams, 2004). Employed women are more likely to be engaged in all three activities, and they commit more hours of care to older relatives, primarily parents, than do employed men (Pyper, 2006). Because women are so prominent as providers of parental support, their increased involvement in the labor force prompts concerns about how these competing demands can be met. Geographic distance overrides work commitments in decisions about which child cares for an older parent (Stern, 1996) and is an additional challenge to caring. Middle-aged long-distance carers to older family members miss time from work or perform below par, incur financial costs for travel or alternative care, and feel guilty and stressed because they are too far away to provide care readily (Neal et al., 2008). Daughters are particularly likely to engage in distance-defying support to their parents, traveling remarkable distances from home or work to offer support in the parental home (Joseph & Hallman, 1996; Phillips & Bernard, 2008). Sons are more inclined to invest extensive commuting time for a distant work destination.

Typically, labor force participants manage parent care by identifying needs and ensuring that some of them are met by others, including paid-for services. Among employed men and women, care management is a common facet of caring for parents and includes orchestrating care and overseeing financial and bureaucratic matters (Rosenthal et al., 2007). Being employed affects how much care is provided by both men and women, explaining some of the gender gap in care to older parents (Sarkisian & Gerstel, 2004). Men are as likely as women to aid their parents, daughters and sons provide similar levels of health care, and sons- and daughters-in-law provide parallel levels of help to their parents-in-law (Ingersoll-Dayton et al., 1996). Daughters provide more socioemotional and home-based support to their parents than do sons, and they are more likely to be primary carers (Neal et al., 1997). Canadian research also finds that personal care is more likely to come from employed women than employed men (Martin Matthews & Campbell, 1995).

Overall, a gendered workplace in which women and men experience different conditions of work, and women's greater responsiveness to variation in their parent's needs, results in more work adjustments by women as they provide more care to parents than do men (Sarkisian & Gerstel, 2004). Women tend to use sick days, miss work-based social events, and pass up opportunities for advancement; men more often interrupt their work days (Martin Matthews & Campbell, 1995). Although both sons and daughters experience stress as a result of taking time off work (Starrels et al., 1997), lost opportunities for advancement have dire long-term consequences for women, as they accumulate fewer pension benefits due to forfeiting promotions, scaling back in work hours, or leaving the labor force (Evandrou & Glaser, 2004; Martin-Matthews, 1999). Women who work outside the home also continue to support their old parents by forfeiting leisure time and sleep, enlisting the help of other family members, and cutting back on housework and nonessential dimensions of family life (Guberman & Maheu, 1999; Ikkink et al., 1999; Martin Matthews & Rosenthal, 1993).

On balance, those who receive care from employed women rather than homemakers receive as much of it but not necessarily directly from their daughters (Doty et al., 1998). Women in the labor force and unpaid workers in the home provide similar levels of help with shopping, transportation, household maintenance, emotional support and service management (Brody et al., 1987), but traditional hands-on care is most usual among housewives. More hours at work decreases both the number of hours of care a woman provides and the total number of hours of care received by a parent (Doty et al., 1998). Despite the juggling act that combining work and caregiving requires, women may find employment a positive counterpoint to caring for a parent (Martin Matthews & Keefe, 1995; Murphy, Schofield, et al., 1997; Phillips & Bernard, 2008; Scharlach, 1994). One daughter observes, "Work is a break. I can finally use my brain. I am so busy, it takes my mind off everything here [at home]. I wouldn't want to give it up" (Merrill, 1997:82). Despite the positive spin-offs of combining work and care for some, the psychological distress of employed midlife women caring for parents could be alleviated if the socially created conflict between work and family were reduced (Marks, 1998).

Class relations must be factored into any discussion about women's paid work. Indeed, in a study of middle-class working couples caring for parents while they still have children under 18 living at home (Neal & Hammer, 2007), hands-on personal care from either husband or wife is minimal. Because the jobs held by working-class women are not as well paying as the careers typical of middle-class and upper-class women, women with lower-status jobs more often leave them in the face of demands for parent care than women with higher education and higher-status jobs (Henz, 2006). Among workers who stay in the labor force, those in blue-collar jobs are most likely to reduce the number of hours they work as an initial strategy for assuming caring responsibilities (Mutschler, 1994). Rearranging schedules is the most common tactic for combining work and care, but managers, professionals and clerks are almost twice as likely to use this approach. The alternative for those in sales, service and blue-collar jobs is to take time off without pay.

Gendered family life plays out in the impact of having children on the middle generation's support for their parents. Having adolescent or older children actually increases the help that fathers and homemaker mothers give to their parents when the child is of the same gender, and to their parents-in-law when the child is of the opposite gender (Gallagher & Gerstel, 2001). Among employed women, however, having children of any age does not alter significantly the amount of help given to their parents or parents-in-law. Their job constraints leave a smaller potential range of variability in time to spend caring for the older generation. Also, mothers make significant time investments in parenting adolescent children as they negotiate protection and increased independence with them (Kurz, 2002). This overlooked phase of parenting presents unique demands because mothers (and fathers) cannot rely on child care workers inside or outside the home as substitutes for their attention.

Longitudinal research suggests that work-related adjustments are prompted as soon as the need for care arises. These adaptations are often temporary, however, as women discover ways to balance work and caregiving or the parents' need for care declines (Franklin et al., 1994). As well, some research indicates adaptation to caring responsibilities over time, based on declines in stress due to caregiving (Martin-Matthews, 1999). Such apparent adaptability should not be the basis for complacency, because the decline in a parent's health can also escalate the number of crises and amount of care required. As well, some adaptations, such as retiring in order to care for an older family member, more common among women than men (Pyper, 2006), are not temporary for many. While women are more likely to compensate for caring through the use of their home and personal time (Phillips & Bernard, 2008), the workplace adjustments made in response to care demands also affect the workload of co-workers (Winton, 2002), widening the circle of lives adversely affected by treating the welfare of older people and their families as a private trouble rather than public issue. The tension between market work and domestic labor that has historically been resolved through gendered social relations requires new solutions (Crompton, 2006).

Consequences of Caring

Power Shifts

When older parents are healthy, exchanges with children typically involve reciprocity (Ikkink et al., 1999). Engaging in mutual assistance helps to sustain continuity in intergenerational ties over time (Becker et al., 2003). When the ability of older parents to reciprocate declines, they lose power in exchanges with their children and may have to resort to invoking guilty feelings in them or complying with their wishes. The irredeemable obligation felt by children can make them responsive to feelings of guilt that parents are quite unaware of evoking (Pyke, 1999). One consequence is that children report more demands for and greater burden from providing care than do their parents.

Children are very aware of how much they have received from their parents and often view support to old parents, including caregiving, as their attempt to repay them (Silverstein et al., 2002). Such delayed reciprocity is evident in the greater support received by parents who gave more support to their children when they were younger (Ikkink et al., 1999). One son observed,

> I was pleased that I was able in some small way . . . to pay her back. I think if she had died of a heart attack, I would never have had the chance to say to myself in some small way I had repaid her for what she did. Not that she ever made me feel like I had to, but I did. (Harris, 1998:347–348)

Children typically feel unable to truly reciprocate the lifetime of support received from their parents, as a daughter's comments illustrate: "I could never give her all of what she has given me, not in a million years" (Sheehan & Donorfio, 1999:171).

Parents vary in their willingness to defer to their children, based on whether they are members of families that are individualist or collectivist in their stance toward familial support (Pyke, 1999). In individualist families, both generations believe strongly in self-reliance and have very low expectations for, and provision of support, to older members. Collectivist families are the opposite; close family ties are valued, and high levels of support are expected and offered. But greater support has its price. The parents in collectivist families have less intergenerational power and exhibit greater deference to their children than is true of parents in individualist families (Pyke, 1999). Parents in individualist families resist receiving support from their children for as long as possible in an effort to maintain autonomy. In both family types, however, if help is provided and parents fail to repay support with compliance, children are resentful and respond by setting limits on the amount of support they are willing to provide. Thus to maintain reciprocity in the caregiving situation, parents must trade power for support or support for power.

Subjective Impact on Children

Results are mixed about the impact on well-being of looking after an older parent, in part because measures of caregiving and well-being, as well as sample characteristics, vary greatly. In a national sample of married adult children, levels of well-being, marital quality, financial resources, and satisfaction with leisure time are similar for those who assume simultaneous obligations to their parents or parents-in-law and children and those who do not (Loomis & Booth, 1995). Those with happier marriages are more likely to take on this responsibility, so these findings may simply reflect the unique situation of married persons with strong relationships. Other research indicates that the well-being of children who have emotional support (Sheehan & Donorfio, 1999) or have partners (Murphy, Schofield, et al., 1997) is not adversely affected by caring for their parents, whereas those without partners are more likely to resent caregiving (Murphy, Schofield, et al., 1997).

Some studies report deteriorating parent-child relations and less happiness among children when help is given to a parent in declining health (Kaufman & Uhlenberg, 1998; Strawbridge et al., 1997). Lower-income children experience greater strain from caring for parents when families experience conflict (Scharlach, Li, and Dalvi, 2006). Adult children with fewer resources must provide more direct care and must rely more on one another, heightening the potential for disagreement among them. Qualitative research indicates that Black American family caregivers, especially daughters, have fewer resources, look after parents with more functional limitations, and give more extensive support (Calderon & Tennstedt, 1998). Not surprisingly, they suffer more emotional, physical and financial strain than is true among White Americans.

Much of the research on caregiving neglects the emotion work of caring (MacRae, 1998; Sheehan & Donorfio, 1999). The focus on caregivers rather than family networks also misses the fact that children who do *not* provide care to parents also feel stressed as a result of their parents' frailty or disability (Amirkhanyan & Wolf, 2006). Although we tend to think of emotions as rather spontaneous and free ranging, "emotions themselves are subject to normative guidelines" (Finch, 1989: 207), which some have termed "feeling rules" (Hochschild, 1983). Failure to manage the mix of emotions that accompanies caring—anger, frustration, sadness, love, guilt, resentment, fear—according to these feeling rules, is itself stressful for caregivers (MacRae, 1998).

Emotional reciprocity may break down when an older parent's illness interferes with the usual ability to follow feeling rules (MacRae, 1998), as is often the case in the later stages of Alzheimer's disease or following a stroke. The ambiguous loss of losing a parent as he or she once was heightens ambivalent feelings as adult children care for parents who are not clearly psychologically present or absent (Boss & Kaplan, 2004). Unresolved conflict between parent and child or between siblings often surfaces, increasing the amount of emotion work as carers try to manage the conflict (MacRae, 1998). Caring for a mentally impaired relative evokes more strain among spouses and more family conflict among children (Scharlach et al., 2006), highlighting the sibling dynamics of negotiating parental care (see Chapter 13).

The emotion work that is fundamental to family caring is also the basis for assigning meaning and for defining rewards as well as costs as part of this experience. Although mother-daughter dyads—including those in which daughters provide care—involve more ambivalent feelings (Willson et al, 2003), caring by the daughter is also the basis for growing tolerance and acceptance of one another (Sheehan & Donorfio, 1999). The additional time together is an opportunity to know one another better and put conflicts aside. Similarly, among sons, the opportunity to repay parents for past support, a sense of purpose and personal growth, and serving as good role models for their children are positive outcomes of looking after parents (Harris, 1998). The vast majority of informal caregivers, including children, view supporting an older family member as an opportunity to give back some of what has been given to them and to strengthen their relationship (Cranswick, 2003).

Gender Variations

Men and women, but women more so, experience feelings of guilt, work-life stress, and burden when combining a higher number of hours of paid work and of caring for older relatives (Pyper, 2006), all indicators of the need to attend to the needs of those who care and of those they care for. Gender, a parent's cognitive and behavioral problems, and the need for extensive care are key determinants of stress (Penning, 1998). As is evident in many studies, daughters experience more stress and strain than do sons, whether homemakers or employed outside the home (Penning, 1998; Scharlach et al., 2006; Starrels et al., 1997). As previously noted, gender differences occur among employed men and women as well; providing managerial care to older relatives, particularly orchestrating care options, creates more stress for women and more job interference for men (Rosenthal et al., 2007). Daughters experience more stress than do sons from caring for parents; they also experience more stress from not caring when parents need help (Amirkhanyan & Wolf, 2006).

Knowing the predictors of stress for men and women is at least as important to our understanding of family dynamics as knowing gender variations in the amount of stress. Both sons and daughters experience more strain as the impact of caregiving on their personal and social lives increases (Mui, 1995). For daughters only, the spillover of caregiving into work and a poor relationship with their parent are critical determinants of emotional strain. For sons, more behavioral problems on the part of the parent and having fewer other informal helpers are key predictors of emotional strain. All things being equal, men and women do not differ substantially in their experience of emotional strain (Kramer & Kipnis, 1995; Mui, 1995). But all things are not equal. Daughters tend to have fewer resources, to provide more intensive support, and to experience more interference with work, all factors that contribute to stress (Merrill, 1997).

Another gender contrast is that parents who are cared for by sons tend to reciprocate by offering assistance more often than parents who are cared for by daughters, possibly because help from daughters is accepted as appropriate (Starrels et al., 1997). Such assistance lowers stress, so once again, sons may enjoy less stressful conditions when caring for a parent. These various gender differences must be placed within the broader social context of structured social relations (Connidis & McMullin, 2002a). On balance, the social construction of gender in the family and workplace creates different caregiving conditions for men and women, leading to greater stress on women that is not an inherent feature of being a man or woman. The fact that caring is considered normative for women does not remove the feeling of ambivalence that results from meeting this obligation (Aronson, 1992).

The Relevance of Race

Some studies find lower levels of stress, burden and depression among non-White caregivers (Connell & Gibson, 1997), whereas others report similar levels of stress (Aranda & Knight, 1997; Bowman et al., 1998; Young & Kahana, 1995). However, the causes of stress may differ by race, reflecting different life circumstances (Aranda & Knight, 1997). For example, among Whites but not African Americans, children suffer more strain than do other relatives when providing care (Bowman et al., 1998). Conversely, being married tends to reduce caregiver strain for Black but not White caregivers. The different impact of these factors may be an outcome of variations in family structures and arrangements, which reflect structured relations based on race.

Impact on Parents

How do older parents feel about being helped and cared for by their children? Emotional support is generally well received by parents and leaves them more satisfied; advice from children has the opposite effect (Lang & Schütze, 2002). The loss of independence can be traumatic for older persons. When care is necessary, receiving it from children may be a desirable option for parents, but having children care for them also takes a psychological toll. Depression is higher among both mothers and fathers who receive support from children than among parents who do not (Dunham, 1995), but marital status and level of care tend to mediate this relationship (Silverstein et al., 1996). Unmarried parents benefit psychologically from receiving support until it moves from moderate to high levels, when children's caring lowers their well-being. Among co-resident parents, when the older mother or father contributes to the family, thereby increasing a sense of personal control, psychological well-being is enhanced (Pruchno et al., 1997b).

There are times when children simply cannot offer the support needed to sustain parents' independence in the community. Institutionalizing an elderly parent can be a very difficult decision and transition period for the parent and child and is usually only entertained after other alternatives have been tried, including co-residence. Once in institutional settings, continued interaction with family is common among those with children, but the degree and type of contact varies (Ball et al., 2005; Keefe & Fancey, 2000). Family members, including children, act as advocates, oversee the care provided in the long-term care facility, are on call if needed, and, less often, develop friendly and supportive relationships with the staff (Keefe & Fancey, 2000). Staying involved with parents through more frequent visits improves children's satisfaction with the care offered by nursing homes (Tornatore & Grant, 2004). A parent's move to a nursing home may actually increase involvement when the selected nursing home is closer to a child than was the parent's previous private home, as was the case for this daughter:

> I would say I try to get here at least six out of seven days a week, unless I am sick. . . . I usually stay, it varies a lot, it could be just a couple of hours, it could be four or five hours. It depends on how my mother is doing. . . . Really most of what I do is just to be here, just kind of support. If she is trying to do something, I will try to help her do it. (Ball et al., 2005:147)

Many of us will not see a day when our parents move to an institutional setting. For most of our lifetimes, the more familiar experience in our relationships with parents will be receiving help from them, not giving it to them.

Parental Support to Adult Children

> *You know, when I first got my little boy, I wanted to live to bring him up, and here I am at 85 still worrying about him.*
>
> —85-year-old widow

When children experience problems or are unable to be truly independent, the potentially active role of parenting in older age is evident. Older parents continue to be a source of advice and often serve as the first personal example of later-life transitions, such as retirement or widowhood. The intergenerational equity debate (see Chapter 14) has spawned greater attention to the various ways in which older parents continue to assist their children, a topic generally neglected in the focus on caregiving. Most older parents remain not only independent but also significant contributors to their children's lives, ranging from emotional support to providing a home. Exchanges of instrumental aid between parents and children either favor children or remain balanced until parents are aged 70 years or more; aid to children drops off markedly after the age of 75 (Stone et al., 1998).

Financial aid between the generations in the form of private wealth transfers strongly favor adult children over older parents (Stone et al., 1998). Add to this transfers through inheritance, and the imbalance is increased manifold (Marshall, 1997). This pattern of giving is established in middle age, when parents are more inclined to provide financial support to their children than to their parents (Wong et al., 1999). Within families, children who are less well-off are more likely to receive financial help from their parents and to receive more of it than their more solvent siblings (McGarry & Schoeni, 1997). Among White, African and Hispanic Americans, Hispanics are most committed to the view that older parents should provide financial assistance to their children (Burr & Mutchler, 1999). An older mothers' help to children, like adult children's help to parents, is influenced by gender, need and reciprocity. Mothers generally give more support to daughters than to sons (Davey et al., 2005), and within families, mothers are more likely to help daughters and children who are unmarried, live near by, have health problems, and have provided help in the past (Suitor et al., 2006).

The tendency to provide help to children based on need means that older parents serve as effective troubleshooters and committed sources of support for their children. This is particularly evident in two situations that highlight the extent to which parents help when required: caring for children who have AIDS and caring for children with long-term disabilities. These are not typical situations for older parents, but they stand as testament to the operation of revocable detachment (see Chapter 1) by which family members honor one another's independence but are ready to provide extensive support if and when it is needed. A third form of support, co-residence, is discussed separately. The contributions that older persons make to their children's lives through their involvement with grandchildren are discussed in Chapter 10.

Supporting Children With AIDS

The spread of AIDS among young and middle-aged adults has created a tragic situation for older parents who must confront their child's illness and often death during the prime of life (Mullan, 1998). For many persons with AIDS, an older mother serves as a critical source of emotional support and when needed, hands-on caring. This is particularly true among homosexual and bisexual African American men who are less likely to be members of gay support networks than their White counterparts (Brown & Sankar, 1998). Similarly, African American women turn for help to their families of origin first and then to their partners. Generally, Hispanic men rely more on their families, whereas White men rely more on extrafamilial ties for support.

Among older mothers of children with AIDS, initial awareness of their child's illness tends to be met with the strong emotions of grief, sadness, shock and fear, coupled with the practical response of seeking information (Thompson, 2000). Despite some older mothers' discomfort with the link between AIDS and being gay (see also Brennan & Moore, 1994), mothers tend to focus on their child's illness rather than his or her sexual orientation. One mother comments,

I try . . . to think of . . . first of all, "What can I do to help?" and that's a mother's instinct, you know, "How can I help?" And "How can I be more understanding of it?," and that's been hard for me to understand—I want to understand more about the disease, and I don't want to know too much more about the lifestyle. (Thompson, 2000:161)

Many mothers whose children are either gay or intravenous drug users fully accept their children and do not assign any blame to them for contracting HIV. But they may have to manage the conflict with spouses or other children that this acceptance creates.

Supporting Children With Special Needs

A particularly demanding case of ongoing support occurs when children have long-term disabilities or illness. Caring for children with developmental disabilities represents a good example of this phenomenon. The demands of caring for these children as youngsters may be typical of all children, and parents often receive support from their parents, as illustrated in Photo 8.1. In stark contrast to the situation of adult children caring for their parents, caring for a child with a long-term disability is often a lifelong responsibility for parents. Increases in survival at birth and in longevity heighten a parent's chances of looking after a child with a developmental disability into old age (Fullmer et al., 1997). Policy shifts that encourage community living, in part to reduce the costs of providing services, increase the pressure on families to provide long-term care for those who are mentally ill and developmentally challenged (Greenberg et al., 1993).

The vast majority of caregivers to such adults are parents, and the vast majority of adults with developmental disabilities or mental illness live with their parents (Greenberg et al., 1993). This is a source of major concern among aging parents who experience ambivalence about their child's present and future living arrangements when there is disagreement among family members about where the child should

Photo 8.1   Having a child with special needs typically means a lifelong commitment to caring by parents, including living together.

live, when there is great emotional pain about an undesirable future for the child, or when they cannot choose between undesirable alternatives (Rietschlin, 2000). Their longer life expectancy makes it more likely that older mothers will carry out this responsibility alone at a time in life when their own needs for support may be increasing. Nonetheless, parents remain committed caregivers to their dependent children, sometimes to the point of remaining silent about abuse at their hands for fear that their children will have nowhere else to live if the abuse is discovered (Pillemer, 1985; re elder mistreatment, see Chapter 14). The course of caring for adult children with intellectual disabilities involves "a cycle of stresses and rewards, demands and invisible contributions" (Grant, 2007:19), as parents discreetly protect their child's integrity and their family's privacy. The stresses and rewards extend beyond the caregiving dyad or triad to other family members, especially other children.

Older parents caring for adult children with disabilities receive little outside assistance (Roeher Institute, 1996). Even when such support is available, several factors inhibit its use by older mothers. The child's condition is one factor. Although most adult children with developmental disabilities who live with their mothers are in day programs or employed, this is true for less than half of co-resident children with mental illness (Greenberg et al., 1993). The child's condition also creates different care demands. Children with developmental disabilities receive a broader range of direct care from their mothers than do children who are mentally ill (Greenberg et al., 1993; Pruchno et al., 1996). Mothers report better relationships with their children when their child has developmental disabilities rather than mental illness, in part because children who are mentally ill exhibit more behavioral problems.

A child's gender is also influential. Mothers of daughters with developmental disabilities are more vigilant caregivers and experience more subjective burden as a consequence of looking after them than do mothers of sons (Fullmer et al., 1997). One reason for this is that mothers of daughters are less likely to use day programs because they worry about their daughters being sexually exploited. Yet mothers of children who are mentally ill or developmentally challenged report better relationships with their daughters than sons (Greenberg et al., 1993).

One family member's situation has repercussions for all family members. The majority of mothers report receiving substantial help from other children in meeting the needs of their child (Fullmer et al., 1997). Mothers with a smaller support group experience more caregiver burden from looking after children with developmental disabilities or mental illness (Greenberg et al., 1993). Ironically, given their greater need, increasing age and disability among mothers of adult children with developmental disabilities make it less likely that their children are in day programs (Fullmer et al., 1997). Mothers who do not use this service also are less inclined to use respite care or to make future plans for their children in the event that they can no longer look after them (Fullmer et al., 1997).

The Subjective Impact of Caring

Generally, providing support to children does not have negative consequences for parents' well-being. Indeed, among widowed and divorced parents, helping children may actually reduce depression (Silverstein et al., 1996). However, there are times when the needs of adult children can be intense and take their toll. The well-being of parents suffers when their children have problems related to mental or physical health, alcohol or drug abuse, financial or marital problems, or stress (Greenfield & Marks, 2006; Pillemer & Suitor, 1991). Older African American mothers experience psychological distress if a son is incarcerated, especially when it leads to financial hardship and looking after grandchildren (Green et al., 2006). Married parents in this situation have poorer relationships with their children; single and unmarried parents feel less positive (Greenfield & Marks, 2006). When compared with parents who enjoy close ties, both mothers and fathers with distant ties to their children are significantly less happy, and fathers are also less satisfied with life (Connidis & McMullin, 1993; Koropeckyj-Cox, 1999).

Clearly, the concept of linked lives continues to apply to parent-child relations across the life course. There are qualitative benefits and costs to being parents in later life and no guarantees that having children will bring happiness at this stage of life. At the same time, parents derive rewards from successfully meeting commitments to their children. Even in the case of caring for a child with a long-term disability or illness, parents experience the gratification that stems from meeting the challenge and making life better for their children (Greenberg et al., 1993).

Co-Residence of Adult Children and Their Parents

The co-residence of parents and adult children may reflect at least four situations: parents and children who have always lived together; parents who are the receivers of help; children who are the receivers of support; and parents and children engaged in mutual support (Choi, 2003). We consider first the situation of older parents living with their adult children and then of adult children living with their parents.

Parents Living With Children

In 2000, 15% of Whites and 22% of African Americans aged 65 years or more lived with an adult child (Ruggles, 2007). From the ages of 60 to 75 years, the likelihood of living with a child decreases, but beyond the age of 75 for women and 80 for men, the chances of living together increase (Schmertmann et al., 2000). An older parent's declining health, loss of a former caregiver or partner, desire for companionship, and lower income are the key reasons for moving into the home of a child (Brody et al., 1995; Wilmoth, 2000). Widowed mothers are more likely to live with a child than are women of other marital statuses, although they prefer not to live with their children in order to protect their relationship with them and to avoid isolation if living with a child means moving to another community (Kestin van den Hoonaard, 2001). They are happy when their children offer them this option, but a decision to co-reside is likely to coincide with other changing circumstances rather than widowhood alone. Counter to popular belief, having a widowed mother move in is more likely to improve than depress the economic well-being of the household, especially among non-Whites (Waehrer & Crystal, 1995).

The marital status of daughters also alters the co-resident care situation (Brody et al., 1995). Married and widowed women more commonly have their mothers move in with them, whereas divorced and separated daughters more often move in with their mothers. For a daughter, a mother's declining ability to cope independently is the primary motivation for co-residence. Because of its association with poorer health, co-residency typically means more intensive caregiving by the adult child (Boaz et al., 1999; Call et al., 1999). Co-resident older parents receive parallel levels of help from daughters and daughters-in-law, despite the fact that daughters feel closer to their parents than daughters-in-law do to their parents-in-law (Peters-Davis et al., 1999). Sons and sons-in-law provide considerably less help than their spouses, but only sons feel guilty about not giving more help (Peters-Davis et al., 1999).

Co-residence is more likely among Asian, Mexican, other Hispanic and Black than among White older persons (Brown & Sankar, 1998; Burr & Mutchler, 1999; Glick & Hook, 2002). This reflects in part a stronger normative commitment among older Hispanic and African Americans, along with Cambodian Americans (Becker et al., 2003), to living together as an appropriate filial obligation (Burr & Mutchler, 1999; Lee, Peek et al., 1998; Zajicek et al., 2006). Such apparent cultural influences may be transitory in the case of Asian and Central and South American families where co-residence is high because older parents are relatively recent immigrants and economically dependent upon their children (Glick & Hook, 2002). The cultural imperative to care held by old parents who are recent arrivals may conflict with the American way of life adopted by their daughters, including labor force participation (Olson, 2003). The more common experience of multigenerational households among Black than White older parents (Belgrave & Bradsher, 1994) relates to variations in marital status, with older and younger Whites more likely to be married (Aquilino, 1990).

Some argue that a stronger sense of responsibility to family among non-Whites is a coping mechanism for dealing with poverty, poor health and discrimination (Burr & Mutchler, 1999). However, strong filial norms and multigenerational households cannot counteract the relative disadvantages faced by older Black parents, including poorer functional ability (see Waite & Hughes, 1999). Instead, these features of family life must be linked to the structurally created inequality that makes them necessary. Comparisons of Mexican and European Americans show that differences in co-residence derive largely from class differences that favor European Americans and lower their likelihood of living with children (Sarkisian et al., 2007). Although research can make attempts to control for the factors that help account for observed differences by race—income, health, living conditions, education, marital status—in real life, these factors operate simultaneously.

Childhood experiences may also influence whether an older parent shares a child's home (Szinovacz, 1997). When compared with children who lived with both parents when they were growing up, those who grew up with remarried fathers are less likely to live with them later. By contrast, children growing up with mothers who were single or remarried makes later co-residence more likely. For sons only, growing up with a single father makes it more likely that they will live together once the son is an adult. Multigenerational living arrangements while a child or young adult create more favorable attitudes toward sharing a home with either an older parent or adult child (Goldscheider & Lawton, 1998).

When parents live with their children, satisfaction with living together is higher for both parent and child when there is greater balance in their relationship (Brackbill & Kitch, 1991). In turn, greater dependence of the parent increases the risk of ending co-residency. Daughters with co-residing parents are especially subject to strain and are more overloaded, more resentful about providing care, and less satisfied than daughters whose parent lives elsewhere (Murphy et al., 1997). Similarly, when economic hardship or poor health leads mothers-in-law to live with their daughters-in-law, their relationship appears to worsen regardless of its quality prior to co-residence (Merrill, 2007).

Children Living With Parents

Growing proportions of adult children live with their parents, either because they delay leaving home, the more common reason, or because they refill the empty nest by returning home after leaving, the so-called boomerang kids. Starting with the Depression-era generation, through to the baby boomers, and then to Generation X, each new wave has taken longer to leave home and is more likely to return (Beaupré et al, 2006a, 2006b). The one exception was the post-World War II era of the 1940s and 1950s, when adult children were leaving home at younger ages, largely because more of them were marrying at younger ages (Mitchell, 2006). This unusual experience of the parents of the baby boom is often treated as the benchmark, making current realities appear more dramatic than they are when put into longer historical perspective.

High unemployment rates and higher education are the key reasons for the delay in leaving home (Cherlin et al., 1997). Intergenerational effects occur as well: parents who themselves left home for good at younger ages tend to see their children follow suit (Turcotte, 2006). Children who take longer to leave home are primarily the offspring of middle-aged parents. In the United States, 20% of men aged 25 to 29 years and 12% of women in this age group have yet to leave their parents' homes (Goldscheider, 1997). Among 18- to 24-year-olds, 50% of men and 43% of women live with parents ("Baby Boomers," 2008), reflecting the greater likelihood of sons to live with their parents. In Canada, almost a third (32%) of parents whose youngest child is between 20 and 34 years old has at least one child living with them, and almost one quarter (24%) has at least one boomerang child (Statistics Canada, 2006).

Children who return home are more likely to be sharing the home of somewhat older parents. Among parents aged 65 years or more, close to 1 in 7 have a child living with them (White & Rogers, 1997). Key reasons for return are to save money, financial setbacks, to finish school, to return to school, unemployment, or a relationship ending (Beaupré et al., 2006a; Mitchell, 2000, 2006). Generally, having an unmarried child, especially one who never married, makes a child living with an older parent more likely; about half of parents who are 65 years or more have such a child, and one-quarter of them have a co-resident child (Aquilino, 1990; White & Rogers, 1997). These marital-status differences help account for the higher probability of older Black persons, including women, to be head of multigenerational households than to be dependent old parents (Becker et al., 2003; Olson, 2003). In Canada, parents born in Asia or South or Central America more often have children return home (Turcotte, 2006). Once again, race and immigration play out in different patterns of co-residence.

Somewhat surprisingly, qualitative aspects of the parent-child relationship (Ward & Spitze, 2007) and of the parents' marriage do not alter the probability of adult children living with their parents, although the continuous marriage of parents does (Beaupré et al., 2006a; White & Rogers, 1997). Mothers engaged in paid work are less likely to have their children delay leaving home or to return once they have left (Beaupré et al., 2006a). Parents in rural areas are also less likely than those in urban areas (where costs are higher) to have their children return home. On balance, the factors that account for either a delay in leaving or a return to the parental home reflect the adult child's need for support.

Although intergenerational exchanges occur when children return to their parents' homes, parents and children agree that parents give more support to their children than their children give to them (Mitchell, 2000), and mothers in particular may experience a return of the second shift (Beaupré et al., 2006b; Turcotte, 2006). This may explain why returning home is more likely when the mother is not in the labor force. The modest contributions by children to housework and finances when living with parents are similar for sons and daughters, who both view living with their parents positively (Ward & Spitze, 1996). Even though children who live with their parents tend to receive more support than they give, when compared with nonresident children, they exchange more support with their parents (White & Rogers, 1997). Co-residing does not affect the quality of parent-child relations (Ward & Spitze, 2007), but when compared with non-resident children, co-resident children trust their mothers less, and they believe that their mothers show them less respect and fairness (White & Rogers, 1997). Co-residing also increases disagreements between parents and their adult children (Ward & Spitze, 2007). Older and employed children find living with their parents a more positive experience than their younger and unemployed counterparts (White & Rogers, 1997). These findings indicate ambivalence in sharing a home, with coexisting strain and emotional attachment, between older parents and their adult children.

Parents who have children living with them are generally satisfied with this arrangement (Aquilino & Supple, 1991; Mitchell, 2000). When parents who share their homes with adult children are compared with parents who do not, they are more likely to feel frustrated by their children but generally do not feel this way, are equally likely to be happy to have children, and are more satisfied with the amount of time that they spend together (Turcotte, 2006). Research in the UK (Evandrou & Glaser, 2004) suggests, however, that living with children who have health problems or are dependent, unemployed, divorced or widowed has negative consequences for parents' health and for involvement in social activities.

Nearly 75% of mothers and 50% of fathers list the companionship and friendship of their children as a key benefit of having a child living at home (Mitchell, 2000). Associated costs for mothers are lack of privacy and independence, the child's failure to help out with household tasks, and the child's lifestyle and dependence. For fathers, key detriments of co-residence are lack of privacy and independence, the child's personality or attitude, and the child's lifestyle. Thus although most parents who have children living at home believe that the arrangement is working out very well, there can be tensions in the arrangement.

Summary

Older parents and their adult children maintain active ties with one another. The meaning of parenthood shifts in old age as parents feel less responsibility for their children. A child's well-being continues to be a central source of concern to older parents, however, and should their children be in need, older parents provide extensive support. In turn, as their parents age, adult children typically provide more help as needed. Most old persons maintain relatively independent lifestyles for most if not all of their lives. Consequently, the picture of the sandwiched generation, caught between the demands of two dependent generations, applies to a relatively small proportion of adult children.

Gender pervades intergenerational ties between older persons and their children, qualitatively and in terms of support exchanges and as reflected in work-life balance and the emotional impact of caring. This does not mean that one gender has better ties to parents than the other, rather that they are different. More recent work points out some of the advantages of sons' support to parents, correcting the bias implicit in the assumption that the type of support provided by daughters is best for parents. At the same time, women continue to carry more of the responsibility for domestic labor, and families that care for elders are often working at capacity, making it very difficult to manage the crises that are a regular feature of ongoing caregiving (Sims-Gould, Martin-Matthews, & Gignac, 2008).

As children age and have growing responsibilities to other family members or to work, parents are less central to their lives than they once were. At the same time, although children are a significant component of older parents' lives, they are not typically the hub of their lives, and having children does not guarantee their happiness. Nonetheless, older parents and their children are critical sources of support to one another, and should old age bring dependency, children serve as reliable sources of emotional and instrumental aid to their parents, often at considerable expense to their present and future well-being, especially among women. Commitment to filial responsibility remains strong.

Gender, race, and class relations affect how the age relations of parent-child ties and support are negotiated. The ambivalence created by the socially created contradictions of balancing work and family, particularly for women who continue to remain heavily involved in care work even when in the labor force, for those with fewer resources, and for men who assume major responsibility for caring, calls for resolution through social change. Resiliency in the face of a challenging situation does not negate the need for a better policy response to the growing number of families who struggle to meet contradictory demands (see Chapter 14).

Shifting patterns of support between generations over time reflect the evolving convoy of the life course. We also saw alternative ways of negotiating similar relationships, depending upon marital status (see also Chapters 6, 12 and 13).

CHAPTER 9

Childless Older Persons

Trends in Childlessness

If children are as important to the lives of older parents as they appear to be, what then of older persons who have never had children? In this chapter, the term *childless* refers to never having any children, but some distinguish between childfree and childless to make the point that some see not having children positively and others negatively. None of these labels captures those who think of themselves simply as people who did not have children (Moir, 2006). Despite the shared pressures of a pronatalist culture experienced by today's older persons, cohort variations among them during their younger years resulted in different rates of childlessness. A high rate of remaining childless (25%) occurred among women who were of childbearing age during the Depression (Heaton et al., 1999; Rowland, 2007). Some years later, rates of childlessness were unusually low (10%) among women in the cohort that bore the baby boom. Thus among the current elderly, there is considerable variation in whether being childless was chosen, either freely or by force of circumstance. The relatively small percentage of persons who remained childless while the baby boom was born suggests that childlessness was mainly involuntary for this cohort.

As we saw in Chapter 2, rates of childlessness are up substantially since the birth of the baby boom. In the early years of this century, about 1 in 5 women aged 35 to 44 were childless, and more of them are voluntarily than involuntarily so (Abma & Martinez, 2006). Previously, women who had not had children by their mid 30s were often assumed to be permanently childless. Now, however, more women are having their first children at substantially older ages, due often to advances in reproductive technology (Friese et al., 2008). These numbers are not enough to offset higher rates of childlessness in younger cohorts, but they caution us that delayed childbearing has an extended deadline. Indeed, among childless women aged 35 to 44 years in 2002, 30% considered themselves temporarily so and another 42% were voluntarily childless, a status that can be subject to change (Abma & Martinez, 2006).

The experiences of today's old childless women provide a partial glimpse into the future for the rising number of younger women who do not have children, remembering that social and historical contexts vary by cohort. Better birth control and changing gender relations promoted by successive waves of feminism give women both more control over fertility and more options to marriage and motherhood, altering the acceptability of choosing to be childless and the parameters for adapting to childlessness (Cain, 2001; Trimberger, 2005). Among men and women currently of childbearing ages, women are more likely to view being childless positively, a gender gap that grows with more education (Koropeckyj-Cox & Pendell, 2007). Greater numbers of voluntarily childfree women are part of the general move toward nonreproductive sexual relations that helps to replace the focus on women with one on gender. This shift simultaneously disassociates women from procreation and babies and associates women with men, women with women, and men with men—we move away from relations of mother and child and toward gender relations (Mitchell, 2007).

The Transition to Childlessness

> *When I was three, I decided not to have children. . . . As it turns out, my choice not to have children has defined my adult life. It's been like hacking through undergrowth while walking down a hardly used, perfectly paved way. . . . In fact, on that path my choice not to be a mother became more of a discovery of a decision. . . . I had to make the choice from so far down in my own core that I was never wholly aware of it. . . . For this is a decision you do not make once, but many times. I would leave the idea of not having children behind, only to face it again and again as I went on.*
>
> —Molly Peacock (1998:1, 9)

Molly Peacock's (1998) memoirs provide a vivid example of childlessness as a transition rather than a discrete event. Indeed, even those who choose parenthood but cannot have children become childless over time (Matthews & Martin Matthews, 1986). Among today's older persons, there are three primary routes to becoming childless: never marrying, involuntary childlessness in a marriage, and voluntary childlessness in a marriage. For the vast majority of today's older persons, staying single meant having no children. Thus these individuals went through two transitions, one to being single (see Chapter 5) and one to childlessness. For many involuntarily childless couples, considerable time and emotion are invested in becoming parents before becoming childless; as options for parenthood diminish, one begins to view oneself as permanently rather than temporarily childless. In recent decades, involuntary childlessness has declined as health and treatments for sexually transmitted diseases have improved (Heaton et al., 1999).

Perceptions of childlessness during childbearing ages involve dimensions of later life in two ways: the assumed pleasure of grandparenthood for their parents and the anticipated merits of having children to provide care in old age (Seccombe, 1991). These tacit benefits of having children are offset by the perceived costs of parenting, including immediate financial costs, and longer-term opportunity costs related to leisure time and the careers of one or both partners. The assumed long-term advantages of having children reflect strongly held cultural beliefs about filial responsibility and the pleasures of grandparenthood that have been highly resistant to changing social conditions.

Although childless persons may still believe that they are negatively stereotyped by their family and friends (Somers, 1993), the longstanding stigma associated with being childless is softening. This is evident in the rising numbers who choose to be childless, with a persistently greater preference for this status among Whites than Blacks (Heaton et al., 1999). As well, current terms to describe childlessness, most notably *childfree* and *childless by choice,* were introduced to capture the more positive side of being without children. Cohabitation rather than marriage may increase the number of couples who do not have children, as marriage is a stronger predisposing factor to having children than is cohabitation. Childlessness, however, can no longer be assumed among the single. A lower-key view of becoming a parent is also suggested by the decreasing stability of decisions about whether to have children, with some of childbearing age switching from a preference for childlessness to either wanting or having children and others drifting into childlessness through perpetual delay (Heaton et al., 1999). Nonetheless, being childless remains an atypical experience for most couples.

Childless old people made the transition to childlessness at a time when the pressure on married persons to have children was very strong, the stigma of not doing so very high, and when far fewer reproductive interventions were available. Adoption was the primary alternative to conceiving a child as the route to parenthood. The extension of biological reproductive technologies means not only the possibility of motherhood at a later stage in the life course (Friese et al., 2008) but also, for those who try to have biological children and do not succeed, a longer transition to defining oneself as forever childless. Involuntary childlessness due to infertility heightens distress among women (McQuillan et al., 2003). Thus, investing lengthier stretches of their adult lives in attempts to become biological parents before concluding that it is not going to happen may complicate negotiating a positive identity as childfree in the future.

Reasons for Being Childless

The high level of childlessness among women born in the early 1900s was due mainly to delaying children for too long while waiting for better economic or more peaceful times, the absence or injury of a spouse, or not remarrying following early widowhood in wartime (Rowland, 2007). The prosperous times post World War II reversed this trend. For all cohorts and in keeping with the life course perspective, delays in leaving home, getting married, and having children increase the prospects of remaining childless (Hagestad & Call, 2007).

Typically, childlessness is treated as involuntary, primarily due to infertility, or voluntary, in which case an individual or couple has chosen not to have children. In fact, however, when asked, older childless persons give a much broader range of reasons for being childless, and their assessment of whether their reasons constitute a choice or circumstance does not always fit the conventional dichotomy of voluntary versus involuntary childlessness (Connidis & McMullin, 1996; Jeffries & Konnert, 2002). Among childless persons aged 55 years or more, 28% define themselves as childless by choice and 72% as childless by circumstance. Widowed women are more likely than all other combinations of gender and marital status to consider childlessness an outcome of circumstances. Conversely, single and divorced women and single and widowed men are most likely to see being childless as a choice. Only those who give physiological reasons for childlessness, the most common response among the ever married, uniformly define themselves as childless by circumstance.

How do specific reasons for being childless compare for those of different marital statuses, and for those who view themselves as childless by choice versus circumstance? Among single persons, about 70% give being single as their reason for not having children; one-quarter of this group sees childlessness as a choice (Connidis & McMullin, 1996). The other single persons who see their situation as a choice view having no children as due to fate, altruism (e.g., not wanting to have children in an overcrowded world), and self-actualization (e.g., wanting to be free to travel). Among single persons who consider being childless a matter of circumstance, being single and altruism are the key reasons for being childless. Among the ever married who chose to be childless, key reasons for their choice include age, their spouse's preferences, and altruism or practical concerns. Those ever married who consider childlessness a consequence of circumstances focus on physiological problems, age and fate (Connidis & McMullin, 1996). Among both single and ever-married childless people, there is overlap in the reasons given for being childless either by choice or by circumstance, indicating the difficulty of assuming that a particular reason for not having children is uniformly an issue of voluntary or involuntary childlessness.

The Impact of Being Childless on Social Activity and Support in Later Life

Being childless has unique implications for the lives of middle-aged and old persons, but the power of marital status (see Chapter 3) and gender relations (see Chapter 1) shapes its impact. Childless couples tend to have higher educations and incomes than couples with children, and childless women tend to be better educated, better off financially, and are more likely to be in the labor force and committed to paid work than mothers (Dykstra & Hagestad, 2007; Dykstra & Wagner, 2007; Koropeckyj-Cox & Call, 2007). Married childless persons of younger and older ages have particularly strong marital ties and rely extensively on one another rather than on an extended network of family and friends (Ishii-Kuntz & Seccombe, 1989; Somers, 1993; on childless men, Connidis & Davies, 1990; Wenger et al., 2007). The restricted support network that results from this focus on the marital dyad leaves either a surviving spouse or the couple vulnerable, if they are both frail (Wenger et al., 2000). In contrast, single childless women tend to be resourceful in negotiating effective and active social support networks over the years, a result of their greater involvement in the broader community, including paid work (Wenger et al., 2000; Wenger et al., 2007). Childless single men tend to rely heavily on the support of a small network, often a sister.

Parents have more friends and family, more contact with family, and receive more help and support than do the childless (Wenger et al., 2007). Yet 90% of older, unmarried, childless Canadians have support available to them from family, friends, or most commonly, family and friends (Wu & Pollard, 1998), and older parents and childless persons are equally likely to report having someone to confide in and to provide assistance, financial aid, emotional support and companionship (Connidis & McMullin, 1994). One difference between them is that childless women aged 55 and over are less likely than mothers to have someone who makes them feel needed and appreciated. Important exceptions among the childless are the very old and those who become frail; they are less likely to have someone to take care of them when needed and more likely to require formal institutional care than are parents (Dykstra & Hagestad, 2007; Johnson & Barer, 1995; Koropeckyj-Cox & Call, 2007; Wenger et al., 2007). Living alone in old age is especially likely for old childless women, increasing their likelihood of entering residential care (Wenger et al., 2000).

Older childless persons and parents share equal levels of involvement in going to public places and traveling and in voluntary organizations and volunteer work, but the childless go on outings more often than do parents (Connidis & McMullin 1992; Wenger et al., 2007). Childless persons are also more likely to find companionship and be in greater contact with other relatives, including siblings, nieces and nephews, than are parents. Childless men and women are more likely than parents to find companionship in their friends (Connidis & McMullin, 1992), and childless women have more frequent contact with their friends than do mothers (Wenger et al., 2007). Generally, childless persons negotiate social participation networks that enhance taking part in activities outside the home.

Friends comprise a larger complement of childless women's confidant and companion networks, and siblings are more dominant in their confidant network than is true for either childless men or mothers (Connidis & Davies, 1990). The companion networks of childless men rely more heavily on friends, whereas their confidant networks favor other relatives to a greater extent than the networks of fathers. As well, sibling pairs in which at least one sibling is childless talk on the phone and discuss important matters more often than do parents (Connidis, 1989a).

The Impact of Being Childless on Quality of Life in Older Age

When asked about whether there are advantages or disadvantages to being childless, nearly three-quarters of 267 older childless men and women said that there are advantages, whereas two-thirds said that there are disadvantages (Connidis & McMullin, 1999). Close to half, 45%, reported both advantages and disadvantages, 25% said that there are only advantages, and 20% see only disadvantages to being childless. These responses suggest a fairly balanced view of being childless that might be mirrored if similar questions were asked of parents about the merits of having children.

Although there are no variations in the probability of seeing disadvantages to childlessness, childless persons who are widowed are less likely than married individuals to report advantages (Connidis & McMullin, 1999). Perhaps, the fact that the single and divorced typically spent more of their younger lives alone than did the widowed created a better opportunity for them to negotiate other ties, whereas the widowed were investing in their marriage. The other significant difference is the higher odds of the childless by choice (86%) reporting advantages to being without children when compared with those who are childless by circumstance (67%). Women who consider themselves voluntarily childless also enjoy higher levels of psychological well-being than women who define their childless status as involuntary (Jeffries & Konnert, 2002).

What are the perceived advantages and disadvantages of childlessness in later life? The top three advantages are fewer worries and problems, financial wealth, and greater freedom. The top-rated disadvantages are lack of companionship, being alone, and loneliness; a feeling of a missed experience or incompleteness; and lack of support and care (Connidis & McMullin, 1999; for similar results re women, see Alexander et al., 1992). The perception of financial advantage is supported by actual experience among those who hold this view; they are indeed better off than those who do not. However, the actual situations of those who report greater loneliness, incompleteness and inadequate support as costs of being childfree do not differ from those who do not observe these disadvantages. They are no lonelier or less satisfied with what they have done in life, and they are as likely to have support available to them. The contrast between perceptions and actual experience, combined with the lack of variation in who reports disadvantages, "suggests that the costs of childlessness are less related to personal experience and more a function of learning widely-held cultural views supporting parenthood and the negative side of being childless" (Connidis & McMullin, 1999:462). For today's older women in particular, regrets about being childless occur in the context of failing to conform to strongly held expectations that women should have children (Alexander et al., 1992).

Despite objective differences in the number of family and friends and amount of help received, those with and without children in old age share similar levels of satisfaction, loneliness and depression (McMullin & Marshall, 1996; Zhang &

Hayward, 2001). When marital and parental status are combined, however, divorced parents are more lonely than divorced childless persons, and divorced mothers are more depressed than women who are divorced and childless (Koropeckyj-Cox, 1998). Married parents are less lonely and depressed than parents and childless persons who are widowed or divorced, but married parents are no better off than either married or never-married childless persons. Once again, the greater opportunity to cultivate other relationships enjoyed by single persons and by divorced childless persons, when compared with divorced parents, may explain why childlessness does not carry the same costs in loneliness and depression for these groups.

Gender relations create further distinctions (Zhang & Hayward, 2001). Divorced and widowed childless old men are lonelier and more depressed than women in parallel situations, and single childless men are lonelier than single childless women. As well, among unmarried men, those who are also childless are in the worst shape as indicated by levels of exercise, depression, sleep patterns and general health (Kendig et al., 2007). For old men, having a partner and an adult child are important links to the social world.

Comparisons of well-being between parents and children pay little attention to variations within the parent and childless categories. When compared with parents who have close ties with their children, those who are childless by choice are just as happy and satisfied with life (Connidis & McMullin, 1993). But those who are childless by circumstance are less satisfied with life than are close parents, childless men are less happy than close fathers, and childless women are more depressed than close mothers. Parents with distant or lower quality ties to their children do not enjoy better well-being than those who are childless (Connidis & McMullin, 1993; Koropeckyj-Cox, 2002). Mothers who have poor relationships with their children and childless women who believe having a child is better than not, are more lonely and depressed than mothers with good ties to children and childless women who do not believe that having a child is preferable (Koropeckyj-Cox, 2002). In short, neither having children nor remaining childless guarantees happiness in later life.

Summary

Having children is not essential to having a satisfying old age. Childless old persons are engaged with the social world and negotiate smaller but active social networks of family and friends. For those who wanted to have children and could not, a sense of regret about being childless may continue into later life and lower subjective well-being. But most older childless persons see advantages to their situation. Gender and marital status shape the experience of childlessness, with single old women leading particularly good lives without children (Dykstra & Hagestad, 2007). Unattached childless men do not fare as well, and childless persons who become very old or frail are more likely to have to turn to formal support than are parents.

Looking ahead, changes already in motion will alter the life course impact of not having children. As more women, with or without children, are active and long-term participants in the labor force and are increasingly positive about being childfree, the current differences between married mothers and married or single childless women are likely to diminish. At an admittedly slower pace, as more women are active players in the labor market, more men are becoming active players as involved fathers. This is likely to increase the divide between fathers and childless men as the experience of fathering deepens men's family connections. For those who want but do not have children due to infertility, heightened expectations for successful reproductive interventions may make negotiating being childless more difficult.

We have seen that siblings are active in the family networks of childless older persons. Unfortunately, we know very little about the intergenerational ties of childless persons aside from those with their older parents. What about ties with the older generation of aunts and uncles and the younger generation of nieces and nephews? Research on siblings (see Chapters 12 and 13) suggests that childless older persons are quite involved with the children of their siblings. Childless persons are subject, however, to the mediating role of their siblings in the cultivation of ties with nieces and nephews, much as grandparents must depend on their children to foster good ties with their grandchildren. Consider this link as we explore grandparent-grandchild ties in the next chapter.

CHAPTER 10

Grandparents and Grandchildren

Research on the grandparent-grandchild tie has followed a route similar to that of parent-child relationships, with its increased emphasis on caregiving. Studies on parent-child exchanges pay disproportionate attention to the help provided *to* older parents, but work on grandparent-grandchild exchanges concerns primarily the help provided *by* grandparents. A recent upsurge in studies of grandparents as caregivers is met by very few studies on the more typical grandparent-grandchild relationship that does not involve intensive caregiving. This means a corresponding emphasis on the experience of grandparenting in midlife rather than old age, when grandchildren are older and often grown up. This chapter begins with information about the availability of grandparents and contact between them and their grandchildren. I then explore the nature of grandparent-grandchild ties, the qualitative aspects of this relationship, and support exchanges. The impact of divorce and remarriage on grandparent-grandchild ties is addressed further in Chapter 11.

Availability of and Contact With Grandparents and Grandchildren

As we saw in Chapter 2, about 80% of older persons are grandparents. The higher rates of childlessness of women born in the early 1900s and of women now in their 30s and 40s create a grandbaby bust for these cohorts (Uhlenberg, 2004). Lower fertility also means more grandparents for fewer grandchildren. Parents of the baby boom are more likely to have had grandchildren through at least one child by the time they were aged 60 to 64 than cohorts before and after them. Baby boomers themselves will have fewer grandchildren, and about 1 in 5 will have no grandchildren. As well, a growing proportion of older people will have only one or two grandchild sets—grandchildren through one or two children—rather than three or four grandchild sets.

From the vantage point of grandchildren, the odds of having grandparents increased dramatically over the 20th century. Only 6% of children in 1900 had four grandparents by the age of 10; by age 30, only 1 in 5 had any surviving grandparents (Uhlenberg, 2004). In 2000, 41% of 10-year-olds had four biological grandparents, and by age 30, 3 in 4 still had at least one grandparent. Over time, having grandmothers has become even more likely, as women's life expectancy increased more dramatically than men's. Differences in life expectancy by race continue, but the negative impact of mortality on the availability of grandparents is offset somewhat by younger ages of childbearing and of becoming grandparents among non-Whites (Szinovacz, 1998).

One thing that has remained quite constant over the past 100 years is the age at which adults become grandparents; the transition to grandparenthood remains a phenomenon of middle, not old, age (Szinovacz, 1998). About half of all grandparents are under the age of 60 (Aldous, 1995). Thus for the majority, grandparenthood is not new in old age (see Photo 10.1). The grandchildren of later-life grandparents are usually teenagers or young adults, and today's grandparents, especially grand-mothers, typically live long enough to see their grandchildren grow up (Falk & Falk, 2002) and often to see them have their own children (Attias-Donfut & Segalen, 2002). Joint survival past the early childhood of grandchildren alters the conditions of relationships with grandparents because older grandchildren can engage independently in the relationship.

The age at which one becomes a grandparent also influences the nature of grand-parenting because those who do so at younger ages are more likely to be engaged in other activities, such as child rearing and paid work; those who are relatively old for this transition tend not to engage in more demanding forms of support, such as looking after their grandchildren (Aldous, 1995). Grandparents have been subject to the same social changes as all age groups. Consequently, across time and across generations

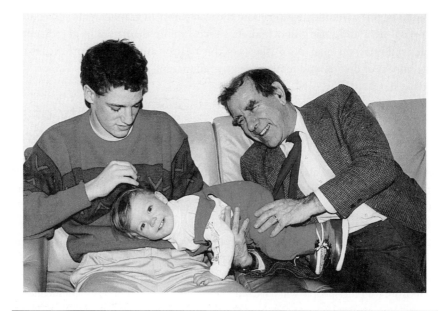

Photo 10.1 Most grandparents acquire grandchildren before they reach old age.

in a family, there are elements of continuity, as a particular family's view of grand-parenting moves from one generation to the next, and of change, as grandparent-grandchild relations respond in different ways to new conditions (Kemp, 2007).

Key changes regarding grandparent-grandchild relations are increased labor force participation among women and increased rates of divorce at all ages. Of married persons with adult children over the age of 18, 40% have a stepgrandparent in the family, more often as a consequence of divorce and remarriage for the grandparent rather than the parent generation (Szinovacz, 1998). Two countertrends potentially increase the time that grandparents have to invest in their grandchildren: retiring at younger ages and the reduced overlap of parenting and grandparenting responsibilities (Szinovacz, 1998). At the same time, more women of all ages are in the labor force, decreasing the availability of grandmothers prior to retirement, and more blended families may mean a greater mix of ages so that overlapping parenting and stepparenting and grand-parenting and stepgrandparenting become more common (see Chapter 11).

Regular contact with at least one grandchild is the norm, with over 80% of grand-parents aged 50 or more seeing an adult grandchild in the past month (AARP, 2000). Among grandparents who are not caregivers to their grandchildren, nearly half (44%) see a grandchild once a week. Telephone contact is also common. Geographic distance is a key determinant of contact; increased distance diminishes both personal and phone contact (Aldous, 1995; Hodgson, 1995; Uhlenberg & Hammill, 1998). Although geographic mobility has not changed much over the past century, a shrink-ing number of grandchild sets (i.e., the number of children through whom one has grandchildren) makes having a grandchild nearby less likely (Uhlenburg, 2004).

Baby boom granddaughters are in greater contact with their grandmothers than with their grandfathers (Mills, 1999), and grandmothers report greater contact and proximity with their grandchildren than do grandfathers (Silverstein & Long, 1998). Grandparents who have better relationships with their children, grand-mothers, and maternal grandparents all enjoy more contact with their grandchildren than do their counterparts (Uhlenberg & Hammill, 1998). Grandparents with more grandchild sets see any one family of grandchildren less often but have more over-all contact with grandchildren than those with fewer grandchild sets. Last, married grandparents see their grandchildren most often, followed, in order, by widowed, remarried, and divorced grandparents. Reflecting current gender relations, these marital-status differences are greater for grandfathers than for grandmothers, who are more likely to sustain contact whatever their marital status.

The grandchild's age is also related to contact frequency. Adult grandchildren see less of their grandparents than do younger grandchildren and less than they did when they were younger, often due to greater geographic distance between them (Mills, 1999; Silverstein & Long, 1998). Several age-related transitions affect grandparent-grandchild contact once grandchildren have grown up. Landing a job decreases contact with grandparents, whereas getting married and divorced both mean more contact with grandparents (Mills, 1999). In general, contact decreases over time, not because of emo-tional detachment but because grandchildren have other commitments, some of which lead them to live farther away (Silverstein & Long, 1998). Thus despite sentimental attachments between them, once grandparents are very old (85 and over), grandchildren are not key sources of instrumental support (Johnson & Barer, 1997).

Still, a majority of grandchildren aged 18 or more have contact with their grand-parents several times a month or more by phone, letter or in person, with greater contact among those who feel emotionally closer to their grandparents (Hodgson, 1995). The growing popularity of e-mail enhances communication with all family members, especially younger generations; e-mail communication between grand-parents and grandchildren is quite frequent and is related to satisfying and close relationships (Soliz et al., 2006).

The Nature of Grandparent-Grandchild Relations

The nature of grandparent-grandchild relations has shifted toward an emotional bond as grandparents have become more autonomous (Uhlenberg, 2004). We must consider the impact on grandparent-grandchild relations of period effects, the consequences of historical and social experience for a particular cohort. Stereotypical views of grand-parents have not caught up with the realities of those born in the 1940s and 1950s who are now becoming grandparents (Attias-Donfut & Segalen, 2002). Their lifetime expe-rience includes more women with access to paid work, contraception and abortion; a greater variety of conjugal relationships; more liberal parenting; and prosperous times.

Norms of noninterference by grandparents and of respect by adult grandchildren dominate expectations of their relationship (Kemp, 2004). Both generations charac-terize their tie as loving and supportive, with an emphasis on assistance flowing from grandparents at the request of their grandchildren. When compared with ties between parents and children, there is greater freedom and choice about how they will be involved with one another (Kemp, 2004; Rossi and Rossi, 1990). The flexible expectations of grandparenthood and a stronger sense of what is not acceptable than of what is expected may create ambiguity, tension and ambivalence. Qualitative analysis of grandparent-adult grandchild relations concludes that current age rela-tions give more agency and power to adult grandchildren, creating intergenerational ambivalence as grandparents avoid interfering and adult grandchildren exercise respect while asserting their independence and right to be left alone (Kemp, 2004).

Tension and conflicts in family relations may also be triggered by different views between grandparents and their children about how grandchildren should be raised and by potential rivalry between paternal and maternal lineages, grandparents on the father's versus the mother's side (Attias-Donfut & Segalen, 2002). Yet most research on grandparent-grandchild relations deals either with the pleasant and rel-atively benign side of this relationship or with the atypical but intense relationships of grandparents who care for grandchildren.

Age of Grandchildren and Parents as Mediators

Much of the research on grandparent-grandchild relations concerns relationships between younger grandparents and grandchildren and focuses on a target grandchild rather than the entire network of grandchildren. Findings from such studies are therefore limited in what they tell us about older grandparent-grandchild relations, although earlier patterns are likely to shape what these relationships become and how members of each generation differentiate among their grandparents and grandchildren. Grandparents are most involved from a grandchild's birth to the teenage years (Cherlin & Furstenberg Jr., 1986). Teenagers withdraw somewhat from their grandparents, and grandparents are less able to assist their grandchildren in their current activities, although adolescent grandchildren may perform errands for their grandparents. The difference that age of grandchildren makes to grandparenting is addressed by a 67-year-old grandmother in one of my studies:

> My two older granddaughters who live near here are 16 and 18. They have their own little worlds now. You don't expect to see as much of them. I miss them and I would love it if they would just drop in, you know. They do occasionally, but I know what it is to be young. I know that . . . they have their own schedules and they are working and going to school . . . and their social lives. But I do enjoy particularly the ones that are too young to be out on their own like that. And I think that they enjoy us. They love to come to Grandma's.

Age of grandchildren also affects the extent to which parents are the linchpins in grandparent-grandchild interactions. Becoming a grandparent is a contingent transition that is typically in the hands of one's children (Troll, 1985), setting the stage for children as mediators in the relationship between grandparents and grandchildren. Virtually all interaction between young grandchildren and their grandparents is dependent on the parents, but preadolescents and early adolescents are less passive and may tell their parents whether they want to see their grandparents (Sprey & Matthews, 1982). In late adolescence and adulthood, grandchildren and grandparents often interact independently, and grandparents may play the role of mediators between their children and grandchildren.

Daughters are more influential mediators than sons when children are young, establishing more involvement with maternal than paternal grandparents. Ties with grandchildren involve negotiating relationships not only with one's children but also with one's children-in-law (Peters et al., 2006). The close mother-daughter bond puts particular pressure on paternal grandparents to develop good relations with their daughters-in-law. In the words of one grandfather figuring out acceptable involvement with his grandchildren, "you have to find out the mood of the spouse, and go from there" (Peters et al., 2006:549). The impact of gender and lineage may be a source of ambivalence in multigenerational ties, as paternal grandparents experience more limits on their interaction with their grandchildren when compared with maternal grandparents. The extent of subsequent independent contact between older grandchildren and their paternal grandparents may also be affected.

The unique situation of today's lesbian and gay grandparents, many of whom have children through previous heterosexual marriages, heightens the significance of adult children as mediators. Lesbian and bisexual grandmothers in a qualitative study believe that intimate and affectionate relationships with their children are pivotal to having close ties with their grandchildren (Orel, 2006). Having grandchildren reopens the issue of disclosure, and some grandmothers follow their own or their child's preference not to reveal their sexual orientation, especially when grandchildren are young. Grandmothers who do not disclose feel greater distance from their grandchildren, find it stressful to hide their sexual orientation, and fear how their grandchildren would react if they knew. Their children's response to their sexual identity is central to such concerns, and generally, these grandmothers do not see their sexual orientation as central to their relationship with their grandchildren. As more future lesbian and gay old persons are grandparents to grandchildren born to or raised by children from same-sex unions, the dynamics of negotiating grandparent-grandchild ties will change.

Dimensions of Grandparenting

For some grandparents, particularly grandfathers (Thomas, 1995), the sense of immortality provided by grandchildren invests the relationship with special meaning. For others, the opportunity for reliving earlier parts of one's life is a valued component of grandparenting (Kivnick, 1985). The link to an older person's younger years is evident in the comments of a 65-year-old grandmother in my community study:

> The babe (grandson) was crying the second night he was home, and I got out of bed and toddled in, and my son is up looking after the babe. I said, "Here, give him to me." So I took him to a rocking chair, and I said, "This makes me think of my Grandma." Whenever we were upset or there was something that we didn't like, or we were unhappy, Grandma used to take us and she would sit one on here, one on one arm and one on the other arm or knee and just rock. And she would sing.

As this grandmother's account suggests, experiences as grandchildren influence the ways in which grandparents are involved with their grandchildren. Grandparents who knew and spent time with their own grandparents, particularly on the maternal side, are more active in the lives of their grandchildren as mentors, companions, providers of instrumental help, and people to talk to about problems and future plans (King & Elder Jr., 1997; Mueller & Elder Jr., 2003).

For grandchildren, contact with grandparents is the primary experience of intergenerational connection across the young-old divide. This connection with old people on the personal or micro level is typically positive and undermines the assumed tension between young and old at the macro level that is part of the intergenerational equity argument (Harper, 2005; see Chapter 14). Adult grandchildren value grandparents as an important source of cultural and ethnic identity (Wiscott & Kopera-Frye, 2000; Zajicek et al., 2006).

Studies of grandparenting styles indicate considerable variation despite their usual samples of Whites and younger grandparents. The *remote* grandparent is not very involved (Roberto & Stroes, 1995), often because of geographic distance from grandchildren (Cherlin & Furstenberg Jr., 1986). In contrast, a small proportion of grandparents has an *involved style* and often assumes parentlike responsibilities, usually in response to a family crisis. The *companionate* or *apportioned style* (Roberto & Stroes, 1995), in which grandparents feels close to their grandchildren without taking on a parental role, is most common (Cherlin & Furstenberg Jr., 1986; Henry et al., 1992).

Of a national sample of grandparents, half of them are companions or friends to their grandchildren, and about one-third give advice, talk about family history and the parent's life as a child, and serve as a confidant (AARP, 2000). According to college-aged grandchildren, such grandparents participate in their lives and development and also indulge them (Roberto & Stroes, 1995). The greater independence and financial security of older people today fosters a companionate style because occupying a similar social status encourages closer bonds. For example, grandchildren pursuing advanced education more often view their grandparents as mentors if their grandparents also have higher education (Crosnoe & Elder Jr., 2002).

A recent study places the grandparent's relationship with a particular grandchild in a broader family context and specifies five types of ties (Mueller & Elder Jr., 2003). *Influential* grandparents are highly involved with and emotionally close to their grandchildren, live nearby, have close ties with their children, knew at least one of their grandparents, and are especially close to the target grandchild. *Supportive* grandparents differ from the influential type in exercising no authority or discipline over their grandchildren and having less contact. They are younger, better off, usually on the maternal side, especially close to the target grandchild, and have coexisting strong emotional closeness and considerable conflict with their children about how their grandchildren are being raised. Ties between *authority-oriented* grandparents and their children exhibit even greater contrasts in combining the closest emotional ties and the most conflict and tension. These grandparents are involved with and close to their target grandchild but distinguish themselves from influential and supportive grandparents by being the most authoritarian, living farther away, and being the youngest of the grandparent groups. *Passive* and *detached* grandparents are not involved with their grandchildren, but passive grandparents believe that they have close ties with their grandchildren and children.

These grandparent types reveal considerable ambivalence in ties between grandparents and their children among those with supportive and authoritarian ties with grandchildren. The coexistence of conflict and tension with emotionally close relationships reflects the complexity of intergenerational relationships and the fact that conflict need not signal a poor relationship either between parents and their adult children or between grandparents and their grandchildren. The significance of the middle and old generations' own intergenerational relationships for shaping current grandparent-grandchild ties and differentiation among grandchildren are also evident.

The predominant style of grandparenting in Black families is *authoritative* or influential and involves extensive support (Hunter, 1997), particularly by grandmothers (Burton, 1992; Kivett, 1993). Grandmothers in African American families are important sources of parental support for both mothers and fathers (Hunter, 1997). About a third of Black mothers and fathers turn to their mothers for parenting advice, almost half of mothers and over a third of fathers turn to them for child care and advice, and the rest rely on their mothers for child care only. Being employed increases such support for fathers but not for mothers, whereas family characteristics, such as closeness and the number of surviving generations, are influential among mothers but not fathers. Thus in the usual course of parenting, grandmothers are an important resource to their children in Black families.

Gender also shapes the nature of grandparenting. Grandmothers and grandfathers are as likely to report aiding and being interested in grandchildren, but grandmothers emphasize closeness, warmth and fun in their relationships with grandchildren (Russell, 1986). Grandfathers place more emphasis on their role as adviser, especially grandfathers on the paternal side. College-aged grandchildren engage in more activities more often with grandmothers than with grandfathers, whether paternal or maternal (Roberto & Stroes, 1995). These activities include short visits for conversation, family gatherings, talking about things that matter to them, and helping with chores. Grandmothers are also seen as having had a greater impact on their values as they grew up, as reflected in adulthood by greater mutual understanding, communication and shared views of life.

Qualitative Aspects of the Grandparent-Grandchild Relationship

If you can keep in touch with young people, it will rub off on you. I get a big kick. My grandchildren will come down tonight—three of them. Now, I will change and I will be laughing. And they are so natural and they are cheerful. And natural rubs off on you, and I think it keeps you young.

—66-year-old grandfather

I have three grandchildren, and my goodness me, there is no generation gap there at all. . . . I say they either make me feel old or they make me feel young. But I will say this, they certainly do keep the wheels lubricated—mentally and physically.

—76-year-old grandmother

Most grandparents are very satisfied with grandparenting and describe their relationships with their grandchildren as warm and close (Russell, 1986). Among both Black and White grandparents, more time spent interacting with grandchildren increases the sense of being effective grandparents (Strom et al., 1995). At the same time, grandchildren who share more time with their grandparents consider their grandparents better teachers and perceive them to be more satisfied with grandparenting.

Grandparents tend to have a positive view of their identities as grandparents, grandmothers especially so (Reitzes & Mutran, 2004). In turn, holding a positive identity as a grandparent is associated with higher self-esteem and lower signs of depression. The positive outcomes for grandfathers and grandmothers suggest a tendency to minimize the significance of being a grandparent to men. This tendency flows in part from a feminized version of grandparenting based on grandmothers' experiences. Mann (2007) argues that men's ways of relating are not captured in the usual vocabulary or questions in research on parent-child or grandparent-grandchild relations. Practices of gender established while parenting may be hard to break (Mann, 2007), but aging and changing times make room for new ways of relating for both grandmothers and grandfathers. Grandfathers may play a significant nurturing role in the lives of single-parent daughters' children, and they describe warm bonds with grandchildren even when using traditional male discourse to do so (Roberto et al., 2001).

A qualitative study of old women suggests that we may also exaggerate the meaning of grandmothers' close ties to grandchildren. Despite their positive contribution to a grandmother's sense of self and of family, grandmothers view grandchildren as peripheral to their everyday lives unless they are providing extensive care to them (Roberto et al., 1999). Thus research on grandparent-grandchild relations must attend to unique gender constructions for men and women, and a critical eye must be cast on the gendered questions asked and assumptions made about grandparents' relationships with their children.

Grandmothers find their relationships with grandchildren more satisfying than do grandfathers (Silverstein & Long, 1998; Thomas, 1995) and are more involved with both grandsons and granddaughters (Cherlin & Furstenberg Jr., 1986). This helps account for the fact that adult grandchildren more often consider a grandmother their emotionally closest grandparent, even when they have both grandmothers and grandfathers (Hodgson, 1995; Kennedy & Kennedy, 1993). The gendered nature of family ties is also reflected in greater closeness to maternal than paternal grandparents and to maternal than paternal grandmothers in particular (Hodgson, 1995). The ongoing advantage of maternal over paternal grandparents in having close relations with their grandchildren stems directly from the closer ties of mothers than fathers to their parents (Chan & Elder, 2000). Grandparents, in turn, are generally closer to their granddaughters than grandsons (Silverstein & Long, 1998).

The middle generation's influence is apparent in grandparents' reports of higher-quality ties with their grandchildren when they have better relationships with their children (King & Elder Jr., 1997). Similarly, older grandchildren who view the relationship between their parents and grandparents as positive and supportive also have better bonds with their grandparents (Hodgson, 1995; King & Elder Jr., 1995). For mothers and fathers, the closer the relationship that they have with their parents, the closer their adult children's relationships with their corresponding grandparents (Monserud, 2008). The only crossing of lineage lines occurs among mothers and their mothers-in-law; closer ties between them are linked to closer ties between grandchildren and their paternal grandmothers (see also Matthews & Sprey, 1985).

Do grandparent-grandchild relations have a comparable impact on the middle generation? Observations made by a 67-year-old woman in my community study suggest that the grandparent-grandchild bond can affect the behavior and views of the middle generation:

> When I was a nurse, I had a patient, and her grandson wanted to take her for a drive. She was recuperating, and they used to keep them in the hospital much longer then, but she was allowed to go out for a drive. The boy's mother, who was the patient's daughter, said, "We don't have time today, son," and he said, "Mum, I will have [more] time for you when you are older than you have for Grandma." Now, she [the grandmother] went for the ride.

The arrival of grandchildren has different effects on parent-child relations, depending on gender. The closeness of ties between fathers and sons and between mothers and daughters seems to be unaffected by the arrival of grandchildren, and the transition to parenthood itself does not alter the closeness of parent-child relationships (Kaufman & Uhlenberg, 1998). However, additional children (beyond the first child) improve mother-son relationships but weaken the father-daughter bond. Similarly, the transition to parenthood among grandchildren tends to draw grandchildren closer to grandmothers but decreases closeness to grandfathers (Mills, 1999). Thus across the parent and grandparent generations, the arrival of children tends to have more positive consequences for the intergenerational relationships of women than of men.

What about patterns of closeness between grandparents and grandchildren over time? Grandparents tend to report closer ties to their grandchildren than grandchildren report to their grandparents. Although levels of closeness are generally high, grandparents' affections for their grandchildren follow a curvilinear pattern over time (Silverstein & Long, 1998). Closeness, mutual understanding, communication and compatibility gradually decline from the ages of roughly 55 to 70 years and then increase modestly when grandparents are in their 70s and 80s. Adult grandchildren report very good relationships with their grandparents, characterized by closeness and feeling loved and appreciated (King & Elder Jr., 1997), and among grandchildren aged 18 to 51 years, many report becoming closer to their grandparents over the years (Hodgson, 1995). When grandchildren pursue higher education, the quality of their relationship with their grandparents improves (Crosnoe & Elder Jr., 2002).

Grandchildren believe that growing up heightened their ability to appreciate their grandparents. For example, one 24-year-old grandson explains his closer feelings toward his grandfather this way: "Now that I'm not a kid, I'm taking the time to really get to know him" (Hodgson, 1995:166). Qualitative research indicates that both grandparents and adult grandchildren view their relationships as distinct ties characterized by love, mutual support and obligation that become more personally meaningful and friendshiplike over time (Kemp, 2005). An exception to this trend occurs among grandchildren who are comfortable with American culture but whose grandparents are not (Silverstein & Chen, 1999). Unlike their grandparents, acculturated Mexican American grandchildren report declines in affection for their grandparents over time.

Longitudinal work suggests that the grandparent's gender alters the impact of age on grandchildren's feelings so that they grow less close to their grandfathers but closer to their grandmothers (Mills, 1999). A personal crisis, more often on behalf of the grandparent, is sometimes the catalyst for greater closeness. One granddaughter reflects on her grandmother's support: "When my husband died, she really helped me through it, and now we're very close" (Hodgson, 1995:166). The combination of these results suggests that the feelings of grandparents, especially grandmothers, and grandchildren for one another become more similar over time.

Grandparents Caring for Grandchildren

Thirty years ago, higher rates of divorce, single parenthood, and labor force participation among women were the basis for predicting a less symbolic and more functional role for middle-class grandparents as they met the changed needs of their children and grandchildren (Clavan, 1978). This prediction has come true, as increasing numbers of older persons have taken on intensive support for their grandchildren.

Roughly 1 in 5 preschoolers who receive regular child care receive it from their grandparents (Uhlenberg, 2004). Grandmothers who provide part-time care for their grandchildren are usually providing child care for working mothers (Bowers & Myers, 1999). They have excellent relationships with their grandchildren and are more likely to be in the labor force themselves and to be satisfied with grandparenting than are grandmothers who are providing help to their grandchildren full time or not at all. The support of grandparents can be pivotal to the lives of their grandchildren. For example, young adults with a parent who suffers from depression are less likely to develop severe depressive symptoms if they are engaged with involved grandparents (Silverstein & Ruiz, 2006).

Relying on a grandparent as the primary source of child care while at work is most common among Black mothers, followed by Hispanic and then White mothers (Ries & Stone, 1992). These differences reflect variations in cultural preferences, the immediate needs of working mothers, and the availability of relatives to provide care. For example, among Mexican and Black American mothers, one reason for turning to kin for child care is having unemployed family members, including grandmothers, who are both available and in need of the reciprocal arrangement of pay for child care (Uttal, 1999).

A hundred years ago, grandmothers often acted as mothers to their grandchildren following the death of their daughters (Uhlenberg, 2004). Though far fewer in number, more grandparents today than in recent history are involved in extensive care for their grandchildren. The increase in grandparent-grandchild co-residence and multigenerational households is one indicator of recent shifts in such commitment (Hobbs, 2005). In the United States, 75% of families that include grandparents and grandchildren are maintained by a grandparent (Bryson & Casper, 1999). Similarly, in Canada, 55% of three-generation families maintained by one person are maintained by a grandparent (Che-Alford & Hamm, 1999).

About 4% of grandparents live with grandchildren (Simmons & Dye, 2003), and 6% of American children up to the age of 18 live in the homes of one or more of their grandparents (Bowers & Myers, 1999; Bryson & Casper, 1999). Neither parent is present in over a third of these families, leaving the care of grandchildren primarily in the hands of their grandparents (Bryson & Casper, 1999). Although still relatively rare, the skipped-generation family in which grandchildren live with grandparents without a parent in the household is the most rapidly growing co-residence arrangement. Such households are less common in Canada, where approximately 4% of children aged 15 and under live in a multigenerational household, and only 12% of co-residing grandparents and grandchildren are in skipped-generation households (Milan & Hamm, 2003). This may reflect lower rates of teen births in Canada than the United States.

In U.S. households in which grandparents and grandchildren live together, 42% involve grandparents caring for their grandchildren; this number drops to 26% for grandparents aged 65 or more (Gist & Hetzel, 2004). The vast majority—94%—of co-residing grandparents who are also primary caregivers are either the heads of the household or that person's spouse (Simmons & Dye, 2003). The odds of caring for grandchildren for a minimum of six months are now over 1 in 10 (Fuller-Thomson, Minkler, and Driver, 1997). Over half of caregiving grandparents have looked after their grandchildren for three or more years, and 1 in 5 have done so for 10 years or more. Time spent in this role increases with age; 55% of co-residing grandparents over the age of 60 have been caring for grandchildren for five or more years, compared with 32% of those under 60 (Simmons & Dye, 2003).

Grandparent-maintained families are most likely to include both grandparents (50%), followed by a grandmother only (43%), and much less often, a grandfather only (6%; Bryson & Casper, 1999). Among co-resident grandparents who care for grandchildren, 63% are women and 71% are under the age of 60 (Simmons & Dye, 2003), reflecting gender relations and grandparenthood of younger children as a middle-aged phenomenon. Grandmothers who are either the sole parental figure or share parenting with their spouses are most involved in caring for their grandchildren (Pearson et al., 1997).

The increase in grandparents caring for grandchildren mimics long-established patterns of race and class relations. In disadvantaged families, the need for family support, including that from grandparents, has always been greater (Fuller-Thomson et al., 1997), and African American families often have a heritage of such caring stemming from West African traditions or from accommodations to family breakup created by slavery (Minkler & Fuller-Thompson, 2005). White grandparents are least likely to co-reside with their grandchildren, and Black, Hispanic, American Indian and Alaska Native Americans are most likely to do so, followed closely by Asian grandparents (Simmons & Dye, 2003). This is only part of the story, because patterns of caring vary among co-residing grandparents and grandchildren. Co-residence is least likely to signal caring for grandchildren among Asian grandparents (20%), followed by Hispanic (35%), White (43%), Black (52%) and American Indian or Alaska Native (56%) American grandparents.

Race and ethnic relations intersect with shifting age, gender and class relations to create unfamiliar and ambivalent caregiving situations for some groups. For example, among Mexican Chicanas, age relations have changed so that the older generation of grandmothers now feels pressured to give support to rather than assume receiving support from younger generations (Zajicek et al., 2006). Changing gender relations mean that more daughters or daughters-in-law are in the labor force, and limited economic resources put grandmothers in high demand as child care providers. But grandmothers are ambivalent about providing extensive care. One way to resolve the ambivalence created by colliding age, ethnic, gender and class relations is for these grandmothers to maintain some independence and limit care to grandchildren by living on their own.

Although more White than Black children live in skipped-generation families, the odds of this situation are higher among African American children, followed by Hispanic and then White children (Minkler, 1999). Grandchildren in families headed by grandparents are more likely to be poor, without health insurance, and to be in families receiving public assistance (Bryson & Casper, 1999). The probability of poverty is highest in grandmother-maintained households, and such families most often have at least two generations of women (the grandmother and mother). Overall, the odds of becoming a caregiving grandparent are highest among women, African Americans, and grandparents whose children have died (Fuller-Thomson et al., 1997; Landry-Meyer, 1999). Among African Americans aged 45 and over, grandparents who care for grandchildren are less educated, poorer, and more likely to be women, native born, to live in overcrowded conditions, and to receive public assistance (Minkler & Fuller-Thompson, 2005). Among grandmothers, those who care are younger and more likely to be out of the labor force and to have functional limitations than those who do not; for grandfathers, those who care are more likely to be married than those who do not. Clearly, the construction of social and family life by gender, race, class and age is reflected in grandparent-grandchild co-resident care patterns.

The traumatic situations that typically precipitate caring for grandchildren represent a tough situation from the start. Grandparents who become parentlike figures to their grandchildren usually do so in response to their children's circumstances, including alcohol or drug abuse; divorce; emotional, mental, and physical health problems; the neglect or abuse of children; teen pregnancy; and imprisonment (Bowers & Myers, 1999; Fuller-Thomson et al., 1997; Hayslip Jr., et al., 1998; Jendrek, 1994; Minkler, 1999; Pruchno, 1999; Sands & Goldberg-Glen, 2000). Less often, grandparents take over the care of their grandchildren following the death of their child, a factor of growing significance in the wake of the AIDS epidemic, especially among grandmothers of color (Draimin & Joslin, 2002; Minkler, 1999). As these reasons indicate, taking on full-time parental responsibilities for grandchildren is rarely a choice. Rather, it is a response to the clear needs of grandchildren and children.

The factors associated with becoming a caregiving grandparent are reflected in the strategies and concerns of grandparents. Among Latino grandparents, multi-generational families typically include an adult child, but that child is most often the grandchild's aunt, not mother, and she provides considerable assistance with child care (Burnette, 1999). Unlike African American families, language may create a barrier to good grandparent-grandchild relations as Latino grandchildren become more assimilated, especially regarding language. The association of caregiving with poverty creates additional concerns among grandparents about the safety of their neighborhoods for their grandchildren, with particular worry about drugs in the streets (Burnette, 1999; Burton, 1992). A 67-year-old grandfather looking after his 4-year-old grandson describes the routine that he has developed to manage this concern:

> I make sure that I get all my business done before the dope dealers get busy around 4 in the afternoon. I let my grandson play outside till about noon. I get him in quick just in case there is some people on dope outside who got an early start. (Burton, 1992:748)

Grandparents worry also about whether they will stay healthy (Landry-Meyer, 1999) and live long enough to see their grandchildren into adulthood: "Every night I pray to God for ten more years of life. By then they [the grandchildren] will be socialized to know what is good and bad. . . . I only hope I can see them through these difficult years" (Burnette, 1999:55). At the same time, looking ahead to the end of one's life often includes the resigned assumption that caring for younger generations will be a lifelong endeavor, as this 82-year-old great-grandmother observes:

> I had my great-grandbaby since she was 2 years old. Now she is 15. Her momma and daddy are still messing with that stuff [drugs]. That's a long time to have somebody's child. I guess she will be with me till I die. (Burton, 1992:749)

Consequences of Caring

Raising grandchildren is equivalent to a second round of parenting. The contradiction inherent in being a parent to a grandchild is noted by grandparents who struggle with violating assumed expectations of what it means to be a grandparent while caring for their grandchildren (Landry-Meyer & Newman, 2004). Qualitative research shows two categories of response to parenting grandchildren, one more positive than the other (Dolbin-MacNab, 2006). Grandmothers who enjoy parenting grandchildren more than they did their children feel more relaxed and freer to develop their own approach to parenting, benefit from being wiser and experienced, and have more time for their grandchildren than they did for their children. Being off-time has advantages for these women.

For other grandmothers, challenges dominate and include lack of energy and physical limitations that they tie to aging (Dolbin-MacNab, 2006). These women typically have competing challenges, including parenting alone, no male role model for their grandchildren, and ongoing parenting. African American grandmothers tend to experience caring for grandchildren as challenging rather than enjoyable (Gibson, 2005), a reflection of the intersecting influence of gender, age, race and class relations. Aging and being off-time combine with contradictory demands to make caring for grandchildren an ambivalent situation.

Grandmothers who look after their grandchildren full-time tend to have good to excellent relationships with them, some growing closer over time (Bowers & Myers, 1999; Goodman & Silverstein, 2004), and to think of themselves as parents or guardians rather than "grandparent caregivers" (Landry-Meyer & Newman, 2004). Caregiving grandmothers feel satisfied, happy, and rewarded by helping their grandchildren and enjoy their company and progress (Pruchno, 1999). Despite this, grandparents report quite high rates of argumentative or aggressive behavior, discipline problems, psychological and medical problems, learning disabilities, and poor school performance among the grandchildren in their care (Pruchno, 1999; Sands & Goldberg-Glen, 2000). Care in general, and care of grandchildren with various problems in particular, diminishes the positive sentiments and increases the stress of being a grandparent (Hayslip Jr., et al., 1998; Sands & Goldberg-Glen, 2000).

Grandparents from various backgrounds who look after grandchildren report poorer health, have a higher probability of depression, and more chronic health problems than those who do not (Minkler, 1999; Strawbridge et al., 1997). Low-income grandmothers who care for grandchildren full-time experience greater burden than their more affluent peers (Bowers & Myers, 1999). Longitudinal data indicate that, although they start out in poorer health than those who are not raising their grandchildren, not all grandparents experience their health getting worse over time due to looking after their grandchildren (Hughes et al., 2007). Grandmothers who look after their grandchildren in skipped-generation households are the significant exception to the rule; they suffer declines in health and increases in depression as a result of parenting their grandchildren.

African American grandparents, especially grandmothers, who serve as parent surrogates are more likely to have personal histories of multigenerational living arrangements and to have peers who are also raising grandchildren (Pruchno, 1999). This helps account for the fact that Black grandparents are less burdened than White grandparents from caring for their grandchildren. In contrast, results from a small sample indicate more symptoms of depression among Native American than European American grandparents, despite a stronger tradition of care by grandparents in many Native American cultures (Letiecq et al., 2008). These differences suggest the ongoing impact of cultural genocide and of substance abuse in the middle generation on the lives of Native American elders. On balance, caregiving exacts a substantial toll among grandparents, especially grandmothers, because they are much more likely than those caring for spouses or children to be providing care following a history of stressful life events on behalf of their grandchildren (Strawbridge et al., 1997).

The considerable confusion about the place of caregiving grandparents in their relations with other family members may result in conflict among children concerning the respective parenting role of parents and grandparents and about the relative attention received by various grandchildren (Burnette, 1999). Grandmothers with parental responsibility for their grandchildren experience considerable ambivalence because care of grandchildren contradicts the expectation of rest later in life (Jendrek, 1994). As well, acting as parents to their grandchildren means acknowledging that their child is an incompetent parent. An overlooked consequence of caring for grandchildren is the impact on the ties between grandparents and other grandchildren who are not care recipients (Hayslip Jr., et al., 1998). Differential treatment of grandchildren creates an additional complication to family dynamics for these grandmothers.

> I am the only one who sees that he gets his vitamins, that he has a normal life, that he gets to bed on time, that he doesn't run wild. Because of all that, I can never be a grandmother. I can't indulge him like I do my other grandchildren. I have to discipline him, so I can't be fun to be around. (Grandmother with full-time responsibility for her five-year-old grandson; Johnson, 1988b:112)

Like parents, the main concerns of grandparents are that their grandchildren are safe, healthy, and on their way to receiving good educations (Landry-Meyer, 1999). Despite the associated costs, most grandparents would make the decision to care for their grandchildren again and view caring for grandchildren as "the Lord's blessing" and an activity that gives life additional meaning (Burton, 1992; Hayslip Jr., et al., 1998).

In turn, despite the challenging circumstances that led grandparents to care for their grandchildren, taking into account other factors, grandchildren raised solely by grandparents appear to fare well when compared with those children raised by a single biological parent (Solomon & Marx, 1995). Even more striking, they do not differ markedly from children raised by both parents in terms of their relationships with teachers, general well-being and health. Indeed, the only substantial difference is in school achievement, with children raised by grandparents performing less well than those raised by parents (Solomon & Marx, 1995). More generally, teenagers who live with a single mother and at least one grandparent compare favorably with teenagers who live with married parents on likelihood of finishing high school and engaging in healthy activities (DeLaire & Kalil, 2002). Mixed results on the impact of such multigenerational living by race make more research on this topic necessary (Dunifon & Kowaleski-Jones, 2007).

The benefits enjoyed by grandchildren may well come home to roost, as in the case of a granddaughter who helps her grandparents daily:

> I am thankful that I can do it. My mother was only 16 years old when I was born and my grandparents took care of me. I will never forget how she [my grandmother] always had time to do things with me. (Dellmann-Jenkins et al., 2000:183)

Little attention is paid to such reciprocity of help flowing from grandchildren to grandparents. As the foregoing quote suggests, adult grandchildren can be important sources of support to their grandparents. Such support does not apply only when grandparents serve an active parentlike role. A lesbian grandmother who lost her partner of 19 years observes, "My granddaughter was in some ways the best support . . . because she was not afraid to talk about and have feelings about Joan [her lesbian partner]" (Whipple, 2006:119). Research on Canadian university students' visits with grandparents in declining or poor health suggests that grandchildren are motivated to visit by the rewards of seeing a grandparent rather than by a strong sense of obligation (Boon & Shaw, 2007) and affirms the more voluntary approach of grandchildren to engaging in their relationships with grandparents.

Summary

In sum, older grandparents and adult grandchildren derive considerable pleasure from their relationships with one another. For most middle-aged and old persons, being a grandparent involves regular and emotionally rewarding contact. For some, being a grandparent involves intensive caring for grandchildren. Age, gender, race and class relations shape the nature of grandparent-grandchild ties, as do the mediating role and relationship history of parents. The greater number of divorces among the middle generation is one of the reasons that more grandparents are playing an active role in the lives of their grandchildren, often at considerable expense, especially among grandmothers who are raising grandchildren on their own.

CHAPTER 11

Divorce, Remarriage, Step Ties, and Intergenerational Relations

The impact of divorce and remarriage on intergenerational relationships reflects the ways that age, gender, race and class relations shape intimate parent-child and grandparent-grandchild ties. The end of other long-term relationships and other forms of repartnering also affect intergenerational relationships, but the bulk of research related to adult ties concerns divorce and remarriage. More unions that include children from prior marriages and relationships offset declining fertility somewhat by increasing the number of families with more than one or two co-resident children. For some childless persons, marriage may also bring parenthood through stepchildren. From the vantage point of grandparents, although the pool of biological grandchildren is in decline (except for parents of the baby boom), the number of step-grandchildren is on the rise.

Gender, time and place are central dimensions to exploring how transitions in partner status affect intergenerational relations (Connidis, 2003b). Regarding generation, our interest in aging leads us to focus on three generations: generation one, grandparents; generation two, parents; and generation three, grandchildren. Partner transitions in one generation reverberate across generations with varying effects, depending upon the generation in which the transition occurs (Connidis, 2003a). This reverberation reflects the life course principle of linked or interdependent lives so that the experiences of one family member are not confined either to that individual or to his or her immediate family circle. For example, a generation two couple's divorce requires renegotiating relationships that involve the divorced couple, each partner and his or her children and parents, siblings, grandparents and grandchildren, the respective in-law ties, and extended ties beyond these.

Following the life course perspective, the second dimension, time, includes the age at which a transition occurs (the life stage principle) and duration, the length of time either between transitions (e.g., between parental divorce and remarriage) or spent in relationships created or affected by a given transition. As an example of life stage, the impact of parental divorce will vary if it occurs when a child is very young, away at university, or in middle age. Duration also matters. For example, do new step ties follow a short or long period since a marital breakup? Are step ties acquired recently or long ago?

The third dimension is place. Where were various family members living at the time of a transition in partner status, and what impact did that transition have on subsequent living arrangements? Co-residence and geographic proximity are pivotal parameters to how relationships are negotiated in the wake of partner transitions. With which parent or parents did children live following divorce? Did a parent's repartnering involve co-residence for the child? Did a new partner bring additional family members to the household or a parent's move to a new location? These are facets of family history from the vantage point of adult children and grandchildren that have lasting effects on intergenerational relations.

In the discussion that follows, keep in mind the dimensions of generation, time (life stage and duration), and place (co-residence and geographic proximity) as we explore the impact of partner transitions on adult intergenerational relations. Consider also the ways in which structured social relations shape the experience of these transitions. For example, reflecting age relations, parents make choices over which children have little control, and the impact of the same transition has variable effects based on gender relations. Much of the following discussion compares the relative risks of particular outcomes for particular groups. Such variations do not mean that all or even most in a particular group experience that outcome, only that their odds of doing so are higher.

The Impact of Divorce on Ties Between Older Parents and Their Children

Unlike death, which is final, the problems of divorce go on and on.

—Twice-married grandmother
(Johnson, 1988b:163)

During the second half of the 20th century, there was a marked increase in divorce rates at all ages, including old age. Divorcing later in life is still relatively uncommon, but a slight increase in divorce among couples aged 50 and over generates large numbers. These divorces are more often prompted by women than men (Bair, 2007; Montenegro, 2004). The far more common divorce experience for older parents is to have divorced earlier in life and to have either continued life as unmarried persons or to have remarried some time ago.

In our attempt to discern general patterns, complexity and variability within groups and even with families is often lost. For example, qualitative work reveals quite different alliances within families, with some adult children of divorced parents more loyal to and understanding of their mothers' situation and others more so with respect to their fathers (Connidis, 2003a). More generally, the experience of divorce, just like marriage, is highly varied. As we paint patterns with broad strokes, remember the diversity that occurs within the big picture.

The view that parents have a stronger obligation to support their children than children have to support their parents after the divorce or remarriage of parents is strongly held (Coleman et al., 1997). Relationships between in-laws are unclear at best, but following divorce, they become even less clear, and expectations of support rest on the degree of emotional closeness between former in-laws (Ganong & Coleman, 1999).

The Impact of Parental Divorce

Romance and Divorce across Generations

Women with divorced parents report more ambivalence, conflict and negativity in their romantic relationships (Jacquet & Surra, 2001). This outcome in turn affects men who are most likely to experience conflict and negativity in their relationships when their romantic partner's parents—not their own—are divorced. Qualitative work shows that some young adult women favor staying single because they will avoid the financial and emotional dependence that their mothers experienced after divorce (Sharp & Ganong, 2007). As well, among young adults, cohabitation is less likely to be followed by marriage if parents are divorced rather than married (Wolfinger, 2001).

What about those who do marry? The greater risk of divorce among children whose parents divorced continues, but the impact of parental divorce is declining (Wolfinger, 2005). The increased risk of divorce is in part because children of divorced parents marry at a younger age (Ross & Mirowsky, 1999) and engage in interpersonal behavior with their spouses, such as anger, jealousy, hurt feelings, and infidelity, that can negatively affect the marriage (Amato, 1996). A more important predictor of divorce in the adult child generation, however, is the state of their parents' marriages prior to divorce: Divorce among adult children is more likely when parental divorce followed low- rather than high-conflict marriages (Amato & DeBoer, 2001). When limited marital discord leads to divorce, parents exemplify lower commitment to marriage, and this is more pivotal than divorce itself to the next generation's behavior. Yet children of divorced parents who remain married are no more or less likely to have good marriages than are children of parents who stay together (Feng et al., 1999).

Parental Divorce and Support Exchanges

How are support exchanges between parents and their adult children affected by parental divorce? Both divorced mothers and fathers, but especially fathers, have less contact than do married parents with their children (Aquilino, 1994; Booth & Amato, 1994; Cooney, 1994; Daatland, 2007; Shapiro, 2003; Uhlenberg, 1990; Webster & Herzog, 1995). Although level of contact is generally unrelated to closeness between older parents and their children, children of divorced parents who feel closer to their parents maintain greater contact with them (Cooney, 1994). This suggests that the tie between adult children and their divorced parents has a more voluntary and less obligatory character, potentially undermining the support exchanges typical of the parent-child relationship. Selection effects also appear to be at work, with couples who eventually divorce having less contact with children both before and after divorce than do couples who stay married (Shapiro, 2003).

Divorced parents are less likely than married ones to receive help from adult children, with stronger effects for fathers (Daatland, 2007). Among divorced parents aged 36 to 72, divorced mothers report receiving much more advice, financial help, emotional support, and service provision from their children than do divorced fathers (Wright & Maxwell, 1991). Almost half of mothers but less than one-fifth of fathers found children to be their most helpful source of support during the divorce process itself (Wright & Maxwell, 1991). Among divorced fathers, parents outrank children as significant support providers. Older divorced fathers (aged 50 to 79) are far less likely than never-divorced fathers to consider their children likely sources of support should they be in need (Uhlenberg, 1990).

Supporting mothers following divorce is often the outcome of patterns begun when children were still at home. Among older women especially, custodial mothers could find themselves in an alien labor market looking for paid work for the first time and raising a family with fewer resources (Connidis, 2003a). In such circumstances, children take on more responsibility, sometimes to the point of becoming parentlike figures to younger siblings. This runs counter to current views of childhood, and yet daughters whose divorced mothers rely heavily on them for emotional support enjoy more equal, close and friendly ties with them (Arditti, 1999). Offering help to divorced parents is unlikely to have the unusual outcome that it did for one woman whose parents divorced decades earlier (Bair, 2007). Both her mother and father developed Alzheimer's disease in their 80s and, as their only child, she felt compelled to offer both of them care in her home. After years apart, and not recognizing each other, they fell in love again and shared stories of their former bad marriage and partners.

Research in the UK underscores the need for more studies on older parents to fully understand the long-term impact of divorce on support from children. There, divorced parents aged 70 and over are just as likely as married parents to receive support from their adult children according to need (Glaser et al., 2008). A recent marital disruption among old people, whether due to widowhood or divorce, actually increases the odds of receiving help from adult children (Tomassini et al., 2007). As Glaser (2008) notes, research in the United States that shows less support from children when parents are divorced tends to use samples of parents aged 50 and over, many of whom do not need much support. By the time that they are in need, children appear to step up to the plate, whatever the prior impact of their parents' divorce may have been. Over time, parents and adult children renegotiate their ties with one another in response to changing circumstances.

Regarding support from parents to their children, divorced parents generally provide less financial aid, instrumental support, advice, and companionship to their adult children than do their married peers, with a greater difference between fathers than mothers of the two marital statuses (White, 1992). Compared with children whose parents remain married, children whose parents divorce leave home at younger ages (Boyd & Norris, 1995), are less likely to return after they have left (Aquilino, 1990), and are less likely to co-reside with parents as young adults (Booth & Amato, 1994). Children who were adults at the time their parents divorced experience a decline in family gatherings and celebrations that would normally bring various factions of the family together (Campbell, 1995). Thus the potential of midlife divorced parents to contribute to the cohesion of their extended family is undermined.

For divorced parents, the level of contact and relationship quality are crucial to the amount of support given to their adult children (White, 1992). Only financial aid is a function of available resources, but even here, divorced parents provide more help to children with whom they are in greater contact and have stronger ties. Thus the parent-child tie is characteristically more voluntary and less obligatory when parents are divorced. What remains unclear is the extent to which parental divorce leads to less support to adult children because of limited resources, competing obligations (e.g., to a new spouse), or a decline in the commitment that divorced parents feel toward their children.

The resources available to parents, and postdivorce family stability while children are growing up, shape outcomes for adult children and indicate the need to differentiate among divorced families. Fewer resources in childhood rather than divorce account for lower educational attainment, income and job prestige among young adults who lived in stable postdivorce families when they were adolescents (Sun & Li, 2008). This was not the case for young adults who lived in unstable postdivorce families. Increased risk of particular outcomes does not mean that they are commonplace among children of divorce. For example, although high school dropout rates are higher among children whose parents divorce than among those whose parents stay married, the majority of both groups finish high school (Wolfinger, 2007). A silver lining of growing up in families in which parents have divorced is greater independence and more awareness of financial issues and responsibilities at an earlier age (Wallerstein, 2007). By their 30s, many have resolved earlier anxieties that they may have had about relationships and are in committed relationships, including marriage.

Parental Divorce and Relationship Quality

What about the quality of relationships between divorced parents and their adult children? Much of the research concerning the impact of parental divorce on adult children concerns divorce that occurred when they were children, involves relatively young adults and middle-aged parents, and too often assesses divorce's impact by drawing comparisons between those from married and those from divorced families without distinguishing among marriages. Consequently, it is important to be cautious about findings, and more research is needed that explores marital history prior to divorce and the impact of parental divorce when it occurs at different ages.

Adult children whose parents are divorced view relationships with both parents more negatively (Kaufman & Uhlenberg, 1998) and more often have discordant than harmonious ties with them (van Gaalen & Dykstra, 2006). Both sons and daughters report more positive ties to their mothers than to their fathers before and after their parents' separation and divorce (Hoffman & Ledford, 1995; Kaufman & Uhlenberg, 1998). Adults see their ties with parents as at their lowest ebb following separation, after which they tend to improve (Hoffman & Ledford, 1995). Divorce affects the quality of ties with fathers more adversely than ties with mothers, with father-child ties characterized by far greater detachment and less closeness, particularly with adult daughters (Aquilino, 1994; Hoffman & Ledford, 1995; Kaufman & Uhlenberg, 1998; Putney & Bengtson, 2003; Silverstein & Bengtson, 1997; Webster & Herzog, 1995). Among Generation Xers, however, closeness to divorced mothers does not have as positive an impact on self-esteem as closeness to married mothers (Putney & Bengtson, 2003).

Gender differences reflect in part the custody and living arrangements following divorce that leave fathers more isolated from their children. Similar and sometimes greater risks of estrangement are faced by children of nonbiological lesbian mothers who, like stepparents (Hans, 2002), are legal strangers to their children; should the relationship with the biological mother end, there is no legal recourse to maintain contact with their child (Allen, 2007b). In law, biological parents have fundamental parental rights, and only two legal parents can be recognized at one time (Skinner & Kohler, 2002). In 2007, the Ontario Court of Appeal granted legal parent status to three parents: the biological mother, the biological father, and the mother's lesbian partner. Subsequent attempts to have the ruling overturned were rejected by the Supreme Court of Canada.

This precedent-setting Canadian case stands as an exception and does not address the ambiguous loss of children through separation or divorce from their parent. For lesbian women, this situation requires the constant effort to normalize the ambivalent situation of having a child who is ever present in their hearts and minds but is neither physically present nor legally (and often, socially) recognized as their child (Allen, 2007a). Legal support of such relationships would enhance the prospects of putting a child first. More generally, cooperative coparenting by former partners benefits children of divorce, as is evident in the better relationships between nonresident fathers and children that accrue from this approach regardless of gender, class and race (Sobolewski & King, 2005).

The unexpected divorce of parents, either because there was little marital discord or because parents were older at the time of divorce, has negative consequences for early adult children. When divorce follows a marriage in which marital conflict was low, adult children's well-being continues to suffer after they no longer live with them (Booth & Amato, 2001). Similarly, in a sample of 84 adult children, the surprise of parents divorcing after decades of marriage left many feeling devastated or angry at their parents for not being able to keep their marriage together (Bair, 2007). Less often, adult children were relieved that a divorce which was a long time coming finally arrived.

When divorce is precipitated by high conflict between parents, the well-being of adult children is enhanced (Booth & Amato, 2001). These children are less likely than children of intact high-conflict parental marriages to experience feeling caught between their parents and the dampening effect that this has on affection for parents and on subjective well-being (Amato & Afifi, 2006). With time, any loyalty conflicts dissipate among those whose parents divorced. These variations suggest that longer-term outcomes of parental divorce are not necessarily direct effects of divorce itself, but rather of the marriage that preceded it. More generally, factors that increase the risk of divorce (e.g., poverty and low maternal education), the process of divorce itself, and particular postdivorce family dynamics are responsible for some of the negative outcomes attributed to divorce (Coontz, 2007; Sun & Li, 2008).

Parental divorce influences how children negotiate other relationships. Once adults, children of divorce are almost two times more likely than those from intact families to have someone who is more like a mother to them than is their biological mother and 13 times more likely to have someone who is more like a father than their biological father (Webster & Herzog, 1995). Blacks are less likely than Whites to have a motherlike figure and more likely to report a fatherlike figure. These results suggest that parental divorce encourages investment in other relationships that may satisfy needs that are not met by biological parents.

The impact of divorce on adult children depends upon the nature of their parents' marriage prior to divorce. Research shows that adult children of parents who have stayed in high-conflict marriages have smaller networks of friends and relatives and less happy intimate relationships than adult children whose parents divorced in the wake of high conflict marriages—but larger networks and happier relationships than adult children whose parents divorced following low-conflict marriages (Booth & Amato, 2001). If parental divorce occurs when children are already adults, the unexpected change disrupts established adult family relationships and requires their renegotiation (Bair, 2007). Older divorced parents also may lean on their adult children for support during the transition out of marriage. Once again, relief from a negative environment has benefits; unexpected disruption does not.

As divorce becomes more normative, its negative effects on individuals and on family ties diminish, and succeeding cohorts of children experience fewer ill effects from their parents' divorces (Wolfinger, 2005). As the stigma of divorce declines, so too does its negative sting.

The Impact of a Child's Divorce

For most parents, a child's divorce is a distressing experience, evoking feelings of shock, sadness, loss, powerlessness, disappointment, confusion, guilt, and for some, bitterness (Hamon & Cobb, 1993; Pearson, 1993). Having no foreknowledge of a child's marital problems and later, not knowing why a child divorced, make parents' adjustment to the divorce more difficult (Hamon & Cobb, 1993). Lack of awareness reflects a cultural preference to maintain intimacy at a distance once children are adults, with both parents and children seeking to respect mutual independence. A child's divorce prompts the need to renegotiate the parent-child relationship.

When the child of divorced parents also divorces, parents often feel both guilty and sad, believing that they bear some responsibility for their child's divorce through the example they set and knowing firsthand the challenges that face their child. In the words of a separated 66-year-old father of a divorced daughter,

> You are saddened by the thought of what your divorced child will have to go through. Well, you kinda know what's ahead for them in a marriage breakup after seeing your own deteriorate. You know there is disappointment; there's heartache, no peace, and your life is really upset. . . . You see all that heavy stuff because you've been there, and they are just starting on that road. (Hamon & Cobb, 1993:83)

The reorganization that follows a child's divorce results in three general family forms (Johnson & Barer, 1988b). The first focuses on the strong intergenerational bond between biological grandparents, the parent, and grandchildren. The second type revolves around the nuclear unit of parent and children. A third option is the formation of a loose-knit network that, unlike the other types, includes friendly relations with in-laws and the ex-spouse, less dependency on parents, and shifting boundaries. These family forms represent alternative and in some cases transitional strategies for renegotiating relationships following divorce. Heavy reliance on parents is for some an effective method of moving from a nuclear family with two parents to one with one parent. Although parents can be particularly helpful in making this transition, their involvement also means more scrutiny of the previously private domain of the child's family, creating ambivalence in the parent-child tie (Johnson & Barer, 1988b).

A Child's Divorce and Support Exchanges

Less research concerns the impact of a child's divorce than a parent's divorce on relationships between adult children and their older parents. In-depth reports of older parents suggest extensive emotional and instrumental support to children in the aftermath of divorce (Hamon, 1995). Divorce clearly introduces ambiguity in family boundaries and ambivalence in parent-child ties, with parents confused about how to interact appropriately with both their child and former child-in-law and feeling conflicted about how involved to be in their child's life (Hamon, 1995; Hamon & Cobb, 1993; Peters et al., 2006). Although parents share a strong desire to support divorced children, some feel overinvolved in the lives of their child following his or her divorce, and others are concerned about the impact it has on their own marriage. One 70-year-old father of a divorced daughter with children observes,

> I don't have the companionship of my wife. I don't have her there to take trips and to do some of the things that I worked for and should be able to enjoy doing now. And instead, we're almost literally tied down with another family. . . . So, we're stuck. (Hamon & Cobb, 1993:81)

There are mixed results regarding the impact of a child's divorce on parent-child relations. Children in happy marriages have better relationships with their parents than do single, divorced, and separated daughters and divorced and separated sons (Kaufman & Uhlenberg, 1998). Some find no difference in support from parents, but others find that divorced adult children receive less support from their parents and have more strained ties with their mothers (Umberson, 1992b). Daughters with custody of children, however, appear to have more contact with and support from their parents (Logan & Spitze, 1996; see also Cooney & Uhlenberg, 1992).

From the parents' perspective, supporting divorced children creates an ambivalent situation when the desire to help is curbed by the fear of interfering (Hamon, 1995; Hamon & Cobb, 1993). Within families, mothers aged 65 to 75 years are more likely to express mixed and torn feelings about children who are ever single or divorced and who do not reciprocate the support that their mothers give (Pillemer et al., 2007). For some, the ambivalent situation created by divorce is resolved by redefining the mother-daughter tie as friendship (Johnson & Barer, 1988b). For others, the conflict that ambivalence provokes is open and accepted as a given. Yet others define the daughter's dependency following divorce as expected and, therefore, a mother's help is defined as appropriate for the situation. Divorced daughters without partners experience more conflict with their mothers if they give more than they receive; this does not hold for either married daughters or previously divorced daughters with new partners (Schwarz, 2006).

Some studies find no change in parental support when children divorce (Dwyer et al., 1992; Logan & Spitze, 1996), but recent research concludes that an upside of having divorced versus married children is greater contact with them and greater emotional, financial and practical help from them (Sarkisian & Gerstel, 2008). For some mothers, the companionship with a daughter that divorce facilitated is interrupted by a new romantic involvement, as in the case of this widowed mother: "I'm glad she's happy, but I still miss her because I don't feel I can just drop in and do things with her" (Kestin van den Hoonaard, 2001:57). The voluntary nature of intergenerational ties is highlighted by the apparent priority assigned to intimate over parental ties. Yet whether it occurs among parents or children, divorce does not preclude care for parents when their need for it is clear.

The Impact of Divorce on Grandparent-Grandchild Ties

Changes that occur in the grandparent-parent-grandchild network following divorce in the middle generation are indicative of the major contribution grandparents often make to the lives of their children and grandchildren and of the dependence of the grandparent-grandchild relationship on the parent as mediator (see Chapter 10). Lineage (maternal versus paternal grandparents), the gendered nature of child custody, timing of divorce, and the age of grandchildren all affect the impact of middle-generation divorce on grandparent-grandchild relations. Most research concerns divorce in the middle generation, but grandparents who are themselves divorced, especially grandfathers, have less contact with their grandchildren than do married grandparents (Attias-Donfut & Segalen, 2002; King, 2003).

Parents are generally saddened by the divorces of their children, but the presence of grandchildren creates additional concern, and grandparents tend to worry about their grandchildren's future (Hamon & Cobb, 1993). The ambiguity created by divorce extends to grandparents as they wonder how to maintain close ties with their grandchildren (Hamon & Cobb, 1993). More divorces, dissolved cohabiting unions, and single mothers (Uhlenberg, 2004) increase the number of children for whom grandparents may play a significant role and raise the issue of grandparents' visitation rights. Now all states in the United States have provisions for recognizing grandparents' rights to see their grandchildren under specified and variable conditions (Falk & Falk, 2002), but the courts' failure to clarify the best interests of the child in grandparent visitation cases contributes to the ambiguous status of grandparents in families (Henderson, 2005). Whatever their level of involvement, grandparents must negotiate a revised relationship with their grandchildren following the dissolution of their child's relationship, in substantial measure, through renegotiating relationships with their child and with their child's former spouse or partner.

When compared with those who do not have grandchildren, grandparents are more likely to feel responsible, guilty or burdened after their children's divorces, and their mixed feelings about the divorces are more inclined to increase over time (Pearson, 1993). Such ambivalence also rests on grandparents being eager to support their grandchildren but not wanting to serve as parents to them (Hamon & Cobb, 1993; Johnson & Barer, 1988b). Grandparents who were relatively uninvolved before a child's divorce are not usually the ones who become very involved afterwards (Ferguson et al., 2004). In turn, grandchildren continue to turn to their parents, especially their mothers, and to their siblings with concerns about the divorce, not to their grandparents.

A key factor differentiating postdivorce grandparental involvement in a range of activities is child custody. Living nearer by and having more frequent contact are associated with greater emotional closeness, and greater contact and closeness are most likely when grandchildren are in the custody of the child rather than child-in-law (Henry et al., 1992; Hilton & Macari, 1997). Under current gender relations, child custody is more often granted to women and reinforces matrilineal ties. The weaker ties between children and fathers that occur when fathers do not live with their children weaken ties between paternal grandparents and their grandchildren (Uhlenberg, 2004). Paternal grandparents often expect to play a more minor role than maternal grandparents in the lives of their shared grandchildren (Ferguson et al., 2004). Grandchildren who were aged 16 or more when their parents divorced act more autonomously, independently initiating contact with their grandparents and seeing their paternal grandparents on their own rather than with their fathers (Cooney & Smith, 1996). Thus, later age of parental divorce appears to minimize the impact of custodial arrangements and reliance on parents as mediators in grandparent-grandchild relations.

Grandparents with multiple grandchild sets are often paternal grandparents to some of their grandchildren (their sons' children) and maternal grandparents to their other grandchildren (their daughters' children). Some divorced parents note a decline in attention from paternal grandparents when they become maternal grandparents to a daughter's new child (Ferguson et al., 2004). More generally, grandparents who have grandchild sets through both daughters and sons may be less involved in the postdivorce families of their sons than those who are paternal grandparents only.

A child-in-law's custody of grandchildren threatens contact between grandparents and grandchildren, and rancor between parents and grandparents magnifies this threat (Kruk, 1995). Thus grandparents are highly motivated to get along with their children-in-law. The extent to which grandparents struggle to maintain contact with their grandchildren is evident in the fact that, following the divorce of their children, contact between fathers and their children falls off more precipitously than between paternal grandfathers and their grandchildren (Kruk & Hall, 1995). Maternal grandmothers are less likely than paternal grandmothers to maintain ties with their children-in-law (Ferguson et al., 2004), less likely to expand their kinship network, and more likely to increase both instrumental and expressive aid to grandchildren following divorce (Johnson & Barer, 1988b). Meanwhile, the maintenance of ties with their daughters-in-law to secure access to grandchildren has the long-term effect of expanding paternal grandparents' kinship networks. The impact of child custody is reflected further in findings that paternal grandparents are more involved than maternal grandparents in single-father families, and maternal grandparents are more involved than paternal grandparents in single-mother families (Hilton & Macari, 1997). Regardless of whether the father or mother has custody, grandmothers spend more time with grandchildren and are more likely than grandfathers to provide child care, help grandchildren with problems, teach new skills, go on outings and provide treats (Hilton & Macari, 1997), as Photo 11.1 reflects.

Photo 11.1   A child's divorce may threaten special times between grandparents and their grandchildren. Grandmothers stay in touch with their grandchildren more than grandfathers do after the divorce.

Despite concern that divorce will interfere with good relationships with grand-children, research using young adult samples of grandchildren finds equally close and involved ties between grandchildren and grandparents, whether or not parents have divorced (Cogswell & Henry, 1995; Cooney & Smith, 1996). Among those with grandparents nearby, maternal grandmothers are seen as more engaged in nurturance and guidance activities by grandchildren whose parents are divorced (Cogswell & Henry, 1995). Last, children of divorce are far more likely than those from intact families to have a significant, nonbiological grandparent figure in their lives, including stepgrandparents (Cogswell & Henry, 1995). This supports the contention that, for grandchildren at least, divorce may have the positive side effect of extending family networks (Riley & Riley, 1996).

Remarriage, Step Ties, and Intergenerational Relations

I've come to the sage knowledge that people who remarry have to make laws beforehand about their own families. No matter how hard I try, I can't make my husband's children like mine. It causes emotional dismemberment.

—Remarried grandmother (Johnson & Barer, 1988b:165)

There is limited research about the impact of remarriage itself on ties with adult children and even less regarding other forms of repartnering. Remarried parents provide less support to their adult children than do continuously married parents (White, 1992). Similarly, the remarriage of adult children following divorce may decrease contact with parents (Logan & Spitze, 1996). For some parents and adult children, this decline may be relative to elevated rates of contact after the child's divorce. These studies focus on relatively short-term effects, and some of the patterns may shift over time, as we saw regarding support to divorced parents in their old versus middle age.

Step Ties and Intergenerational Relations

Remarriage makes family relationships more complex, typically adding a constellation of new ties in the form of step- and sometimes half-kin, while creating permutations in old ones. For the person who remarries, a new spouse means, potentially, new in-laws (parents- and siblings-in-law) and new step relations (acquiring stepchildren and becoming stepparents). In turn, other family members experience parallel changes in their family composition. Children may acquire stepsiblings and stepgrandparents as well as a stepparent and, eventually, half siblings. Parents of the remarried child may now have stepgrandchildren, along with a new son- or daughter-in-law. Existing relationships are likely to be altered. For example, an adult child's remarriage may spur changes in the relationship between biological or adoptive grandparents and their grandchildren. Thus there are many facets to the consequences of remarriage when one considers the range of relationships that are affected. Our focus here is on adult intergenerational ties.

The significance of family history (Finch, 1989) takes on new heights in the study of step relationships. Important and unique conceptual issues regarding step kin that do not apply to blood or, usually, adoptive ties must be addressed. In the case of biological and adoptive parents, for example, the bond between parent and child typically begins at birth or when the child is very young and involves two parents who share the same relationship to the child, either biological or chosen. Of course, there are exceptions, most notably, single mothers and lesbian or straight couples in which one partner is the biological parent. Determining when a step tie begins is not a simple matter, as step family members do not always consider a marriage the starting point of feeling that they were engaged in familylike relationships (Braithwaite et al., 2006). Nonetheless, both age at which a step relationship begins (life stage) and its duration are important considerations. The gendered nature of family relations makes the issue of who is biologically and who is step related significant. Is the combination a biological mother and stepfather or a biological father and stepmother? This relates to custody and co-residence, which tend also to be gendered, especially for today's older persons.

Just as referring to aging or gay or lesbian families is limiting, so too is referring to step families (Dimmock et al., 2004). No family consists solely of step ties. Rather, family histories create a mixture of ties and may include some that are step ties. Parents' marital histories create different family structures that have consequences for how various step ties are negotiated. One parent may remarry and another not, one or both parents may remarry more than once, and one or both parents may have additional children with new spouses, adding half siblings to the family constellation. The mix of step, blood, adoptive and other types of relations within a family network is a compositional feature that influences the negotiation of family relationships, just as combinations based on age, gender, and sexual orientation are. Failure to address these dimensions of step relations in studies that compare biological and step ties raises a red flag about their results.

The foregoing facets of step ties have both short- and long-term consequences for family ties, extending to inheritance decisions by older parents and grandparents who have a mix of biological and stepchildren and grandchildren (Bornat et al., 1999; Finch & Mason, 2000), and to care decisions by adult children who have both biological and stepparents. Attitudes that stress biological kinship as a basis for inheritance except when step kin have very close emotional relationships (Ganong & Coleman, 1999) suggest an additional burden of proof to step ties that parallels that of same-sex versus straight unions (see Chapter 4). The concept of ambivalence is particularly relevant to understanding the complex negotiations that must occur as families work out relatively uncharted territory.

Stepparent–Adult Stepchild Ties

About one fifth of children in the United States are in families that include step ties, and two-fifths of them live with a step parent (Ferguson et al., 2004). Usual estimates of step ties focus on married adults with minor children living at home;

6% of them are in this situation. When this is expanded to include those who cohabit and those with nonresident stepchildren, 14% of married and cohabiting adults have stepchildren (Stewart, 2001). Stepparent-stepchild ties are not a new phenomenon. What is new is the greater likelihood that they will follow divorce than widowhood, increasing co-survival of multiple parents and grandparents. This difference reverses the gender composition of stepparent-parent couples. When childbirth was a primary cause of death among women, widowed men remarried, creating the more typical combination of the time: a father and step-mother. Now that divorce is the more likely precursor of remarriage and given that custody more often goes to the mother than father, the more typical couple combi-nation is a mother and stepfather. Thus co-residence with a stepparent during childhood is much more likely to involve a stepfather than stepmother. On balance, current social trends and arrangements make mothers more involved than fathers, but stepfathers more involved than stepmothers, in the daily lives of children.

Following the life course perspective, this has implications for adult children's ties with stepparents. What are they? A qualitative study of adult stepchildren whose relationship with a stepparent began in childhood shows how gender is played out in mother-stepfather and stepmother-father couples (Schmeeckle, 2007). In both situations, adult stepchildren recall that mothers and stepmothers dominated the management of their activities, as well as their nurturing and discipline. Mothers and stepmothers also emerge as primary kinkeepers, making arrangements for visits and investing in the relationships with their children and stepchildren. Stepmothers are sometimes instrumental in the later renegotiation of ties of stepchildren with their father as well. For some stepchildren, the active involvement of their stepmothers has fostered a more involved tie in adulthood with them than with their fathers.

Finch (2007:67) argues that, along with doing family, we also engage in display-ing family, a term that refers to presenting our relationships as familylike. Successful displays require "demonstrating that relationships between individuals are effective in a familylike way. . . . Defining 'my family' is also an evaluative statement about the positive character of these relationships" (Finch, 2007:70). Success also depends on having a display of familylike qualities confirmed as such by an external audi-ence. Displays of so-called good family relationships are especially important claims to legitimacy among those whose familylike connections are marginalized. Efforts of same-sex (Weeks et al., 2001) or lesbigay families (Carrington, 1999) exemplify the desire of those in unconventional relationships and networks to have their chosen families recognized as family.

Similarly, step relatives may be especially motivated to display their relationships as just like non-stepfamilies (Finch, 2007). The extent to which they do is likely to vary according to when the relationship started and whether it involved co-residing. Stepparents of young children are more likely to strive to be accepted as families, for example, than are those who become stepparents to adult stepchildren. Attempts to display as family may reveal ambivalence in step ties stemming from marginal legal status and from different feelings that family members may have about displaying their relations as familylike. The numerous stepfamilies that try to mimic first-marriage families, labeled Brady Bunch stepfamilies, are likely to be more committed to displaying family than either those families with engaged parents and disengaged stepparents or couple-focused stepfamilies (Ganong & Coleman, 2004).

In research on stepparent-stepchild relations involving adult stepchildren, support exchanges are a primary concern. Attitudes concerning the obligation to help parents favor biological parents over stepparents, regardless of race and ethnicity. But helping stepparents is also considered appropriate, particularly when stepchildren lived with their stepparents while they were growing up and when they have received help from their stepparents and feel close familylike ties to them (Coleman et al., 2006; Ganong et al., 1998). Although Asian and African Americans endorse stronger norms of filial support than do European and Latino Americans, all groups share the view that more help should go to parents than to stepparents (Coleman et al., 2006). African Americans, in contrast, are as likely to see themselves as indebted to stepparents as to parents for having raised them, a reflection of the significant place of stepparents in their lives. Stepchildren are less likely to feel familylike bonds to stepparents acquired later in life, and beliefs about helping them depend upon their obligation to their parent, having a very good relationship with their stepparent, and their stepparent's need for help being minimal (Ganong & Colemen, 2006).

Similar patterns apply regarding stepparent support to stepchildren. Expressed support for the obligation of stepparents to help their adult stepchildren is more substantial than the reverse obligation, but it still falls far short of obligations to biological children (Rossi & Rossi, 1990). Stepparents are influenced by the same factors as stepgrandchildren—familylike close ties, previous help received, and co-residence when stepchildren were younger—in their expectations of help from stepchildren (Clawson & Ganong, 2002).

How do attitudes compare with actual exchanges? Qualitative work indicates that the same factors that shape attitudes are influential in the actual provision of support to stepparents (Clawson & Ganong, 2002). Transfers of financial gifts are more likely from parents to adult children than from stepparents to adult stepchildren, and the average amount of the gifts is also higher from parents to children, but in both cases transfers from stepparents to adult stepchildren are substantial (Killian, 2004). Adult stepchildren of mother and stepfather couples are more likely to receive such financial transfers than are stepchildren of stepmother and father couples (30% versus 21%). Qualitative research indicates the view of adult children that stepfathers invest equally in their step and biological children or more in their stepchildren but stepmothers invest more in their biological than stepchildren (Schmeeckle, 2007). These differences reflect the influence of gendered parent-child relations, including differences in co-residence patterns earlier in life based on gendered custody.

Studies of intergenerational transfers that involve stepparents and stepchildren tend not to consider that, unlike children whose original parents stay married, stepchildren may be receiving support from multiple sources—each parent as well as one or more stepparents. Adult stepchildren do not differ from other children in the amount of support that they give to and receive from parents when all parental support is included (Logan & Spitze, 1996).

Which factors shape familylike relations between stepparents and adult stepchildren? Among adult stepchildren, 31% consider their current stepparent fully family, and another 25% think of stepparents as quite a bit like family (Schmeeckle et al., 2006). They are less likely to think of their current stepparents as parents: 18% do so fully and another 16% quite a bit. The relative precariousness of stepparents as family members is indicated by the much smaller percentages who think of former stepparents as family (7% fully, 9% quite a bit) or parents (3% fully, 6% quite a bit). Adult stepchildren are more inclined to think of their stepparents as fully family and fully parents if their stepparent is married to rather than cohabiting with their parent and if they co-resided when they were young. Co-residence with former stepparents also enhances current, independently negotiated, familylike ties with them. Thus familylike practices of marrying and co-residing tend to enhance adult stepchildren's view of their stepparents as family and parents, and ties to stepparents once children are adults do not require the mediation of biological parents.

Grandparent-Grandchild Relations

At first glance, information from grandparents presents a picture of declining contact between grandparents and grandchildren when a parent remarries (Gladstone, 1991). About half of grandparents whose child remarried report less contact with their grandchildren following their child's remarriage, whereas one-quarter report more contact However, key reasons for fewer visits are greater geographic distance, a grandchild getting older, and their child not having custody of the grandchildren, rather than remarriage per se. The perception of grandchildren's shifting needs is also a factor. In some families, remarriage addresses needs of both the grandchildren and children that grandparents had previously helped meet. Greater contact is also attributed to the increasing age of grandchildren, in this case, because grandchildren have reached an age when contact does not require the involvement of their parents.

Among college students, the tie to the closest grandparent is strongest among grandchildren with a parent and stepparent, followed by those from single-parent families and then those from intact families (Kennedy & Kennedy, 1993). In 4 out of 5 stepfamilies, the closest grandparent is the parent of the co-resident, biological parent. The closer grandparent-grandchild ties in stepfamilies are interpreted as an ever-deepening link with at least one grandparent as the grandchild moves from an intact family, to a single-parent family, to a stepfamily (Kennedy & Kennedy, 1993). The fact that grandchildren in stepfamilies are also more likely to have been cared for by grandparents or to have lived with them while growing up suggests that the support offered by grandparents may facilitate the remarriage of their children in the first place.

About 40% of American families include stepgrandparents, but over half of African American families do so (Szinovacz, 1998). There are three paths to becoming stepgrandparents: marrying someone who is a grandparent, acquiring stepgrandchildren through a child's marriage to someone who has children, and gaining stepgrandchildren through a stepchild's children (Ganong & Coleman, 1999). Before confronting the arrival of stepgrandchildren through their child's remarriage, older persons have had to deal with their child's divorce, subsequent status as a single parent, and the emerging relationship with a new partner (Henry et al., 1993). Close ties between stepgrandparents and stepgrandchildren help foster closer ties between the stepgrandparents and their adult stepchildren (Clawson & Ganong, 2002).

Another perspective on grandparent-grandchild relations following remarriage is that of the middle generation. An abiding concern of parents who form blended families is the relative attention received by children versus stepchildren. Recently remarried mothers perceive both maternal and paternal grandmothers to be more engaged with original grandchildren than with stepgrandchildren, although they believe that their own mothers provide similar levels of instrumental support to their biological and stepgrandchildren (Henry et al., 1992). When older mothers treat their son's children and stepchildren acquired through his marriage as equals, ties between mother-in-law and daughter-in-law are positive (Merrill, 2007). Daughters-in-law who have estranged relationships with their current mothers-in-law are most inclined to report special treatment of their husband's children over theirs.

Among maternal grandmothers, ties to stepchildren through sons-in-law are remote, but paternal grandmothers are as likely to have an apportioned or remote style in relation to their stepchildren through daughters-in-law (Henry et al., 1992). The greater involvement of paternal than maternal grandmothers with their stepchildren may reflect the fact that mothers are more likely than fathers to have their children living with them. Thus sons are more likely to be living with their stepchildren than are daughters, potentially enhancing ties between paternal grandmothers and their stepgrandchildren through greater contact.

Finally, for a growing number of grandparents, step ties with grandchildren are a function of the grandparents' remarriage many years ago or in later life. In the former case, grandchildren were acquired at birth, when they were born to their stepchild. For grandparents who negotiated an involved parental tie with their stepchildren, the term *step* may be a technical one only. This is the experience of a grandfather in his 70s who married his then-widowed wife and became stepfather to her young daughter: "I'm a great-grandfather step! But . . . the word step doesn't come into my vocabulary now" (Dimmock et al., 2004:84).

Chapter Summary

Generation (in which generation did divorce, remarriage, or acquiring step ties occur?), time (life stage and relationship duration) and place (co-residence and geographic proximity) are pivotal to exploring how transitions in intimate relationships affect intergenerational ties. More research is needed to clarify our understanding of the long-term consequences of divorce for intergenerational relations. Recent work indicates that by the time children are in middle age, they and their parents have renegotiated their relationships to involve more support in both directions.

Divorce, remarriage, and their impact on negotiating step ties highlight the gendered nature of family life, including practices of custody and of responsibility toward raising children. In addition to their concerns about the welfare of their children following divorce, grandparents worry about their grandchildren's future. The response to this worry by many grandparents is to step in and offer support and stability to the grandchildren. This intervention appears to have lasting effects on the grandparent-grandchild tie, with good relations continuing after the remarriage of the middle-generation parent. In more extreme cases, divorce may result in the grandparent meeting parental responsibilities.

More research is needed on the impact of transitions in other forms of intimate relationships on intergenerational ties, including the dissolution of cohabiting and same-sex relationships or transitions into these relationships following divorce or dissolution. More sophisticated studies indicate conditions and processes that enhance intergenerational relations, whether ties are biological, adoptive or step, and encourage more research in this direction (Lansford et al., 2001). Changes in union formation and changing parenting practices are reshaping the consequences of union dissolution for intergenerational step ties.

Summary and Conclusion to Part III

The majority of older persons has children and is engaged in exchange relationships with them. However, with age, parents and children become less focused on one another as they attend to other commitments and interests. However, should needs for support escalate in either generation, the other generation is generally available and willing to provide help, often at extensive levels.

The lives of adult children remain an ongoing concern for older parents, whose contentment can rise and fall depending on the successes and problems of their children. Having children, by itself, is no guarantee of happiness in old age, but having close relations with children enhances quality of life. Adult children with either temporary or long-term needs for housing, financial support, and care generally find ready allies and advocates in their parents. Increasing age and declining health may lead to an imbalance in the exchange, with parents more dependent on children toward the end of their lives. Although providing parental care may create considerable strain, a sense of filial duty motivates children, especially daughters, to provide care whether or not they have competing obligations, such as children and jobs.

Those who chose to be childless are happier in later life than those who did not, but on balance, regardless of whether it was a choice, most old childless persons lead contented lives. The childless have fewer sources of care and support in old age, but childless older persons tend to meet their needs through the smaller number of support persons that they do have, and their social activity levels are at least as high as those of parents. Most old persons believe that there are both advantages and disadvantages to not having children. Perceived advantages are more likely to be founded on actual experience, whereas perceived disadvantages tend to reflect long-held cultural assumptions about the merits of having children. Just as having children is no guarantee of happiness, not having children does not spell unhappiness in later life.

Most old persons are grandparents and derive considerable pleasure from the flexibility and emotional focus of their relationship with grandchildren. Typically, grandparents engage in low-key, companionate ties with their grandchildren. Geographic proximity is important to this relationship, enhancing contact, emotional closeness and involvement. Adult grandchildren tend to report close ties to their grandparents, especially on the maternal side and to grandmothers. The potential extensiveness of support from the older to younger generations is most evident among the growing numbers of grandparents who effectively raise their grandchildren when their children cannot. There are important ways in which the burdens of caring can be redressed through social policy (see Chapter 14). As more grandparents see their grandchildren reach their 20s, 30s, and 40s, more attention should be paid to the support that adult grandchildren give to their grandparents.

The growing variety and turnover of unions adds a complex web of step ties to the constellation of family relationships. Two sets of parent-child relationships (generation one and generation two, and generation two and generation three) and grandparent-grandchild ties are engaged in negotiating the ambivalence that is more evident in step ties.

Throughout this discussion of intergenerational relationships, several key themes repeat themselves. First, gender fundamentally shapes familial ties because gender is the basis for structuring both family and work. The consequence is that women dominate in care situations, particularly as adult children and grandmothers. Men and women differ in terms of the nature of the care they provide, the support received from others when providing it, and the consequences of caring.

Second, differences in intergenerational relations are also a result of how race structures social life. The association of race with advantage or disadvantage and with different cultural traditions creates additional complexity to understanding how families work. The greater involvement of non-White parents and grandparents in assisting and supporting younger generations presents a particular challenge, given their relative lack of resources. Yet cultural traditions appear to help offset the costs of caring in these families. As with gender, alleviating the burden of support can only occur through fundamental social change.

Third, meeting the substantial challenges faced by family members in providing support to one another is either impeded or facilitated by access to resources. Class and economic situation are intricately bound to the demands on women and on family members of color as support providers. Limited access to resources and a position of disadvantage over generations combine to make support provision more necessary and more difficult to elude. In turn, providing extensive, unpaid support further undermines the capacity to improve one's resource base.

Last, social change is reshaping family structure across gender, class and race divisions. Focusing on change rather than judgmental terms, such as the decline of the family, deepens our understanding of different family forms and their relative strengths and weaknesses from the vantage point of different players in the family.

A family structure that better serves the interests of some groups is bound to be assessed as a better family form by those groups. Our examination of family ties following divorce suggests both costs and benefits for various family members. Costs include disrupting family ties, the increase in support demanded of others in the family, such as parents or grandparents, and the heartache associated with longer-term separation or isolation from loved ones. But there are also benefits: relief from unhealthy relationships, the satisfaction of seeing family members through difficult times, the greater closeness that comes from increased involvement, and the addition of new family members who enrich lives in unanticipated ways.

PART IV

Sibling Relationships

CHAPTER 12

Sibling Ties in Middle and Later Life

Siblings influence each other's thoughts, feelings, and actions even without being present. Shared family and interpersonal history means that sibling ties have the potential to be active even without contact. Daily experiences trigger memories of siblings or remind us of things only our siblings would understand.

—Walker, Allen, and Connidis, 2005:177

You may not yet have a long-term partner, be married, or have children or grandchildren, but you are very likely to have at least one brother or sister. If not, you are close to someone who does. Although personal reflections have limited utility as a basis for drawing general conclusions about sibling ties, they are good touchstones for comparison and for raising unanswered questions as you consider what we know so far. For most of us, the sibling relationship is the first experience of an intimate relationship with a peer and is likely to shape our future perspective on family living.

The life course interplay of structured social relations, ambivalence and agency creates a dynamic perspective on sibling relationships over time (Connidis, 2005b). The concept of ambivalence captures the mixed emotions and socially structured contradictions that typify sibling relationships. Throughout this and the next chapter, consider how the theoretical perspective outlined in Chapter 1 applies to adult sibling relationships.

Longer lives and more alternative unions and changes in partner status are likely to make sibling ties more significant in middle and later life. For certain, greater diversity will result as more half (siblings who share one biological parent) and step (related by a parent's marriage) siblings are added to family constellations over a lengthier and more complex life course. Yet the limited research available on older siblings typically focuses on either biological siblings or on all those who are considered siblings, without distinguishing among them, leaving a major gap in research regarding adult ties involving half and step siblings. There are also step sibling equivalents in nonmarital same-sex and opposite-sex unions.

Because the law differentiates among parents based on whether they have biological ties to their children, the law also differentiates among siblings. The ambiguous legal standing of a step tie heightens ambivalence because step relations are expected to act like family even though they are not legally sanctioned as full family members (Connidis, 2005b). Adoptive siblings are more like biological siblings in being legally recognized as children and in usually starting out with two parents since infancy or early childhood. When full, half or step siblings share a home, ambiguity and ambivalence are especially high (Ahrons, 2004; Stewart, 2005). Such changes in family structure are likely to have particularly significant long-term effects on sibling ties (Matthews, 2002a). In this chapter, we explore the availability and qualities of adult sibling relationships. In Chapter 13, support exchanges involving siblings in mid and later life are discussed. When possible, available information on step and half sibling ties, as well as siblings of different sexual orientations, is included in both chapters.

Unique Features of Sibling Ties

A unique feature of the sibling relationship is its duration when compared to other family ties. As the longest-lasting tie most of us will have, there is the potential for shared experiences over a lifetime, providing a ready basis for reminiscence as we age. Mutual reminiscing is associated with positive emotions, especially among older persons (Pasupathi & Carstensen, 2003). The enduring quality of the sibling relationship can also provide a sense of continuity over the life course, confirming a sense of ourselves in older age as persons still engaged in the world and as objects of affection and caring (Goetting, 1986; Moss & Moss, 1989; Ross & Milgram, 1982). In the wake of higher rates of divorce and of remaining single, these features may become especially valued. Studying the sibling tie makes a contribution to our general understanding of family ties in emphasizing the connection between our family lives as children and as adults.

Unlike other relationships, those among most siblings include the sharing of a common cultural background, early experiences of family belonging, and for biological siblings, the same genetic pool (Cicirelli, 1995). Thus siblings can play a substantial role in continuing the family sentiments of youth into adulthood and old age. In addition to shared sentiments, siblings share important structural positions in the larger social world, such as age and race. At the same time, there are often important differences between them, and we must be cautious not to over-draw the similarity of experience between siblings, especially once adults.

Another unique characteristic of the sibling relationship is its egalitarian nature. This reflects the horizontal nature of the tie between siblings, in contrast to the vertical tie between parents and children. Such horizontal ties are characterized by the relatively equal power of both parties and an emphasis on sociability (Cumming & Schneider, 1961). This suggests that, of all family ties, the sibling relationship most closely parallels the characteristics of friendship. Most sibling relationships weather a variety of changes and witness many phases of family life (Connidis, 1992). At the same time, sibling ties are characterized by contradiction, as we will see.

Diversity Among Siblings

Because of the usual focus on the sibling ties of childhood, we risk assuming more uniformity among them as adults than we should. Variations among adult siblings and in sibling constellations or configurations are notable, including the variations based on being full, half or step siblings already noted. Full siblings share the same race, but half and step siblings may not. Gender and sexual orientation vary within sibling networks, as do partner and parent status. A sibling network may be all sisters, all brothers, or a combination of brothers and sisters; it may be all straight, all gay or lesbian, or a combination and so on. There is also significant inequality among European and African American adult siblings in social class, as indicated by education, occupation and income (Conley, 2004; Hauser et al., 1999; Heflin & Pattillo, 2006). Class variations contradict the assumed egalitarianism of sibling ties and may engender ambivalent feelings about siblings (Connidis, 2007). Thus we must consider whether and how structured social relations make a difference to sibling relationships both across and within families.

Sibling Rivalry and Birth Order

Sibling rivalry and birth order are very popular topics. In both cases, the usual focus is childhood. Goetting (1986) argues that resolving rivalry is a key task of siblings in old age, along with companionship, shared reminiscence and mutual aid. Typically, sibling rivalry declines or is managed effectively with increasing age (Cicirelli, 1995). Large families tend not to promote sibling rivalry to the same extent as smaller ones, primarily because parents of many children do not have time to serve as arbitrators in disputes among siblings (Bossard & Boll, 1956). Instead, siblings are left to sort things out on their own, thus promoting cooperation and minimizing rivalry. The more positive relationships with siblings reported by young adults from larger families (Riggio, 2006) raise questions about future sibling ties, given the growing number of two-sibling families.

Birth order studies usually explore the consequences of relative positions as siblings during childhood for longer-term individual outcomes. Who hasn't been intrigued by contemplating what it meant to grow up as the oldest or middle or youngest child? Mass media coverage, such as *Time* magazine's (2007) cover story on "The Secrets of Birth Order: New research shows how your family's pecking order really does shape your destiny," appeals to this curiosity and reflects the dramatic claims that some make about birth order's profound and long-lasting effects (Sulloway, 1996). On balance, research does not support a strong birth order effect on individual outcomes (Steelman et al., 2002). Given the focus on family ties, however, the central question is, Does birth order have lasting repercussions for relationships with siblings and with other family members? To date, the evidence is mixed, at best (Cicerilli, 1995).

When children are young, families can lead relatively isolated lives in which siblings are major players and key reference points, although this is changing as child care and preschool settings increase exposure to other children and families at earlier ages. A study of young adults with a mean age of 22 years suggests that the younger sibling in families of two, and those reporting on eldest siblings, are less positive about their siblings than those in other birth order positions or those referring to younger siblings (Riggio, 2006). This sample of university students, however, reported on only one sibling, chosen as the sibling who had either the greatest negative or positive impact on their lives. Research on sisters across age groups indicates growing equality among them once they are in their 20s and in response to adult life transitions (Stark, 2006). As well, although older siblings are more likely to help younger ones with odd jobs and to give them advice, this only lasts until middle age (Voorpostel et al., 2007). By middle and old age, siblings have collectively experienced a range of experiences that are likely to outweigh any impact of birth order on their relationships.

Relationships evolve in response to changing times and circumstances, making the determination of birth order in later life more problematic. What counts as your birth order if you gain a second round of step or half siblings or if a sibling dies? A first-born sister may see the assumed power of being oldest disappear when her younger brother becomes a successful lawyer. A second child may assume new status as the rebellious behavior that led to mediocre school grades leads to success in the business world because she is willing to take necessary risks. The youngest sibling who marries a wealthy partner may no longer seem like the baby of the family. A two- or three-year age difference may matter greatly in the sandbox but not much in a retirement community. Thus even if birth order were significant for individual outcomes and in childhood, and that is a big if (Steelman et al., 2002), its impact on adult sibling relationships is likely to fade as structured social relations and cumulative life experience trump birth order in shaping sibling and other family ties.

Availability of and Contact With Siblings

As mentioned in Chapter 2, most of today's older persons have at least one living sibling (80% of those aged 65 and more). A high proportion of the baby boom generation, whose older members are now approaching old age, has siblings. Looking ahead, the distribution of family size rather than birth rates is the key to having biological siblings (Connidis, 2005b). In Canada and the United States, most of those who have children have two or three of them, ensuring a sibling for most of us into old age. In cohorts following the baby boom, however, many more people will have one rather than two or more siblings, a change in family structure that has significant consequences for sibling ties. For example, dyads do not allow for the formation of coalitions based on gender, age or interests. The greater complexity of family structure makes counting siblings more of a challenge, as individuals and researchers grapple with whether to include biological, half and step siblings in one category; to count them separately; or to distinguish among siblings on qualitative grounds (White,

1998). Canadian data indicate that over 1 in 5 persons aged 25 to 34 have a step, adoptive or half sibling, compared with 1 in 10 aged 65 to 74 (Statistics Canada, 2002b).

As well as having siblings, many older persons have a sibling who lives nearby. Over 40% of those aged 65 or over have a sibling living nearby (within 30 minutes; Murphy, 2004). In my community study, 70% of respondents aged 65 years or more who had living siblings had at least one sibling less than a day's drive away. A large panel study in the United States found declines in geographic proximity from the ages of 18 to 50, when proximity stabilized (White, 2001). From age 50 and up, 55% have at least one sibling living within 25 miles. Closer proximity to at least one sibling occurs among those with less education, those with more siblings, nonimmigrants, African Americans, and following divorce or widowhood (White, 2001).

Geographic proximity tends to have a particularly strong impact on sibling contact, with much higher contact in person and by phone among siblings who live near each other (Connidis & Campbell, 1995; Kalmijn, 2006; Lee et al., 1990; Spitze & Trent, 2006; White, 2001). As a 67-year-old sister put it when comparing her closer tie to one sister than the other,

> Living in the same city, of course, you see each other every day or phone every day. I think that is the big bonus. With Susan, she was away for so many years. . . . You are not in touch or as close as you are when you are in the same city.

The significance of proximity reflects the more voluntary nature of sibling relationships when compared with the more obligatory ties to parents or children.

What about sibling contact over time? Across seven countries, including the United States, variations in sibling contact occur with age for men but not women (Murphy, 2004). Among women, sibling contact is stable across age groups from the mid-30s into old age, with one-third reporting at least weekly contact. Social class variations are minimal. Panel data in the United States show that aging leads to a decline in sibling contact that plateaus in middle age (White, 2001), but less of a decrease occurs among women, African Americans (see also Becker et al., 2003), Latinos, the less educated, and nonimmigrants. Closer proximity accounts for much of the greater contact with siblings among the less educated, African Americans, and Latinos (White, 2001).

Individuals with an average age of 42 and who have only one sibling visit their siblings in person an average of three times a month (Spitze & Trent, 2006). Increasing age leads to fewer visits in person but not by phone, and Black respondents and those who grew up with both of their parents have more visits with their siblings than their counterparts. The latter finding suggests change ahead in sibling relationships, given the increased likelihood of not growing up with both parents in the same household.

Gender is strongly related to sibling contact. At age 65 and over, women are in greater contact with siblings than are men (Murphy, 2004), even when proximity is taken into account (White, 2001). In two-sibling families, gender of the adult sibling pair is unrelated to contact in person, but phone contact is more frequent for women with a sister than for other gender combinations (woman with a brother, man with a sister, man with a brother; Spitze & Trent, 2006). In an older sample of varying family sizes, contact with the sibling who is seen most often and contact with the entire sibling network is more frequent among middle-aged and older women than men, and sisters interact more often than other gender combinations (Connidis, 1989a; Connidis & Campbell, 1995; Lee et al., 1990; Scott, 1983).

Although most siblings maintain contact with one another over the life course, the amount of sibling interaction is subject to competition from the family of procreation, so that when demands in the procreative family are higher, sibling interaction is lower (Gold, 1987). Having a spouse or partner decreases personal and phone contact, and having children under 18 decreases visits with siblings among those with one sibling (Spitze & Trent, 2006). Across seven countries, contact with siblings is about twice as high among single as among ever-married siblings, and older persons without children have considerably more contact with their siblings than do parents (Murphy, 2004; re the UK, see Wenger et al., 2000; Wenger & Burholt, 2001). When compared with divorced older persons, single older persons see their siblings more often (Strain & Payne, 1992). Greater contact with siblings following marital dissolution or widowhood is accounted for in substantial measure by moving closer to siblings, when this occurs (White, 2001).

The constellation of marital and parent statuses in sibling dyads and networks of those aged 55 and over also makes a difference, independent of emotional closeness (Connidis & Campbell, 1995). For the sibling seen most often, contact is greatest between single respondents and a single sibling, followed by divorced persons with a single sibling, and then widowed respondents with a single sibling. Interaction is lowest between married respondents and their married siblings (see also Lee et al., 1990) and between widowed individuals with either a widowed or a divorced sibling. Thus being unmarried per se does not lead to greater interaction; rather, being single (never married) is key. Results for contact with all siblings are similar; interaction with their sibling networks is greater for single respondents than for all other marital-status groups. Regarding parent-status constellations, those who have only childless siblings see their siblings more often than those whose sibling networks include parents (Connidis & Campbell, 1995). Pairs of childless siblings see each other most often, followed by pairs in which one sibling is a parent and one is childless, and then by two parents (Connidis, 1989a).

The marital and childbearing history of parents affects sibling contact. Among siblings aged 18 and over, although some contact is maintained whether full, half, or step, full siblings enjoy significantly greater levels of contact than half or step siblings (White & Riedmann, 1992a). Even the full siblings in families with step ties see each other less often than full siblings in original families do. More research is needed to determine the impact of the age at which siblings become step or half siblings, whether they lived together, and the age gaps between them to appreciate just what it is about not being full siblings or in intact families that accounts for these differences.

Fewer hours of paid work enhance contact among adult siblings (Spitze & Trent, 2006), and retirement affords an opportunity for greater sibling contact for many older individuals. However, the confining impact of health problems and decreased mobility, especially where distance is a factor, generally leads to a decline in contact in the oldest stages of life (Cicirelli, 1995; Scott, 1983). Different types of interaction may be possible or impossible, depending on circumstances such as health or financial situation, and do not bear upon the quality of the relationship. For example, an 81-year-old man in the London study observed,

There are nine of us [brothers and sisters] in the family, and we kind of cling together. Especially when you move around, you know, you have got to stay together. I haven't made as many friends, but we have each other. . . . They are all so far away now . . . we don't see much of each other.

There are also cases where extensive contact does not reflect closeness but rather is a function of a shared sense of family commitment among siblings (McGhee, 1985). The relatively voluntary nature of sibling ties and the limited institutional support for them when compared with marriage and parent-child relations makes them a somewhat elusive adult tie (Mauthner, 2000). As the opening quote indicates, siblings do not have to be physically present to be influential (Walker et al., 2005). Indeed, being at once active and dormant, close and distant are among the contradictions of this relationship.

The Nature of Sibling Ties in Later Life

Social expectations that pose major contradictions for sibling ties start in childhood. Equity, maturity, loyalty and individuality are four major issues in childhood sibling relationships (Handel, 1994). These issues reflect strongly held but conflicting cultural views about the nature of sibling ties and can be viewed as two pairs of dialectical opposites. In the first, the expectation that siblings should be treated equitably by their parents is made difficult by the fact that, being different ages, siblings are at different levels of maturity and cannot, therefore, be treated in the same way. In the second, the expectation of loyalty between siblings conflicts with the need to develop as individuals. These fundamental contradictions make sibling ties inherently ambivalent (Bedford, 1989).

To some extent, aging itself reduces ambivalence by minimizing the significance of maturity and individuality as issues to be dealt with in the sibling relationship. Although the closer ties to parents, adult children and siblings are more likely to evoke ambivalence than more distant ties (Fingerman et al., 2004), the mixed feelings about siblings that are more common among teenagers give way to primarily positive sentiments among old persons (Fingerman & Hay, 2004). As siblings grow older, age ceases to be a major factor in their relationship, a shift observed frequently by respondents in my sibling dyad study. The following quote from a woman of 60 about her relationship with her 70-year-old brother is a good example:

He left home when I was 9 years old so we had very little relationship growing up. He was 10 years older than I and so he was 19. He went away from home and then he was in the army and went overseas for 6 years. And then came back and went to university . . . so our relationship has become closer as we got older rather than a continuum. . . . It would have been 35 years ago [that our father died]. At that point, we hadn't seen much of each other and at that age a 10-year age difference . . . is quite an age difference. The age difference doesn't matter as much as you get older.

As well, despite stereotypical depictions that present a uniform image of older people, the older we get, the more diverse we become as different arrays of life experience accumulate. Thus the need to actively strive for individuality declines with time. Nonetheless, expectations regarding the sibling tie in childhood are extended into adult life when the sibling relationship is viewed as egalitarian and as more voluntary than ties to spouses, parents, or children (Cicirelli, 1995).

Types of Sibling Relationships

The considerable variations in the type of relationships that siblings negotiate with one another occur across and also within families, reflecting the different points of view that can be held by members of one family. Qualitative data from 60 older individuals were used to create a typology of sibling relationships based on degrees of closeness, envy, resentment, instrumental support, emotional support, acceptance, psychological involvement, and contact (Gold, 1986, 1989; Gold et al., 1990). Five types of sibling ties were identified: intimate, congenial, loyal, apathetic, and hostile (Gold, 1986, 1989). The variation of sibling types underlines the folly of attempting to develop one characterization of the sibling bond.

The majority of older persons have intimate, congenial, or loyal ties with siblings. However, Blacks are more likely to emphasize positive and supportive dimensions of sibling ties, whereas Whites more often refer to envy and resentment when talking about their siblings (Gold, 1990). This contrast may reflect long-standing differences rooted in childhood and early adulthood, periods during which Black siblings offer extensive support to one another. Loyal sibling relationships have several features parallel to those of friendship: actively trying to be with each other; cooperation, sympathy and mutual helpfulness; a unique language generally not shared with others; and defense of each other against outsiders (Bank & Kahn, 1982). Given that 77% of older individuals consider at least one sibling a close friend (Connidis, 1989b), many older persons appear to enjoy loyal sibling relationships. A review of research on adult siblings concludes that they qualify as a nonsexual intimate relationship because they involve cognitive and emotional connections that stem from shared experiences and they can be sustained despite limited proximity and contact (Bedford & Avioli, 2001).

Closeness Among Siblings in Later Life

For many, the sibling tie has the potential for being a warm and close relationship over the life course and into old age, as reflected in Photo 12.1. A strong sense of family membership and closeness to particular siblings is permanently shaped by shared childhood experiences for many adults, including eating and playing games together, going to church, family crises, and special events (Gold, 1987).

Closeness rarely develops in old age; instead, siblings who are close as adults tend to have been close in childhood (Scott, 1983). A range of studies illustrates closeness among a majority of siblings across the adult life course. In a sample of younger adults aged 19 to 33, 65% report being close or extremely close to their

Photo 12.1   For many brothers and sisters, sibling ties are closer in older age when there is time to invest in them once more.

siblings (Milevsky, 2005). Of adults with a mean age of 42 and one sibling, 80% get along with their sibling, and over half consider their sibling among their closest friends (Spitze & Trent, 2006). Among adults aged 55 and over, 70% say they are somewhat, very, or extremely close to at least one of their siblings (Connidis, 1994a). By middle age, increasing age means greater closeness to siblings (Connidis & Campbell, 1995), and by old age, attachment to siblings appears to rebound from lulls experienced when other relationships took precedence (Cicirelli, 1995; Doherty & Feeney, 2004). These patterns over time are described by a married father, aged 64:

> When we were younger, we were all quite close. And I mean right up through our early married years. And then, for some reason that none of us know about—and we've actually discussed it—we drifted apart. We really did drift apart. And we had very little in common. I think Mary (wife) and I being out of town contributed to it. But starting again, oh, I don't know, 10, 12 years ago or something, we've really got back and got pretty much the relationship we had when we were kids. But we did come full circle and we've actually talked about it, you know, "How come?" There was a period of 6 or 8 years that we hardly ever even talked to each other on the telephone, never mind directly.
>
> We'd meet occasionally at family things and what not. I think it was partly . . . job related; I think it was partly because of what our children were involved in. Just for no real reason. Just drifted apart.

Despite the drifting apart noted by this brother, he also talks about working together with his siblings to handle the closing of their father's business after his death and to settle the estate of their mother after her death. In both instances, siblings were brought closer together. The various health problems of this man and his siblings have had a similar effect.

A widowed mother in her 60s describes a similar pattern of closeness over time but emphasizes changing responsibilities as the reason for growing closer again later in life:

> If you develop relationships in the community where you live and you're very involved with your family, you don't have much time for siblings. But then, after your children grow up, you probably think of your siblings more just because you are fond of each other, and you just want to maintain that relationship. . . . You don't want to lose it. After your responsibilities are fewer, you want to renew and strengthen the relationship with your siblings. That's the way I feel about it.

Those who have more siblings are generally more likely to consider at least one of them a close friend but less likely to think of all of their siblings as close friends, indicating selectivity among siblings (Connidis, 1989b). Aging minimizes barriers to closeness created by age differences when they were young (Gold, 1987), but within families, older siblings appear to feel closer to a sibling who is closer in age and shares more common interests (Folwell et al., 1997). The comments of a 66-year-old man are illustrative:

> My father died when I was two and that makes a difference. And the different age groups in a large family, from the youngest—I'm the second youngest—to the oldest. . . . I never skated with any of them on the river or went swimming with them, so we have no memories of the things that we had done together when we were children. I am closer to the young one, my brother that died. I was quite close to him because we grew up together. And my sister. We used to go dancing together. Now, I was fairly close to those two, the ones that I grew up with. The other ones weren't there, so I couldn't be close to them.

Those with more siblings are significantly closer to their emotionally closest sibling than are those from smaller families (Connidis & Campbell, 1995).

Geographic distance tends to hamper sibling closeness (Lee et al., 1990). In two-sibling families, living nearer by enhances getting along and thinking of one's sibling as a close friend (Spitze & Trent, 2006), but in larger families, proximity enhances closeness to the sibling network overall but not to the emotionally closest sibling (Connidis & Campbell, 1995). Having a proximate sibling appears to increase indirect communication about the entire sibling network, enhancing general closeness to siblings. Speaking first of his sister and then of his brother, a 71-year-old man in one of my studies recounts,

> Then they [sister and her husband] came to live here permanently . . . and of course, we were physically close, and we saw more of them. My brother moved . . . and I saw much less of him . . . so that . . . changed the relationship. If you are going to continue a relationship, you have to see each other.

Indeed, the link of geographic proximity to greater contact is the key reason for greater emotional closeness (White & Riedmann, 1992a).

Marital and parent status also influence sibling intimacy. Those who are unattached and childless are especially likely to have strong attachments to their siblings (Doherty & Feeney, 2004). Widowed siblings stand out as the emotionally closest siblings of middle-aged and older persons (Connidis & Campbell, 1995). More generally, those who are widowed, single, or childless are closer than married parents to their siblings (Chappell & Badger, 1987). The high rate of widowhood among older people makes siblings pivotal or focal kin for many in old age, particularly women. Furthermore, the special place of siblings in the lives of unattached and childless older persons may extend to other members of a sibling's family. For example, a childless aunt of 68 moved in order to be near to her sister and family. She says,

> I am very close to my nieces and nephews. They're like my own, and I'm very fond of them. They used to come to Toronto to stay with my mother and me. I'd take them around Toronto, and they really enjoyed that.

Parents' marital status may also have long-term implications for sibling ties. Among siblings aged 19 to 33 years, those whose parents are divorced are less close emotionally and communicate less often than is true of those whose parents stay together (Milevsky, 2004).

Research on gender composition and its impact on sibling ties yields mixed results. Compared to men, middle-aged and older women are closer to their siblings, regardless of gender (Connidis & Campbell, 1995). However, there are contradictory results about whether sisters, same-sex, or mixed-gender (sister-brother) siblings are closer to one another. The tie between sisters is generally seen to be closer (Cicirelli, 1995; Goetting, 1986), followed by brother-sister ties and then by brothers. However, some conclude that both men and women feel closer to a sibling of the same sex, with women feeling closer to their sisters than men do to their brothers (Gibson & Mugford, 1986).

Two problems haunt studies of gender variations in emotional closeness. One is that there are likely to be gender differences in what closeness means and in willingness to speak openly about it, with men more reticent to discuss the emotional side of relationships (Matthews, 1994). When one focuses on the emotionally closest sibling, for example, older women report being closer to their sibling, whether brother or sister, than do men (Connidis & Campbell, 1995). Similarly, in two-sibling families with an average age in their early 40s, women with sisters stand out because they are more likely than men with brothers to say that they get along and more likely than men with brothers or sisters to consider their siblings among their closest friends (Spitze & Trent, 2006). But there are not significant differences between women with sisters and women with brothers. In other words, the gender of the respondent rather than the gender combination may be more critical to determining closeness. The other problem is that the entire configuration of the sibling network is rarely taken into account when determining how close siblings are to one another. Families vary in gender composition so that some have siblings of the same sex only, some have opposite-sex siblings only, and some have both brothers and sisters. As we shall see when we discuss the sharing of parental care (Chapter 13), such gender configurations are important in shaping sibling relationships.

This said, the tie between sisters tends to have a unique capacity for intimacy, starting early in life:

> Later in life, the close proximity of sisters in childhood may be recreated. Women tend to outlive their male partners by several years, and many widowed and retired sisters end up living together again in the same kind of intimacy as they shared in childhood. At the end of her life, as at the beginning, a sister may be privy to the small, personal details about the other—her eating, sleeping and washing habits—to which possibly no other person, except a long-term sexual partner, ever has access. Over a whole lifetime such intimacy contributes to a rare and special kind of closeness. (McConville, 1985:56)

Several respondents in my study of sibling dyads, both men and women, talk about the difference that gender makes, including the observation that gender simply makes a difference but does not make sibling ties better or worse. A 60-year-old woman with one sister and two brothers, speaking of her sister and one of her brothers, says,

> The person I talk to the most is Rose. But I'm definitely not fonder of her. Rose and John are both [close]—perhaps Rose a little bit more because I talk to her a little bit more. And perhaps two women, you know, talk perhaps a little bit more. . . . I can say anything at all to John. Anything. . . . For a man, he is extremely understanding. I mean, there are very few men that would sit around and discuss relationships.

A 71-year-old man compares his relationships with his sister and brother and concludes,

> They are different, but I wouldn't say one was closer. The distance, of course, and the fact that my brother is a male. There are some personal feelings that I don't confide in anyone, but I discuss some things with my brother that I wouldn't with my sister. It's just different.

Changing attitudes toward gender relations are sometimes raised as older persons reflect on their sibling ties. For example, a 72-year-old woman observes,

> I imagine maybe [my brothers] were at one time closer than I was to either of them. . . . It used to be different, how you talk to a woman and a man, but nowadays, things are so much more open than it used to be. I guess you can say whatever, male or female.

Just as some childless older persons make culturally based assumptions about the benefits of having children (see Chapter 9), some older persons without a same-sex sibling make assumptions about how positive the experience would be. A woman of 72 with brothers only says,

> Maybe if I had a sister, it would be different. I think having a sister would have been great. A sister you would feel closer to than you would brothers. Your interests would be more the same. They [my brothers] were always playing ball, and I wasn't much of a sports fan.

A 64-year-old man begins a similar reverie but catches himself:

> I have to keep a balanced attitude. It's hard to do when you're a brother [with] sisters, because I don't have brothers. I've often speculated what it would have been like to have had a brother. But it's funny, I'm looking back now on the two sons I have. . . . They don't speak to each other. They don't get along.

Last, emotional closeness is usually regarded as a dependent variable, with researchers trying to understand what factors lead to closer ties. However, feeling close to siblings is also likely to encourage certain behaviors, such as contact and confiding. The focus on egalitarianism in the sibling tie minimizes some of the obligatory component that typifies other family relationships, especially those between parents and children. Thus our sentiments or emotional attachment to siblings are likely to play important roles in our adult relationships with brothers and sisters. Indeed, among those aged 55 and over who have siblings, those who are emotionally closer to their siblings confide in and see each other more than those who are less close (Connidis & Campbell, 1995; see also Lee et al., 1990). Similarly, those who consider a sibling a friend see that sibling more often (White & Riedmann, 1992b). The significance of emotional closeness for increasing contact makes the sibling tie a more precarious source of support than those relationships imbued with a stronger sense of obligation.

What happens when there are significant social status differences among siblings? A qualitative study suggests that middle-aged siblings sustain close ties with one another despite substantial differences in material resources if they had interdependent relationships as children, when parents did not differentiate among them based on gender or personal characteristics, and when they share upward mobility in relation to their parents despite variation among themselves in socioeconomic status (Connidis, 2007). These conditions foster greater closeness among siblings, an attachment that is valued over material differences.

Siblings as Confidants and Companions

Siblings are important confidants in later life, with a general preference for sisters over brothers (Wenger & Jerome, 1999). However, because siblings are peers, living into old age may require turning to younger kin to replace lost siblings. Among old persons who have someone that they trust and confide in, 22% list a sibling as one of their key confidants (Connidis & Davies, 1992). If we look at the composition of the confidant network, siblings comprise a larger portion of the confidant network of childless persons, of single women, and of parents whose children live farther away. Among persons aged 55 and over, the chances of confiding in a sibling are higher among women, the childless, those whose children live far away, and those whose siblings live nearby (Campbell et al., 1999). In terms of network composition, among those whose nearest sibling lives within an hour's drive, siblings are a larger portion of the confidant network of single men (55%) than single women (40%) and compose about one-fifth of the network of divorced men and women. Among the married and widowed, siblings are more dominant in the confidant networks of women than of men.

Siblings are more likely to serve as confidants than companions in later life (Connidis & Davies, 1992), in part because companionship requires proximity. Siblings compose a larger portion of the companion network of single women than of any other group (Connidis & Davies, 1990). Among those aged 55 and over, women and those with a proximate sibling are more likely than their counterparts to list a sibling as a companion (Campbell et al., 1999). If siblings are nearby, they follow friends as the second most dominant tie in the companion network of single persons and are a sizeable portion (23%) of this network for widowed women. Once again, siblings emerge as especially salient in the lives of women, as well as among single and childless persons.

The Sibling Ties of Gay and Lesbian Adults

The scant research attention to how variations in sexual orientation are negotiated among siblings over time is partly a function of the understandable focus on gay and lesbian partnerships and parenting in discussions of gay family ties (Allen & Demo, 1995). Both of these relationships have involved political struggle for formal legislation, for example, through legalization of same-sex marriage and the right of gay and lesbian individuals or couples to adopt children. Same-sex partnerships, and the absence of support from the partners' families of origin in some cases, were discussed in Chapter 4. Although accounts of rejection due to sexual orientation abound, we must be careful not to overstate the case. Joan Laird (1996:90), a mother, grandmother, and partner of a lesbian, argues,

> Ours is not an unusual story. Lesbian and gays come from families and are connected to these original families. . . . Most of us are not cut off from our families—not forever rejected, isolated, disinherited. We are daughters and sons, siblings, aunts and uncles, parents and grandparents. Like everyone else, most of us have continuing, complicated relationships with our families. We participate in negotiating the changing meanings, rituals, values, and connections that define kinship.

A key reason for framing the sentiment of families toward their gay or lesbian members as one of rejection is the common focus on coming out as the defining moment of this relationship (Laird, 1996). Yet over time, many gay and lesbian persons with families work out good relations with both their parents and siblings. Indeed, dominant family forms among older lesbians and gays include the family of origin (Fullmer, 1995; see Chapter 4).

For families that include diversity in sexual orientation, working out family relations requires negotiating the stigmatized social status of a gay or lesbian family member (Connidis, 2003b). Multiple meanings of family may be the outcome. In a case study of a three-generation family, a lesbian's middle-aged siblings are part of the effort to manage her identity in encounters with their parents, aunts and uncles. Sharing the view that her sexual orientation would be problematic for their old parents, they protect her very close relationship with her parents by not naming her sexual identity (Connidis, 2005a). Among gay men, increasing age decreases the likelihood of being out with their families. About three-quarters of men aged 24 to 29 years are out to their families compared with about two-thirds of gay men over 60, but they are not necessarily out to all members of their families (Bergling, 2004:234): "I came out to my siblings around thirty-five, but my parents still don't know. Well, I'm almost sure they do know, but they just don't talk about it. . . . They're not stupid, just silent" (44-year-old male).

In a selective sample of older lesbians, of 22 who mentioned their ties with siblings, 13 reported good ties with sisters or brothers, 6 reported nonexistent ties with siblings, and 3 reported bad relationships with brothers (Claassen, 2005). Comparisons of gay and lesbian adults with their same-gender siblings indicate some interesting differences between them. Among women with a mean age in their 30s but ranging from their 20s to 60s, lesbians are more educated, more geographically mobile, more likely to live in urban areas, more likely to hold high prestige jobs, and have higher self-esteem than their straight sister who is closest in age (Rothblum et al., 2004; Rothblum et al., 2006; Rothblum & Factor, 2001). Their straight sisters are more likely to have ever married and to be married, to have been in longer relationships, to have children and to be living with children, to identify with a religion, and to be better paid. Comparisons of gay and straight brothers are less conclusive because the sample is smaller (Rothblum et al., 2004). One reason for this is the number of gay men who are closer to their sisters and did not want to have their brothers included in the study (Rothblum et al., 2004). When compared with the straight brother closest in age, gay men with a mean age in their late 30s are better educated and more likely to live in large cities (Rothblum et al., 2004; Rothblum et al., 2006). Their straight brothers are more likely to have ever married and be married and to have children and be living with them.

These comparisons indicate the different life paths that siblings of differing sexual identities follow, despite a similar starting point. At the same time, the lower likelihood of having partners and, particularly, children may make gay and lesbian adults attentive siblings. The combination of higher education and higher-prestige jobs but lower pay among lesbians, and between higher education and lower pay among gay men when compared with their own siblings lends some support to Conley's (2005) contention that sexual orientation is likely to affect social mobility (Rothblum et al., 2006). The greater geographic mobility and propensity to live in large cities among lesbian and gay adults is an effective use of place to negotiate ambivalence in relationships with straight parents and siblings (Connidis, 2003b).

Clearly, there is much to explore about sibling ties among gay and lesbian adults. Does the peership of siblings make acceptance of and support to a gay or lesbian sibling more likely than is true of a parent's response to a child? Does the coming out of a brother or sister mark a key transition in the sibling tie that persists over time? Are siblings important players in the family networks of older gays and lesbians? Such questions demand answers if we are to have a complete picture of family ties across the life course.

CHAPTER 13

Life Transitions and Sibling Ties

Social expectations are never perfectly reproduced in our social relationships but are instead only one factor taken into account in the negotiation of family ties (Finch, 1989). Their variable interpretation is one reason for differences between and within families. As we have seen, adult sibling relationships are negotiated in diverse ways, depending upon such factors as gender, marital and parent status, class and race. This variation is downplayed considerably by the two models of support that dominated gerontological work on social support for some time: the hierarchical compensatory model and the task-specific model (see Chapter 8). When the functional-specificity-of-relationships model is combined with the convoy model, alternative ways of negotiating particular relationships by different groups of people at different points across the life course are highlighted. For some older persons, and at some points in time, siblings may be a particularly important source of support.

Such variation does not mean the absence of a socially constructed hierarchy of relationships. A fairly widespread ranking of obligation toward given family members is evident in Western culture: children, a spouse and parents are at the top of the obligation hierarchy (see Rossi & Rossi, 1990). Other ties, including those to siblings, follow. Obligations to family members lower in the hierarchy can be avoided when claims of obligation to family members higher in the hierarchy can be made. Thus the cost of a more voluntary relationship, such as that between siblings, is that it carries less of an obligation to provide support. As was true of the grandparent-grandchild relationship (Chapter 10), greater latitude in more voluntary relations makes for less certain expectations that must be clarified through negotiations.

We have seen that involvement with siblings ebbs during the early and middle adult years. How do the transitions typical of the family life course affect the sibling tie? This chapter focuses on support exchanges involving middle-aged and old siblings. The changing needs of parents and of siblings as they age often mark pivotal

241

transitions in sibling relationships as they work out how to support parents or one another. Siblings typically approach these transitions with a history of renegotiating their ties in response to marriage and other forms of partnering, having children, and relationship dissolution. What are the consequences of these transitions for ties between sisters and brothers? A brief consideration of shifts in marital and parental status precedes our focus on support exchanges.

The Impact of Changes in Marital and Parental Status

In Chapter 12, the discussion of proximity, contact and closeness among siblings underscored the significant effects of marital and parental status. Retrospective data from my sibling dyad study reflect the experience of individuals who ranged in age from 25 to 89 years (Connidis, 1994a). Forty percent of them believed that their sibling ties were affected by their own or a sibling's marriage. About half of this group made positive comments referring to improved or enhanced relationships and becoming closer emotionally due to maturing, doing more together, sharing the experience of being married, and good relations with siblings-in-law. When asked about the impact of his marriage on his sibling relationships, a 63-year-old man replied,

> Oh God, much improved! Very simple . . . Rita, Mary, and Bob have said to me, "You know, you'd really have a problem if you decided to split from June. We like you very much, but we love June."

The other half of those who note the impact of marriage on sibling ties focus on its diminution. In some cases, getting married creates distance in sibling ties. A 53-year-old childless woman observed,

> I was more close with my sister when I was . . . living with her. After I got married, I moved out. . . . It's not the same as if you live in the same house. It takes you a little bit out of the family. . . . You've got another person to spend more time with.

Comments regarding less closeness apply more often to the marriage of a sibling than a respondent's marriage (35% versus 20%). Conversely, reduced contact with siblings comes up more often in comments about one's own marriage than about siblings' marriages that are usually cast in neutral tones as an outcome of being busier, having other obligations, or being farther away. For some, even though sibling ties remain close, there is regret about less contact, as a 67-year-old woman illustrates:

> When I got married, my husband didn't see it was all that necessary to see anybody that much, and I missed [my brother]. . . . It's funny, but I didn't ever think about it or even diagnose it really. But in later years, I sort of did.

This woman's comments indicate our changing responses to the same situation as we age.

The birth of a child may extend family boundaries to include siblings who have their own claims as aunts and uncles to their new niece or nephew (Connidis, 1994b). Once again, two-fifths of the respondents in the sibling dyad study believe that the arrival of children, either theirs or their siblings', affected their sibling ties. In this case, however, the vast majority of comments focus on positive consequences: Almost 75% report greater emotional closeness, improved relations, and greater contact. Children bring families together, provide new companions for younger siblings or cousins, and are the basis for common concerns. Greater sharing with siblings is noted by a 64-year-old father:

> After I had children, I guess there's more understanding, and there's more sharing in the same problems, "Oh, my child did this and my son did that." . . . When individuals . . . have children, they have common problems and common worries and common concerns. They're a little bit more able to share and to understand what the other people are going through and perhaps support one another.

For a minority, the arrival of children spelled less closeness and contact, primarily because they were the first to have children, so parenthood was a unique rather than a shared experience, and they had less free time. Although some parents experience a decline in emotional closeness to their siblings as their children grow up and become companions in their own right, over a third of the observations reflect greater emotional closeness, with a history of shared experiences with siblings and their children cementing the sibling bond (Connidis, 1994b).

Bonds between aunts and uncles and their nieces and nephews tend to grow out of close sibling relationships (Wenger & Burholt, 2001). Contact with nieces and nephews usually occurs as part of contact with siblings, and emotionally close bonds are more common among childless old persons. Contact varies over time and, in old age, may focus on a particular niece or nephew, often anticipated to be the heir. Following the death of a very close sibling, ties with particular nieces or nephews may intensify. For childless older persons, nieces and nephews are a significant link with the next generation (Wenger et al., 2007). Close ties among childless persons with their nieces and nephews appear especially salient to older Latinos and African Americans, as in the case of a Latina woman who says, "I have never gotten married. . . . My nephews are like my grand-kids. They care about me" (Becker et al., 2003). When compared with other groups, a higher proportion of Hispanic aunts and great-aunts provide intensive help to their (great) nieces and nephews (Minkler, 1999). Gay and lesbian older persons who are childless are also likely to invest in relationships with nieces and nephews (Cohler et al., 1998). This intergenerational link between childless aunts or uncles and their nieces and nephews provides an important antidote to the usual experience of age segregation in most other social and cultural spheres (Hagestad & Uhlenberg, 2005).

Very little research concerns the nature of the aunt or uncle and niece or nephew tie. A qualitative study of midlife uncles and young adult nephews finds a range of involvement (Milardo, 2005). Some uncles act as surrogate fathers, others as friends, others as mentors and supplements to parents. Uncles may be effective intergenerational buffers, providing insight and smoothing relationships between parents and their children. In turn, nephews sometimes provide uncles with insights regarding their siblings. Reports of young adult nieces and nephews indicate that aunts also mediate relationships with other family members and range from being best friends to mother figures (Sotirin & Ellingson, 2006). More research on older nephews and nieces and their aunts and uncles is needed to see how this relationship evolves over time.

Divorce and widowhood are more likely than either marriage or having children to affect sibling ties (Connidis, 1994b; see Chapter 6). The intimacy of sibling ties allows open sharing of painful transitions. A 61-year-old widow says, "You don't mind having them [siblings] know what you've gone through. This is something that you need to talk about inside the family." Indeed, following divorce and widowhood, siblings are often a helpful source of support, bringing brothers and sisters closer together (re older divorced parents, see Wright & Maxwell, 1991; re widowed women, see Martin Matthews, 1991). By the time that siblings may have to confront their parents' growing need for care, their relationships have already experienced considerable ebb and flow in response to other life transitions.

Sharing Caring for Parents

The growing need for support by aging parents can signal a transition in the sibling relationship, as sisters and brothers seek ways of providing support to their mothers or fathers or both (Connidis, 1994a). Typically, this is a gradual transition, but a health crisis or death of one parent may mark a dramatic shift in sibling involvement to meet the immediate demands of the situation. Ideally, siblings, who are now primarily middle-aged adults, figure out ways of sharing responsibility for their parents. For some, however, negotiating commitments to parents is the basis for conflict about what constitutes equitable contributions (Strawbridge & Wallhagen, 1991), as letters to advice columnists regularly attest.

Helping older parents often involves mutual assistance among siblings (Cicirelli, 1995) and reestablishes greater interaction among siblings in middle and older age, as compared to the earlier adult years. Although they do not always do as they say, most children profess the view that the responsibility of supporting parents means "doing one's share of the caregiving as well as attending to the needs of other family members, not just those of the older person" (Piercy, 1998:116). Close sibling relations tend to facilitate the parent-caring process, as those who are close are most likely to share the care (Matthews, 2002a). Siblings unable to share equally in caring for parents can offer relief to the sibling shouldering the responsibility by visiting the parent or parents. Typically, siblings provide a wide range of support to a sibling who serves as the primary helper (Penrod et al., 1995). Women who are primary caregivers to an older adult are most likely to name sisters as their main helper, men to name their wives (Sims-Gould, Martin-Matthews, & Rosenthal, 2008).

Nonetheless, both men and women name siblings as key helpers to them in the care that they provide to an older relative, including household help and home maintenance.

How do brothers and sisters work out caring arrangements for their parents? A number of research issues confound studies of care to older parents. First, older persons vary greatly in their needs for help, and samples of older parents differ in the amount of help that they require. Thus some samples contain a cross-section of older persons (Stoller et al., 1992), not all of whom need help. Others focus on parents who require daily help with basic activities, such as meal preparation, bathing and moving around the house (Wolf et al., 1997). Second, some research seeks to explain who is likely to help older persons (Stoller et al., 1992), whereas others examine what leads to differences in the amount of support provided to older parents (Connidis et al., 1996; Wolf et al., 1997). Third, some studies obtain information from older parents (Stoller et al., 1992; Wolf et al., 1997), whereas others rely on the reports of the person providing support (Connidis et al., 1996). Fourth, studies tend to focus on the types and styles of support that are more common among women at the risk of underestimating the support offered by men, in this case, brothers (Matthews, 2002b; Thompson, 2002).

Caring for parents takes place in a network of relationships, and arrangements may shift over time. Yet most research focuses on primary caregivers and on one point in time (cross-sectional) and therefore fails to consider the range of involvement among siblings and how their arrangements may change over time. Some important exceptions include Matthews's (2002a) work on parental support in which adults are studied as both siblings and adult children, a study by Ingersoll-Dayton and her colleagues (2003) that explores sibling dyads and the negotiation of care, and a study by Sims-Gould and her colleagues (2008) that looks at the web of caring by exploring direct and indirect support and both primary and supportive caregivers. Variations in research questions, samples, methodology and analysis help to explain some of the contradictory findings in the literature.

Do siblings have plans for the care of their parents? Qualitative research indicates limited communication among siblings about the eventuality of caring for parents and quite disparate views among them about who would do what if a parent should require care (Connidis & Kemp, 2008). Siblings share a sense of filial responsibility but usually identify one sibling (not always the same one) as the likely key provider. Support to parents is not anticipated to be equal, and siblings with family and paid work responsibilities are seen to have a legitimate excuse for not providing care. In mixed-gender sibling networks, sisters are more often identified as likely care providers, and past practices (who has helped parents in the past) and proximity are also influential. Despite the attention that researchers and the media pay to caregiving, siblings do not appear to anticipate how they will support their parents, and their arrangements may often be worked out in the midst of suddenly changing conditions, such as a parent's health crisis.

The discussion in Chapter 8 about the help that adult children give to their older parents reviewed an array of factors that affect support to parents. We know, for example, that daughters are more likely than sons to provide support and in larger quantities. When exploring the sibling relationship, the entire family is of greater interest than the traits of individual siblings, because we can then address questions about how support to parents is determined within the context of family negotiations. What are the factors that shape which siblings provide what support to older parents? Examining the impact of family composition, such as number of brothers and sisters, is one way to approach this question.

Among parents aged 65 and over ($n = 584$) with varying levels of independence, having at least one proximate child is the most important determinant of reporting a child as one of their "biggest helpers" (Stoller et al., 1992). Although this seems straightforward enough, there may be differences among sisters and brothers in their likelihood of moving to be closer to their parents when help is needed. As well, parents, given a choice, may be more inclined to move near a daughter than a son when they require support. Thus although the significance of geographic proximity appears to be gender neutral, proximity itself may be gendered, just as White adult children and their parents are less likely than their Black or Hispanic counterparts to live near one another.

For married parents, greater need for support and having a child living nearer by make naming a child a key or primary helper more likely (Stoller et al., 1992). Previously married mothers are more likely than married parents to name a child as a helper, even if children live far away. Parents who have both sons and daughters are most likely to consider a son the primary helper if there are proximate sons in combination with distant daughters. Married parents tend not to have a gender preference, but widowed mothers do, preferring daughters over sons when they are equally available. Thus while both parents are living, sisters may feel no more pressure than their brothers to help their parents. But a father's death may precipitate gender-specific pressures to aid a widowed mother, altering the nature of sibling ties in the process.

A Canadian study of 1,015 employed workers who help parents for at least one hour per week examined the effects of number of brothers and number of sisters on helping patterns (Connidis et al., 1996). Among women particularly, those with more sisters provided *more* hours of help to both parents, but for both men and women, having more sisters made sharing care for mothers more likely and being the primary helper less likely. The number of brothers also increased the amount of help given but only to fathers. Those with more brothers were more likely to have someone share in the help given to mothers and, for men and married women, less likely to be the primary helper. These findings underscore the fact that the help shared among siblings is not a zero-sum game; instead, the amount of help increases with family size. Sisters appear to have a stronger ethos of support (Connidis et al., 1996). Such an ethos may be a function of family size as well. Women with more siblings are more likely to give financial help to their parents, and both men and women with more siblings are more likely to receive financial help from their parents, women more so (Sarkisian & Gerstel, 2008). An even stronger association is evident for practical help: Men and women with more siblings are more likely to exchange such help with their parents, to both give and receive it.

A study of unmarried parents who need help and have at least two children focuses on the parent's report of the one person who helps "most of the time" with activities of daily living (e.g., bathing, getting out of bed, eating) and the two people who help most with instrumental activities of daily living (e.g., preparing meals, shopping, managing money; Wolf et al., 1997). The parent's need for care is most central to predicting the number of hours of care that siblings provide. The net effect of having more children is to receive more support because, for every additional hour one sibling helps his or her parent, other siblings reduce the care they give by only about five minutes. Because daughters provide more hours of help than do sons, networks with more sisters provide more support to an unmarried parent.

What is unclear from this and other studies that focus on one point in time is the extent to which siblings rotate responsibility for parent care over time. Indeed, siblings do collaborate with one another by either taking turns or by dividing the help that parents require (Ingersoll-Dayton et al., 2003). As well, when one sibling serves as the primary helper to a parent, others assist that sibling (Sims-Gould, et al., 2008). Like sisters, brothers may be involved in caring for parents as helpers or as co-providers (Hequembourg & Brallier, 2005).

Qualitative analysis indicates differences in gender preference among parents, depending on the nature of the support that is required (Stoller et al., 1992). Parents whose needs are minimal do not favor sons or daughters, but parents who need help with household labor tend to favor daughters over sons. In cases where sons are the primary helpers, much of the help is actually provided by women, typically daughters-in-law or granddaughters (see Chapter 8). Sisters provide a range of help to their parents that equals or exceeds that given by their brothers, regardless of their relative competing commitments. The exceptional cases where brothers provide more varied parental help than their sisters are explained by greater proximity.

Factors relevant to sibling contributions to parental care occur in relational context. Variations in sibling configurations make gender salient in families of both sisters and brothers; if there are only sisters or brothers, then gender cannot be a basis for deciding which sibling will do what. Sibling configurations or constellations reflect the relative attributes of a sibling network, including gender, proximity, employment status, marital status and in-law ties, other family responsibilities, health status and social class (Matthews, 2002a). On balance, when there is variety among siblings, women, those who live nearer by, those who are unattached, those in better health, those who have more income (for financial assistance), and those with no job or with jobs that are less demanding, more flexible or relevant to the caregiving situation are likely to carry more of the responsibility for parental support.

The impact of gender structure and the number of siblings on the division of parent care is documented in both qualitative and quantitative studies (Coward & Dwyer, 1990; Dwyer & Coward, 1991; Matthews, 2002a). Families with only two sisters share the care of parents most equitably (Matthews, 2002a). In larger families, two sisters provide most of the care, whereas the others provide periodic help when needed or none at all. In families of brothers and sisters, it is the sisters who provide most of the care, with brothers providing occasional or no care. Consequently, primary caregivers who have brothers only are most likely to receive little or no sibling support (Matthews, 2002a). This difference is magnified among sisters because they are reluctant to seek help from their siblings, taking the view that "I shouldn't have to ask; they should just pitch in" (Merrill, 1997:57). In contrast, brothers who serve as the primary helper tend to simply demand support from their siblings. As one brother puts it, "Family is family, but I won't let it take over my life. I make sure the others help, and they listen. I just tell them, 'This is the way it has to be'" (Merrill, 1997:57).

The discrepancy between the help offered by brothers versus sisters is exaggerated by a tendency to focus on the types of help more typically provided by sisters (Matthews, 1995; 2002a). Although lone sisters with brothers are more likely to be "in charge" of parental care and to provide more of the personal and housekeeping support, brothers are active in providing the more traditionally male forms of help, such as financial management, visiting, and sometimes, more personal forms of care for fathers but not mothers. Because such efforts do not fit the traditional image of caregiving, they tend to be minimized by the sister and her brothers.

Gender differences in approaches to caring for parents are also reflected in the way that men in families with brothers only negotiate care arrangements for their parents. Unlike sisters, brothers tend to deal directly with their parents rather than with each other about their parents' situation unless there is a crisis, in which case they coordinate their efforts (Matthews & Heidorn, 1998; Matthews, 2002a). Brothers are more reactive than proactive, leaving it to parents to let them know what help is needed rather than seeking out ways in which to assist. Usual forms of support are masculine or gender neutral, and sons typically minimize the significance of the help they provide. The approach taken by sons in brothers-only families fosters more independence among their parents, leading them to negotiate other sources of help to reduce their reliance on sons and to be active participants in decisions about what and how much help they receive (Matthews & Heidorn, 1998). Clearly, the gender configuration of siblings has a substantial impact on both the process and the form of providing care to older parents. Whether one configuration is better or worse from the parent's point of view is an open question. Certainly, involving parents in decision making regarding their care respects their autonomy. It also allows siblings to collaborate with one another more effectively based on shared information about their parents' preferences (Ingersoll-Dayton et al., 2003).

The substantially greater involvement of sisters than brothers in the care of parents reflects the gendered nature of family care. In a cultural context where looking after family members is seen as women's work (Matthews, 1995), women are less able than men to claim legitimate excuses to avoid parental caring. In the family context, marital status is an additional source of inequality (Connidis & Campbell, 1995). Although inequities of marital status may be a central facet of the inequities based on gender, marital status provides a dimension to family dynamics that is not entirely reducible to gender. For example, when negotiating responsibilities toward parents, being married and having assumed obligations toward a spouse has currency as a legitimate excuse from providing support (see Finch, 1989), especially when compared to a single sibling. In this sense, marital status is a source of differential power in negotiating family relationships. The fact that unmarried children outstrip their married counterparts in the amount of support that they provide to their parents (Silverstein & Litwak, 1993), especially among women (Connidis et al., 1996), supports this argument. Indeed, an unmarried child is more likely to be the only one assisting a mother and to be the primary helper to a father.

Gay and lesbian siblings may be especially likely to care for their parents, in part because of their assumed single status (Kimmel, 1992). A review of the limited available data on gay and lesbian caregivers to older parents (Hunter, 2005) indicates that gay and lesbian family members may resent their siblings' assumption that they are somehow more available because they are not married or parents. A study of gay and lesbian caregivers to adults compares them with gay and lesbian adults who are not providing care (Fredriksen, 1999). Only 16% of the recipients are parents, compared with 60% who are friends. Lesbians are more likely to be caring for elder family members, gays for working-age adults who are often ill due to HIV/AIDS. One in four lesbian and gay caregivers receives support from all of their biological family members, and two-thirds receive support from some of them.

There is also an affective component to the provision of parent care. Siblings who are emotionally close to one another are more likely to share in the care they provide to parents and to accept inequities among siblings in the division of parental care (Connidis & Kemp, 2008; Matthews, 2002a). A 60-year-old married mother in my sibling dyad study said that her family was close during her childhood, but she observes,

> We probably drew closest together during the time that we looked after our elderly mother. We shared responsibility for looking after her. He [respondent's brother] looked after her, and I would take her for a month or so. Then, I looked after her for a couple of years or so, and he would take her. We did it together. It was a joint decision. And the finances. We decided jointly and then we agreed that if she outlived her money, then we would jointly do whatever needed to be done. And she did outlive her money, but, you know, it all worked out.

In this case, a history of closeness was the basis for sharing parental care amicably. Qualitative research suggests that emotionally close siblings are more inclined to consider the legitimate excuses that their sisters and brothers have for not being able to care for parents; distant siblings focus more on their own legitimacy claims for not being able to provide care (Connidis & Kemp, 2008).

In some families, the need to support parents leads to conflict and stress, usually over the relative amount of help offered by siblings but also over having caregiving efforts criticized or having different views about the option of institutionalization (Avioli, 1989; Bedford, 1995; Lerner et al., 1991; Merrill, 1997; Strawbridge & Wallhagen, 1991). Working-class siblings more often note conflict, in part perhaps because failure to care violates a more strongly held commitment to filial obligation (Merrill, 1997). Sibling pairs in which both members were involved in parental support report the situation as reasonably manageable and fair to both siblings until asked specific questions about whether caregiving is equitable and whether the sharing of care could be fairer (Lerner et al., 1991). Then, substantial discrepancies surface between siblings. Most siblings believe that their own contribution is greater than their sibling's and that they cannot increase the amount of help that they give. They also believe that their sibling could contribute more but will not. Such sentiments are more common among women than men, among those who are less close to their sibling, and when caregiving is more demanding. Even in families described as close, the needs of parents can be the basis for disagreement. A 56-year-old married father with six siblings observes,

> . . . what my mother should do with her house. . . . We're all telling her different things, and I had a bit of an argument with my brother . . . about trying to get things done and sorted out for her. So I've just sort of withdrawn and let him run things.

Here, disagreement is the basis for different levels of involvement in parental support but not necessarily for animosity between siblings. Indeed, general reports of fairness in the sharing of care to parents, despite believing that contributions are unequal, suggest a shared desire among siblings to maintain good relations with one another during trying times (Lerner et al., 1991). Emotionally close siblings place less emphasis on equal contribution in their assessments of their siblings' contributions to parental support as fair (Matthews, 2002a). When attempts to forge equity by asking siblings who give less to give more fail, siblings often preserve their ties to one another by changing how equity is perceived (Ingersoll-Dayton et al., 2003).

Following the death of a parent, previously weak ties may lead to the dissolution of the sibling relationship. More often, ties are strengthened on the loss of parents, in part because siblings offer the only remaining ties to the original family (Connidis, 1994b). Siblings who experienced the death of a parent before the age of 19 are more likely than those who grew up with both parents to consider their siblings as among their closest friends as adults (Mack, 2004). However, a parental death may lead to new or renewed conflict among siblings as they debate appropriate inheritance from their parents or feel bitterness about their parents' legacy. Court cases document the distress that results when siblings believe that their contribution to a parent's care was impeded by the undue influence of other siblings or was underestimated, as reflected in lower proceeds from an inheritance (Lashewicz et al., 2007). Again, such conflict and its extent will depend on the nature of sibling ties prior to the parent's death. As we have seen (Chapter 12), emotional closeness can be its own force in how siblings respond to ambivalent situations, an effect that extends to how adult children respond to their parents' will. Those with close emotional ties focus on preserving their relationship in the wake of the potentially negative impact of unequal treatment in a parent's will (Stum, 1999; re transfer of property see Taylor & Norris, 2000). Thus, emotional closeness is important beyond its immediate rewards.

Support Exchanges Among Siblings

Sadie and Bessie Delaney, two single African American sisters who lived to be over 100 years old, both attributed their survival to their sister's support (Delany & Delany, 1993). According to their accounts, they literally lived for one another, Sadie so that she could keep Bessie living and Bessie so that she wouldn't disappoint Sadie. Their mutual support helped them to transcend the realities of racism and poverty that characterized their lives. Class variations among siblings occur for African and European American adults, but the likelihood of having siblings across the class divide between poor and middle class varies (Heflin & Pattillo, 2006). Poor Blacks are less likely than poor Whites to have a middle-class sibling (50% versus 66%), but middle-class Blacks are more likely than middle-class Whites to have a poor sibling (41% versus 16%). As a result, "African-Americans are less likely to have a sibling to turn to for help if they are poor, but more likely to have a sibling turn to them for assistance if they are middle class" (Heflin & Pattillo, 2006:818). This cross-cutting of class and race relations has important implications for support between siblings.

As Finch (1989:45) notes, whether siblings provide support "depends very much upon personal circumstances and personal liking. . . . Except perhaps in rather trivial matters, there is no real sense that one can expect assistance from someone just because they are your brother or sister." Yet as the Delany sisters exemplified, for some, the tie to siblings is very powerful and supportive. Because sibling ties are relatively voluntary and egalitarian, there is considerable variability in the likelihood of helping siblings (Wellman, 1992), siblings tend to keep their exchanges equitable (Scott, 1983), and help from siblings in older age is usually in response to specific situational demands (Goetting, 1986). Even when siblings live together, they are typically quite independent (Chappell & Badger, 1987).

Nonetheless, a very important facet of the sibling relationship in older age is the common view that siblings are potential caregivers (Chappell & Badger, 1987), particularly in the absence of a spouse or child who can provide help (Cicirelli, 1992). Among persons aged 55 or more, one-fifth of those with one sibling and one-quarter of those with two or more siblings report that they could live with one of their siblings if needed (Connidis, 1994b). In turn, 60% of respondents say that a sibling could live with them if needed. Over half of those with one sibling and three-quarters of those with two or more say that their siblings would provide help during a crisis. In addition, longer-term help due to illness is perceived to be available from a brother or sister by one-fifth of those who have one sibling and one-third of those who have two or more. Single and widowed persons are more likely than married individuals to consider siblings a potential source of long-term support due to illness. Single, widowed and divorced persons are also more likely than their married counterparts to say that a sibling could live with them, thereby serving as a resource in later life. As well, having sisters rather than brothers and living near a sibling heighten the view that siblings are potential sources of help. Thus for many, having a sibling provides a sense of having an "insurance policy" for support in older age (Hochschild, 1973) and helps to stave off loneliness in old age (Gold, 1987).

What about actual exchanges of support between siblings in later life? Generally, siblings are more active as providers of emotional than instrumental support (Miner & Uhlenberg, 1997), in part because emotional support is less subject to geographic proximity (Eriksen & Gerstel, 2002). More involved sibling ties among some racial and ethnic groups, such as Latinos, tend to translate primarily into emotional rather than instrumental support (Olson, 2003). Poorer ties with parents are linked with more emotional support among siblings, and more positive sibling ties are associated with more practical help (housework and odd jobs; Voorpostel & Blieszner, 2008; Voorpostel & Van der Lippe, 2007).

A U.S. sample of adults aged 24 to 76 indicates that a vast majority provided some form of practical, personal or material help—broadly defined—to their siblings in the past year (Eriksen & Gerstel, 2002; see also Voorpostel & Van der Lippe, 2007). The most frequently cited forms of help are giving a gift, talking about problems, and sharing a meal, activities that one might categorize as the usual exchanges of close relationships rather than the labor of caregiving. Less often, support to a sibling in the past year was given in the form of help when sick (28%), giving money (25%), and doing laundry (8%). In my community study of persons aged 55 and over, only a minority reported having received direct aid from their siblings (Connidis, 1994b). About one-fifth have received help when ill, and less than 1 in 10 have received financial aid from siblings.

A U.S. panel study with a large sample aged 18 to 85 years found aging effects on giving help to and receiving help from siblings, with dramatic differences based on geographic proximity (White, 2001). Note that these findings concern change over time, not absolute amounts of help exchanged. Among those with at least one sibling living within 25 miles, help from and to a sibling declined from the ages of 20 to 70 and then rebounded. Those who are more educated, those with more siblings, and women are mostly likely to experience this pattern in giving and receiving over time. More help is received from nearby siblings when marriages end and when parents die. Among siblings who live farther apart, the decline in receiving help is less pronounced, but there is also not an increase in old age (White, 2001). But women, people who have more siblings and the more highly educated receive sustained levels of help from siblings over time. Generally, siblings are more likely to be providers of emotional and instrumental support and to serve as confidants and companions for middle-aged and older women than men (Campbell et al., 1999; Miner and Uhlenberg, 1997). Women give more personal and practical support to siblings than do men (Eriksen & Gerstel, 2002).

In the context of the gender composition of sibling dyads, the most emotionally supportive adult ties are between sisters (Lee et al., 1990; White & Riedmann, 1992b). Sister pairs are also more likely to exchange advice and child care; odd jobs are more commonly performed for siblings, especially brothers, by men (Spitze & Trent, 2006; Voorpostel et al., 2007). Among those with only one sibling, help during an illness is more likely between a pair of older sisters than any other gender combination (Connidis, 1994b).

Marital status has a substantial bearing on sibling support. Those with only one sibling have a higher incidence of receiving support when sick if that sibling is divorced (Connidis, 1994b). Among those with two or more siblings, single and widowed respondents are more likely than those who are married to have received sibling support during an illness. More generally, single older persons exceed married individuals in the probability of receiving instrumental help from siblings (Campbell et al., 1999). Siblings are also the largest portion of the instrumental support networks of single persons, especially for single women, and place second (after children) in the networks of widowed persons and divorced women when siblings live nearby. In a Dutch sample of adults ranging in age from 18 to 80, dyads of siblings with partners are least involved with one another (Voorpostel et al., 2007).

Siblings without partners receive more support than siblings with partners from both siblings with and without partners. Thus, siblings emerge as especially significant ties for adults without partners across the life course.

Parent status also plays a role in sibling support (Voorpostel et al., 2007). Among old adults, siblings who are childless are the most likely source of advice. For respondents with two or more siblings, childless persons are more likely than parents to have received help from siblings during an illness (Connidis, 1994b). In terms of overall network composition, siblings compose a larger portion of the instrumental support networks of childless persons than of those who are parents (Campbell et al., 1999), demonstrating that childless individuals negotiate particularly supportive sibling ties that continue into old age. In turn, those who have at least one childless sibling are more likely to have received other forms of help from a sibling (Connidis, 1994b).

Older individuals who are unmarried and childless, especially those who have always been single, are most likely to live with siblings (Chappell & Badger, 1987). A 72-year-old widow from one of my studies highlights the full family membership of a co-resident brother:

> My brother and I get along very well. . . . He has lived with me a number of years. He never got married, and my mother died when he was just a baby, you see. When I got married, he came to live with me about 2 years after. . . . Yes, he's family, with the grandchildren and everything. He's one of our family. He is not excluded from anything. That's the way we live.

There are important differences in the features of co-residence, depending on whether older persons are living with a brother or sister. Siblings may live together and not have a particularly good relationship, as is the case of a 79-year-old widow and her widowed brother: "We get along all right, but he is very short tempered, and sometimes it doesn't work too well. I am just beginning to get to the stage where I am thinking seriously about selling my home." Among persons aged 60 and over, those who live with a brother both perceive their sibling as available for support and receive support from him (Chappell, 1991). Those who live with a sister are generally well off, are more likely to be women, and are more likely to profess independence but actually receive support from their sister.

Having a sibling with a developmental disability has lifelong consequences for sibling ties. Qualitative research of sisters aged 22 to 66 years who have a sibling with a developmental disability finds that adult sisters invest heavily in presenting the disability of their sibling positively, at the expense of adopting a gender ideology that makes them more responsible than brothers for providing care (McGraw & Walker, 2007). These sisters often see themselves as mother figures and emphasize their sibling's potential, minimize the cost of caring, and focus on how their special sibling has enhanced their lives. Siblings aged 33 to 79 years who have a sibling with a developmental disability often report that things have improved over the years, with greater acceptance of those with disabilities (Karasik, 2006). Their childhood experience often involved family isolation due to their sibling being ostracized, and there is considerable variability in current sibling attachment, with some acting as parents to their sibling and others having no contact. Growing up together generally makes their current relationship stronger, and these ties can involve mutual emotional support, as in the case of an old woman who says of her sister with a developmental disability, "She makes me feel like I'm the most special person in the entire universe . . . it's a very special relationship we have . . . I wouldn't ever want to lose it" (Karasik, 2006:F15).

On balance, the results concerning sibling support uphold the view that the same relationship can be negotiated quite differently, depending on an individual's circumstances. The fact that siblings are particularly good at offering emotional support suggests that the sibling tie is best suited to socioemotional support, in keeping with the task-specificity model (see Chapter 8). However, the variability among older persons in the relative significance of siblings as support providers illustrates considerable flexibility in how particular ties are negotiated. For those who are not married, especially single (Cicirelli et al., 1992) and widowed persons, and for childless older persons, siblings can be especially important sources of support in later life. At the same time, older persons without spouses or children are also distinguished by their greater availability as potential helpers to their siblings.

Summary and Conclusion to Part IV

Most older people have a living sibling. Sibling contact is typically pleasurable, motivated by seeking enjoyable company, and there is evidence of sibling closeness and loyalty, most notably between older sisters. The more voluntary nature of sibling ties makes them more variable. Consequently, differences in gender, class, race, geographic proximity, marital status and parent status all affect the amount and nature of sibling interaction. Sibling ties are especially significant for women, those who are not married (particularly single persons) and the childless. These groups both rely more on their siblings and are more available to them. Nonetheless, most older persons enjoy warm ties with their siblings, often reestablishing contact and closeness with them once the demands of the early and middle adult years are met. Working out the care of parents involves negotiating new understandings, often bringing siblings together. However, this situation can trigger conflict as well.

The concepts of intimacy at a distance and revocable detachment, developed to characterize the North American family (see Chapter 1), apply particularly well to the adult sibling relationship. Although a relatively small proportion of older persons actually receive extensive support from siblings, many more consider a sibling someone they could turn to should the need arise. The supportive behavior of many siblings following a divorce or widowhood suggests that siblings can and do become more involved when demanded by the situation.

The sibling relationship illustrates that the hierarchical depiction of family relationships provides an overly monolithic, static and deterministic representation of relationships in action. At the very least, one must take into account that different groups are likely to have different hierarchies of relationships. Moreover, the hierarchies themselves vary, depending on the nature or form of the interaction (for example, companionship versus confiding versus help during an illness).

Several other factors combine to make the negotiation of family obligations a very dynamic process. Circumstances change. Various family members have different needs at different times. Obligations to someone higher in the obligation hierarchy might be met by someone else, freeing siblings to support each other. A married mother in her 50s addresses this possibility:

> Because of my sister's circumstances—and I certainly would never want her to know this—but because she is on her own, I think that if my sister were sick and one of the [children] were ill, I know where I'd be. I'd be with my sister because there are other people that would be with my [children]. My husband would go to my kids, but I would be with my sister. And that may sound strange to you but . . . I just feel she hasn't married, and . . . my husband is always here if something happens to me or the children. And so, it would be my sister I would go to.

The sibling tie links our present to our past, providing a sense of continuity over time that very few relationships can rival.

Several trends may have important implications for sibling ties in the future. Because larger families tend to promote sibling loyalty and reduce sibling rivalry, the tendency toward smaller families in the past two decades could result in reduced loyalty and increased competition between siblings. This possibility may be heightened by the combination of full sibling ties with half and step siblings in a growing number of families. Conversely, having one sibling may heighten the interdependence and intensity of the sibling relationship.

The increased labor force participation of women may offset or reinforce these possibilities. On the one hand, work outside the home can be expected to limit the amount of time mothers spend with their children, including time spent mediating sibling disputes. This mimics the situation found in larger families where parents cannot play such a role, with the consequence that cooperation among siblings is necessary. On the other hand, if age-graded day care outside the home is required, the opportunity for sibling interaction is also limited. This may minimize the development of strong sibling loyalties based on accessibility and shared experiences. Among children for whom care is provided in the home, the effect of mothers working outside the home could be the enhancement of sibling closeness. Divorce may also be expected to have a surprisingly positive effect on sibling relationships. The absence of one parent and the decreased availability of the remaining parent may lead to a greater reliance on siblings, thereby engendering greater closeness and loyalty. Again, this may be offset by the arrival of step and half siblings. Such differences in childhood experiences probably extend into the later years.

Among divorced adults, the absence of spouses may lead to reestablishing sibling bonds earlier than usual. The importance of sisters to women following divorce suggests that this support and bonding may be more common among women than men. In general, heightened awareness of the possibility of divorce among children and adults alike may enhance the importance of the durability of the sibling relationship over time. Last, the greater longevity of women means more years of living without spouses and more years spent in the company of other women, including sisters.

PART V

Research and Policy

CHAPTER 14

Research and Policy

Issues and Directions

In research and in practice, families should not be isolated from other social domains, such as work, and old people should not be isolated from other age groups. This makes any discussion of related policy a broad one, with a tangle of policies and regulations designed to meet the needs of old people (for example, retirement age, pension and welfare entitlements, health care, formal and informal support) and of families (such as obligations to provide care, guardianship, regulations concerning marriage and divorce, family-related welfare entitlements and benefits, policies regarding domestic violence, regulations regarding adoption, inheritance law). We can add policies in the areas of work, housing, education, policing, and health care that are also relevant to older persons and their families. Clearly, covering all of the research and policy issues that relate to family ties and aging in one chapter is impossible. As this partial list shows, a vast array of federal or national, state or provincial and municipal policies and programs have implications for older persons and their family relationships.

Research and policy initiatives can range from the macro (What should the state do? How do we respond to globalization?) to the micro (What are our responsibilities as individuals—for looking after ourselves and for looking after members of our families?) and the social institutions in between (How can family, paid and unpaid work, and other social arrangements be altered so that individuals can negotiate optimal family relationships across the life course?). As well, policy questions may concern the general welfare of old people as a group or may target the needs of specific subgroups, such as those with advanced dementia and the family members who care for them.

An important starting point for theory, research and policy is knowing what we are exploring. What is the question or objective that we seek to address? What are the meanings of the terms included in that question or objective? As Hendricks (2005:515) observes, "As problems are defined, so will they be resolved." What is our framework for thinking about the question or objective that we are concerned about? In order to produce good research findings and good social policy, we need a framework in which our key terms are clearly defined, the information we gather is clearly related to those definitions, and our definitions and data are clearly linked to theoretical concepts and perspectives that help us to understand what we see and what we choose to do about it. As noted in Chapter 1, a critical perspective in combination with life course and feminist approaches encourages us to consider multiple levels of analysis across time and to question what we see, in part by taking into account structured social relations that create different opportunities and constraints in the choices we make. This framework also encourages us to be clear about the link between theory and practice. How do our theoretical understandings inform our decisions regarding the appropriate directions for social policy? How do we move beyond a dichotomy of private versus public responsibility to a model that views individual and societal interests as a more complementary process of shared responsibility?

One topic that has held the interest of students, researchers, professionals, politicians, concerned citizens, family members, and the old themselves is elder mistreatment. Following a broader discussion of research and policy issues, I use elder mistreatment as a case study that exemplifies the challenges of formulating clear definitions, the fallout of unclear definitions for research, and the consequent challenges to creating social policy when its targets are unclear. In the process, I also consider what we know and need to know about elder mistreatment. I conclude with some general reflections.

Most research is not motivated by a desire to address questions of social policy, but good research provides essential, valid and reliable information that, ideally, counters the impact of incorrect assumptions and cultural biases on social policy. Unsubstantiated biases are especially likely to run deep on the topic of family relationships because these ties are so central to our daily lives and so close to morally loaded issues, such as sexuality. As the editors of the most recent *Sourcebook of Family Theory and Research* (Bengtson et al., 2005:616) note, "Family scholars are theorizing about issues that affect people in their bedrooms, around their kitchen tables, in the courts, and in places of worship; thus family theories are entwined with the political nature of those ideas." Similarly, the power relations of age make aging intensely personal and challenging, as individuals grapple with creating both a positive personal and social identities in a culture that does not support them (Estes et al., 2003). As we have seen, the cross-cutting of age with gender, class and race relations creates additional social worlds with unique experiences of aging and family ties. Enduring family relationships are a central facet of negotiating old age.

Improving research and theory on aging and family ties enhances both our understanding of the older person in a family context and the knowledge base necessary for formulating more effective and innovative social policy. One outcome of attending to research concerns is a more informed basis for establishing programs and policies that suit the varied needs of older persons and their families. Because they are read, interpreted, and politicized by those who take an active interest in promoting various visions of family life, research results must not be left to speak for themselves. Researchers have a heavy responsibility to provide clear interpretations of their work and its application to the real world.

Research Issues

Research concerns can be divided into three categories: the topics and questions chosen for exploration, the methods of data collection and types of analysis employed, and the theoretical frameworks used to direct questions and interpret results.

Research Questions

The questions that researchers choose to address create a sense of urgency about some topics and minimize the importance of others. When many researchers decide that a particular topic warrants their attention, the proliferation of studies that result shapes priorities, in this instance, about the issues related to aging and family ties about which something must be done. Some examples over the past few decades are the crisis of retirement for men, the emptiness of the nest when children grow up and leave home, and the burden of caring carried by the sandwiched generation. Are these issues important? Yes. Do they reflect the real experiences of most old persons and their families? No. These questions typically arise from deeply embedded social beliefs about what matters (or should matter) to various groups in our society and reflect inadequate information about how prevalent particular situations were and are.

Research about family ties and aging has made remarkable progress over the past 20 years. Greater sophistication and flexibility in thinking, researching and theorizing about families, about aging, and about their interconnection have advanced markedly our understanding and orientation to this topic. Based on sound research, we can now conclusively dispel many myths and downplay many exaggerations about family life. Here is what the research shows:

The vast majority of old people are active family members, including those who are single, divorced and childless.

The typical experience of being an older family member is to be engaged in relationships characterized by reciprocity, not dependency.

Across the life course, relationships are negotiated and renegotiated in response to life transitions, changing circumstances, and the availability of various ties and opportunities.

Older persons have not been deserted by their families.

Diversity in family life does not necessarily denote superior and inferior alternatives but rather, proactive strategies for dealing with varying circumstances.

Family forms that are yet to be officially legitimated carry many of the hallmarks of idealized family life, such as the caring, support and love evident in gay and lesbian partnerships or between stepparents and their stepchildren.

The field has also matured to the point where researchers can admit to overzealous attempts to convince others of the significance of aging and family life. Several authors have documented how we have unwittingly oversold the so-called problems related to changes in family life (Rosenthal, 2000), intergenerational caregiving (Martin-Matthews, 2000b), the refilled nest (Mitchell, 2000), and intergenerational equity (McDaniel, 2000). For example, only a minority of families are in the structural position of having both older parents and children of young ages, and even fewer experience the simultaneous dependence of parents and children to the point of requiring care (see Chapter 8). Clearly, for those who do, the demands are pressing and sometimes overwhelming. But recent work also recognizes the rewards of caring and the genuine interest that family members have in helping to ensure the comfort and well-being of their loved ones, including older parents.

Researchers' questions have tended to be tradition bound, particularly when it comes to older persons. Social scientists have a long history of asking questions about relationships between married partners, between parents and children, and between grandparents and grandchildren. One outcome is that very little is known about the intimate relationships of the unmarried in later life, although there has been noted improvement in the past few years (see Chapters 4 & 5). We researchers have only recently begun to explore questions about other ties, such as those between siblings (Chapters 12 & 13), or to consider the place of single (Chapter 5) and childless (Chapter 7) individuals as family members rather than as individuals left behind when others marry and have children. Siblings are central to the lives of older persons who do not have partners or children, and siblings without such attachments are particularly valuable resources for other family members. To best appreciate what it is to be single in later life, we should explore variations in the experience of being single over the life course for different groups and for different cohorts.

As a society and as researchers, we have only recently begun to conceive of alternative family forms as simply alternatives rather than as dysfunctional versions of an ideal family. This includes asking new and different research questions about families headed by single parents, about the impact of divorce on family life, and about the rights of gay and lesbian persons to have their partnerships and families formally recognized. One reason that we know very little of the family lives of older gay and lesbian individuals is that we have failed to ask about them. This requires going beyond discussion of same-sex relationships to considering the larger family networks of which gay and lesbian adults are a part, as old people and as members of their families (see Chapters 7, 8, and 12).

More studies that examine the impact of divorce on the lives of older persons are needed. Such research must take into account the duration of the marriage prior to divorce, the age at divorce, and differences across cohorts in the repercussions of divorce. The long-term consequences of remarriage earlier in life and of remarriage in older age also require further investigation. To date, we have focused on remarriage following divorce rather than widowhood and on the consequences of both divorce and remarriage for younger children. What are the long-term effects on ties between parents and children and between full versus half and step siblings (see Chapter 11)? Related questions concern cohabitation involving older couples.

Another trend with significant implications for family life is women's participation in the labor force. Although the impact of women's paid work on caregiving to young children and to old parents has received considerable attention, we know little about the impact of lifelong work on partnerships, on ties with adult children, and on relationships with grandchildren. The combination of older women working and higher divorce rates among their children could have major repercussions for the transitions that occur after divorce in both generations.

Research Methods

At the same time that we limit our understanding of the full range of family life through the questions that we ask and do not ask, we also obscure our perception through the kinds of research that we do. Confining ourselves to favored research methodologies hampers our ability to observe the complexity and dynamism of family life. Our capacity for witnessing family processes is dampened by our focus on individuals rather than family relationships. As I have mentioned, we have moved forward in our attempts to take into account the bigger family picture through examinations of family composition and through having multiple sources of information about one family or relationship.

Nonetheless, much research continues to focus on a key informant (such as the primary caregiver, the child or sibling of greatest contact, the grandchild who lives nearest by) rather than an entire family. Because we have yet to develop one research methodology that addresses all of our concerns about family life, we must combine multiple research strategies to create a better composite picture. This involves valuing the important contributions that various quantitative *and* qualitative research strategies can make to our understanding of family ties and aging. Having succeeded in minimizing the dogma of positivist quantitative work, we must be cautious not to become dogmatic about approaches to qualitative research (LaRossa, 2005; Matthews, 2005b).

A major problem in aging research, including that related to family ties, is the dependence on results from cross-sectional studies. Because a cross-sectional design involves obtaining information from a sample at one point in time, one can only reach definitive conclusions about the state of affairs at that point in time. This is useful for some purposes, such as knowing the characteristics of a particular older population in order to estimate needed services, but cross-sectional designs are an uncertain basis for drawing conclusions about change over time. Longitudinal studies involve obtaining data at different times, either from the same sample or from different samples that represent the same population. Such an approach is unduly costly and time consuming when the need is for data about current circumstances. But if the objective is to observe continuity and change over time, longitudinal work is essential.

The development of several longitudinal studies using both local and national samples has made a substantial contribution to our understanding of family ties over the life course (Hofferth, 2005). Knowing which changes over the life course are a function of aging and which are responses to other situational factors improves our understanding and the accuracy of our projections for the future. A critical feminist approach and a life course perspective on aging and family ties encourage more longitudinal work and emphasize the need to consider the link between individual lives, historical time and social structure.

Theoretical Issues

Broadening our definition of family ties, moving from a focus on individuals to one on relationships, and expanding the array of research questions and methods should improve our understanding of family ties and of families as a dynamic process of negotiating a network of relationships. They do not guarantee, however, that we will place families within a larger social context. This connection can be achieved partly through the research that we do but is most likely to occur through the application of theoretical frameworks that focus on the connections between broader social processes and family life (see Chapter 1).

Inequitable structural arrangements based on age, gender (including sexual orientation), race, ethnicity and class are reproduced in families and often overpower individual objectives and initiatives, making it very difficult for some to create and maintain desired familial arrangements. For example, differential expectations of familial commitment based on gender, extreme differences in economic resources based on race and class, and varying legal rights and privileges based on age, marital status, and sexual orientation cross-cut one another to create ambivalent and sometimes conflicting situations for family members. Yet, remarkably in some cases, the family has remained a resilient social institution, in part because of the strong efforts of family members to make their families work despite structural pressures that militate against their success. Our theoretical work must incorporate this essential tension between individual agency and social structure, in part with the objective of recommending ways in which social arrangements can be altered to reduce inequity and better support a range of family forms.

Just as appreciating diversity is central to our understanding of family life at the societal level, so too is diversity in relationships essential to all family members, including older persons. As our discussion has clearly shown, family ties remain central to the social life of Americans and Canadians. At the same time, all of us benefit from having social networks that extend beyond family. A critical life course perspective that incorporates a feminist approach reveals the limits to family as a social institution, particularly for some groups. For example, the often dire circumstances that many women face in old age after a lifetime of committing themselves to family members attest to the shortcomings of extreme dependence on families in old age. Changes such as increases in paid work among women and in divorce have been seen primarily as threats to the welfare of families in general and of children in particular. Yet one might argue that these changes represent important transitions toward an expanded ability to negotiate a lifetime of varied relationships more independently. Theoretical perspectives must provide room for alternatives to established ways of doing family as potential avenues for actually strengthening family relationships and improving the chances for independence in later life. Social policy has an important role to play in enhancing such independence.

Social Policy

Reforms always are the product of political struggle and negotiation. Hence, they invariably generate positive as well as negative effects that, in turn, are mediated by gender, race, class, sexual orientation, age, and (dis)ability.

—Chunn (2000:226)

Public Issue or Private Trouble?

Problems encountered by members of society can be perceived and treated as private troubles or public issues (Mills, 1959). When treated as private troubles, they are the problems of individuals for which they and their families are typically held responsible. Holding individuals accountable for solving their problems can have the effect of implicitly blaming them for their problems, thereby abdicating society of responsibility for providing remedies (Ryan, 1971). When problems are treated as public issues, there is acceptance at the social level for some responsibility in providing solutions. A primary concern about postmodern society is the retrenchment of the welfare state and the increase in individual responsibility and, consequently, individual risk (Estes et al., 2003; Katz, 2005). A similar retreat is evident in the private sector, where employers are now providing less security to their employees in order to protect themselves from market risks (O'Rand, 2003).

Only rarely is a particular event or circumstance entirely a private trouble or a public issue. Instead, most situations have elements of both. Perhaps, no area better exemplifies the delicate balance between private troubles and public issues than transitions and challenges that arise in family life. When families are considered the logical source for solutions to the problems of their members, this is essentially treating problems as private troubles. When social polices are developed to support individuals and families in the resolution of problems, there is evidence of treating problems as public issues. The privacy and autonomy accorded to families complicate their treatment as targets for social policy. At the same time, the importance of the family as a social institution has been the basis for considering it an ideal focus for policy initiatives.

Widowhood, a predominantly female experience, provides a good example of these issues. Although a widow is rarely blamed for the death of her husband, the initial adjustment to widowhood is indeed an intensely personal process of bereavement (a private trouble) to be surmounted by the widow, with support from her family and close friends (see Chapter 6). At the same time, some of the repercussions of widowhood, such as the poverty experienced by many widows, are more accurately considered public issues because they are, in substantial measure, socially created.

The distinction between private and public responsibility has taken on new urgency in debates about support to older persons and their families. We have observed the great extent to which older individuals and their families treat changes accompanying aging as private troubles for which they assume responsibility.

Family members increase their support in response to poor health, divorce, the birth of a child, retirement, widowhood, remarriage, and other life events and transitions. Several factors combine to potentially limit the future ability of families to provide care for older members. First, the net effect of fewer children (except for parents of the baby boom) and living longer is an increase in the proportion of old individuals who do not have working-age children, typically the best source of support. Second, although labor force participation does not lead women to abandon their parents, it alters the ways in which care is provided and increases the need for support from other sources. Third, divorce clearly negates the support of a spouse but also may lower the amount of support exchanged between generations, undermining adult children as a resource in old age.

At the same time as the reservoir of familial support is shrinking (except for the parents of the baby boom), the potential needs of the older population are expanding. Differences in life expectancy between men and women are shrinking but continue, and longevity keeps going up. This means that there will continue to be a large number of widows and an ever-aging older population. Thus, although the older population as a whole (i.e., those over 65) may be healthier, wealthier, and more educated in the future, the more rapid growth of the oldest age group (those 75 plus) will counter-balance some of this improvement, because health and income are lower in this age cohort, especially among widows. Yet at a time when the very trends that increase the need for support also impede the ability of family members to provide more of it, governments are cutting back publicly funded programs, effectively transferring care to families (Gee, 2000; Gerstel & Gallagher, 1994).

The Intergenerational Equity Debate

The intergenerational equity debate centers on the view that each generation must receive its fair share of government spending or public transfers (Kohli, 2005). On one side are those who argue that the old are receiving too much, at the expense of the young. On the other are those who disagree and believe that discussions of equity must include more than current government expenditures (Marshall et al., 1993; see Chapter 1). The view of intergenerational inequity as a problem has strong roots in the United States where, in 1984, Americans for Generational Equity (AGE) was formed with the objective of applying Thomas Jefferson's view that each generation should ensure that the succeeding one enjoys similar or greater levels of prosperity (Bengtson, 1993). In Britain, Johnson et al. (1989) argued that old people are "parasitic upon the state and ultimately on taxpayers" and paralleled AGE's effect in the United States of encouraging governments to carry through on their commitment to cut state benefits and services while laying "part of the blame for the economic crisis on elderly people" (Arber & Ginn, 1991:54).

Comparisons of Canadian and U.S. policy have cast Canada as more publicly minded, collectivist and egalitarian (Clark, 1993). Sadly, however, claims that the intergenerational equity debate does not apply to Canada (Marshall et al., 1993; Schulz, 1997) now ring hollow as both countries have shared trends in deficit and tax reduction, downsizing, and cost cutting in the public and private spheres. An outcome of these trends is a renewed focus on methods for reducing public support, such as espousing a philosophy of community-based rather than institutional care. In an economic climate where funds do not match rhetoric (Chappell, 1993), this philosophy typically means an increased reliance on family members who are often already overextended. Another result is further entrenchment of the intergenerational equity debate, as one age group is cast against another as more or less deserving of government funds in the face of a general reluctance to increase support to all age groups.

Claims of intergenerational inequity might be supportable if one considers only one point in time and only public transfers to old people, particularly the very old (Cornman & Kingson, 1996). But these claims stand up very poorly if one expands the horizon to include a lifetime of contributions to society, including to the public purse (Cornman & Kingson, 1996; Townson, 2001), as well as the private transfers that older people make, particularly to their families, over their lifetimes (Gee, 2000; Kohli, 2005; Marshall, 1997; Marshall et al., 1993; McDaniel, 1997; Stone et al., 1998). These lifelong and continuing efforts of older people make it impossible to claim lack of individual initiative. They also help account for the general lack of intergenerational conflict that supposed inequities are assumed to create (Attias-Donfut & Arber, 2000). Yet the push for so-called fiscal responsibility, and the resulting cuts in programs of all kinds that have ensued, have stymied the groundswell of growing demands to humanize, personalize, integrate, and expand social programs that arose in the 1980s (Dobell & Mansbridge, 1986).

Supporting the young and old need not be treated as a zero-sum game; meeting the needs of one group will assist the other, and meeting the needs of both groups is essential. Social policies that provide for one age group tend to benefit other generations because assets are shared within families. Financial transfers to older persons do not only decrease their dependence on family members; they also increase older persons' financial contributions to children and grandchildren (Foner, 2000). Grandparents often face considerable hardship when caring for grandchildren in families experiencing a spate of challenges, including poverty, racial discrimination, drug use and divorce (see Chapter 10). Social policies that support either children or older persons help the other generation; helping both children and older persons multiplies the reciprocal benefits to both generations. As well, the personal concern of younger persons for their older relatives fosters a willingness to contribute to public programs for older people (Attias-Donfut, 2000; Foner, 2000).

Age-Based Versus Needs-Based Social Policy

One of the problems of the intergenerational equity debate is the assumption of similarity within a generation when there is, in fact, great disparity (Kohli, 2005). Indeed, if there is a risk of conflict, it is one based on class rather than generational, differences (Kohli, 2006). One way to address diversity is to base social policy on need rather than on age, but there is some debate about this alternative. Some time ago, Marshall (1981) discussed two scenarios of what the future holds for older persons, a best case and a worst case, foreshadowing current discussions of whether we are moving toward an age-integrated society (Riley & Riley, 2000; Uhlenberg, 2000).

In the best case, described more recently as the scenario of postmodern optimism (Giddens, 1991), age will become irrelevant because of the improved health, education and status of older people. Thus, age-based policies will become increasingly unnecessary and, indeed, are to be avoided both now and in the future because they reinforce age segregation. In the worst case, also dubbed the nightmare scenario (Giddens, 1991), significant differences among age groups will continue, and because these differences place older persons at a disadvantage, age-based policies to counter them will still be required.

The postmodern view that characterizes old age as a time of endless possibilities (Estes et al., 2003; Walker, 2006) and the emphasis on successful aging that is part of what is being referred to as the new gerontology (Holstein & Minkler, 2003) ignore the continuing influence of age relations and the great disparity among old people in their ability to act on their preferences. Holding out such possibilities does a particular disservice to those who are marginalized—older women, those who are poor, and those of color—by trivializing the difficulties of their situations (Holstein & Minkler, 2003). This stance does coalesce nicely, however, with current trends to turn public issues into private troubles by withdrawing state support and increasing individual risk. In the end, the postmodern emphasis on the many potential options of old age presents a paradox: It is a great time to be old if you can continue to produce and consume, as you did when you were younger. If you cannot, you are on your own.

As long as there are age-based limits to labor market accessibility in the form of the common practice of retirement by the age of 65 or the reluctance to hire older workers, claims of age irrelevance are hard to justify. The inability of some to continue working for health reasons also suggests some responsibility on behalf of the state to ensure economic viability in later life. The age set for either mandatory (in some parts of Canada) or customary retirement (indirectly through age requirements for benefits such as social security in the United States) can serve as an economic safety valve. In times of high unemployment, an earlier age is either encouraged or required. An economic upswing results in both increased employment and a move to an older retirement age. So too does an aging population and concerns about a shrinking labor force. If current moves to delay both retirement and eligibility for pension benefits continue (Henretta, 2000), government responsibility may once again be replaced by private earnings. However, if subtle or overt discrimination against older workers continues (Guillemard, 2000), such changes in policy are unlikely to be met by corresponding changes in employment eligibility of more than a year or two beyond current retirement ages.

Providing services in response to need reflects a view recommended by Cain (1987:291) that the "proper quest for policy makers is to provide equal concern and respect—not necessarily equal resources or access to services—to members of various age categories." Hence, groups of any age who have particular circumstances that necessitate public support should receive it. For older persons, the principles of basing support on age and on need are reflected in social policy. Eligibility for social insurance programs rests on age and is exemplified by social security and Medicare in the United States (Meyer & Bellas, 1995) and by the Canada/Québec Pension

Plan in Canada (Street & Connidis, 2001). Social assistance programs are based on need, as in the case of supplemental security income and Medicaid in the United States or the Guaranteed Income Supplement in Canada. Determining whether older persons are in need tends to be a humiliating process, and such social assistance programs are likely to pit taxpayer against welfare recipient. Social insurance programs, although expensive, are generally more popular because all contributors are beneficiaries. Despite their apparent universality, social security and Medicare as well as the Canada/Québec Pension Plan leave some groups vulnerable, most notably women, Blacks, Hispanics, immigrants and the poor, because they are tied to previous labor force involvement; long-term care can quickly deplete their limited benefits (Estes, 2001; Ginn et al., 2001; Meyer & Bellas, 1995; Street & Connidis, 2001). Increased privatization of such schemes would make matters even worse for these groups (Estes, 2001; Townson, 2001), because the safety net provided by assistance programs does not catch all of those who need additional support.

Tax-based programs, such as deductions for retirement savings plans, are another form of public support that benefits those with more resources at the same time that it diminishes the tax base that could be used for support programs (Street & Connidis, 2001). Tax deductions for those who care for relatives may be used as an incentive for informal caring, but they yield limited results (Linsk et al., 1995). As well, there are private transfers, including private and public pension plans, employment-based health benefits, and the extensive range of support offered by family and friends.

The need for support is the most compelling reason that public programs should be augmented. Encouraging older persons' dependence on family members, particularly children, is inconsistent with a culture that places such high value on independence. We know that parents derive greater satisfaction from their relationships with children when there is reciprocity rather than dependency. As well, studies from several Western nations show that today's older population favors formal over informal support for personal and long-term care (Daatland, 1990; Wielink et al., 1997). Providing assistance, including funds, directly to older individuals helps them to maintain their position in exchange relationships instead of becoming more dependent and subservient (Brubaker & Brubaker, 1995; Kane & Penrod, 1995; Pyke, 1999). Indeed, intergenerational investment has been proposed as a counter to the concept of intergenerational equity and views age-based public supports to older persons as a large insurance benefit that protects younger generations from the personal debt they would accrue if their older relatives were sick or poor (Greene & Marty, 1999).

Connecting Informal and Formal Support

A major impetus for promoting informal support from families to older persons is the view that formal support from publicly funded services *replaces* the support that family members provide, despite evidence to the contrary (Penning & Keating, 2000; Walker, 1991). According to this view, formal support should not be offered prematurely because it prompts families to leave the care of their older members entirely in the hands of professionals and service providers. This rests on a model that separates informal from formal care and independence from dependence; an older person is assumed to move to formal support when informal support is no longer feasible due to his or her growing dependence. The implicit assumption is that it is only old adults who receive formal support in response to their growing dependency. If one imagined a continuum of such a support model, informal support, independence and youth would be on the left end and formal support, dependence and old age on the right end.

In fact, we avail ourselves of both informal and formal support across the life course and remembering this helps to correct the undue focus of the intergenerational equity proponents on old people as the primary recipients of formal support. I have noted in previous chapters that reciprocity characterizes intergenerational relationships and that access to formal support does not typically lead a spouse or children to leave their partner or parent entirely in the hands of professional staff. A life course view encourages a model of informal and formal support as two parallel and interacting continua in which both are present simultaneously. As responsibilities, social networks, and needs vary over the life course (not necessarily in a linear fashion), the balance between informal and formal support shifts. In this model, the life course would be represented with the young on the left and the old on the right as each end of the continuum. Simple versions of the two models are shown in Figure 14.1.

The + signs of the informal support continuum indicate the growing informal social network as one moves from childhood, to adolescence, young adulthood, middle age, and old age. The − signs depict losses from the informal network. Clearly, one may gain additional friends and family ties at multiple points across the life course, and there are substantial variations from the life course trajectory shown here. The point is that at all ages, we have an informal support network, and this network has elements of both continuity and change over time (see Chapter 8).

The formal support network continuum also indicates a lifetime of receiving various forms of publicly funded support. As with informal support, the particular form of support may vary over time, but whatever our age, we rely to some extent on formal as well as informal support. Some forms of support are age related, but I have not included lost sources of formal support because the changing life course may mean that, for example, education is not as strictly associated with youth as it once was. Nonetheless, educational resources are more likely to be utilized by young rather than old citizens.

Our tendency to treat informal and formal (or private and public) support as two separate worlds misses the essential connection between them. Successful implementation of social policy depends on good relationships among family members, professionals, friends and neighbors. Ideally, informal and formal support networks complement one another as needed. In reality, there are often gaps, in part because of competing ideologies regarding the wisdom of offering state-supported programs for what is seen by some to be a family responsibility.

Meeting Diverse Needs

Diversity has become a buzz word of our time. The call to respect the significant variations among us in a society characterized by agism, sexism and heterosexism, and racism is irresistible. However, a focus on diversity and the call to celebrate

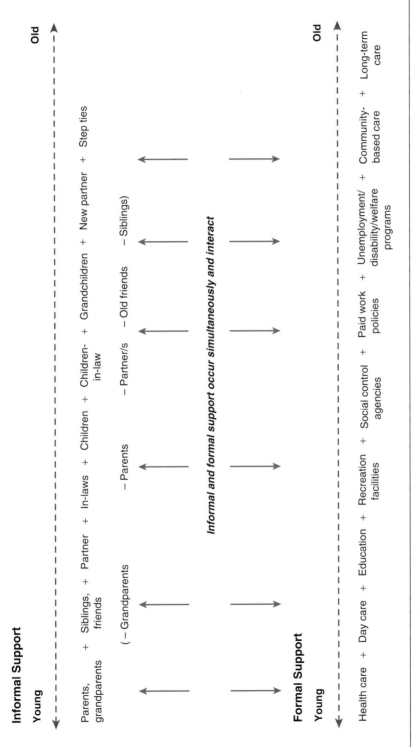

FIGURE 14.1 Models of Informal and Formal Support

difference runs paradoxical risks. In his provocative discussion of this trend, Michaels (2006) argues that the significance of growing economic inequality has been supplanted by attending instead to honoring differences such as those based on race. Rather than strive to eliminate discrimination and inequality, we are encouraged to respect the differences that are their object and the pride in cultural identities that such respect is assumed to allow. The inequalities embedded in current social arrangements and social relations are thus protected from a critical gaze, an appealing stance to those with resources because the obligation to respect diversity requires only that we be nice to each other, not that we share unequal resources. Yet as Michaels (2006:10) observes, classes "are not like races or cultures, and treating them as if they were like races or cultures—different but equal—is one of our strategies for managing inequality rather than minimizing or eliminating it. White is not better than black, but rich is definitely better than poor."

In my view, the challenge is to appreciate the cross-cutting of class with other power relations, including those of race and gender, in order to appreciate that there is not simply economic inequality but that it is systematically related to other forms of inequality. Thus, dealing with significant differences based on gender and race is also related to unequal resource distribution. Men and women or Blacks and Whites or straight and gay people do not have to be the same as each other, but respecting their difference at the expense of addressing how that difference is related to unequal economic and social security misses an opportunity for appropriate policy intervention and social change. The framework I espouse, with its emphasis on multiple, interconnected structured social relations and on multiple levels of analysis, helps us to avoid the dichotomous view of focusing either on racial (or gender, or age, or sexual) identity or on economic inequality.

We must consider various connections to privilege, such as recognition in law, opportunities in the workplace, expectations regarding unpaid labor, and access to education and health care. As well, shared ethnicity and race are important grounds for political activism, and as our society becomes more ethnically and racially diverse, the intersection of aging, ethnicity, race and politics has significant implications for public policy (Torres-Gil, 2005). As Whites continue to be an ever-shrinking proportion of the population (see Chapter 2), longstanding White elderly advocacy groups are more likely to build alliances with minority and immigrant elderly groups at the same time that minority elderly advocacy groups must reach out to their younger counterparts. Shared interests based on age and on ethnicity are more likely to coalesce as cooperation becomes a growing imperative for all groups. Old immigrants face particular challenges because they have less money and education than do native-born Americans (Jackson et al., 2005). A helpful strategy among Hispanic and Asian immigrants is to build strong networks of fictive kin with whom support is exchanged, including care responsibilities in old age (Ebaugh & Curry, 2000). As the goals of various advocacy groups for the old underscore, honoring difference is an unacceptable substitute for economic (Michaels, 2006) and social equality.

A central critique of the intergenerational equity premise is the focus on differences *between* age groups rather than the substantial differences *within* age groups based on gender, race, class and health status (Bengtson & Murray, 1993; Marshall,

1997; Stone et al., 1998). One appeal of focusing on intergenerational equity is the greater simplicity of altering age-based government transfers than of tackling more fundamental but thorny challenges, such as poverty and racism. The most wrenching demands on familial relationships tend to be made on those who have the fewest resources. As well, it is in these families that the older generation is most likely to be giving more support than it is receiving (Jackson & Kalavar, 1993). A critical life course perspective reveals the advantages *and* disadvantages that accrue over a lifetime, creating even more disparity among the old than among the young (Dannefer, 2003; O'Rand, 2006). A life course view also signals the wisdom of meeting the needs of old age by targeting policies and programs at key transition points across the life course, such as those from education to paid work, from paid work to parenting, from domestic to paid labor, from paid work to unemployment and back again, and from paid labor to retirement and ongoing domestic responsibilities (Cooke, 2006; Law Commission, 2004). It is at these junctures that individuals face substantial risk and when setbacks can have lifetime consequences from which many cannot fully recover.

The substantial drop in financial status experienced by older persons generally, and the high poverty rates among visible minority seniors and older women in particular, can only be redressed if treated as public issues. The growing ethnic and racial diversity among older persons is one reason that the improved standard of living among today's seniors must not be the basis for a complacent stance toward cutbacks in publicly funded support to older persons. Yet dealing with inequality based on race and ethnicity poses a unique quandary. How does one strike the right balance between recognizing the negative consequences of socially created structural conditions that leave some in a position of relative disadvantage and respecting the effective adaptation of familial arrangements as a proactive strategy?

If the disadvantages faced by particular groups, such as Black and Hispanic Americans, are emphasized too much, there is a risk of promoting the view that their familial arrangements are dysfunctional. But if the focus is placed too heavily on successful culturally based reliance on extended family relationships, there is the risk of relying too much on strong family ties and failing to acknowledge social responsibility for structurally created conditions (Burnette, 1999). An overly monolithic view of particular minority groups also risks minimizing the substantial historical and cultural diversity within them (Dilworth-Anderson & Burton, 1999). On balance, the impact of minority status, poverty, and accessibility appear to loom larger than cultural preferences in explaining the long-term care arrangements of older persons (Mui et al., 1998) and the lesser accessibility to good institutional options among African Americans (Cantor & Brennan, 2000; Olson, 2003).

In the longer term, more racial and gender equality in the labor force today will benefit younger generations and reduce their dependence on older generations. However, such initiatives at the early stages of employment must extend as well to the end of work careers. Although Black and White men and women have all retired at earlier ages over the past few decades (Gendell & Siegel, 1996), Black and Hispanic older persons and women are more likely to experience early involuntary exit from the labor force. This early exit often becomes retirement and reduces years of earnings and subsequent pensions in old age (Flippen & Tienda, 2000). Poverty lies at the heart of many of the dilemmas confronted by older persons and their families and is particularly high among those who engage most in support exchanges with kin (Minkler, 1999).

As with race, gender cross-cuts concerns about social policy from the perspective of both the older person and the caregiver. In old age, women face more economic hardship, in substantial measure because they are more likely to be alone for longer periods as a result of being widowed or divorced (see Chapter 6). Of course, the reason that being on their own has such dramatic consequences is that most of today's older women did not accumulate their own wealth during their younger years. Instead, they spent most of their lives engaged in caring for others, work that is both undervalued and unpaid (Ginn et al., 2001; Hooyman & Gonyea, 1995).

The structural and cultural context of gender relations encourages a strategic selection process that favors domestic work among women, either instead of or in conjunction with labor force participation (Moen & Spencer, 2006). Limited paid work minimizes access not only to benefits through work but also to state-based support that rests on financial contributions in earlier years. Even among middle-aged, full-time paid workers with pension coverage, men's accumulated pension wealth is significantly greater than women's, reflecting the dual labor market and the more checkered employment histories of women (Ginn et al., 2001; Johnson et al., 1999; Street & Connidis, 2001). The treatment of caring as a personal trouble for families (women) to manage continues to have a firm hold, despite other social changes. Yet only when caring is respected as an issue to be dealt with at the societal level can women escape the costs of caring that follow them into old age (Hooyman & Gonyea, 1995; Neysmith, 1991).

Women are particularly in need of financial support through public policy and through changes in the private sector, such as improvements in eligibility for and value of work-based pensions. The collision between caring responsibilities and labor force participation reveals the essential tension between work and family when they are treated as two independent, rather than overlapping, spheres of social life. If family caregiving is to remain viable, there must be more latitude in the work place.

The gendered structure of our society also oppresses men but in quite different ways (Calasanti, 2004). For example, divorced men tend to be especially isolated in old age, a situation shaped considerably by the fact that during their younger years, their former spouses typically received custody of their children. Restructuring society based on equitable gender relations is likely to enhance the social networks of men, giving them the opportunity to develop more involved familial ties. As the case of old divorced men illustrates, such changes must occur across the life course, including caring for children. Inequities cannot be corrected at the end of life through targeted social programs—for women or men.

A hallmark of social policy must be variety. I have noted the substantial differences in family dynamics and old age that result from inequities based on gender, race, ethnicity, and class. When these intersect with each other and with age, relative social disadvantage is compounded. A strategy of serving older persons and their families that rests on one approach, however popular it might be, cannot succeed because the needs and situations of older individuals are too variable. One aspect of variety includes a necessary mix of privately and publicly funded care. Just as claims that only families can provide good care leave gaps, relying solely on government as the answer is likely to limit care options and to underestimate the potential of the private sector to meet some of the needs for care (England, 2005).

Support for Caregivers and Community-Based Support

One reason that families cannot be considered true substitutes for other social programs for the elderly is that caregivers also require support, especially if care is given for a long time. In November of 2006, between 30 and 38 million adults in the United States provided an average of 21 hours of help a week to an adult with a limitation in daily living (Gibson & Houser, 2007). Over the course of that year, the total number of Americans providing such help would be about 50% higher. These numbers include adults who are helping older (e.g., parents) and younger (e.g., children) adult family members. Family caregivers want to help older persons, and formal support does not serve as a substitute for their efforts (Brody, 1995; Miller, 1998; Penning & Keating, 2000). Like those they care for, caregivers also receive extensive help from other family members, but they require help from formal services as well. Informal caregiving delays the use of formal support and saves millions of taxpayer dollars, but the personal costs of caregiving often include direct out-of-pocket expenses, lost income and health problems (Gibson & Houser, 2007). More extensive support to and from older persons among ethnic and racial minorities and among those in the lower classes, particularly through co-residence (see Chapters 8 and 10), makes special efforts to provide support to these caregivers essential. Because qualifying for limited formal support services often requires children to emphasize the burden of caring for their parents, relations between older parents and their adult children can be undermined. As well, the complicated access routes to fragmented services lead many caregivers to give up trying to obtain formal support (Miller, 1998).

As combining paid work and family become normative for working adults, employers are becoming more aware of and responsive to the needs of those employees caring for older family members (Neal et al., 1993). Recent changes in Canada include the introduction of Compassionate Leave in the province of Ontario. Workers can take unpaid leave from the labor force in order to care for a terminally ill relative. No such legislation exists in the United States for workers in firms of fewer than 50 employees. Unpaid leaves like those covered by the Family and Medical Leave Act in the United States (used primarily as maternity leave) and Ontario's Compassionate Leave have lower take-up rates among those with fewer resources because they cannot afford to take time from paid work (Wisensale, 2001).

Globalization and the new economy bring new challenges to balancing paid work and family as competition drives long work hours and technology increases the expectation of being available 24/7, cutting into family time and caring (Blair-Loy & Jacobs, 2003). New fields, such as information technology, threaten the return to a more traditional division of domestic labor among male workers who depend upon their spouses to assume more of the domestic labor as a way of meeting work demands (Connidis & Kemp, forthcoming). We cannot take for granted the advances that women have made in paid labor and the consequent assumption of their improved situation in old age. In both the United States and Canada, there is much room for expanding work-based policies that facilitate meeting the simultaneous demands of employment and family caring. Favored benefits to help balance work and family commitments among employees include time off without pay, flexible time, compressed work weeks, personal days with pay, part-time work that permits maintenance of regular benefits (Martin-Matthews, 1999), and being able to work at home (Merrill, 1997). Such benefits are crucial to long-distance caregiving by children (Neal et al., 2008). As well, there is the critical issue of respecting the value of reproductive labor by ensuring economic security for those who commit much of their lives to caring for both young and old family members.

Direct financial support to carers, through tax incentives or actual payment, relieves some of the strain and enhances the autonomy of those committed to caring for an older member, but it is unlikely to encourage more families to provide care or to avert institutionalization (Kapp, 1995). The ethical debate about paying individuals who already have a moral obligation to care is one reason that some states forbid financial compensation to family caregivers. Paying family caregivers who have few resources has the merit of redistributing income (Kane & Penrod, 1995; Linsk et al., 1995) but runs the risk of reinforcing elder care as women's work within the family rather than making major changes in the balance of individual and collective responsibility (Olson, 2003).

A number of programs share the common goal of bolstering the ability of older individuals to remain in the community, either independently or with the support of family. These include homemaker services, meal preparation (meals-on-wheels, wheels-to-meals), personal in-home care, telephone information and assistance, assistance for minor household repairs, transportation, and day care and respite care programs. To the extent that some of these services enhance the independence of elderly individuals (e.g., transportation), they reduce dependence on families. Support such as day care and respite care provides either daily or periodic relief from caregiving. Although respite care does not improve caregiver well-being appreciably, it is lauded by those who use it and meets short-term needs for additional support (Kane & Penrod, 1995; Linsk et al., 1995). Day care programs have the additional advantage of providing the older individual with a social outlet. As well, these programs are an independent source of activity that is not family based and are, therefore, more likely to enhance self-esteem.

Home care (formal support offered in the home of the client) is also a successful strategy for supporting older clients and the family members who care for them. Home care can help to relieve the pressures of balancing employment and caring and may improve relationships between adult children and the parents they care for (Martin-Matthews, 2007). It also appears to be an effective method of alleviating some of the disparities by race in accessing other forms of care (White-Means & Rubin, 2004). Personal experience and public policy connect when funding shortages and the poor working conditions of home care workers bring policy issues at the levels of government and work organizations into the intimate setting of clients' homes (Martin-Matthews, 2007).

Even when services and programs are available in many communities, a key problem is their coordination (Kane & Kane, 2005). Elders and their families often face difficulties in finding services, not because they do not exist but because they cannot locate them. Furthermore, the support provided by family and by the formal sector is far more effective if properly coordinated (Brubaker & Brubaker, 1995). Higher labor force participation rates among women threaten the viability of volunteer labor as a resource for service delivery, but paid work among women increases the ability of some families to purchase care for their members, young and old.

Consequences of health care cutbacks in Canada, as elsewhere, are declines in community-based support, the transfer of public responsibility to private enterprise and thereby the individual, and heightened demands for family-based care (Chappell & Penning, 2005). The result is disproportionate costs for those most likely to be both in need of care and providers of it: women, aboriginal and other ethnic and racial minorities, and those who are financially insecure. Such trends and outcomes "amplify existing inequalities of class, gender, race, and ethnicity" (Chappell & Penning, 2005:461).

Rather than viewing any form of care as the ideal, we must instead work toward coordinating complementary support from various sources. A value shift in this direction is evident in policy paradigms that focus on caring partnerships in which all caregivers, whether formal or informal, coordinate their efforts; and on client-centered care, in which older persons are clients rather than patients and are considered partners in the caring process (Keating et al., 1997). This approach is at the heart of the assisted living initiative launched from 1990 to 2000 (Kane & Wilson, 2007). Assisted living is intended to provide desirable housing and to maximize independence while providing services. The current variability in both definition and service delivery makes assessment of outcomes difficult. Both home care and nursing home delivery methods have learned from assisted living approaches, particularly regarding the capacity to function at home despite extensive needs for support and ways of making the nursing home environment more homelike (Kane & Wilson, 2007).

The Ongoing Need for Institutional Options

Thus far, we have focused attention on family caregiving and community-based support for older persons and their families. But the philosophical and financial appeal of community-based programs has not been matched by necessary funding (Olson, 2003), and it does not erase the ongoing and potentially heightened need for improvements in institutional care, including nursing homes, as the oldest of the old are the fastest growing segment of the older population (Kane & Kane, 2005). Over 40% of those aged 65 years and over are expected to spend some time in a nursing home (Olson, 2003). More and better institutional alternatives are needed for those with limited options for familial support and for those whose care requirements exceed what family members and community-based programs can handle.

As we look ahead, growing numbers of old people and of groups that are more likely to use formal care in institutional settings, such as the unattached and childless, will increase the need for more formal (paid) care workers. With more job prospects for women than was true in the past and the shrinking labor force that population aging brings, the pool of potential workers is declining. Better pay, better health care and child care, better work environments, more appreciation and recognition for a job well done, and better training are all needed in order to make good formal care for old family members viable (Ball et al., 2005; Callahan, 2001; Kane & Kane, 2005). Better screening of employees, better staff training, and stronger advocacy efforts on behalf of patients are recommended strategies for improving conditions for nursing home residents (Harris & Benson, 2006). Better working conditions with more pay and more time per patient would also improve staff–resident relations in nursing home settings.

The need for more formal caregivers occurs in a global market in which immigrants—both legal and illegal—are filling the gap between demand and available workers (Olson, 2003), creating additional issues of worker oppression and the disruption of family ties in the countries of origin.

A changing ethnic mix of old people has varied effects on the need for informal and formal support. Because Hispanics depend more than other groups on informal support, their growing numbers will not have a major impact on the demand for formal support (Alecxih, 2001). However, Blacks rely more than Whites on community-based services, so their increased proportion of the population pushes demand for more of this kind of support. On the other hand, Blacks are less likely than Whites to avail themselves of nursing homes or assisted living, despite their apparent greater need for them, in part because of their substantial cost (Ball et al., 2005; Olson, 2003). As well, a study of assisted living facilities in Georgia finds that African American elders prefer being in a facility that has a "distinctively African American cultural milieu" (Ball et al., 2005).

This preference for feeling at home with one's people, as well as the costs of formal care, may be central to understanding the limited appeal of nursing homes in the Black community, given their predominantly White clientele. Similarly, language barriers are a key impediment to seeking formal care, particularly residential care, among Asian elders, despite a growing acceptance of formal care in principle (Olson, 2003). Such concerns speak to the unique importance of cultural diversity, including language, in policy planning.

Legal Intervention in Family Ties

The law serves as a vehicle for change and a reflection of our cultural beliefs about family life and the obligations of family members to one another. In Canada, all 10 provinces have legislation regarding support obligations of adult children to their older parents, either as a separate Parents' Maintenance Act or as part of a Family Law Reform Act. Such acts reflect a belief in reciprocity between parent and child and, unlike earlier acts, do not require evidence of parental destitution due to specified circumstances, such as mental illness. However, very few cases under parents' maintenance acts are ever brought to court, and even fewer result in an order to provide support to a parent or third party on behalf of the parent (Parsons & Tindale, 2001). When parents do succeed at obtaining support from children through the courts, the cases typically involve financial need by the parents, financial capacity of the children, and a history of adequate parental support to the child (Martin-Matthews, 2000a). In legislative efforts in the United States, the Health Care Financing Administration allows state Medicaid offices to curtail nursing home expenses by passing "family responsibility" laws that require family members to help cover costs (Linsk et al.,

1995). However, to date, the few attempts to apply such statutes have resulted in very little capital accruing to nursing homes (Kapp, 1995).

Although legislation that directly concerns family caregiving to older persons is very limited, there are other ways in which the law has been used as a vehicle to change family ties across the life course. Two current issues stand as examples: attempts to secure visitation and custody rights for grandparents and attempts to have gay and lesbian relationships and parenthood legally recognized. Statutes concerning grandparents' visitation rights are in place in all 50 states, but they usually require a divorce, separation, or death of a parent or parents for grandparents to make a claim (Wacker, 1995). If parents and children are together, grandparents cannot seek visitation rights in any state. Parental rights continue to take precedence, and grandparents may well be denied access when parents argue their rights to privacy and to judge appropriate levels of grandparental access to their children (Aldous, 1995). The isolation of grandparents from their grandchildren, particularly following the awarding of custody to a child-in-law, has prompted the creation of advocacy groups aimed at securing additional grandparent rights (Bender & Brannon, 1994; Hilton & Macari, 1997). The policy implications of growing numbers of single-parent families is one incentive for governmental support of grandparents' desire to carry out their ongoing commitment to their grandchildren (Aldous, 1995).

Although grandparents do not have the rights of access to grandchildren that parents do to children, when serving as caregivers, the fact that they are relatives often limits accessibility to financial assistance (Landry-Meyer, 1999). Given that grandparents caring for grandchildren are often poor, it is not surprising that one of their overwhelming concerns is whether they can afford to look after their grandchildren. Obtaining legal custody of grandchildren can prove difficult and costly and is a significant issue for grandparents who are raising their grandchildren (Landry-Meyer, 1999). Some states have instituted alternative legal relationships between grandparents and grandchildren that grant grandparents parental authority without going through a custody case.

The changing role of grandparents in the lives of their grandchildren is but one outcome of the changing face of families. Rising numbers of divorce, remarriage and cohabitation have meant changes in family structure, including a growing number of families that involve various step relationships (Milan, 2000). Changes in public policy, including legal rights and obligations, must keep pace with the emergence of these new ties (Mason & Mauldon, 1999). Current inconsistencies include the contrast between the *stranger* model of some policies, in which co-resident stepparents have no rights or responsibilities, and the *dependency* model, in which it is assumed that a co-resident father is providing financial support (Mason, 1998).

Historical and current resistance to instituting gay and lesbian relationships as marriage in both the United States and Canada demonstrates the significance of sexual orientation as a basis for establishing rights and obligations (see Chapter 4). The backlash following the 1996 passage of same-sex unions in Hawaii (repealed in a 1999 final ruling) and the rise of the family values debate during the Dole-Clinton campaign was so strong that the Defense of Marriage Act was passed (Schwartz & Rutter, 1998). This federal law explicitly does not recognize same-sex relationships as marriage, thus denying access to related benefits, and states are not required to recognize same-sex marriages that take place in other states. This sets a precedent of federal involvement in state powers by breaking with the long-standing requirement of the states to recognize marriages and divorces that occur in other states. To date, only the state of Massachusetts has legalized same-sex marriage (Allen, 2007b). As of November 2008, Connecticut followed suit, and California failed to do so.

In Canada, same-sex marriage was legalized in 2005, following years of evolution in rights for gay and lesbian Canadians. Attempts to revisit and repeal the legislation have failed, but they speak to the need to avoid complacency about the permanence of such change. The quite different situation in the United States, where the prospect of same-sex marriage has created a backlash against it, reflects the resurging impact of fundamentalist religion and a move to the right in politics. Yet the United States stands as an anomaly when one considers worldwide trends in the legalization of same-sex unions. One effect of globalization is the potential to "challenge unjust or inadequate national laws and policies" (Phillipson, 2006:55). Gay and lesbian couples have made claims to the right to receive benefit entitlements and to marry based on having married legally in another country. For example, in 2006, Israel's High Court of Justice ruled that five gay couples who married in Canada should have their unions recognized in Israel (CBC News, 2007a). In New York State, the appellate court ruled that a lesbian couple from New York State who married in Canada should have that marriage recognized as legal, entitling one partner access to the workplace spousal benefits of the other (Boswell, 2008). A growing list of countries, including Denmark, the Netherlands, Spain and South Africa, now recognizes same-sex marriage.

Being in unsanctioned same-sex partnerships can undermine the familial commitments that many gay and lesbian couples desire. Legal marriage includes myriad state and federal entitlements, including a spouse's pension, social security survivor benefits, inheritance, bereavement leave, child custody, divorce protection, and sick leave to care for a spouse (Demian, 2000). A growing number of employers now offer spousal benefits to same-sex partners of their employees, and legal domestic partnerships in some municipalities give cohabiting couples access to benefits, whatever their gender or sexual orientation (Allen, 2007b; Stacey, 1998; Wisensale, 2001). Women; Whites; younger persons; those who are childfree; and those who have divorced, separated, cohabited or stayed single are more supportive of same-sex marriage than men, Blacks, older persons, parents, and married persons (Brumbaugh et al., 2008).

The absence of legally sanctioned same-sex couple relationships undermines the parental rights of both biological and nonbiological lesbian or gay parents, whose intimate relationships often serve as justification for denying custody (Allen, 2007b; Millbank, 1997, see Chapter 6). In some countries, same-sex partners can legally adopt children, even in countries like New Zealand where same-sex couples cannot marry but do have the same custody rights as married straight couples (CBC News, 2007a). In addition to maintaining custody, current legal efforts by lesbians and gays include obtaining second-parent (the nonbiological parent) adoption rights. In 2007, a lesbian partner in Ontario, Canada, won the right to be recognized as a third legal parent, along with her partner (the biological mother) and the biological father who donated sperm.

In terms of social programs targeted at older people, gay and lesbian individuals face difficult situations as they confront discriminatory attitudes among those who administer resources and services (Brotman et al., 2003; Ehrenberg, 1997). Although all sexual activity in institutional settings tends to be shunned by staff, this is particularly true of gay and lesbian relations. Limited acceptance is one reason that older gay and lesbian persons generally favor living in a gay or lesbian retirement community over one for gay and straight residents (Quam & Whitford, 1992). Thus the progress that has been made in increasing the number of social, educational and outreach services directed toward older gay and lesbian persons (Jacobson & Grossman, 1996) must continue.

Elder Mistreatment: A Case Study of Research and Policy Issues and Future Directions

Elder mistreatment provides a good example of the links between different social domains, in this case, the link between the informal world of families and the formal one of professional care, and of the links between different levels of analysis. At the macro level, this includes the social construction of old age that dominates Western culture and society, the view of the State about appropriate intervention, and the impact of structured social relations on one's risk of being mistreated *and* of mistreating others and on the likelihood of having someone do something about it. At the meso level are the challenges of dealing with elder mistreatment in families, in communities, and in formal institutional settings. Being an older individual who is mistreated or a family member who either abuses or is aware of abuse at the hands of others are central concerns at the micro level.

The fact that current anthologies on elder abuse and mistreatment (see e.g., Loseke et al., 2005a) still rely heavily on works published in the 1980s for the stronger statements on and conceptualizations of mistreatment in old age indicates the continuing challenges of studying this topic. Elder mistreatment is a good case study of the issues that are fundamental to sound research and policy: defining key terms, stating clear research questions, conducting research that can properly address these questions, relating research findings to policy initiatives, and developing and applying appropriate theoretical frameworks.

As is true of many subjects, preferred terminology regarding elder mistreatment has changed over the years. The terms *elder mistreatment* (particularly in North America) and *elder maltreatment* (more common in the United Kingdom) are favored over *elder abuse*. I use the three terms interchangeably for variety. Key research questions regarding elder mistreatment include, What is it? How much is there of which types? What are the conditions that increase the risk of mistreatment? Who are most likely to be victims and perpetrators of abuse? What can we do about it?

What Is Elder Mistreatment?

Elder mistreatment is complicated conceptual terrain. Although official bodies, including the Congress of the United States, use 60 years of age to signify elder status (Barnett et al., 2005), debate continues regarding which cutoff age makes someone a victim of *elder* abuse. The quandary of whether to isolate elder from other forms of mistreatment exemplifies the larger issue of constructing concepts that are both theoretically and pragmatically grounded. The fact that policies and research-funding agencies currently target old age is a pragmatic criterion for isolating elder mistreatment for separate study. Legal definitions are another. Typically, those studying elder abuse are interested in a broader range of behavior than is found in legal definitions that include assessments of culpability and intent. Yet if the aim is to be relevant to policy and practice, research definitions should have some connection to legal and statutory ones (Bonnie & Wallace, 2001; Steinmetz, 2005). Thus an important pragmatic issue is to define elder mistreatment in a way that is relevant beyond the research community.

Defining elder mistreatment is difficult because it concerns "covert and overt conflict in social relationships, private (in domestic settings), semi-public (in the special settings of residential homes and related forums), and public (in the wider society). . . . There will always be a degree of selectivity in whom we decide is being abused, and in what we see as representative of abuse" (Biggs et al., 1995:8). Power relations within families and between care workers and their clients are an important dimension of this selectivity.

Isolating elder mistreatment as a novel category of abuse creates conceptual dilemmas. If the perpetrator is a spouse, are we witnessing a case of aging spousal abuse or a new pattern in the spousal relationship that is brought on by increased dependency and caring? If the perpetrator is an adult child, is the mistreatment brought on by an older parent's growing dependency, or might it reflect a family history of abuse in which the tables have now turned? We must balance the interests of older persons who are newly vulnerable to mistreatment by family members against overstated estimates of elder abuse that treat all mistreatment later in life as unique to old age.

A life course perspective encourages us to question whether mistreatment has first emerged in old age or is a continuation of earlier patterns. It also improves the prospects of having policy and program initiatives address real situations and target appropriate intervention points in the life course. Solutions to long-term spousal abuse are likely to be quite different from those geared toward mistreatment that *begins* in old age as a function of changing circumstances. When age is the primary defining feature of elder abuse, the important issue of dependency is not specified (Steinmetz, 2005). Some clarify the relevance of 'elder' through the concept of vulnerability (Bonnie & Wallace, 2001). Age-associated vulnerability refers to an elder's diminished ability for self-care or self-protection and distinguishes elder from other forms of mistreatment. Defining elder mistreatment based on an assumption of increased vulnerability in old age risks further marginalization of the old. We must be clear that vulnerability is associated with specific age-related phenomena (isolation, memory loss, physical or mental impairment) and not old age per se. In the United States, some states have chosen to have protection legislation that does not specify age but rather offers protection from abuse to all adults who are considered vulnerable or incapacitated (Hafemeister, 2001).

The category of elder mistreatment includes a broad range of abuses, including physical, psychological and financial abuses as well as neglect (Wolf, 2001). Clear distinctions among them are essential because the etiology, consequences and solutions are likely to differ among them. Given our focus on family ties, a broad definition that suits our purposes here refers to elder mistreatment as

> intentional actions that cause harm or create a serious risk of harm (whether or not harm is intended) to a vulnerable elder by a caregiver or other person who stands in a trust relationship to the elder or . . . failure by a caregiver to satisfy the elder's basic needs or to protect the elder from harm. The term . . . is meant to exclude . . . self-neglect . . . and also cases involving victimization of elders by strangers. (Bonnie & Wallace, 2001:1)

The same authors confine the terms *abuse* and *neglect* to their legal meanings. Thus abuse is "conduct by responsible caregivers or other individuals that constitutes 'abuse' under applicable state or federal law," and neglect refers to "an omission by responsible caregivers that constitutes 'neglect' under applicable federal or state law" (Bonnie & Wallace, 2001: 39). Awareness of the distinction between research and legal definitions reminds us of the disconnection between them and the limits to law in dealing with the larger issue of elder mistreatment.

How Much Elder Mistreatment Is There?

We still do not have reliable figures of exactly how many older persons are victims (Barnett et al., 2005; Stein, 2006). It is estimated that from 3% to 10% of older persons suffer some form of mistreatment and that the more extreme forms—physical abuse and neglect—are the least common (Biggs et al., 1995; Wolf, 2001). Limited sound, national data over time makes it impossible to know whether apparent increases in mistreatment are real or a function of increased awareness and reporting (Wolf, 2001). Many studies continue to rely on cases reported to agencies despite knowing the weaknesses of these data (Stein, 2006). Older persons and rural residents set a higher threshold point than do their younger, urban counterparts in the extent of mistreatment required to be perceived as abusive (Stones & Bédard, 2002), suggesting a possible increase in future reports of abuse.

Family violence is particularly disconcerting and controversial (Loseke et al., 2005b). Historically invisible, private behavior within families has gradually reached the public eye through altered views about family, gender and violence. Attempts to assess the prevalence of family violence exemplify the dilemma of separating elder from general abuse. In the case of intimate partner violence, for example, recent research in the United States that distinguishes among lifetime, past-five-year and past-year prevalence succeeds in establishing when abuse occurred but not when it *began* (Bonomi et al., 2007). Although 26.5% of a sample of women aged 65 years and over report lifetime partner violence (defined to include both actual and threatened physical, sexual and psychological abuse), this number drops to 3.5% for past-five-year prevalence and 2.2% for the past year.

Several studies indicate that rates of intimate partner violence (Mouton, 2003) and physical and verbal abuse against women by family members or close friends (Mouton et al., 2004) are similar among younger and older women. In this instance, old persons who are abused by their spouses or partners are victims of partner abuse who happen to be old, not victims of a catchall category of elder mistreatment. However, the fact that over a quarter of older women report partner violence at some point in their lifetimes signals the need to attend to this issue in old age as well as earlier stages in the life course.

Three possible reporters of mistreatment are the perpetrator, the victim, and a third party. Understandably, perpetrators are unlikely to report their behavior to others. Victims may also be reluctant to let others know about being mistreated because they fear looking foolish (especially in the case of financial abuse); they fear further abuse, retaliation or the withdrawal of needed support; or they know the perpetrator and feel either partly responsible for his or her behavior or protective of the abuser, a common scenario regarding younger family members (Hafemeister, 2001). Professionals may also report abuse, particularly health care and social workers who witness the results of physical abuse and for whom reporting is legally required. When the reporting of mistreatment is not legally required, as in the case of financial professionals, underreporting often results. Third parties may also be other family members.

Media reports tend to pay particular attention to financial mistreatment, often in the form of scams directed at old people. Financial abuse is often perpetrated by family members and others in trusted relationships. Unlike other forms of abuse, it typically involves the older person's tacit awareness and consent (Hafemeister, 2001). Domestic financial abuse ranges from cashing pension checks without permission and misusing funds and credit cards, to forgery and denying older persons access to their money or to care without the promise of money or property (Hafemeister, 2001). Of substantiated elder abuse in the United States, about 30% was financial, and Canadian data show financial abuse to be the most common form of elder mistreatment.

What Are the Conditions That Increase the Risk of Mistreatment? Who Are Most Likely to Be Victims and Perpetrators of Abuse?

A critical research issue is uncovering who is most likely to abuse and be abused, where mistreatment is likely to occur, and what types of relationships and families are most prone to which forms of elder mistreatment (Sprey & Matthews, 1989). The difficulty of first defining mistreatment and then determining how many older persons are mistreated makes identifying causes precarious and the term *risk* preferable to *causal factors* (Schiamberg & Gans, 2000). Women and those who are in poorer health, who are living with someone else (including a spouse), who have no one to turn to (and hence are isolated and may suffer undetected neglect), and who are the source of needed resources (particularly financial, often due to the health problems of the abuser), are at higher risk of being mistreated (Biggs et al., 1995). Married persons are at particular risk because they live with someone who could be a potential abuser, even though protection against abuse is afforded by having a larger social network (Biggs et al., 1995). Studies suggest that mistreatment by adult children has overtaken that by a spouse (Schiamberg & Gans, 2000), and sons appear more likely than daughters to abuse a parent (Biggs et al., 1995).

Vulnerability to financial abuse is heightened by membership in minority populations, notably among Korean immigrants and Black elders (Hafemeister, 2001). However, the most likely victims of financial abuse are very old white women who live alone. In addition to the consequences for older victims, financial abuse has ramifications for other family members who would have inherited assets that are no longer there.

What are the conditions that are likely to result in the informal (personal relationships) and formal (professional service providers) mistreatment of old family members or clients? Answering this question regarding mistreatment that is unique to later life (as opposed to long-term patterns) helps us to identify important targets for social policy initiatives. Potential risk factors that look to *relationships* rather than individual characteristics in trying to understand the dynamics of elder mistreatment are on the right track. In the case of families, concerns about elder mistreatment focus on relationships with a spouse, a child who is providing care, and a child who depends on the older person (Steinmetz, 2005). A somewhat counterintuitive finding is that the dependency of older persons and caregiver stress do *not* distinguish between those who do and do not abuse old family members (Biggs et al., 1995; Pillemer, 2005). Thus we must resist the easy explanation that caring for a dependent older person is itself enough to prompt mistreatment and, at the same time, avoid equating elder abuse with a problem of family caregiving (Pillemer, 2005). Those who *perceive* caring as stressful are more likely to abuse an old relative (Schiamberg & Gans, 2000; Steinmetz, 2005), but the perception of the situation as stressful and the abuse may share the same source.

Evidence suggests that dependency *upon* an older person makes mistreating that person more likely (Biggs et al., 1995; Pillemer, 1986, 2005). Similarly, relying on a family member with substance abuse problems, who is unemployed, or who is the only person providing support increases risk, as does having a child or grandchild who depends on you for housing and other forms of support (Hafemeister, 2001). Gender of the perpetrator does not appear to be a factor in the willingness to take financial advantage of an old family member. When the obligation to care for an old family member is not softened by affection for that person, perfunctory and conflicted relationships between the carer and cared for are more likely (Biggs et al., 1995). Caregiver responses to the ambivalence of caring when a relationship is characterized by obligation and conflict may include providing care and engaging in conflict simultaneously, neglecting care provision, an on-and-off approach to caring, and ideally, caring while at the same time trying to resolve conflict.

Our particular interest is in abuse that occurs in family relationships, but mistreatment in the hands of formal service providers is also a significant family issue. Formal care provision may occur in the home or in a variety of institutional settings, including nursing homes. At any one time, about 6% of old Americans live in a nursing home, but about one-fifth of all men and one-third of all women will have at least one stay in a nursing home before they die (Harris & Benson, 2006). Nursing home placement is typically a last resort for both older persons and their families and can be a costly option, given that only a small portion of nursing home care is covered by Medicare in the United States. Viewing formal support as an option for an old family member is influenced by concerns about whether that person will be treated well in an institutional setting.

Family and professional support providers share the challenges of competing demands, too little time, cost constraints, and resulting frustration. Whether informal or formal, mistreatment occurs in the context of power relations, including the conditions of both paid and unpaid labor that make women more likely to be caring for others (Neysmith, 1995). When the opportunity for communication between staff and clients beyond that necessary to take care of the business at hand is limited, a direct outcome of scarce resources, mistreatment of old clients is more likely, and morale among both clients and staff members is lower (Biggs et al., 1995). Nursing home residents are sometimes the victims of physical, psychological and financial mistreatment, including theft of personal items. According to a nationwide survey of abuse in nursing homes in the United States, 30% of nursing homes were cited for violations over a two-year period from 1999 to 2001 (Harris & Benson, 2006). A range of figures on the prevalence of abuse in nursing homes is produced by different methods of data collection. For example, regarding the theft of personal items belonging to old clients, estimates range from 1.5% based on employee reports, 5.7% based on staff observations of other employees, to 19% based on reports by clients' family members (Harris & Benson, 2006).

The potential for building relationships is pivotal to successful operations in institutional settings. Nursing home staff are often drawn to their work by a desire to help others (Pillemer & Moore, 1990), an objective that is quickly quashed in environments where staff are poorly trained, underpaid and overworked. Like other forms of formal personal care, this typifies much of the employment in the institutional care setting, particularly the working conditions of nursing aides who are predominantly women and do the bulk of the work but are at the bottom of the pay scale (Harris & Benson, 2006). The resulting burnout, staff turnover and under-staffing create a downhill spiral that undermines both the staff and their clients. The potential for mistreating old residents is also increased by limited outside contact on behalf of the old client (Biggs et al., 1995), highlighting the significant link between informal and formal support.

What Can We Do About It? Relating Research Findings to Policy Initiatives

An effective response to elder mistreatment starts with addressing ageist views at the societal level for, in the end, they allow us to be complacent about the welfare of old people in general, even if not about the old family members in our personal lives (Biggs et al., 1995). When we fail to consider how our society treats older people until we are confronted with the immediate needs of an older person we care about, we discover that it is too late to put in place the kind of caring world that we would like for the ones that we love and for ourselves.

Intervention efforts intended to deal with elder mistreatment typically take three forms: legislative change regarding adult protection services, modeled after efforts to respond to child abuse; community services aimed at coordinating legal, medical and psychosocial services for seniors at risk, modeled after efforts to respond to domestic violence; and prevention through education, advocacy and empowering old people (Wolfe, 2001). Following the earlier discussion, the need to distinguish elder mistreatment from other forms of abuse means that social policy designed to deal with elder abuse cannot rely on existing services that target child abuse and domestic violence (Biggs et al., 1995:92). For example, financial abuse of old people does not fit either a child or spousal abuse model (Hafemeister, 2001). Physical rather than financial abuse is the focus of concerns related to mistreating children, who are assumed not to have the capacity to act on their own behalf. Making the latter distinction about older people contributes to infantilizing them. Unlike adult physical abuse, financial abuse is more likely to be at the hands of children and grandchildren or of strangers than of a spouse, placing limits on a spousal abuse model for responding to financial mistreatment.

The United States was ahead of most Western nations in the attention it paid to elder abuse in the late 1970s, but fiscal challenges and debates over national versus state responsibility continue to hamper consistent social policy across the country (Biggs et al., 1995). Nonetheless, all 50 states have some form of legislation aimed at reducing elder mistreatment, and Congress and the media share an interest in this topic. Yet the Elder Justice Act, designed to protect older persons, in part by offering better care options and supporting related research, is still waiting to be ratified by Congress. Other countries, including some in Europe, the UK, and Australia, have relied less on finding perpetrators and more on protective interventions for old people, either through existing agencies or by forming new ones.

A tendency to rely on criminalizing abuse through such measures as mandatory reporting laws as a primary policy response misses cases of neglect and can undermine efforts to better understand the dynamics that create abusive relationships (Biggs et al., 1995). Generally, legal responses to elder abuse, especially when it involves violence, have not been particularly successful (Barnett et al., 2005; Harbison & Morrow, 1998), in part because both reporting abuse and successful engagement in mediation processes designed to resolve it assume a degree of power on behalf of the victim that is rare (Neysmith, 1995). Recognizing the limits to legislative and legal responses to elder abuse forces us to focus on the power dynamics in families and institutions and make them the target for changing the conditions that foster mistreatment (Neysmith, 1995).

Dependency upon the individual who is the source of mistreatment and fear of being placed in an institutional setting inhibit the reporting of elder mistreatment by the victims (Biggs et al., 1995; Wolfe, 2001). Inadequate provisions for senior citizens and limited community-based alternatives for delivering support encourage silence when the ticket to remaining in the home is reliance on an abusive caregiver. As Wolfe

(2001:520) notes, "intervention after the fact is seldom satisfactory to the individual, the family, or the community. . . . Individual autonomy and special needs . . . profit from stability, continuity of caregivers, and a supportive family and community environment." Efforts must go beyond responding to individual victims to discovering methods for improving care relationships through broader population-based research on how best to meet the needs of older persons and those who care for them.

What about elder mistreatment in institutional settings? In order for facilities such as nursing homes to be viable alternatives to intensive informal support, families need the assurance that their older members will be cared for properly. Some suggest that institutional living, by its nature, is abusive because adults are removed from their communities and placed under the control of professional staff and organizational routines aimed at meeting the needs of the institution and collective clientele, not the individual (Biggs et al., 1995). Cooperation by those who run institutions is enhanced when the objective of exposing mistreatment is to work on improving conditions rather than shutting down institutions (Biggs et al., 1995). Conditions that enhance the care of old clients are likely to be the same measures that enhance the workplace culture and morale of staff members, creating a better *relationship* between clients and staff that benefits both groups. Sufficient training, regular supportive supervision, better pay and more reasonable caseloads are routes for improving both the provision and receipt of care in institutional settings (Biggs et al., 1995). Enhancing the working conditions of employees in institutional settings enhances staff-client relationships, an essential focus for minimizing mistreatment in both informal and formal care settings.

The drawbacks of institutional living have been at the ethical center of moving toward community-based care, with strong support from those seeking ways to contain the costs of caring. The failure to offer adequate resources for community-based care in an environment in which this is the prevailing policy response to providing formal support is also mistreatment. The focus on community-based support has limited investment in improving institutional conditions, creating immense pressures on the staff who work in institutional settings, including hospitals. Attempts to deal with overworked employees and overcrowded institutions may create additional pressures that threaten the welfare of old clients and patients. For example, nursing home placement in another community as a means of alleviating a hospital bed shortage (CBC News, 2007b) leaves families less able to provide support to their older members, nursing home residents more isolated and vulnerable, and nursing home staff more overloaded because the informal assistance often provided by families shrinks. Such conditions may heighten the potential for elder mistreatment, particularly in the form of neglect. This domino effect illustrates the need to think broadly when addressing the issue of elder mistreatment and related social policy.

The untenable working conditions of many homecare workers parallel those of the poorly paid, overworked, and predominantly female staff in institutional settings, especially as more care is transferred to the community without commensurate changes in funding (Neysmith, 1995). Power relations apply to the ties between old clients and home care workers who "frequently come from different cultural and linguistic backgrounds. The situation can become a pressure cooker where elderly persons and their care providers experience, at the personal level, the gender, class and racial inequities that riddle the larger society" (Neysmith, 1995:54).

In sum, elder mistreatment goes beyond the bounds of interpersonal relationships to the broader reality of structured social relations. Age relations structure a social world in which old people face growing dependency as a consequence of restricted access to the labor market and greater reliance on both informal and formal support systems to provide care in the face of failing health. Gender relations play out in the interpersonal dynamic of caring and mistreatment in which women are more likely to be both informal and formal carers and victims of mistreatment. Race and ethnicity structure access to support for both carers and cared for, a reflection of how structured social relations at the macro level are embedded in institutional arrangements for providing formal support (Forbat, 2004). Regarding race, an analysis of policy documents in the UK leads Forbat (2004:314) to propose "a reconceptualization of abuse—away from individualistic understandings . . . toward an institutional one, where 'race' is seen to mediate access to statutory services. Accountability for abuse is therefore aligned with institutions and organizations rather than individuals." A move in focus from individuals to institutions means assuming social as well as personal responsibility for change.

In a recent review of two books on elder abuse, Stein (2006) asks the question, What does the elder abuse field need? She answers,

> We need to reliably know the true national incidence and prevalence of elder abuse and neglect. We need to know the effects of changes in public policy on elder abuse. We need to develop an accurate methodology for measuring, and then measure, the true public and private costs of elder abuse and neglect. And we need to present what we learn in a manner that shocks . . . the American public into action about a socially deplorable phenomenon that harms . . . all of us. . . . This year, Ralph Nader is 72. Ralph, if you're itching for your next 'good fight,' . . . here it is. (703)

As murky as the research findings regarding the prevalence and risks of elder mistreatment are, there is no doubt that too many old people suffer at the hands of others. Sometimes these others have been the beneficiaries of an elder's care for a lifetime. An essential challenge for social policy is to negotiate the private–public boundary between family and community in a way that honors both those who need care and those who provide it. As well, social policy makers must avoid assuming that all instances of mistreatment involve a caregiving situation.

Conclusion

The family values debate of the past two decades and the rise of postmodernism in various disciplines cast the family as an institution in decline. Yet a long view of family life, aided by taking the vantage point of older family members, suggests a timeless quest to develop and invest in familial relationships. As this chapter has illustrated, policy initiatives designed to benefit older persons and their families can cast a broad net. Although some programs are clearly targeted at meeting the immediate demands of particular situations, these can only be effective if built on a foundation of income adequacy and accessibility to health care—regardless of age, race, gender, sexual orientation, ethnicity, class and marital status. Thus to address the challenges faced by older persons and their family members, we must address these fundamental social issues.

Ultimately, a caring environment cannot be legislated. In a society where the independence and support of all adult members are valued, policies that increase the ability of older persons to help themselves and that support families in the comprehensive help that they offer their senior members best serve the interests of all. More active promotion and funding of a full array of services would help seniors and family members avoid undue delays in discovering appropriate community and institutional support. If families are to continue to meet the needs of their members, young and old, family interests must be permitted to coexist with, and sometimes supersede, those of other domains.

Only fundamental shifts at the macro level of structured social relations, of embedded cultural ideologies that support them, and of state policies can change the inequality that characterizes our society (King & Calasanti, 2006). When we add to this the view that solutions to the challenges of aging must be addressed in a global context (Phillipson, 2006), the task is truly daunting. But there is much that can and must be done now for today's older citizens and for the younger generations who care about them and whose current situations are shaping their future as old people. When we recommend workplace policies that support parents and partners, not only mothers and spouses; when we recommend policies that address need and not only age; when we fight for equal pay for work of equal value; when we encourage action that is based on appreciating the long-term consequences of experiences early in the life course, we are addressing fundamental social processes that currently inhibit the options available to many old people and their families. When we open up options, we optimize the willing and supportive individual efforts that are evident in family relationships across the life course.

References

Abma, Joyce C., & Gladys M. Martinez. 2006. Childlessness among older women in the United States: Trends and profiles. *Journal of Marriage and Family* 68:4:1045–1056.

Acock, Alan C., Manfred M. H. van Dulmen, Katherine R. Allen, & Fred P. Piercy. 2005. Contemporary theory and emerging research methods in studying families. Pp. 59–89 in Bengtson, Vern L., Alan C. Acock, Katherine R. Allen, Peggye Dilworth-Anderson, & David M. Klein (Eds.), *Sourcebook of family theory & research.* Thousand Oaks, CA: Sage.

Adelman, Marcy. 1991. Stigma, gay lifestyles, and adjustment to aging: A study of later-life gay men and lesbians. Pp. 7–32 in John Alan Lee (Ed.), *Gay midlife and maturity.* New York: Haworth.

Ade-Ridder, Linda. 1990. Sexuality and marital quality among older married couples. Pp. 48–67 in Timothy H. Brubaker (Ed.), *Family relationships in later life,* 2nd ed. Newbury Park, CA: Sage.

Ade-Ridder, Linda, & Timothy H. Brubaker. 1983. The quality of long-term marriages Pp. 77–90 in Timothy H. Brubaker (Ed.), *Family relationships in later life.* Beverly Hills, CA: Sage.

Ahrons, Constance R. 2004. *We're still family: What grown children have to say about their parents' divorce.* New York: HarperCollins.

Akiyama, Hiroko, Toni Antonucci, Keiko Takahashi, & Elizabeth S. Langfahl. 2003. Negative interactions in close relationships across the life span. *Journal of Gerontology: Psychological Sciences* 58B:2:P70-P79.

Aldous, Joan. 1994. Someone to watch over me: Family responsibilities and their realization across family lives. Pp. 42–68 in Eva Kahana, David Biegel, & May Wykle (Eds.), *Family caregiving across the lifespan.* Thousand Oaks, CA: Sage.

Aldous, Joan. 1995. New views of grandparents in intergenerational conflict. *Journal of Family Issues* 16:1:104–122.

Alecxih, Lisa. 2001. The impact of sociodemographic change on the future of long-term care. *Generations* 25:1:7–11.

Alexander, Baine B., Robert L. Rubinstein, Marcene Goodman, & Mark Luborsky. 1992. A path not taken: A cultural analysis of regrets and childlessness in the lives of older women. *The Gerontologist* 32:5:618–625.

Allen, Katherine R. 1989. *Single women/family ties: Life histories of older women* Newbury Park, CA: Sage.

Allen, Katherine R. 2005a. Gay and lesbian elders. Pp. 482–489 in Malcolm L. Johnson (Ed.), *The Cambridge handbook of age and ageing.* Cambridge, UK: Cambridge University Press.

Allen, Katherine. 2005b. My view: Theorizing as contextual, relevant, and imaginative. P. 11 in Bengtson, Vern L., Alan C. Acock, Katherine R. Allen, Peggye Dilworth-Anderson, & David M. Klein (Eds.), *Sourcebook of family theory & research.* Thousand Oaks, CA: Sage.

Allen, Katherine. 2007a. Ambiguous loss after lesbian couples with children break up: A case for same-gender divorce. *Family Relations* 56:2:175–183.

Allen, Katherine R. 2007b. The missing right to same-sex divorce. *National Council on Family Relations Report* 52:4:F2 & F17.

Allen, Katherine R., & David H. Demo. 1995. The families of lesbians and gay men: A new frontier in family research. *Journal of Marriage and Family* Feb:11–127.

Allen, Katherine R., & Robert S. Pickett. 1987. Forgotten streams in the family life course: Utilization of qualitative retrospective interviews in the analysis of lifelong single women's family careers. *Journal of Marriage and Family* 49:Aug:517–526.

Allen, Katherine R., & Alexis J. Walker. 2006. Aging and gender in families: A very grand opening. Pp. 155–174 in Toni M. Calasanti & Kathleen F. Slevin (Eds.), *Age matters: Realigning feminist thinking.* New York: Routledge.

Allen, Katherine R., & Alexis J. Walker. Forthcoming. Theorizing about families and aging from a feminist perspective. In V. Bengtson, M. Silverstein, N. Putney, & D. Gans (Eds.), *Handbook of theories of aging.* New York: Springer.

Allen, Susan M. 1994. Gender differences in spousal caregiving and unmet need for care. *Journal of Gerontology: Social Sciences* 49:4:S187-S195.

Allen, Susan M., Frances Goldscheider, & Desiree A. Ciambrone. 1999. Gender roles, marital intimacy, and nomination of spouse as primary caregiver. *The Gerontologist* 39:2:150–158.

Amato, Paul R. 1996. Explaining the intergenerational transmission of divorce. *Journal of Marriage and Family* 58:3:628–640.

Amato, Paul R. 2000. The consequences of divorce for adults and children. *Journal of Marriage and Family* 62:1269–1287.

Amato, Paul. R. 2005. Family change: Decline or resilience. Pp. 112–117 in Vern L. Bengtson, Alan C. Acock, Katherine R. Allen, Peggy Dilworth-Anderson, & David M. Klein (Eds.), *Sourcebook of family theory & research*, Thousand Oaks, CA: Sage.

Amato, Paul R. 2007. Divorce and the well-being of adults and children. *National Council on Family Relations Report* 52:4:F3-F4, F18.

Amato, Paul R., & Tamara D. Afifi. 2006. Feeling caught between parents: Adult children's relations with parents and subjective well-being. *Journal of Marriage and Family* 68: 222–235.

Amato, Paul R., & Danelle D. Deboer. 2001. The transmission of marital instability across generations: Relationship skills or commitment to marriage? *Journal of Marriage and Family* 63:4:1038–1051.

Amato, Paul R., & Bryndl Hohmann-Marriott. 2007. A comparison of high- and low-distress marriages that end in divorce. *Journal of Marriage and Family* 69:3:621–638.

Ambert, Anne-Marie. 2005. Divorce: Facts, causes, and consequences. *Contemporary family trends*. Ottawa, Canada: Vanier Institute of the Family.

Ambert, Anne-Marie. 2006. One parent families: Characteristics, causes, consequences, and issues. *Contemporary Family Trends*. Ottawa, Canada: Vanier Institute of the Family.

American Association of Retired Persons. 1999a. Modern maturity talks about sex! *Modern Maturity* (Sept-Oct). Web edition. http://www.aarpmagazine.org/lifestyle/relationships/great_sex.html

American Association of Retired Persons. 1999b. Ms.behavin' again. *Modern Maturity* (May-June). Web edition. http://www.aarpmagazine.org/modern_maturity.html

American Association of Retired Persons. 1999c. Life lines: Everything you wanted to know about sex after 50. *Modern Maturity* (September-October). Web edition. http://www.aarpmagazine.org/lifestyle/relationships/great_sex.html

American Association of Retired Persons. 2000, January 4. AARP survey: *Grandparents, grandchildren have strong bond, visit often*. News release. http://www.aarp.org/press/2000/nr010400.html

Amirkhanyan, Anna A., & Douglas A. Wolf. 2006. Parent care and the stress process: Findings from a panel study. *Journal of Gerontology: Social Sciences* 61B:5:S248-S255.

Angel, Jacqueline L., Nora Douglas, & Ronald J. Angel. 2003. Gender, widowhood, and long-term care in the older Mexican American population. *Journal of Women & Aging* 15:2/3:89–105.

Angel, Jacqueline L., Maren A. Jiménez, & Ronald J. Angel. 2007. The economic consequences of widowhood for older minority women. *The Gerontologist* 47:2:224–234.

Angel, Ronald J., & Jacqueline L. Angel. 2006. Diversity and aging in the United States. Pp. 94–110 in Robert H. Binstock & Linda K. George (Eds.), *Handbook of aging and the social sciences*, 6th ed. Burlington, MA: Elsevier.

Angel, Ronald J., Jacqueline L. Angel, & Christine L. Himes. 1992. Minority group status, health transitions, and community living arrangements among the elderly. *Research on Aging* 14:4:496–521.

Angel, Ronald J., Jacqueline L. Angel, Judi L. McClellan, & Kyriakos S. Markides. 1996. Nativity, declining health, and preferences in living arrangements among elderly Mexican Americans: Implications for long-term care. *The Gerontologist* 36:4:464–473.

Antonucci, Toni C. 1990. Social supports and social relationships. Pp. 205–226 in Robert H. Binstock & Linda K. George (Eds.), *Handbook of aging and the social sciences*, 3rd ed. New York: Academic Press.

Antonucci, Toni C., & Hiroko Akiyama. 1995. Convoys of social relations: Family and friendship within a life span context. Pp. 355–372 in Rosemary Blieszner & Victoria Hilkevitch Bedford (Eds.), *Handbook of aging and the family*. Westport, CN: Greenwood.

Antonucci, Toni C., Rebecca Fuhrer, & James S. Jackson. 1990. Social support and reciprocity: A cross-ethnic and cross-national perspective. *Journal of Social and Personal Relationships* 7:519–530.

Aquilino, William S. 1990.The likelihood of parent-adult child coresidence: Effects of family structure and parental characteristics. *Journal of Marriage and Family* 52 (May): 405–419.

Aquilino, William S. 1994. Later life parental divorce and widowhood: Impact on young adults' assessment of parent-child relations. *Journal of Marriage and Family* 56:908–922.

Aquilino, William S., & Khalil R. Supple. 1991. Parent-child relations and parent's satisfaction with living arrangements when adult children live at home. *Journal of Marriage and Family* 53:1:13–27.

Aranda, Maria P., & Bob G. Knight. 1997. The influence of ethnicity and culture on the caregiver stress and coping process: A sociocultural review and analysis. *The Gerontologist* 37:3:342–354.

Arber, Sara. 2004. Gender, marital status, and ageing: Linking material, health, and social resources. *Journal of Aging Studies* 18:91–108.

Arber, Sara, Kate Davidson, & Jay Ginn. 2003. Changing approaches to gender and later life. Pp. 1–14 in Sara Arber, Kate Davidson, & Jay Ginn (Eds.), *Gender and ageing: Changing roles and relationships*. Philadelphia: Open University Press.

Arber, Sara, & Jay Ginn. 1991. *Gender and later life*. London: Sage.

Arber, Sara, Debora Price, Kate Davidson, & Kim Perren. 2003. Re-examining gender and marital status: Material well-being and social involvement. Pp. 148–167 in Sara Arber, Kate Davidson & Jay Ginn (Eds.), *Gender and ageing: Changing roles and relationships*. Philadelphia: Open University Press.

Archer, Margaret S. 2007. *Making our way through the world*. Cambridge, UK: Cambridge University Press.

Arditti, J. A. 1999. Rethinking relationships between divorced mothers and their children: Capitalizing on family strengths. *Family Relations* 48:2:109–119.

Aronson, Jane. 1992. Women's sense of responsibility for the care of old people: "But who else is going to do it?" *Gender and Society* 6:1:8–29.

Askham, Janet. 1995. The married lives of older people. Pp. 86–97 in Sara Arber & Jay Ginn (Eds.), *Connecting gender and ageing: A sociological approach.* Buckingham, UK: Open University Press.

Atchley, Robert C., & M. Powell Lawton. 1997. Is gerontology biased toward a negative view of the aging process and old age? YES: Robert C. Atchley, NO: M. Powell Lawton. Pp. 197–208 in Andrew E. Scharlach & Lenard W. Kaye (Eds.), *Controversial issues in aging.* Boston: Allyn & Bacon.

Attias-Donfut, Claudine. 2000. Cultural and economic transfers between generations: One aspect of age integration. *The Gerontologist* 40:3:270–272.

Attias-Donfut, Claudine, & Sara Arber. 2000. Equity and solidarity across the generations. Pp. 1–21 in Sara Arber & Claudine Attias-Donfut (Eds.), *The myth of generational conflict: The family and state in aging societies.* London: Routledge.

Attias-Donfut, Claudine, & Martine Segalen. 2002. The construction of grandparenthood. *Current Sociology* 50:2:281–294.

Attias-Donfut, Claudine, & François-Charles Wolff, 2005. Generational memory and family relationships. Pp. 443–454 in Malcolm L. Johnson (Ed.), *The Cambridge handbook of age and ageing.* New York: Cambridge University Press.

Auger, Jeanette A. 1995. Lesbians and aging: Triple trouble or tremendous thrill. Pp. 105–114 in Robynne Neugebaurer-Visano (Ed.), *Seniors and sexuality: Experiencing intimacy in later life.* Toronto: Canadian Scholar's Press.

Avioli, Paula S. 1989. The social support functions of siblings in later life: A theoretical model. *American Behavioral Scientist* 33:45–57.

Baars, Jann, Dale Dannefer, Chris Phillipson, & Alan Walker. 2006. Introduction: Critical perspectives in social gerontology. Pp. 1–14 in Jan Baars, Dale Dannefer, Chris Phillipson, & Alan Walker (Eds.), *Aging, globalization and inequality: The new critical gerontology.* Amityville, NY: Baywood.

Baby boomers and their boomerang kids. 2008, January 7th. *BabyBoomer-Magazine*.com. Retrieved October 29, 2008. http://www.babyboomermagazine.com/news/117/ARTI CLE/117/2008-01-08.html

Bair, Deirdre. 2007. *Calling it quits: Late-life divorce and starting over.* New York: Random House.

Ball, Mary M., Molly M. Perkins, Frank J. Whittington, Carole Hollingsworth, Sharon V. King, & Bess L. Combs. 2005. *Communities of care: Assisted living for African American elders.* Baltimore: Johns Hopkins University Press.

Balsam, Kimberly F., Theodore P. Beauchaine, Esther D. Rothblum, & Sondra E. Solomon. 2008. Three-year follow-up of same-sex couples who had civil unions in Vermont, same-sex couples not in civil unions, and heterosexual married couples. *Developmental Psychology* 44:1:102–116.

Bank, Stephen, & Michael D. Kahn. 1982. Intense sibling loyalties. Pp. 251–266 in Michael E. Lamb & Brian Sutton-Smith (Eds.), *Sibling relationships: Their nature and significance across the lifespan.* Hillside, NJ: Lawrence Erlbaum.

Barber, Jennifer S. 2000. Intergenerational influence on the entry into parenthood: Mothers' preferences for family and nonfamily behavior. *Social Forces* 79:1:319–348.

Barker, Judith C., Joelle Morrow, & Linda S. Mitteness. 1998. Gender, informal social support networks, and elderly urban African Americans. *Journal of Aging Studies* 12:2:199–222.

Barnett, Ola, Cindy L. Miller-Perrin, & Robin D. Perrin. 2005. *Family violence across the lifespan: An Introduction,* 2nd ed. Thousand Oaks, CA: Sage.

Barrett, Anne E. 1999. Social support and life satisfaction among the never married. *Research on Aging* 21:1:46–72.

Barrett, Anne E., & Scott M. Lynch. 1999. Caregiving networks of elderly persons: Variation by marital status. *The Gerontologist* 39:6:695–704.

Bass, Scott A. 2007. The emergence of the golden age of gerontology? *The Gerontologist* 47:3:408–412.

Baumbusch, Jennifer L. 2004. Unclaimed treasures: Older women's reflections on lifelong singlehood. *Journal of Women & Aging* 16:1/2:105–121.

Baxter, Leslie A., Dawn O. Braithwaite, Tamara D. Golish, & Loreen N. Olson. 2002. Contradictions of interaction for wives of elderly husbands with adult dementia. *Journal of Applied Communication Research* 30:1:1–26.

Beaton, John M., Joan E. Norris, & Micheal W. Pratt. 2003. Unresolved issues in adult children's marital relationships involving intergenerational problems. *Family Relations* 52:143–153.

Beaupré, Pascale, Pierre Truscotte, & Anne Milan. 2006a. Junior comes back home: Trends and predictors of returning to the parental home. *Canadian Social Trends* 82:28–34. Ottawa, Canada: Statistics Canada.

Beaupré, Pascale, Pierre Truscotte, & Anne Milan. 2006b. When is junior moving out? Transitions from the parental home to independence. *Canadian Social Trends* 82:9–15. Ottawa, Canada: Statistics Canada.

Becker, Gay, Yewoubdar Beyene, Edwin Newsom, & Nury Mayen. 2003. Creating continuity through mutual assistance: Intergenerational reciprocity in four ethnic groups. *Journal of Gerontology: Social Sciences* 8B:3:S151-S159.

Bedford, Victoria H. 1989. Sibling ambivalence in adulthood. *Journal of Family Issues* 10:211–224.

Bedford, Victoria H. 1995. Sibling relationships in middle and old age. Pp. 201–222 in Rosemary Blieszner & Victoria Hilkevitch Bedford (Eds.), *Handbook of aging and the family.* Westport, CT: Greenwood.

Bedford, Victoria Helkevitch, & Paula Smith Avioli. 2001. Variations in sibling intimacy in old age. *Generations* 25:2:34–40.

Belgrave, Linda Liska, & Julia E. Bradsher. 1994. Health as a factor in institutionalization: Disparities between

African Americans and Whites. *Research on Aging* 16:2:115–141.

Belgrave, Linda Liska, May L. Wykle, & Jung M. Choi. 1993. Health, double jeopardy, and culture: The use of institutionalization by African-Americans. *The Gerontologist* 33:3:379–385.

Bender, William N., & Lynn Brannon. 1994. Victimization and non-custodial parents, grandparents, and children as a function of sole custody: Views of the advocacy groups and research support. *Journal of Divorce and Remarriage* 21:3/4:81–114.

Bengtson, Vern L. 1993. Is the "contract across generations" changing? Effects of population aging on obligations and expectations across age groups. Pp. 3–23 in V. L. Bengtson, & W. A. Achenbaum (Eds.), *The changing contract across generations.* New York: Aldine De Gruyter.

Bengtson, Vern L., Alan C. Acock, Katherine R. Allen, Peggye Dilworth-Anderson, & David M. Klein. 2005. Theory and theorizing in family research: Puzzle building and puzzle solving. Pp. 3–29 in Vern L. Bengtson, Alan C. Acock, Katherine R. Allen, Peggye Dilworth-Anderson, & David M. Klein (Eds.), *Sourcebook of family theory & research.* Thousand Oaks, CA: Sage.

Bengtson, Vern L., Roseann Giarrusso, J. Beth Mabry, & Merril Silverstein. 2002. Solidarity, conflict, and ambivalence: Complementary or competing perspectives on intergenerational relationships? *Journal of Marriage and Family* 64:3:568–576.

Bengtson, Vern L., Roseann Giarrusso, Merril Silverstein, & Haitao Wang. 2000. Families and intergenerational relationships in aging societies. *Hallym International Journal of Aging* 2:1:3–10.

Bengtson, Vern L., & Tonya M. Murray. 1993. "Justice" across generations (and cohorts): Sociological perspectives on the life course and reciprocities over time. Pp. 111–138 in Lee M. Cohen (Ed.), *The changing contract across generations.* New York: Aldine De Gruyter.

Bengtson, Vern L., Carolyn J. Rosenthal, & Linda M. Burton. 1996. Paradoxes of family and aging. Pp. 253–282 in R. H. Binstock & L. K. George (Eds.), *Handbook of aging and the social sciences,* 4th ed. New York: Academic Press.

Bengtson, Vern L., & S. Schrader. 1982. Parent-child relations: The measurement of intergenerational interaction and affect in old age. In D. J. Mangen & W. Peterson (Eds.), *Research instruments in social gerontology.* Minneapolis: University of Minnesota Press.

Berger, Raymond M. 1996. What are older homosexual men like? Pp. 155–199 in Raymond M. Berger (Ed.), *Gay and grey: The older homosexual man,* 2nd ed. New York: Harrington Park.

Bergling, Tim. 2004. *Reeling in the years: Gay men's perspectives on age and ageism.* New York: Harrington Park.

Berkowitz, Dana, & William Marsiglio. 2007. Gay men: Negotiating procreative, father, and family identities. *Journal of Marriage and Family* 69:2:366–381.

Berman, Harry J. 1987. Adult children and their parents: Irredeemable obligation and irreplaceable loss. *Journal of Gerontological Social Work* 10:1/6:2:21–34.

Bernard, Jessie. 1972. *The future of marriage.* New York: Bantam.

Bess, Irwin. 1999. Widows living alone. *Canadian Social Trends* (Summer): 2–5. Ottawa, Canada: Statistics Canada. Cat. No. 11–008.

Bettinger, Michael. 2006. Polyamory and gay men: A family systems approach. Pp. 161–181 in Jerry J. Bigner (Ed.), *An introduction to GLBT family studies.* New York: Haworth.

Bianchi, Suzanne M., & Lynne M. Casper. 2005. Explanations of family change: A family demographic perspective. Pp. 93–117 in Vern L. Bengtson, Alan C. Acock, Katherine R. Allen, Peggye Dilworth-Anderson, & David M. Klein (Eds.), *Sourcebook of family theory & research.* Thousand Oaks, CA: Sage.

Biggs, Simon, Chris Phillipson, & Paul Kingston. 1995. *Elder abuse in perspective.* Buckingham, UK: Open University Press.

Biggs, Simon, & J. L. Powell. 2001. A Foucauldian analysis of old age and the power of social welfare. *Journal of Aging and Social Policy* 12:93–112.

Blair-Loy, M., & Jacobs, J. A. (2003). Globalization, work hours, and the care deficit among stockbrokers. *Gender & Society* 17:230–249.

Blieszner, Rosemary. 1993. A socialist–feminist perspective on widowhood. *Journal of Aging Studies* 7:2:171–182.

Blieszner, Rosemary, & Brian de Vries. 2001. Introduction: Perspectives on intimacy. *Generations* 25:2:1–2.

Boaz, Rachel F., Jason Hu, & Yongjia Ye. 1999. The transfer of resources from middle-aged children to functionally limited elderly parents: Providing time, giving money, sharing space. *The Gerontologist* 39:6:648–657.

Bograd, R., & B. Spilka 1996. Self-disclosure and marital satisfaction in mid-life and late-life remarriages. *International Journal of Aging and Human Development* 42:3:161–172.

Bonnie, Richard J., & Robert B. Wallace (Eds.). 2001. *Elder mistreatment: Abuse, neglect, and exploitation in an aging America.* National Research Council Panel to Review Risk and Prevalence of Elder Abuse and Neglect. Washington, DC: The National Academies Press.

Bonomi, Amy E., Melissa L. Anderson, Robert J. Reid, David Carrell, Paul A Fishman, Frederick Rivara, & Robert S. Thompson. 2007. Intimate partner violence in older women. *The Gerontologist* 47:1:34–41.

Bookwala, Jamila, & Melissa M. Franks. 2005. Moderating role of marital quality in older adults' depressed affect: Beyond the main-effects model. *Journal of Gerontology: Psychological Sciences* 60B:6:P338-P341.

Boon, Susan D., & Megan J. Shaw. 2007. Reasons young adults visit (and do not visit) impaired grandparents. *Canadian Journal on Aging* 26:4:357–366.

Booth, Alan, & Paul R. Amato. 1994. Parental marital quality, parental divorce, and relations with parents. *Journal of Marriage and Family* 56:1:21–34.

Booth, Alan, & Paul R. Amato. 2001. Parental predivorce relations and offspring postdivorce well-being. *Journal of Marriage and Family* 63:197–212.

Bornat, Joanna, Brian Dimmock, David Jones, & Sheila Peace. 1999. The impact of family change on older people: The case of stepfamilies. Pp. 248–262 in Susan McRae (Ed.), *Changing Britain: Families and households in the 1990s.* New York: Oxford University Press.

Borell, Klas, & Sofie Ghazanfareeon Karlsson. 2003. Reconceptualizing intimacy and aging: Living apart together. Pp. 47–52 in Sara Arber, Kate Davidson & Jay Ginn (Eds.), *Gender and aging: Changing roles and relationships.* Philadelphia: Open University Press.

Boss, Pauline, & Lori Kaplan. 2004. Ambiguous loss and ambivalence when a parent has dementia. Pp. 207–224 in Karl Pillemer & Kurt Lüscher (Eds.), *Intergenerational ambivalence: New perspectives on parent-child relationships in later life.* New York: Elsevier.

Bossard, James H. S., & Eleanor S. Boll. 1956. *The large family system.* Philadelphia: University of Pennsylvania Press.

Boswell, Randy. 2008. Gay marriage ruling sparks border dispute. *The National Post.* February 25. A5.

Bould, Sally. 1993. Familial caretaking: A middle-range definition of family in the context of social policy. *Journal of Family Issues* 14:1:133–151.

Bowers, Bonita F., & Barbara J. Myers. 1999. Grandmothers providing care for grandchildren: Consequences of various levels of caregiving. *Family Relations* 48:3:303–311.

Bowman, Karen F., C. Seth Landefeld, Linda M. Quinn, Robert M. Palmer, Jerome Kowal, & Richard H. Fortinsky. 1998. Strain in African American and White American caregivers of hospitalized elderly: Implications for discharge planning. *Research on Aging* 20:5:547–568.

Boyd, Monica, & Doug Norris. 1995. Leaving the nest? The impact of family structure *Canadian Social Trends* 28:14–19. Ottowa, Canada: Statistics Canada.

Brackbill, Yvonne, & Donna Kitch. 1991. Intergenerational relationships: A social exchange perspective on joint living arrangements among the elderly and their relatives. *Journal of Aging Studies* 5:1:77–97.

Braithwaite, Dawn O., Paul Schrodt, & Leslie A. Baxter. 2006. Understudied and misunderstood: Communication in stepfamily relationships. Pp. 153–170 in Kory Floyd & Mark T. Morman (Eds.), *Family circle: New research in family communication.* Thousand Oaks, CA: Sage.

Bramlett, Matthew D., & William D. Mosher. 2001, May 31. First marriage dissolution, divorce, and remarriage: United States. *Advance Data CDC* (Advance Data From Vital and Health Statistics) No. 323. Hyattsville, MD: National Center for Health Statistics.

Brehm, Sharon Stephens. 1992. *Intimate Relationships*, 2nd ed. New York: McGraw-Hill.

Brennan, Patricia Flatley, & Shirley M. Moore. 1994. Caregivers of persons with AIDS. Pp. 159–177 in Eva Kahana, David E. Biegel, & May L. Wykle (Eds.), *Family caregiving across the lifespan.* Thousand Oaks, CA: Sage.

Brines, J., & K. Joyner. 1999. The ties that bind: Principles of cohesion in cohabitation and marriage. *American Sociological Review* 64 (June): 333–355.

Brockmann, Hilke, & Thomas Klein. 2004. Love and death in Germany: The marital biography and its effect on mortality. *Journal of Marriage and Family* 66:3:567–581.

Brody, Elaine M. 1995. Prospects for family caregiving. Pp. 15–28 in Rosalie A. Kane & Joan D. Penrod (Eds.), *Family caregiving in an aging society: Policy perspectives.* Thousand Oaks, CA: Sage.

Brody, Elaine M., Morton H. Kleban, Pauline T. Johnsen, Christine Hoffman, & Claire B. Schoonover. 1987. Work status and parent care: A comparison of four groups of women. *The Gerontologist* 27:2:201–208.

Brody, Elaine M., Sandra J. Litvin, Christine Hoffman, & Morton Kleban. 1995. Marital status of caregiving daughters and co-residence with dependent parents *The Gerontologist* 35:1:75–85.

Broman, Clifford L. 1993. Race differences in marital well-being. *Journal of Marriage and Family* 55 (August): 724–732.

Brotman, Shari. 1998. The incidence of poverty among seniors in Canada: Exploring impact of gender, ethnicity and race. *Canadian Journal on Aging* 17:2:166–185.

Brotman, Shari, Bill Ryan, Shannon Collins, Line Chamberland, Robert Cormier, Danielle Julien, Elizabeth Meyer, Allen Peterkin, & Brenda Richard. 2007. Coming out to care: Caregivers of gay and lesbian seniors in Canada. *The Gerontologist* 47:4:490–503.

Brotman, Shari, Bill Ryan, & Robert Cormier. 2003. The health and social service needs of gay and lesbian elders and their families in Canada. *The Gerontologist* 43:2:192–202.

Brown, Diane R., & Andrea Sankar. 1998. HIV/AIDS and aging minority populations. *Research on Aging* 20:6:865–884.

Brown, Lester B., Steven G. Sarosy, Terry Clark Cook, & J. Gerramy Quarto. 1997. *Gay men and aging.* New York: Garland.

Brown, S. L., J. Roebuck Bulanda, & G. R. Lee, 2005. The significance of nonmarital cohabitation: Marital status and mental health benefits among middle-aged and older adults. *Journal of Gerontology: Social Sciences* 60:S21-S29.

Brown, Susan L., Gary R. Lee, & Jennifer Roebuck Bulanda. 2006. Cohabitation among older adults: A national portrait. *Journal of Gerontology: Social Sciences* 61B:2:S71-S79.

Brubaker, Ellie, & Timothy H. Brubaker. 1995. Critical policy issues. Pp. 235–247 in G. C. Smith, S. S. Tobin, E. A. Robertson-Tchabo & P. W. Power (Eds.), *Strengthening aging families: Diversity in practice and policy.* Thousand Oaks, CA: Sage.

Brubaker, Timothy H. 1990. An overview of family relationships in later life. Pp. 13–26 in Timothy H. Brubaker (Ed.), *Family relationships in later life,* 2nd ed. Newbury Park, CA: Sage.

Brumbaugh, Stacey M., Laura A. Sanchez, Steven L. Nock, & James D. Right. 2008. Attitudes toward gay marriage in states undergoing marriage law transformation. *Journal of Marriage and Family* 70:2:345–359.

Bryant, Chalandra M., & Rand D. Conger. 1999. Marital success and domains of social support in long-term relationships: Does the influence of network members ever end? *Journal of Marriage and Family* 61:2:437–450.

Bryson, Ken, & Lynne M. Casper. 1999. Coresident grandparents and grandchildren. Pp. 23–198 in *Current population report: Special studies*. Washington, DC: U.S. Census Bureau.

Bucx, Freek, Frits Van Wel, Trudie Knijn, & Louk Hagendoorn. 2008. Intergenerational contact and the life course status of young adult children. *Journal of Marriage and Family* 70:1:144–156.

Bulcroft, Richard A., & Kris A. Bulcroft. 1991. The nature and functions of dating in later life. *Research on Aging* 13:2:244–260.

Burnette, Denise. 1999. Social relationships of Latino grandparent caregivers: A role theory perspective. *The Gerontologist* 39:1:49–58.

Burr, Jeffrey A., & Jan E. Mutchler. 1999. Race and ethnic variations in norms of filial responsibility among older persons. *Journal of Marriage and Family* 61:3: 674–687.

Burton, Linda. 1992. Black grandparents rearing grandchildren of drug-addicted parents: Stressors, outcomes, and social service needs. *The Gerontologist* 32:6:744–751.

Burton, Linda, Judith Kasper, Andrew Shore, Kathleen Cagney, Thomas LaVeist, Catherine Cubbin, & Pearl German. 1995. The structure of informal care: Are there differences by race? *The Gerontologist* 35:6:744–752.

Buunk, Bram P., & Barry van Driel. 1989. *Variant lifestyles and relationships*. Newbury Park, CA: Sage.

Buxton, Amity P. 2006. A family matter: When a spouse comes out as gay, lesbian, or bisexual. Pp. 67–87 in Jerry J. Bigner (Ed.), *An introduction to GLBT family studies*. New York: Haworth.

Byrne, Anne, & Deborah Carr. 2005. Caught in the cultural lag: The stigma of singlehood. *Psychological Inquiry* 16:2&3:84–91.

Cain, Leonard D. 1987. Alternative perspectives on the phenomena of human aging: Age stratification and age status. *Journal of Applied Behavioral Science* 23:2:277–294.

Cain, Leonard. 2003. Age-related phenomena: The interplay of the ameliorative and the scientific. Pp. 295–326 in Richard Settersten, Jr. (Ed.), *Invitation to the life course: Toward new understandings of later life*. Amityville, NY: Baywood.

Cain, Madelyn. 2001. *The childless revolution*. Cambridge, MA: Perseus.

Calasanti, Toni M. 1996. Incorporating diversity: Meaning, levels of research, and implications for theory. *The Gerontologist* 36:2:147–156.

Calasanti, Toni M. 2003. Masculinities and care work in old age. Pp. 15–30 in Sara Arber, Kate Davidson, & Jay Ginn (Eds.), *Gender and ageing: Changing roles and relationships*. Philadelphia: Open University Press.

Calasanti, Toni M. 2004. Feminist gerontology and old men. *Journal of Gerontology: Social Sciences* 59B:6:S305-S314.

Calasanti, Toni M. 2006. Gender and old age: Lessons from spousal care work. Pp. 269–294 in Toni M. Calasanti & Kathleen F. Slevin (Eds.) *Age matters: Realigning feminist thinking*. New York: Routledge.

Calasanti, Toni M., & Neal King. 2007. Taking 'women's work' 'like a man': Husbands' experiences of care work. *The Gerontologist*. 47:4:516–527.

Calasanti, Toni M., & Kathleen F. Slevin. 2001. *Gender, social inequalities, and aging*. Walnut Creek, CA: AltaMira Press.

Calasanti, Toni M., & Kathleen F. Slevin. 2006. *Aging matters: Realigning feminist thinking*. New York: Routledge.

Calasanti, Toni M., & Anna M. Zajicek. 1993. A socialist-feminist approach to aging: embracing diversity. *Journal of Aging Studies* 7:2:117–131.

Calderon, Vanessa, & Sharon Tennstedt. 1998. Ethnic differences in the expression of caregiver burden: Results of a qualitative study. Pp. 159–178 in Melvin Delgado (Ed.), *Latino elders and the twenty-first century*. New York: Haworth.

Call, Kathleen T., Michael A. Finch, Shirley M. Huck, & Rosalie Kane. 1999. Caregiver burden from a social exchange perspective: Caring for older people after hospital discharge. *Journal of Marriage and Family* 61:3:688–699.

Callahan Jr., James J. 2001. Policy perspectives on workforce issues and care of older people. *Generations*. 25:1:12–16.

Campbell, Lori D., Ingrid Arnet Connidis, & Lorraine Davies. 1999. Sibling ties in later life: A social network analysis. *Journal of Family Issues* 20:1:114–148.

Campbell, Marjorie. 1995. Divorce at mid-life: Intergenerational issues. *Journal of Divorce and Remarriage* 23:1/2:185–202.

Cantor, Marjorie. 1979. Neighbors and friends: An overlooked resource in the informal support system. *Research on Aging* 1:434–463.

Cantor, Marjorie, & Mark Brennan. 2000. *Social care of the elderly: The effects of ethnicity, class, and culture*. New York: Springer.

Carlson, Marcia J., & Frank F. Furstenberg Jr. 2006. The prevalence and correlates of multipartnered fertility among urban U.S. parents. *Journal of Marriage and Family* 68:3:718–732.

Carpenter, Brian D., & Wingyun Mak, 2007. Caregiving couples. *Generations* 31:3:47–53.

Carpentier, Laura M., Constance A. Nathanson, & Young J. Kim. 2006. Sex after 40?: Gender, ageism, and sexual partnering in midlife. *Journal of Aging Studies* 20:2:93–106.

Carr, Deborah. 2004a. Black/White differences in psychological adjustment to spousal loss among older adults. *Research on Aging* 26:6:591–622.

Carr, Deborah. 2004b. Gender, preloss marital dependence, and older adults' adjustment to widowhood. *Journal of Marriage and Family* 66:1:220–235.

Carr, Deborah. 2004c. The desire to date and remarry among older widows and widowers. *Journal of Marriage and Family* 66:4:1051–1068.

Carr, Deborah, & Rebecca Utz. 2004. Late-life widowhood in the United States: New directions in research and theory. Pp. 19–46 in Kate Davidson & Graham Fennell (Eds.), *Intimacy in later life*. New Brunswick, MA: Transaction.

Carrière, Yves, & Louis Pelletier. 1995. Factors underlying the institutionalization of elderly persons in Canada. *Journal of Gerontological Sciences* 50B:3:S164-S172.

Carrington, Christopher. 1999. *No place like home: Relationships and family life among lesbians and gay men.* Chicago: University of Chicago Press.

Carroll, Jason S., Stan J. Knapp, & Thomas B. Holman. 2005. Theorizing about marriage. Pp. 263–288 in Vern L. Bengtson, Alan C. Acock, Katherine R. Allen, Peggye Dilworth-Anderson, & David M. Klein (Eds.), *Sourcebook of family theory & research.* Thousand Oaks, CA: Sage.

Cauce, Ana Mari. 2005. The demographics of the 21st century family: Examining race, ethnicity, and culture within geographic and generational context. Pp. 206–208 in Vern L. Bengtson, Alan C. Acock, Katherine R. Allen, Peggye Dilworth-Anderson, & David M. Klein (Eds.), *Sourcebook of family theory & research.* Thousand Oaks, CA: Sage.

Causey, Kelly A., & Candan Duran-Aydintug. 1997. Tendency to stigmatize lesbian mothers in custody cases. *Journal of Divorce and Remarriage* 28:1/2:171–182.

CBC News. 2007a. In depth. *Same-sex rights: World Timeline.* Retrieved October 29, 2008. http://www.cbc.ca/news/background/samesexrights/timeline_world.html

CBC News. 2007b, January 12. "Stop moving patients to other hospitals, Ontario ministry tells overcrowded sites: Other options should solve overcrowding spokesperson says." Retrieved October 29, 2008. http://www.cbc.ca/canada/ottawa/story/2007/01/12/hospital.html

CDC National Center for Health Statistics. 2001. *Vital Statistics of the United States, 2001* (Vol. 1, Natality. Table 1–7). http://www.cdc.gov/nchs/data/statab/natfinal2001.annvol1_07.pdf

CDC National Center for Health Statistics. 2006, November 21. New report shows teen births drop to lowest level ever. *Fact Sheets and Media Advisories.* Hyattsville, MD: Author. Retrieved January 20, 2008. http://www.cdc.gov/nchs/pressroom/06facts/births05.htm

CDC National Center for Health Statistics. 2007, December 5. *Teen birth rate rises for first time in 15 years.* News Release. Hyattsville, Maryland. Retrieved January 20, 2008. http://www.cdc.gov/nchs/pressroom/07newsrelease/teenbirth.htm

Chambers, Pat. 2005. *Older widows and the life course: Multiple narratives of hidden lives.* Burlington, VT: Ashgate.

Chan, Christopher G., & Glen H. Elder. 2000. Matrilineal advantage in grandchild-grandparent relations. *The Gerontologist* 40:2:179–190.

Chappell, Neena L. 1991. In-group differences among elders living with friends and family other than spouses. *Journal of Aging Studies* 5:1:61–76.

Chappell, Neena L. 1992. *Social support and aging.* Toronto: Butterworths.

Chappell, Neena L. 1993. Implications of shifting health care policy for caregiving in Canada. *Journal of Aging and Social Policy* 5:1&2:39–55.

Chappell, Neena L., & Mark Badger. 1987. *Non-traditional living arrangements among the elderly.* Unpublished Manuscript.

Chappell, Neena, & Valerie K. Kuehne. 1998. Congruence among husband and wife caregivers. *Journal of Aging Studies* 12:3:239–254.

Chappell, Neena L., & Margaret J. Penning. 2005. Family caregivers: Increasing demands in the context of 21st-century globalization? Pp. 455–462 in Malcolm L. Johnson (Ed.), *The Cambridge handbook of age and ageing.* Cambridge, UK: Cambridge University Press.

Chapple, M. J., S. Kippax, & G. Smith. 1998. "Semi-straight sort of sex:" Class and gay community attachment explored within a framework of older homosexually active men. *Journal of Homosexuality* 35:2:65–83.

Cheal, David. 1991. *Family and the state of theory.* Toronto: University of Toronto Press.

Cheal, David. 1993. Unity and difference in postmodern families. *Journal of Family Issues* 14:1:5–19.

Cheal, David. 2005. Theorizing family: From the particular to the general. Pp. 29–33 in Vern L. Bengtson, Alan C. Acock, Katherine R. Allen, Peggye Dilworth-Anderson, & David M. Klein (Eds.), *Sourcebook of family theory & research.* Thousand Oaks, CA: Sage.

Che-Alford, Janet, & Brian Hamm. 1999. Under one roof: Three generations living together. *Canadian Social Trends* (Summer): 6–9. Ottawa, Canada: Statistics Canada.

Chen, Zeng-Yin, & Howard B. Kaplan. 2001. Intergenerational transmission of constructive parenting. *Journal of Marriage and Family* 63:1:17–31.

Cherlin, Andrew J. 1992. *Marriage, divorce, remarriage,* 2nd ed. Cambridge, MA: Harvard University Press.

Cherlin, Andrew J. 2004. The deinstitutionalization of American marriage. *Journal of marriage and family* 66:4:848–861.

Cherlin, Andrew J., & Frank F. Furstenberg Jr. 1986. *The new American grandparent: A place in the family, a life apart.* New York: Basic Books.

Cherlin, Andrew J., Eugenia Scabini, & Giovanna Rossi. 1997. Still in the nest: Delayed home leaving in Europe and the United States. *Journal of Family Issues* 18:6:572–575.

Chevan, Albert. 1995. Holding on and letting go: Residential mobility during widowhood. *Research on Aging* 17:3:278–302.

Chevan, Albert. 1996. As cheaply as one: Cohabitation in the older population. *Journal of Marriage and Family* 58 (Aug): 656–667.

Choi, Namkee G. 2003. Coresidence between unmarried aging parents and their adult children. *Research on Aging* 25:4:384–404.

Chunn, Dorothy E. 2000. Politicizing the personal: Feminism, law, and public policy. Pp. 225–259 in Nancy Mandell & Ann Duffy (Eds.), *Canadian families: Diversity, conflict, and change,* 2nd ed. Toronto: Harcourt Brace.

Cicirelli, Victor G. 1992. *Family caregiving: Autonomous and paternalistic decision making.* Newbury Park, CA: Sage.

Cicirelli, Victor G. 1995. *Sibling relationships across the life span.* NewYork: Plenum.

Cicirelli, Victor G., Raymond T. Coward, & Jeffrey W. Dwyer. 1992. Siblings as caregivers for impaired elders. *Research on Aging* 14:3:331–350.

Claassen, Cheryl. 2005. *Whistling women: A study of the lives of older lesbians.* New York: Haworth.

Claes, J. A., & W. R. Moore. 2001 Caring for gay and lesbian elderly. Pp. 217–229 in L. Katz Olson (Ed.), *Age through ethnic lenses: Caring for the elderly in a multicultural society.* New York: Rowman & Littlefield.

Clark, Margaret S., & Steven M. Graham. 2005. Do relationship researchers neglect singles? Can we do better? *Psychological Inquiry* 16:2&3:131–136.

Clark, Phillip G. 1993. Moral discourse and public policy in aging: Framing problems, seeking solutions, and "public ethics." *Canadian Journal on Aging* 12:4:485–508.

Clarke, Edward J., Mar Preston, Jo Raksin, & Vern L. Bengtson. 1999. Types of conflict and tensions between older parents and adult children. *The Gerontologist* 39:3:261–270.

Clarkwest, Andrew. 2007. Spousal dissimilarity, race, and marital dissolution. *Journal of Marriage and Family* 69:3:639–653.

Clavan, Sylvia. 1978. The impact of social class and social trends on the role of grandparents. *The Family Coordinator* (October): 351–357.

Clawson, Julie, & Lawrence Ganong. 2002. Adult stepchildren's obligations to older stepparents. *Journal of Family Nursing* 8:50–73.

Clunis, D. Merilee, Karen I. Fredriksen-Goldsen, Pat A. Freeman, & Nancy Nystrom. 2005. *Lives of lesbian elders: Looking back, looking forward.* Binghamton, NY: Haworth.

Cochran, Donna L., Diane R. Brown, & Karl C. McGregor. 1999. Racial differences in the multiple social roles of older women: Implications for depressive symptoms. *The Gerontologist* 39:4:465–472.

Cogswell, Carolyn, & Carolyn S. Henry. 1995. Grandchildren's perceptions of grandparental support in divorced and intact families. *Journal of Divorce and Remarriage* 23:3/4:127–149.

Cohler, Bertram J. 2004. The experience of ambivalence within the family: Young adults 'coming out' gay or lesbian and their parents. Pp. 255–284 in Karl Pillemer & Kurt Lüscher (Eds.), *Intergenerational ambivalences: New perspectives on parent-child relations in later life.* New York: Elsevier.

Cohler, Bertram J. 2006. Life-course social science perspectives on the GLBT family. Pp. 23–49 in Jerry J. Bigner (Ed.), *An introduction to GLBT family studies.* New York: Haworth.

Cohler, Bertram J., & Karen Altergott. 1995. The family of the second half of life: Connecting theories and findings. Pp. 59–94 in Rosemary Blieszner & Victoria Hilkevitch Bedford (Eds.), *Handbook of aging and the family.* Westport, CT: Greenwood.

Cohler, Bertram J., A. J. Hostetler, & A. M. Boxer. 1998. Generativity, social context, and lived experience: Narratives of gay men in middle adulthood. Pp. 265–309 in D. P. McAdam & E. de St. Aubin (Eds.), *Generativity and adult development.* Washington, DC: American Psychological Association.

Coleman, Marilyn, Lawrence Ganong, & Susan M. Cable. 1997. Beliefs about women's intergenerational family obligations to provide support before and after divorce and remarriage. *Journal of Marriage and Family* 59:1:165–176.

Coleman, Marilyn, Lawrence H. Ganong, & Tanja C. Rothrauff. 2006. Racial and ethnic similarities and differences in beliefs about intergenerational assistance to older adults after divorce and remarriage. *Family Relations* 55:576–587.

Collins, Patricia Hill. 2000. *Black feminist thought*, 2nd ed. New York: Routledge.

Conley, Dalton. 2004. *The pecking order: Which siblings succeed and why.* New York: Pantheon.

Conley, Dalton. 2005. *The pecking order: A bold new look at how family and society determine who we become.* New York: Knopf.

Connell, Cathleen M., & Gloria D. Gibson. 1997. Racial, ethnic, and cultural differences in dementia caregiving: Review and analysis. *The Gerontologist* 37:3:355–364.

Connell, R. W. 1995. *Masculinities.* Los Angeles: University of California Press.

Connidis, Ingrid. 1989a. Contact between siblings in later life. *Canadian Journal of Sociology* 14:4:429–442.

Connidis, Ingrid Arnet. 1989b. Siblings as friends in later life. *American Behavioral Scientist* 33:1:81–93.

Connidis, Ingrid Arnet. 1992. Life transitions and the adult sibling tie: A qualitative study. *Journal of Marriage and Family* 54 (Nov): 972–982.

Connidis, Ingrid Arnet. 1994a. Growing up and old together: Some observations on families in later life. Pp. 195–205 in Victor Marshall & Barry McPherson (Eds.), *Aging: Canadian perspectives.* Peterborough, Ontario: Broadview.

Connidis, Ingrid Arnet. 1994b. Sibling support in older age. *Journal of Gerontology: Social Sciences* 49:6:S309-S317.

Connidis, Ingrid Arnet. 2001. *Family ties & aging.* Thousand Oaks, CA: Sage.

Connidis, Ingrid Arnet. 2002. The impact of demographic and social trends on informal support for older persons. Pp. 105–132 in David Cheal (Ed.), *Aging and demographic change in Canadian context.* Toronto: University of Toronto Press.

Connidis, Ingrid Arnet. 2003a. Divorce and union dissolution: Reverberations over three generations. *Canadian Journal on Aging* 22:4:353–368.

Connidis, Ingrid Arnet. 2003b. Bringing outsiders in: Gay and lesbian family ties over the life course. Pp. 79–94 in Sara Arber, Kate Davidson, & Jay Ginn (Eds.), *Gender and ageing: Changing roles and relationships.* Philadelphia: Open University Press.

Connidis, Ingrid Arnet. 2004. Stability and change in childhood and parenting: Observations across three generations. *Annual Review of Gerontology & Geriatrics* 24:98–119.

Connidis, Ingrid Arnet. 2005a. *Diversity among adult siblings: Negotiating multiple meanings of family.* Paper presented at the Annual Meeting of the National Council on Family Relations. November. Phoenix, Arizona.

Connidis, Ingrid Arnet. 2005b. Sibling ties across time: The middle and later years. Pp. 429–436 in Malcolm

Johnson (Ed.), *The Cambridge handbook of age and ageing.* Cambridge, UK: University of Cambridge Press.

Connidis, Ingrid Arnet. 2006. Intimate relationships: Learning from later life experience. Pp. 123–153 in Toni M. Calasanti & Kathleen F. Slevin (Eds.), *Age matters: Realigning feminist thinking.* New York: Routledge.

Connidis, Ingrid Arnet. 2007. Negotiating inequality among adult siblings: Two case studies. *Journal of Marriage and Family* 69:2:482–499.

Connidis, Ingrid Arnet, & Lori D. Campbell. 1995. Closeness, confiding, and contact among siblings in middle and late adulthood. *Journal of Family Issues* 16:6:722–745.

Connidis, Ingrid Arnet, & Lorraine Davies. 1990. Confidants and companions in later life: The place of family and friends. *Journal of Gerontology: Social Sciences* 45:4:S141–149.

Connidis, Ingrid Arnet, & Lorraine Davies. 1992. Confidants and companions: Choices in later life. *Journal of Gerontology: Social Sciences* 47:3:S115–122.

Connidis, Ingrid Arnet, & Candace L. Kemp. Forthcoming. Negotiating work and family. Julie Ann McMullin (Ed.), *Working in information technology firms: Intersections of gender and aging.* Vancouver, Canada: UBC Press.

Connidis, Ingrid Arnet, & Candace L. Kemp. 2008. Negotiating actual and anticipated parental support: Multiple sibling voices in three-generation families. *Journal of Aging Studies* 22:3:229–238.

Connidis, Ingrid Arnet, & Julie Ann McMullin. 1992. Getting out of the house: The effect of childlessness on social participation and companionship in later life. *Canadian Journal on Aging* 11:4:370–386

Connidis, Ingrid Arnet, & Julie Ann McMullin. 1993. To have or have not: Parent status and the subjective well-being of older men and women. *The Gerontologist* 33:5:630–636.

Connidis, Ingrid Arnet, & Julie Ann McMullin. 1994. Social support in older age: Assessing the impact of marital and parent status. *Canadian Journal on Aging* 13:4:510–527.

Connidis, Ingrid Arnet, & Julie Ann McMullin. 1996. Reasons for and perceptions of childlessness among older persons: Exploring the impact of marital status and gender. *Journal of Aging Studies* 10:3:205–222.

Connidis, Ingrid Arnet, & Julie Ann McMullin. 1999. Permanent childlessness: Perceived advantages and disadvantages among older persons. *Canadian Journal on Aging* 18:4:447–465.

Connidis, Ingrid Arnet, & Julie Ann McMullin. 2002a. Ambivalence, family ties, and doing sociology. *Journal of Marriage and Family* 64:3:594–601.

Connidis, Ingrid Arnet, & Julie Ann McMullin. 2002b. Sociological ambivalence and family ties: A critical perspective. *Journal of Marriage and Family* 64:3:558–567.

Connidis, Ingrid Arnet, Carolyn J. Rosenthal, & Julie Ann McMullin. 1996. The impact of family composition on

providing help to older parents: A study of employed adults. *Research on Aging* 18:4:402–429.

Connidis, Ingrid Arnet, & Alexis J. Walker. Forthcoming. (Re)visioning aging families: Gender, age, and aging in families. Sally A. Lloyd, April L. Few, & Katherine R. Allen (Eds.), *Handbook of feminist family studies.* Thousand Oaks, CA: Sage.

Cooke, Martin. 2006. Policy changes and the labour force participation of older workers: evidence from six countries. *Canadian Journal on Aging* 25:4:387–400.

Cooney, Theresa M. 1994. Young adults' relations with parents: The influence of recent parental divorce. *Journal of Marriage and Family* 56:1:45–56.

Cooney, Theresa M., & Lori Ann Smith. 1996. Young adults' relations with grandparents following recent parental separation. *Journal of Gerontology: Social Sciences* 51B:2:S91-S95.

Cooney, Theresa M., & Peter Uhlenberg. 1992. Support from parents over the life course: The adult child's perspective. *Social Forces* 71:1:63–84.

Coontz, Stephanie. 2007. Divorce and dissolution: Recognizing reality. *National Council on Family Relations Report* 52:4: (Family Focus) F5-F6.

Cornman, John M., & Eric R. Kingson. 1996. Trends, issues, perspectives, and values for the aging of the baby boom. *The Gerontologist* 36:1:15–26.

Cotten, Shelia. 1999. Marital status and mental health revisited: Examining the importance of risk factors and resources. *Family Relations* 48:3:225–233.

Coward, Raymond T., & Jeffrey W. Dwyer. 1990. The association of gender, sibling network composition, and patterns of parent care by adult children. *Research on Aging* 12:158–181.

Cranswick, Kelly. 2003. *General social survey cycle 16: Caring for an aging society.* Ottawa, Canada: Minister of Industry. Statistics Canada Catalogue No. 89-582-XIE.

Crompton, Rosemary. 2006. *Employment and the family: The reconfiguration of work and family life in contemporary societies.* New York: Cambridge University Press.

Crompton, Susan, & Anna Kemeny. 1999. In sickness and in health: The well-being of married seniors. *Canadian Social Trends.* Winter. Ottawa, Canada: Statistics Canada. Cat. No. 11-008.

Crosnoe, Robert, & Glen H. Elder Jr. 2002. Life course transitions, the generational stake, and grandparent-grandchild relationships. *Journal of Marriage and Family* 64:4:1089–1096.

Cruikshank, Margaret. 1991. Lavender and grey: A brief survey of lesbian and gay aging studies. Pp. 77–87 in John Alan Lee (Ed.), *Gay midlife and maturity.* New York: Haworth.

Cumming, Elaine, & M. Schneider. 1961. Sibling solidarity: A property of American kinship. *American Anthropologist* 63:498–507.

Cunningham, J. D., & J. K. Antill. 1995. Current trends in nonmarital cohabitation: In search of the POSSLQ. Pp. 148–172 in J. T. Wood & S. Duck (Eds.). *Understudied relationships: Off the beaten track.* Thousand Oaks, CA: Sage.

Cunningham, Mick. 2001. Parental influences on the gendered division of housework. *American Sociological Review* 66:184–203.

Curran, Sara R. 2002. Agency, accountability, and embedded relations: What's love got to do with it? *Journal of Marriage and Family* 64:3:577–584.

Current Population Reports. 2002. *The older foreign-born population in the United States: 2000.* Washington, DC: U.S. Department of Health and Human Services and U.S. Department of Commerce. September.

D'Augelli, A. R., S. L. Hershberger, & N. W. Pilkington. 1998. Lesbian, gay, and bisexual youth and their families: Disclosure of sexual orientation and its consequences. *Journal of Orthopsychiatry* 68:3:361–371.

D'Erasmo, Stacey. 2004. The good marriage; or, the kiss of the fat man. Pp. 59–72 in Kathy Pories (Ed.), *The M word: Writers on same-sex marriage.* Chapel Hill, NC: Algonquin.

Daatland, Svein Olav. 1990. What are families for? On family solidarity and preferences for help. *Aging and Society* 10:1–15.

Daatland, Svein Olav. 2007. Marital history and intergenerational solidarity: The impact of divorce and unmarried cohabitation. *Journal of Social Issues* 63:4:809–825.

Dailey, Nancy. 2006. Divorce is economic suicide. Pp. 229–241 in Nan Bauer-Maglin (Ed.), *Cut loose: (Mostly) older women talk about the end of (mostly) long-term relationships.* New Brunswick NJ: Rutgers University Press.

Danigelis, Nicholas L., Melissa Hardy, & Stephen J. Cutler. 2007. Population aging, intracohort aging, and sociopolitical attitudes. *American Sociological Review* 72:5:612–830.

Dannefer, Dale, 2003. Cumulative advantage/disadvantage and the life course: Cross fertilizing age and social science theory. *Journal of Gerontology: Social Sciences* 58B:6:S327-S337.

Darroch, A. Gordon, & Michael Ornstein. 1984. Family and household in nineteenth century Canada: Regional patterns and regional economics. *Journal of Family History* (Summer) 158–179.

Davey, Adam, M. Janke, & J. Savla. 2005. Antecedents of intergenerational support: Families in context and families as contexts. Pp. 29–54 in M. Silverstein, R. Giarrusso, & V. L. Bengtson (Eds.), *Annual review of gerontology and geriatrics: intergenerational relations across time and place.* New York: Springer.

Davidson, Kate. 2001. Late life widowhood, selfishness and new partnership choices: A gendered perspective. *Journal of Aging Studies* 21:297–317.

Davidson, Kate. 2004. Gender differences in new partnership choices. Pp. 65–84 in Kate Davidson & Graham Fennell (Eds.), *Intimacy in later life.* London: Transaction Publishers.

Davidson, Kate, Tom Daly, & Sara Arber. 2003. Exploring the social worlds of older men. Pp. 168–185 in Sara Arber, Kate Davidson, & Jay Ginn (Eds.), *Gender and ageing: Changing roles and relationships.* Philadelphia: Open University Press.

Davidson, Kate, & Graham Fennell. 2004. Introduction: New intimate relationships in later life. Pp. vii–xv in Kate Davidson, & Graham Fennell (Eds.), *Intimacy in later life.* London: Transaction Publishers.

Davies, Lorraine. 1995. A closer look at gender and distress among the never married. *Women and Health* 23:2:13–30.

Davies, Lorraine. 2003. Singlehood: Transitions within a gendered world. *Canadian Journal on Aging* 22:4:343–352.

Davis, Ann. 1980. Whoever said life begins at 40 was a fink or, those golden years—phooey. *International Journal of Women's Studies* 3:6:583–589.

de Jong Gierveld, Jenny. 2004a. Remarriage, unmarried cohabitation, living apart together: Partner relationships following bereavement or divorce. *Journal of Marriage and Family* 66:1:236–243.

de Jong Gierveld, Jenny. 2004b. The dilemma of repartnering: Considerations of older men and women entering new intimate relationships in later life. Pp. 85–104 in Kate Davidson & Graham Fennell (Eds.), *Intimacy in later life.* London: Transaction Publishers.

de Vries, Brian. 2006. Home at the end of the rainbow: Supportive housing for LGBT elders. *Generations* 29:4:64–69.

de Vries, Brian. 2007. LGBT couples in later life: A study in diversity. *Generations* 31:3:18–23.

DeLaire, Thomas, & Ariel Kalil. 2002. Good things come in 3s: Multigenerational coresidence and adolescent adjustment. *Demography* 39:393–413.

Delany, Sarah, & E. Elizabeth Delany. 1993. *Having our say: The Delany sisters' first 100 years.* With Amy Hill Hearth. New York: Kodansha America.

Dellmann-Jenkins, Mary, Maureen Blankemeyer, & Odessa Pinkard. 2000. Young adult children and grandchildren in primary caregiver roles to older relatives and their service needs. *Family Relations* 49:2:177–186.

Demian. 2000. *Quick facts on legal marriage for same-sex couples: Partners task force for gay and lesbian couples.* http://www.buddybuddy.com/quick.html

Demo, David H., William S. Aquilino, & Mark A. Fine. 2005. Family composition and family transitions. Pp. 119–142 in Vern L. Bengtson, Alan C. Acock, Katherine R. Allen, Peggye Dilworth-Anderson, & David M. Klein (Eds.), *Sourcebook of family theory & research.* Thousand Oaks, CA: Sage.

Dentinger, Emma, & Marin Clarkberg. 2002. Informal caregiving and retirement timing among men and women. *Journal of Family Issues* 23:7:857–879.

DePaulo, Bella M., & Wendy L. Morris. 2005. Singles in society and in science. *Psychological Inquiry* 6:2&3:57–83.

Depner, Charlene E., & Berit Ingersoll-Dayton. 1985. Conjugal social support: Patterns in later life. *Journal of Gerontology* 40:6:761–766.

DeWit, David J., Andrew V. Wister, & Thomas K. Burch. 1988. Physical distance and social contact between elders and their adult children. *Research on Aging* 10:1:56–80.

Diamond, Lisa M. 2006. The intimate same-sex relationships of same-sex minorities. Pp. 293–312 in Anita L. Vangelisti, & Daniel Perlman (Eds.), *The Cambridge handbook of personal relationships.* New York: Cambridge University Press.

Dickson, F. C. 1995. The best is yet to be: Research on long-lasting marriages. Pp. 22–50 in J. T. Wood & S. Duck (Eds.), *Under-studied relationships: Off the beaten track.* Thousand Oaks, CA: Sage.

Didion, Joan. 2005. *The year of magical thinking.* New York: Knopf.

Dilworth-Anderson, Peggye, Beverly H. Brummett, Paula Goodwin, Sharon Wallace Williams, Redord B. Williams, & Ilene C. Siegler. 2005. Effect of race on cultural justifications for caregiving. *Journal of Gerontology: Social Sciences* 60B:5:S257-S262.

Dilworth-Anderson, Peggye, & Linda Burton. 1999. Critical issues in understanding family support and older minorities. Pp. 93–105 in Toni P. Miles (Ed.), *Full-color aging: Facts, goals, and recommendations for America's diverse elders.* Washington, DC: Gerontological Society of America.

Dilworth-Anderson, Peggye, Linda M. Burton, & David M. Klein. 2005. Contemporary and emerging theories in studying families. Pp. 35–50 in Vern L. Bengtson, Alan C. Acock, Katherine R. Allen, Peggye Dilworth-Anderson, & David M. Klein (Eds.), *Sourcebook of family theory & research.* Thousand Oaks, CA: Sage.

Dimmock, Brian, Joanna Bornat, Sheila Peace, & David Jones. 2004. Intergenerational relationships among stepfamilies in the UK. Pp. 82–94 in Sarah Harper (Ed.), *Families in ageing societies: An Interdisciplinary approach.* New York: Oxford University Press.

Dobell, A. R., & S. H. Mansbridge. 1986. *The social policy process in Canada.* Montreal, Canada: Institute for Research on Public Policy.

Doherty, Nicole E., & Judith A. Feeney. 2004. The composition of attachment networks throughout the adult years. *Personal Relationships* 11:469–488.

Doka, Kenneth J. 2002a. Introduction. Pp. 5–22 in Kenneth J. Doka (Ed.), *Disenfranchised grief: New directions, challenges, and strategies for practice.* Champaign, IL: Research Press.

Doka, Kenneth J. 2002b. The role of ritual in the treatment of disenfranchised grief. Pp. 135–147 in Kenneth J. Doka (Ed.), *Disenfranchised grief: New directions, challenges, and strategies for practice.* Champaign, IL: Research Press.

Doka, Kenneth J. 2002c. How we die: Stigmatized death and disenfranchised grief. Pp. 323–336 in Kenneth J. Doka (Ed.), *Disenfranchised grief: New directions, challenges, and strategies for practice.* Champaign, IL: Research Press.

Dolbin-MacNab, Megan L. 2006. Just like raising your own? Grandmothers' perceptions of parenting a second time around. *Family Relations* 55:5:564–575.

Dorfman, Lorraine T. 1992. Couples in retirement: Division of household work. Pp. 159–173 in Maximiliane Szinovacz, David J. Ekerdt, & Barbara H. Vinick (Eds.), *Families and retirement.* Newbury Park, CA: Sage.

Doty, Pamela, Mary E. Jackson, & William Crown. 1998. The impact of female caregivers' employment on patterns of formal and informal eldercare. *The Gerontologist* 38:3:331–341.

Doudna, Christine, & Fern McBride. 1981. Where are the men for the women at the top? Pp. 21–34 in Peter J. Stein (Ed.), *Single life: Unmarried adults in social context.* New York: St. Martin's.

Draimin, Barbara, & Daphne Joslin. 2002. Their second chance: Grandparents caring for their grandchildren. Pp. 151–169 in Daphne Joslin (Ed.), *Invisible caregivers: older adults raising grandchildren in the wake of HIV/AIDS.* New York: Columbia University Press.

Dugan, Elizabeth, & Vira R. Kivett. 1994. The importance of emotional and social isolation to loneliness among very old rural adults. *The Gerontologist* 34:3:340–346.

Dunham, Charlotte Chorn. 1995. A link between generations: Intergenerational relations and depression in aging parents. *Journal of Family Issues* 16:4:450–465.

Dunham, Charlotte Chorn, & Julie Harms Cannon. 2008. 'They're still in control enough to be in control': Paradox of power in dementia caregiving. *Journal of Aging Studies* 22:1:45–53.

Dunifon, Rachel, & Lori Kowaleski-Jones. 2007. The influence of grandparents in single-mother families. *Journal of Marriage and Family* 69:465–481.

Dupre, Matthew E., & Sarah O. Meadows. 2007. Disaggregating the effects of marital trajectories on health. *Journal of Family Issues* 28:5:623–652.

Duvall, Evelyn Mills. 1967. *Family development,* 3rd ed. Toronto: J. B. Lippincott.

Dworkin, Sari H. 2006. The aging bisexual: The invisible of the invisible minority. Pp. 36–52 in Douglas Kimmel, Tara Rose, & Steven David (Eds.), *Lesbian, gay, bisexual, and transgender aging: Research and clinical perspectives.* New York: Columbia University Press.

Dwyer, Jeffrey W., & Raymond T. Coward. 1991. Multivariate comparisons of the involvement of adult sons versus daughters in the care of impaired parents. *Journal of Gerontology: Social Sciences* 46:5:S259-S269.

Dwyer, Jeffrey W., John C. Henretta, Raymond T. Coward, & Amy J. Barton. 1992. Changes in the helping behaviors of adult children as caregivers. *Research on Aging* 14:351–75.

Dwyer, Jeffrey W., Gary R. Lee, & Thomas B. Jankowski. 1994. Reciprocity, elder satisfaction, and caregiver stress and burden: The exchange of aid in the family caregiving relationship. *Journal of Marriage and Family* 56:1:35–43.

Dwyer, Jeffrey W., & Karen Seccombe. 1991. Elder care as family labor. *Journal of Family Issues* 12:2:229–247.

Dye, Jane Lawler. 2005. *Fertility of American women: June 2004.* Current Population Reports, P20–555. Washington, DC: U.S. Census Bureau. http://www.census.gov/prod/2005pubs/p20–555.pdf

Dykstra, Pearl A. 1990. Disentangling direct and indirect gender effects on the supportive network. Pp. 55–65 in C. P. M. Knipscheer & T. C. Antonucci (Eds.), *Social network research: Substantive issues and methodological questions* Amsterdam: Swets & Zeitlinger.

Dykstra, Pearl A. 1995. Loneliness among the never and formerly married: The importance of supportive friendships and a desire for independence. *Journal of Gerontology: Social Sciences* 50B:5:S321-S329.

Dykstra, Pearl A., & Gunhild O. Hagestad. 2007. Childlessness and parenthood in two centuries: Different roads – different maps? *Journal of Family Issues* 28:11:1518–1532.

Dykstra, Pearl A., & Michael Wagner. 2007. Pathways to childlessness and late-life outcomes. *Journal of Family Issues* 28:11:1487–1517.

Ebaugh, Helen Rose, & Mary Curry. 2000. Fictive kin as social capital in new immigrant communities. *Sociological Perspectives* 43:2:189–209.

Edwards, Marie, & Eleanor Hoover. 1974. *The challenge of being single.* New York: New American Library.

Ehrenberg, Miriam. 1997. Living with aging: Review and prospects. Pp. 627–638 in Martin Duberman (Ed.), *A queer world: The Center for Lesbian and Gay Studies reader.* New York: New York University Press.

Eisenhandler, Susan A. 1992. Lifelong roles and cameo appearances: Elderly parents and relationships with adult children. *Journal of Aging Studies* 6:3:243–257.

Elder, Glen Jr. 1991. Lives and social change. Pp. 58–85 in Walter Heinz (Ed.), *Theoretical advances in life course research.* Weinham, Germany: Deutscher Studies Verlag.

Elder, Glen Jr., & Monica Kirkpatrick Johnson. 2003. The life course and aging: Challenges, lessons, and new directions. Pp. 49–81 in Richard Settersten, Jr. (Ed.), *Invitation to the life course: Toward new understandings of later life.* Amityville, NY: Baywood.

Elliott, Sinika, & Debra Umberson. 2008. The performance of desire: Gender and sexual negotiation in long-term marriages. *Journal of Marriage and Family* 70:2:391–406.

Elwert, Felix, & Nicholas A. Christakis. 2006. Widowhood and race. *American Sociological Review* 71 (February): 16–41.

England, Paula. 2005. Emerging theories of care work. *Annual Review of Sociology* 31:381–399.

Eriksen, Shelley, & Naomi Gerstel. 2002. A labor of love or labor itself: Care work among adult brothers and sisters. *Journal of Family Issues* 23:7:836–856.

Estes, Carroll L., & Associates. 2001. *Social policy & aging: A critical perspective.* Thousand Oaks, CA: Sage.

Estes, Carroll L., Simon Biggs, & Chris Phillipson. 2003. *Social theory, Social policy and ageing: A critical introduction.* Berkshire, UK: Open University Press.

Evandrou, Maria, & Karen Glaser. 2004. Family, work and quality of life: Changing economic and social roles through the lifecourse. *Ageing & Society* 24:771–791.

Falk, Ursula Adler, & Gerhard Falk. 2002. *Grandparents: A new look at the supporting generation.* Amherst, NY: Prometheus.

Faludi, Susan. 1991. *Backlash: The undeclared war against American women.* New York: Crown.

Felstein, I. 1970. *Sex and the longer life.* London: Penguin.

Feng, Du, Roseann Giarrusso, Vern L. Bengtson, & Nancy Frye. 1999. Intergenerational transmission of marital quality and marital instability. *Journal of Marriage and Family* 61:2:451–463.

Ferguson, Neil, Gillian Douglas, Nigel Lowe, Mervyn Murch, & Margaret Robinson. 2004. *Grandparenting in divorced families.* Bristol, UK: Policy Press.

Finch, Janet. 1989. *Family obligations and social change.* Cambridge, MA: Basil Blackwell.

Finch, Janet. 2007. Displaying families. *Sociology* 41:1:65–81.

Finch, Janet, & Jennifer Mason. 1990. Divorce, remarriage, and family obligations. *Sociological Review* 38:2: 219–246.

Finch, Janet, & Jennifer Mason. 1991. Obligations of kinship in contemporary Britain: Is there normative agreement? *British Journal of Sociology* 42:3:345–367.

Finch, Janet, & Jennifer Mason. 1993. *Negotiating family responsibilities.* New York: Tavistock/Routledge.

Finch, Janet, & Jennifer Mason. 2000. *Passing on: Kinship and inheritance in England.* New York: Routledge.

Fincham, Frank D., & Thomas N. Bradbury. 2005. Studying marriages longitudinally. Pp. 274–276 in Bengtson, Vern L., Alan C. Acock, Katherine R. Allen, Peggye Dilworth-Anderson, & David M. Klein (Eds.), *Sourcebook of family theory & research.* Thousand Oaks, CA: Sage.

Fingerman, Karen L. 2000. 'We had a nice little chat': Age and generational differences in mothers' and daughters' descriptions of enjoyable visits. *Journal of Gerontology: Psychological Sciences* 55B:2:P95-P106.

Fingerman, Karen L., Pei-Chun Chen, Elizabeth Hay, Kelly E. Cichy, & Eva S. Lefkowitz. 2006. Ambivalent reactions in the parent and offspring relationship. *Journal of Gerontology: Psychological Sciences* 61B:3:P153-P160.

Fingerman, Karen L., & Elizabeth L. Hay. 2004. Intergenerational ambivalence in the context of the larger social network. Pp. 133–151 in K. Pillemer & K. Lüscher (Eds.), *Intergenerational ambivalences: New perspectives on parent-child relations in later life.* New York: Elsevier.

Fingerman, Karen L., Elizabeth L. Hay, & Kira S. Birditt. 2004. The best of ties, the worst of ties: Close, problematic, and ambivalent social relationships. *Journal of Marriage and Family* 66:3:792–808.

Fisher, Carla, & Michelle Miller-Day. 2006. Communication in mother-adult daughter relationships. In Kory Floyd & Mark T. Morman (Eds.), *Widening the family circle: New research on family communication.* Thousand Oaks, CA: Sage.

Fisher, Linda, & Montenegro, Xenia. 2003. Results from our singles survey. *AARP The Magazine Online.* http://www.aarpmagazine.org/lifestyle/Articles/a2003-09-23-survey_results.html

Fitting, Melinda, Peter Rabins, M. Jane Lucas, & James Eastham. 1986. Caregivers for dementia patients: A comparison of husbands and wives. *The Gerontologist* 26:3:248–252.

Fletcher, G. 2002. *The new science of intimate relationships.* Malden, MA: Blackwell.

Flippen, Chenoa, & Marta Tienda. 2000. Pathways to retirement: Patterns of labor force participation and labor market exit among the pre-retirement population by race, Hispanic origin, and sex. *Journal of Gerontology: Social Sciences* 55B:1:S14-S27.

Flying solo—More women are deciding that marriage is not inevitable, that they can lead a fulfilling life as a single. 2000. *Time*, August 28.

Folsom, Joseph K. 1937. Changing values in sex and family relations, *American Sociological Review* 2:5:717–726.

Folwell, Annette L., Leeva C, Chung, Jon F. Nussbaum, Lisa Sparks Bethea, & Jo Anna Grant. 1997. Differential accounts of closeness in older adult sibling relationships. *Journal of Social and Personal Relationships* 14:843–849.

Foner, Anne. 2000. Age integration or age conflict as society ages? *The Gerontologist* 40:3:272–276.

Forbat, Liz. 2004. The care and abuse of minoritized ethnic groups: The role of statutory services. *Critical Social Policy* 24:3:312–331.

Franklin, Susan T., Barbara D. Ames, & Sharon King. 1994. Acquiring the family eldercare role: Influence on female employment adaptation. *Research on Aging* 16:1:27–42.

Fredriksen, Karen I. 1999. Family caregiving responsibilities among lesbians and gay men. *Social Work* 44:2:142–155.

Freedman, Vicki A. 1996. Family structure and the risk of nursing home admission. *Journal of Gerontology: Social Sciences* 51B:2:S61–S69.

Friedan, Betty. 1963. *The feminine mystique.* New York: Dell.

Friedan, Betty. 2000. *Life so far.* New York: Simon & Schuster.

Friedland, Robert B., & Laura Summer. 1999. *Demography is not destiny.* Washington, DC: National Academy on an Aging Society.

Friend, Richard A. 1996. Older lesbian and gay people: A theory of successful aging. Pp. 277–298 in Raymond Berger (Ed.), *Gay and grey: The older homosexual man,* 2nd ed. New York: Harrington Park.

Friese, Carrie, Gay Becker, & Robert D. Nachtigall. 2008. Older motherhood and the changing life course in the era of assisted reproductive technologies. *Journal of Aging Studies* 22:1:65–73.

Frisco, Michelle L., & Kristi Williams. 2003. Perceived housework equity, marital happiness, and divorce in dual-earner households. *Journal of Family Issues* 24:1:51–73.

Froschl, Merle. 2006. Left alone: Deserted by death or divorce. Pp. 261–264 in Nan Bauer-Maglin (Ed.), *Cut loose: (Mostly) older women talk about the end of (mostly) long-term relationships.* New Brunswick NJ: Rutgers University Press.

Fuller-Thomson, Esme, Meredith Minkler, & Diane Driver. 1997. A profile of grandparents raising grandchildren in the United States. *The Gerontologist* 37:3:406–411.

Fullmer, Elise M. 1995. Challenging biases against families of older gays and lesbians Pp. 99–119 in G. C. Smith, S. S. Tobin, E. A. Robertson-Tchabo, & P. W. Power (Eds.), *Strengthening aging families: Diversity in practice and policy.* Thousand Oaks, CA: Sage.

Fullmer, Elise M., Sheldon S. Tobin, & Gregory C. Smith. 1997. The effects of offspring gender on older mothers caring for their sons and daughters with mental retardation. *The Gerontologist* 37:6:795–803.

Gallagher, Sally K., & Naomi Gerstel. 2001. Connections and constraints: The effects of children on caregiving. *Journal of Marriage and Family* 63:1:265–275.

Ganong, Lawrence H., & Marilyn Coleman. 1999. *Changing families, changing responsibilities: Family obligations following divorce and remarriage.* Mahwah, NJ: Lawrence Erlbaum.

Ganong, Lawrence H., & Marilyn Coleman. 2004. *Stepfamily relationships: Development, dynamics, and interventions.* New York: Kluwer/Plenum.

Ganong, Lawrence H., & Marilyn Coleman. 2006. Obligations to stepparents acquired in later life: Relationship quality and acuity of needs. *Journal of Gerontology: Social Sciences* 61B:2:S80–S88.

Ganong, Lawrence H., Marilyn Coleman, Annette Kusgen McDaniel, & Tim Killian. 1998. Attitudes regarding obligations to assist an older parent or stepparent following later-life remarriage. *Journal of Marriage and Family* 60:3:595–610.

Gans, Daphna, & Merril Silverstein. 2006. Norms of filial responsibility for aging parents across time and generations. *Journal of Marriage and Family* 68:4:961–976.

Garnets, Linda, & Letitia Anne Peplau. 2006. Sexuality in the lives of aging lesbian and bisexual women. Pp. 70–91 in Douglas Kimmel, Tara Rose, & Steven David (Eds.), *Lesbian, gay, bisexual, and transgender aging: Research and clinical perspectives.* New York: Columbia University Press.

Gee, Ellen. 1995. Families in later life. Pp. 77–113 in Roderic Beaujot, Ellen M. Gee, Fernando Rajulton, & Zenaida R. Ravanera (Eds.), *Family over the life course: Current demographic analysis.* Ottawa, Canada: Statistics Canada Demography Division.

Gee, Ellen M. 2000. Population and politics: Voodoo demography, population aging, and social policy. Pp. 5–25 in Ellen M. Gee & Gloria M. Gutman (Eds.), *The overselling of population aging: Apocalyptic demography, intergenerational challenges, and social policy.* Don Mills, Ontario, Canada: Oxford University Press.

Geller, Jaclyn. 2001. *Here comes the bride: Women, weddings and the marriage mystique.* New York: Four Walls Eight Windows Press.

Gendell, Murray, & Jacob S. Siegel. 1996. Trends in retirement age in the United States, 1955–1993, by sex and race. *Journal of Gerontology Social Sciences* 51B:3:S132–S139.

George, Linda. 1980. *Role transitions in later life.* Monterey, CA: Brooks/Cole.

George, Linda K. 1995. The last half-century of aging research—and thoughts for the future. *Journal of Gerontology B: Social Sciences* 50:S1–S3.

George, Linda K. 2003. Life course research: Achievements and potential. Pp. 671–680 in Jeylan T. Mortimer & Michael J. Shanahan (Eds.), *Handbook of the life course.* New York: Kluwer/Plenum.

George, Linda K. 2006. Perceived quality of life. Pp. 320–336 in Robert L. Binstock & Linda K. George (Eds.), *Handbook of aging and the social sciences,* 6th ed. New York: Elsevier.

Gerstel, Naomi, & Sally Gallagher. 1994. Caring for kith and kin: Gender, employment and the privatization of care. *Social problems* 41:519–539.

Gerstel, Naomi, & Sally K. Gallagher. 2001. Men's caregiving: Gender and the contingent character of care. *Gender and Society* 15:2:197–217.

Ghazanfareeon Karlsson, Sofie, & Klas Borell. 2004. Intimacy and autonomy, gender and ageing: Living apart together. Pp. 1–18 in Kate Davidson & Graham Fennell (Eds.), *Intimacy in later life*. London, UK: Transaction Publishers.

Gibson, Diane, & Stephen Mugford. 1986. Expressive relations and social support. Pp. 63–84 in Hal L. Kendig (Ed.), *Aging and families: A social networks perspective*. Boston: Allen & Unwin.

Gibson, Mary Jo, & Ari Houser. 2007. *Valuing the invaluable: A new look at the economic value of family caregiving*. Research Report. Washington DC: AARP Public Policy Institute.

Gibson, Priscilla A. 2005. Intergenerational parenting from the perspective of African American grandmothers. *Family Relations* 54:280–297.

Giddens, Anthony. 1991. *Modernity and self-identity*. Cambridge, MA: Polity.

Giddens, Anthony. 1992. *The transformation of intimacy: Sexuality, love and eroticism in modern societies*. Stanford, CA: Stanford University Press.

Gillis, John R. 1996. *A world of their own making: Myth, ritual, and the quest for family values*. Cambridge, MA: Harvard University Press.

Ginn, Jay, & Sara Arber. 1995. "Only connect": Gender relations and aging. Pp. 1–14 in Sara Arber & Jay Ginn (Eds.), *Connecting gender and aging: A sociological approach*. Philadelphia: Open University Press.

Ginn, Jay, Debra Street, & Sara Arber. 2001. Cross-national trends in women's work. Pp. 11–30 in Jay Ginn, Debra Street, & Sara Arber (Eds.), *Women, work and pensions: International issues and prospects*. Philadelphia: Open University Press.

Gist, Yvonne J., & Lisa I. Hetzel. 2004. *We the people: Aging in the United States*. U.S. Census Bureau, Census 2000 Special Reports, CENSR-19. Washington, DC: U.S. Government Printing Office.

Gladstone, James W. 1991. An analysis of changes in grandparent-grandchild visitation following an adult child's remarriage. *Canadian Journal on Aging* 10:2:113–126.

Glaser, Karen. 2008. Kids do care for divorced parents. *The Globe and Mail,* May 15. Globe Life, 1 & 3.

Glaser, Karen, Rachel Stuchbury, Cecilia Tomassini, & Janet Askham. 2008. The longterm consequences of relationship dissolution for support in later life in the United Kingdom. *Ageing & Society* 28:329–351.

Glenn, Norval D. 1998. The course of marital success and failure in five American 10-year marriage cohorts. *Journal of Marriage and Family* 60 (August): 569–576.

Glick, Jennifer E., & Jennifer Van Hook. 2002. Parents' coresidence with adult children: Can immigration explain racial and ethnic variation? *Journal of Marriage and Family* 64:1:240–253.

Goetting, Anne. 1986. The developmental tasks of siblingship over the life cycle. *Journal of Marriage and Family* 48:703–714.

Gold, Deborah T. 1986, November. *Sibling relationships in old age: A typology*. Paper presented at the Gerontological Society of America annual meeting, Chicago.

Gold, Deborah T. 1987. Siblings in old age: Something special. *Canadian Journal on Aging* 6:3:199–215.

Gold, Deborah T. 1989. Sibling relations in old age: A typology. *International Journal of Aging and Human Development* 28:1:37–51.

Gold, Deborah T. 1990. Late-life sibling relationships: Does race affect typological distribution? *The Gerontologist* 30:6:741–748.

Gold, Deborah T., Max A. Woodbury, & Linda K. George. 1990. Relationship classification using grade of membership analysis: A typology of sibling relationships in later life. *Journal of Gerontology: Social Sciences* 45:2:S43-S51.

Goldberg, Abbie E. 2007. Talking about family: Disclosure practices of adults raised by lesbian, gay, and bisexual parents. *Journal of Family Issues* 28:1:100–131.

Goldberg, Abbie E., & Maureen Perry-Jenkins. 2007. The division of labor and perceptions of parental roles: Lesbian couples across the transition to parenthood. *Journal of Social and Personal Relationships* 24:2:297–318.

Goldscheider, Frances. 1990. The aging of the gender revolution: What do we know and what do we need to know? *Research on Aging* 12:4:531–545.

Goldscheider, Frances. 1997. Recent changes in U.S. young adult living arrangements in comparative perspective. *Journal of Family Issues* 18:6:708–724.

Goldscheider, Frances K., & Leora Lawton. 1998. Family experiences and the erosion of support for intergenerational coresidence. *Journal of Marriage and Family* 60:3:623–632.

Goodman, Catherine Chase, & Merril Silverstein. 2004. Grandmothers who parent their grandchildren: An exploratory study of close relations across three generations. *Journal of Family Issues* 22:557–578.

Goodman, Marcene, & Robert L. Rubinstein. 1996. Parenting in later life: Adaptive illusion in elderly mothers of one child. *Journal of Aging Studies* 10:4:295–311.

Gordon, Tuula. 1994. *Single women: On the margins?* New York: New York University Press.

Gott, Merryn, & Sharon Hinchliff. 2003. Sex and ageing: A gendered issue. Pp. 63–78 in Sara Arber, Kate Davidson & Jay Ginn (Eds.), *Gender and aging: Changing roles and relationships*. Philadelphia: Open University Press/McGraw-Hill.

Gouldner, Alvin J. 1967. Reciprocity and autonomy in functional theory. Pp. 141–169 in N. J. Demerath III, & Richard A. Peterson (Eds.), *System, change and conflict*. New York: Free Press.

Grant, Gordon. 2007. Invisible contributions in families with children and adults with intellectual disabilities. *Canadian Journal on Aging* 26 (Suppl.1): 15–26.

Gratton, Brian, & Carole Haber. 1993. In search of "intimacy at a distance": Family history from the perspective of elderly women. *Journal of Aging Studies* 7:2:183–194.

Green, Adam Isaiah. 2006. Until death do us part? The impact of differential access to marriage on a sample of urban men. *Sociological Perspectives* 49:2:163–189.

Green, Kerry M., Margaret E. Ensminger, Judith A. Robertson, & Hee-Soon Juon. 2006. Impact of adult sons' incarceration on African American mothers' psychological distress. *Journal of Marriage and Family* 68:2:430–441.

Green, Laura R., Deborah S. Richardson, Tanya Lago, & Elizabeth C. Schatten-Jones. 2001. Network correlate of social and emotional loneliness in young and older adults. *Personality and Social Psychology* 27:3:281–288.

Greenberg, Jan S., Marsha Mailick Seltzer, & James R. Greenley. 1993. Aging parents of adults with disabilities: The gratifications and frustrations of later-life caregiving. *The Gerontologist* 33:4:542–550.

Greene, Vernon L., & Kristina Marty. 1999. Editorial essay. Generational investment and social insurance for the elderly: Balancing the accounts. *The Gerontologist* 39:6:645–647.

Greenfield, Emily A., & Nadine Marks. 2006. Linked lives: Adult children's problems and their parents' psychological and relational well-being. *Journal of Marriage and Family* 68:2:442–454.

Greenwell, Lisa, & Vern L. Bengtson. 1997. Geographic distance and contact between middle-aged children and their parents: The effects of social class over 20 years. *Journal of Gerontology: Social Sciences* 52B:1:S13-S26.

Grossman, Arnold H. 1997. The virtual and actual identities of older lesbians and gay men. Pp. 615–626 in Martin Duberman (Ed.), *A queer world: The Center for Lesbian and Gay Studies reader.* New York: New York University Press.

Grote, N. K., & Frieze, I. H. 1998. 'Remembrance of things past': Perceptions of marital love from its beginnings to the present. *Journal of Social and Personal Relationships* 15:91–109.

Groves, E. R. 1934. The marriage panacea. *Social Forces* (Marriage and the Family) 12:3:406–412.

Guberman, Nancy, & Pierre Maheu. 1999. Combining employment and caregiving: An intricate juggling act. *Canadian Journal on Aging* 18:1:84–106.

Gubrium, Jaber F. 1974. Marital dissolution and the evaluation of everyday life in old age. *Journal of Marriage and Family* 36:1:107–113.

Gubrium, Jaber F. 1975. Being single in old age. *International Journal of Aging and Human Development* 6:1:29–41.

Guillemard, Anne-Marie. 2000. Age integration in Europe: Increasing or decreasing? *The Gerontologist* 40:3:301–302.

Guillemette, Yvan. 2003. *Slowing down with age: The ominous implications of workforce aging for Canadian living standards.* Toronto: Howe Institute.

Haber, Carole. 2006. Old age through the lens of family history. Pp. 59–75 in Robert H. Binstock & Linda K. George (Eds.), *Handbook of aging and the social sciences,* 6th ed. New York: Academic Press.

Hafemeister, Thomas L. 2001. Financial abuse of the elderly in domestic settings. Pp. 382–445 in Richard J. Bonnie & Robert B. Wallace (Eds.), *Elder mistreatment: Abuse, neglect, and exploitation in an aging America.* Washington DC: National Academies Press.

Hagestad, Gunhild O. 2003. Interdependent lives and relationships in changing times: A life-course view of families and aging. Pp. 135–159 in Richard Settersten

Jr. (Ed.), *Invitation to the life course: Toward new understandings of later life.* Amityville, NY: Baywood.

Hagestad, Gunhild O., & Dale Dannefer. 2001. Concepts and theories of aging: Beyond microfication in social science approaches. Pp. 3–21 in Robert H. Binstock & Linda K. George (Eds.), *Handbook of aging and the social sciences,* 5th ed. New York: Academic Press.

Hagestad, Gunhild O., & Peter Uhlenberg. 2005. The social separation of old and young: A root of ageism. *Journal of Social Issues* 61:343–360.

Hagestad, Gunhild O., & Vaughn R. A. Call. 2007. Pathways to childlessness: A life course perspective. *Journal of Family Issues* 28:10:1338–1361.

Hahn, Beth A. 1993. Marital status and women's health—The effect of economic marital acquisitions. *Journal of Marriage and Family* 55:495–504.

Hammond, Ron J., & Greg O. Muller. 1992. The late-life divorced: Another look. *Journal of Divorce and Remarriage* 16:3/4:135–150.

Hamon, Reanna R. 1995. Parents as resources when adult children divorce. *Journal of Divorce and Remarriage* 23:1/2:171–183.

Hamon, Reanna R., & Laurel L. Cobb. 1993. Parents' experience of and adjustment to their adult children's divorce: Applying family stress theory. *Journal of Divorce and Remarriage* 21:1/2:73–94.

Handel, Gerald. 1994. Central issues in the construction of sibling relationships. Pp. 493–523 in Gerald Handel & Gail G. Whitchurch (Eds.), *The psychosocial interior of the family,* 4th ed. New York: Aldine de Gruyter.

Hans, Jason D. 2002. Stepparenting after divorce: Stepparents' legal position regarding custody, access, and support. *Family Relations* 51:4:301–307.

Hansson, Robert O., & Margaret S. Stroebe. 2007. Coping with bereavement. *Generations* 31:3:63–65.

Harbison, Joan, & Marina Morrow. 1998. Forum: Re-examining the social construction of 'elder abuse and neglect': A Canadian perspective. *Ageing and Society* 18:691–711.

Hareven, Tamara K. 1991. The history of the family and the complexity of social change. *American Historical Review* 96:95–124.

Hareven, Tamara K. 1996. Introduction: Aging and generational relations over the life course. Pp. 1–12 in Tamara K. Hareven (Ed.), *Aging and generational relations over the life course.* New York: Walter de Gruyter.

Hareven, Tamara K., & Kathleen Adams. 1996. The generation in the middle: Cohort comparisons in assistance to aging parents in an American community. Pp. 272–293 in Tamara K. Hareven (Ed.), *Aging and generational relations over the life course.* New York: Walter de Gruyter.

Harper, Sarah. 2005. Grandparenthood. Pp. 422–428 in Malcolm L. Johnson (Ed.), *The Cambridge handbook of age and ageing.* New York: Cambridge University Press.

Harrington Meyer, Madonna, Douglas A. Wolf, & Christine L. Himes. 2006. Declining eligibility for social security spouse and widow benefits in the United States? *Research on Aging* 28:2:240–260.

Harris, Diana K., & Michael L. Benson. 2006. *Maltreatment of patients in nursing homes*. New York: Haworth.

Harris, Phyllis Braudy. 1998. Listening to caregiving sons: Misunderstood realities. *The Gerontologist* 38:3: 342–352.

Hatch, Laurie Russell. 2000. *Beyond gender differences: Adaptation to aging in life course perspective*. Amityville, NY: Baywood.

Hauser, R. M., J. T. Sheridan, & J. R. Warren. 1999. Socioeconomic achievements of siblings in the life course. *Research on Aging* 21:338–378.

Hayslip, Jr., Bert, R. Gerald Shore, Craig E. Henderson, & Paul L. Lambert. 1998. Custodial grandparenting and the impact of grandchildren with problems on role satisfaction and role meaning. *Journal of Gerontology: Social Sciences* 53B:3:S164-S173.

Heaphy, Brian, & Andrew K. T. Yip. 2006. Policy implications of ageing sexualities. *Social Policy and Society* 5:4:443–451.

Heaton, Tim B., Cardell K. Jacobson, & Kimberlee Holland. 1999. Persistence and change in decisions to remain childless. *Journal of Marriage and Family* 61:2:531–539.

Heflin, Colleen M., & Mary Pattillo. 2006. Poverty in the family: Race, siblings and socioeconomic heterogeneity. *Social Science Research* 35:804–822.

Heilbrun, Carolyn G. 1997. *The last gift of time: Life beyond sixty*. New York: Ballantine.

Heinemann, Gloria D., & Patricia L. Evans. 1990. Widowhood: Loss, change, and adaptation. Pp. 142–168 in Timothy H. Brubaker (Ed.), *Family relationships in later life*, 2nd ed. Newbury Park, CA: Sage.

Heinz, Walter R. 2001. Work and the life course: A cosmopolitan-local perspective. Pp. 3–22 in Victor W. Marshall, Walter R. Heinz, Helga Kruger, & Anil Verma (Eds.), *Restructuring work and the life course*. Toronto: University of Toronto Press.

Henderson, Tammy L. 2005. Grandparent visitation rights: Justices' interpretation of the best interests of the child standard. *Journal of Family Issues* 26:5:638–664.

Hendrick, S. S., & C. Hendrick. 2000. Romantic love. Pp. 203–215 in C. Hendrick & S. Hendrick (Eds.), *Close relationships: A sourcebook*. Thousand Oaks, CA: Sage.

Hendricks, Jon. 2005. Moral economy and ageing. Pp. 510–517 in Malcolm L. Johnson (Ed.), *The Cambridge handbook of age and ageing*. Cambridge, UK: Cambridge University Press.

Henkens, Kene. 1999. Retirement intentions and spousal support: A multi-actor approach. *Journal of Gerontology: Social Sciences* 54B:2:S63-S73.

Henretta, John C. 2000. The future of age integration in employment. *The Gerontologist* 40:3:286–292.

Henry, Carolyn S., Cindi Penor Ceglian, & D. Wayne Matthews. 1992. The role behavior, role meanings, and grandmothering styles of grandmothers and stepmothers: Perceptions of the middle generation. *Journal of Divorce and Remarriage* 17:3/4:1–22.

Henry, Carolyn S., Cindi Penor Ceglian, & Diane L. Ostrander. 1993. The transition to stepgrandparenthood. *Journal of Divorce and Remarriage* 19:3/4:25–44.

Henz, Ursula. 2006. Informal caregiving at working age: Effects of job characteristics and family configuration. *Journal of Marriage and Family* 68:2:411–429.

Hequembourg, A., & S. Brallier. 2005. Gendered stories of parental caregiving among siblings. *Journal of Aging Studies* 19:53–71.

Hequembourg, Amy L., & Michael P. Farrell. 2001. Lesbian motherhood: Negotiating marginal-mainstream identities. Pp. 126–148 in Janet Lehmann (Ed.), *The gay and lesbian marriage and family reader: Analyses of problems and prospects for the 21st century*. Lincoln: Gordian Knot Books/University of Nebraska Press.

Herdt, Gilbert, & Brian de Vries. 2004. (Eds.) *Gay and lesbian aging: Research and future directions*. New York: Springer.

Heuveline, Patrick and Jeffrey M. Timberlake. 2004. The role of cohabitation in family formation: The United States in comparative perspective. *Journal of marriage and family* 66:5:1214-1230.

Hiedemann, Bridget, Olga Suhomlinova, & Angela M. O'Rand. 1998. Economic independence, economic status, and empty nest in midlife marital disruption. *Journal of Marriage and Family* 60 (February): 219–231.

Hilton, Jeanne M., & Daniel P. Macari. 1997. Grandparent involvement following divorce: A comparison in single-mother and single-father families. *Journal of Divorce and Remarriage* 28:1/2:203–224.

Himes, Christine L. 1994. Parental caregiving by adult women: A demographic perspective. *Research on Aging* 16:2:191–211.

Himes, Christine L., Dennis P. Hogan, & David J. Eggebeen. 1996. Living arrangements of minority elders. *Journal of Gerontology: Social Sciences* 15:1:S42-S48.

Hobbs, Frank. 2005. *Examining American household composition: 1990–2000*. U.S. Census Bureau, Census 2000 Special Reports, CENSR-24. Washington, DC: U.S. Government Printing Office.

Hochschild, Arlie R. 1973. *The unexpected community*. Berkeley: University of California Press.

Hochschild, Arlie R. 1983. *The managed heart*. Berkeley: University of California Press.

Hodgson, Lynne Gershenson. 1995. Adult grandchildren and their grandparents: The enduring bond. Pp. 155–170 in Jon Hendricks (Ed.), *The ties of later life*. Amityville, NY: Baywood.

Hofferth, Sandra L. 2005. Secondary data analysis in family research. *Journal of Marriage and Family* 67:4:891–907.

Hoffman, Charles D., & Debra K. Ledford. 1995. Adult children of divorce: Relationships with their mothers and fathers prior to, following parental separation, and currently. *Journal of Divorce and Remarriage* 24:3/5:41–57.

Hohman, Leslie B. and Bertram Schaffner. 1947. The sex lives of unmarried men. *The American Journal of Sociology* 52:6:501–507.

Holden, Karen C., & Hsiang-Hui Daphne Kuo. 1996. Complex marital histories and economic well-being: The continuing legacy of divorce and widowhood as the HRS cohort approaches retirement. *The Gerontologist* 36:3:383–390.

Holstein, Martha B., & Meredith Minkler. 2003. Self, society, and the "New Gerontology." *The Gerontologist* 43:6:787–796.

Hooker, Karen, Deborah J. Monahan, Sally R. Bowman, Leslie D. Frazier, & Kim Shifren. 1998. Personality counts for a lot: Predictors of mental and physical health of spouse caregivers in two disease groups. *Journal of Gerontology: Psychological Sciences* 53B:2:P73-P85.

Hooyman, Nancy R., & Judith Gonyea. 1995. *Feminist perspectives on family care: Policies for gender justice.* Thousand Oaks, CA: Sage.

Hooyman, Nancy, & J. Asuman Kiyak. 1999. *Social gerontology: A multidisciplinary perspective,* 5th ed. Boston: Allyn & Bacon.

Hostetler, A. J. 2004. Old, gay and alone? The ecology of well-being among middle-aged and older single gay men, Pp. 143–176 in G. Herdt & B. de Vries (Eds.), *Gay and lesbian aging: Research and future directions.* New York: Springer.

Hughes, Mary Elizabeth, Linda J. Waite, Tracey A. LaPierre, & Ye Luo. 2007. All in the family: The impact of caring for grandchildren on grandparents' health. *Journal of Gerontology: Social Sciences* 62B:2:S108-S119.

Hull, Kathleen E. 2005. *Same-sex marriage: The cultural politics of love and law.* Cambridge & New York: Cambridge University Press.

Hunter, Andrea G. 1997. Counting on grandmothers: Black mothers' and fathers' reliance on grandmothers for parenting support. *Journal of Family Issues* 18:3:251–269.

Hunter, Ski. 2005. *Midlife and older LGBT adults: Knowledge and affirmative practice for the social services.* Binghamton, NY: Haworth.

Hurd Clarke, Laura. 2005. Remarriage in later life: Older women's negotiations of power, resources and domestic labor. *Journal of Women & Aging* 17:4:21–41.

Huston, M., & P. Schwartz. 1995. The relationships of lesbians and of gay men. Pp. 89–121 in Julia T. Wood & Steve Duck (Eds.), *Under-studied relationships: Off the beaten track.* Thousand Oaks, CA: Sage.

Huyck, Margaret Hellie. 1995. Marriage and close relationships of the marital kind. Pp. 181–200 in Rosemary Blieszner & Victoria Hilkevitch Bedford (Eds.), *Handbook of aging and the family.* Westport, CT: Greenwood.

Huyck, Margaret Hellie. 2001. Romantic relationships in later life. *Generations* 25:2:9–17.

I am single—More Canadians than ever before are choosing to live alone—and liking it. *Maclean's Magazine,* May 8, 2000.

Ikkink, Karen Klein, Theo van Tilberg, & Kees C. P. M. Knipscheer. 1999. Perceived instrumental support exchanges in relationships between elderly parents and their adult children: Normative and structural explanations. *Journal of Marriage and Family* 61:4:831–844.

Ingersoll-Dayton, Berit, Ruth Campbell, Yikiko Kurokawa, & Masahiko Saito. 1996. Separateness and togetherness: Interdependence over the life course in Japanese and American marriages. *Journal of Social and Personal Relationships* 13:3:385–398.

Ingersoll-Dayton, Berit, Maragaret B. Neal, Jun-hwa Ha, & Leslie B. Hammer. 2003. Collaboration among siblings providing care to adult parents. *Journal of Gerontological Social Work* 40:3:51–65.

Ingersoll-Dayton, Berit, Marjorie E. Starrels, & David Dowler. 1996. Caregiving for parents and parents-in-law: Is gender important? *The Gerontologist* 36:4:483–491.

Ishii-Kuntz, Masako, & Karen Seccombe. 1989. The impact of children upon social support networks throughout the life course. *Journal of Marriage and Family* 51 (Aug): 777–790.

Jackson, James S., Edna Brown, Toni C. Antonucci, & Svein Olav Daatland. 2005. Ethnic diversity in ageing: Multicultural societies. Pp. 476–481 in Malcolm L. Johnson (Ed.), *The Cambridge handbook of age and ageing.* Cambridge, UK: Cambridge University Press.

Jackson, James S., & Jyotsna Kalavar. 1993. Equity and distributive justice across age cohorts—A life-course family perspective: Comment on Bengtson and Murray. Pp. 175–183 in Lee M. Cohen (Ed.), *Justice across generations: What does it mean?* Washington, DC: American Association of Retired Persons.

Jackson, Richard, & Neil Howe. 2003. *An assessment of the capacity of twelve developed countries to meet the aging challenge.* Washington, D.C. Center for Strategic and International Studies.

Jacobson, Sharon, & Arnold H. Grossman. 1996. Older lesbians and gay men: Old myths, new images, and future directions. Pp. 345–373 in Ritch C. Savin-Williams & Kenneth M. Cohen (Eds.), *The lives of lesbians, gays, and bisexuals.* New York: Harcourt Brace.

Jacoby, S. 2005. Sex in America. *AARP The Magazine.* July/August. Retrieved October 29, 2008. http://www.aarpmagazine.org

Jacquet, Susan E., & Catherine A. Surra. 2001. Parental divorce and premarital couples: Commitment and other relationship characteristics. *Journal of Marriage and Family* 63:3:627–638.

Jeffries, Sherryl, & Candace Konnert. 2002. Regret and psychological well-being among voluntarily and involuntarily childless women and mothers. *International Journal of Aging and Human Development* 54:2:89–106.

Jendrek, Margaret Platt. 1994. Grandparents who parent their grandchildren: Circumstances and decisions. *The Gerontologist* 34:2:206–216.

Johnson, Colleen Leahy. 1985. The impact of illness on late-life marriages. *Journal of Marriage and Family* 47 (Feb): 165–172.

Johnson, Colleen Leahy. 1988a. Active and latent functions of grandparenting duties during the divorce process. *The Gerontologist* 28:2:185–191.

Johnson, Colleen Leahy. 1988b. *Ex familia: Grandparents, parents, and children adjust to divorce.* New Brunswick, NJ: Rutgers University Press.

Johnson, Colleen L. 1997. Should grandparents assume full parental responsibility? Pp. 178–183 in Andrew E. Scharlach & Lenard W. Kaye (Eds.), *Controversial issues in aging.* Boston: Allyn & Bacon.

Johnson, Colleen L., & Barbara M. Barer. 1995. Childlessness and kinship organization: Comparisons of very old Whites and Blacks. *Journal of Cross-Cultural Gerontology* 10:289–306.

Johnson, Colleen L., & Barbara M. Barer. 1997. *Life beyond 85 years: The aura of survivorship.* New York: Springer.

Johnson, Malcolm L. 1995. Interdependency and the generational compact. *Ageing and Society* 15:243–265.

Johnson, Paul, Christopher Conrad, & David Thomson. 1989. *Workers versus pensioners: Intergenerational justice in an ageing world.* Manchester, UK: Manchester University Press.

Johnson, Richard W., Usha Sambamoorthi, & Stephen Crystal. 1999. Gender differences in pension wealth: Estimates using provider data. *The Gerontologist* 39:3:320–333.

Joseph, A., & B. Hallman. 1996. Caught in the triangle: The influence of home, work and elder location on work-family balance. *Canadian Journal on Aging* 15:393–413.

Julien, Danielle, Elise Chartrand, & Jean Begin. 1999. Social networks, structural interdependence, and conjugal adjustment in heterosexual, gay, and lesbian couples. *Journal of Marriage and Family* 61 (May): 516–530.

Juska, Jane. 2003. *A round-heeled woman: My late-life adventures in sex and romance.* New York: Villard.

Kaiser, Cheryl R., & Deborah A. Kashy. 2005. The contextual nature and function of singlism. *Psychological Inquiry* 16:2&3:122–126.

Kalmijn, Matthijs. 2006. Educational inequality and family relationships: Influences on contact and proximity. *European Sociological Review* 22:1:1–16.

Kalmijn, Matthijs, & Wim Bernasco. 2001. Joint and separated lifestyles in couple relationships. *Journal of Marriage and Family* 63:3:639–654.

Kalmijn, Matthijs, Paul M. De Graaf, & Anne-Rigt Poortman. 2004. Interactions between cultural and economic determinants of divorce in the Netherlands. *Journal of Marriage and Family* 66:1:74–89.

Kane, Robert L., & Rosalie A. Kane. 2005. Long term care. Pp. 638–646 in Malcolm L. Johnson (Ed.), *The Cambridge handbook of age and ageing* Cambridge, UK: Cambridge University Press.

Kane, Rosalie A., & Joan D. Penrod. 1995. Toward a caregiving policy for the aging family. Pp. 144–185 in Rosalie A. Kane & Joan D. Penrod (Eds.), *Family caregiving in an aging society: Policy perspectives.* Thousand Oaks, CA: Sage.

Kane, Rosalie A., & Keren Brown Wilson. 2007. Improving practice through research in and about assisted living: Implications for a research agenda. *The Gerontologist* 47 (Special Issue) III:4–7.

Kapp, Marshall B. 1995. Legal and ethical issues in family caregiving and the role of public policy. Pp. 123–143 in Rosalie A. Kane & Joan D. Penrod (Eds.), *Family caregiving in an aging society: Policy perspectives.* Thousand Oaks, CA: Sage.

Karasik, Rona J. 2006. Siblings of adults with developmental disabilities: Views from middle age and later life. *Report* 51:3:F15-F16.

Katz, Marilyn Ogus. 2006. What's really going on here? The therapist's perspective. Pp. 211–228 in Nan Bauer-Maglin (Ed.), *Cut loose: (Mostly) older women talk about the end of (mostly) long-term relationships.* New Brunswick NJ: Rutgers University Press.

Katz, Ruth, Ariela Lowenstein, Judith Phillips, & Svein Olav Daatland. 2005. Theorizing intergenerational family relations: Solidarity, conflict, and ambivalence in cross-national contexts. Pp. 393–407 in Vern L. Bengtson, Alan C. Acock, Katherine R. Allen, Peggye Dilworth-Anderson, & David M. Klein. (Eds.),

Sourcebook of family theory and research. Thousand Oaks, CA: Sage.

Katz, Stephen. 2005. *Cultural aging: Life course, life style, and senior worlds.* Peterborough, Ontario, Canada: Broadview.

Katz, Stephen H., & Barbara Marshall. 2003. New sex for old: Lifestyle, consumerism and the politics of aging well. *Journal of Aging Studies* 14:2:135–151.

Kaufman, Gayle, & Hiromi Taniguchi. 2006. Gender and marital happiness in later life. *Journal of Family Issues* 27:6:737–757.

Kaufman, Gayle, & Peter Uhlenberg. 1998. Effects of life course transitions on the quality of relationships between adult children and their parents. *Journal of Marriage and Family* 60 (November): 924–938.

Keating, Norah C., & Priscilla Cole. 1980. What do I do with him 24 hours a day? Changes in the housewife role after retirement. *The Gerontologist* 20:1:84–89.

Keating, Norah C., Janet E. Fast, Ingrid A. Connidis, Margaret Penning, & Janice Keefe. 1997. Bridging policy and research in eldercare. *Canadian Journal on Aging/Canadian Public Policy* (Suppl.): 22–41.

Keefe, Janice, & Pamela Fancey. 2000. The care continues: Responsibility for elderly relatives before and after admission to a long term care facility. *Family Relations* 49:3:235–244.

Keith, Pat M. 1985. Financial well-being of older divorced/separated men and women: Findings from a panel study. *Journal of Divorce* 9:1:61–72.

Keith, Patricia M., & Robert B. Schafer. 1985. Equity, role strains, and depression among middle-aged and older men and women. Pp. 37–39 in Warren A. Peterson & Jill Quadagno (Eds.), *Social bonds in later life.* Beverly Hills, CA: Sage.

Keith, Pat M., Robert B. Schafer, & Robbyn Wacker. 1995. Outcomes of equity/inequity among older spouses. Pp. 9–19 in Jon Hendricks (Ed.), *The ties of later life.* Amityville, NY: Baywood.

Kelley, Harold H. 1981. Marriage relationships and aging. Pp. 275–300 in James G. March, Robert W. Fogel, Elaine Hatfield, Sara B. Kiesler, & Ethel Shanas (Eds.), *Aging, stability and change in the family.* Toronto: Academic Press.

Kemp, Candace L. 2003. The social and demographic contours of contemporary grandparenthood: Mapping patterns in Canada and the United States. *Journal of Comparative Family Studies* 34:2:187–212.

Kemp, Candace L. 2004. 'Grand' expectations: The experiences of grandparents and adult grandchildren. *Canadian Journal of Sociology* 29:4:499–525.

Kemp, Candace L. 2005. Dimensions of grandparent-adult grandchild relationships: From family ties to intergenerational friends. *Canadian Journal on Aging* 24:2:161–178.

Kemp, Candace L. 2007. Grandparent-grandchild ties: Reflections on continuity and change across three generations. *Journal of Family Issues* 23:855–881.

Kendig, Hal L. 1986. Intergeneration exchange. Pp. 85–109 in Hal L. Kendig (Ed.), *Ageing and families: A social networks perspective.* Boston: Allen & Unwin.

Kendig, Hal, Pearl A. Dykstra, Ruben I. van Galen, & Tuula Melkas. 2007. Health of aging parents and childless individuals. *Journal of Family Issues* 28:11:1457–1486.

Kennedy, Gregory E., & C. E. Kennedy. 1993. Grandparents: A special resource for children in stepfamilies. *Journal of Divorce and Remarriage* 19:3/4:45–68.

Kestin van den Hoonaard, D. 2001. *The widowed self: The older woman's journey through widowhood.* Waterloo, Ontario, Canada: Wilfrid Laurier University Press.

Kestin van den Hoonaard, D. 2007. Aging and masculinity: A topic whose time has come. *Journal of Aging Studies* 21:4:277–280.

Killian, Timothy S. 2004. Intergenerational monetary transfers to adult children and stepchildren: A household level of analysis. *Journal of Divorce & Remarriage* 42:1/2:105–130.

Kimmel, D. C. 1992. The families of older gay men and lesbians. *Generations* (Summer): 37–38.

Kimmel, Michael S. 2000. *The gendered society.* New York: Oxford University Press.

King, Neal, & Toni Calasanti. 2006. Empowering the old: Critical gerontology and anti-aging in a global context. Pp. 139– 157 in Jaan Baars, Dale Dannefer, Chris Phillipson, & Alan Walker (Eds.), *Aging, globalization and inequality: The new critical gerontology.* Amityville, NY: Baywood.

King, Valarie. 2003. The legacy of a grandparent's divorce: Consequences for ties between grandparents and grandchildren. *Journal of Marriage and Family* 65:170–183.

King, Valarie, & Glen H. Elder Jr. 1995. American children view their grandparents: Linked lives across three rural generations. *Journal of Marriage and Family* 57:1:165–178.

King, Valarie, & Glen H. Elder Jr. 1997. The legacy of grandparenting: Childhood experiences with grandparents and current involvement with grandchildren. *Journal of Marriage and Family* 59 (November): 848–859.

King, Valarie, & Mindy E. Scott. 2005. A comparison of cohabiting relationships among older and younger adults. *Journal of Marriage and Family* 67:2:271–285.

Kinsella, Kevin. 1995. Aging and the family: Present and future demographic issues. Pp. 32–56 in Rosemary Blieszner & Victoria Hilkevitch Bedford (Eds.), *Handbook of aging and the family.* Westport, CT: Greenwood.

Kirsi, Tapio, Antti Hervonen, & Marja Jylhä. 2000. A man's gotta do what a man's gotta do: Husbands as caregivers to their demented wives: A discourse analytic approach. *Journal of Aging Studies* 14:2:153–169.

Kitson, Gay C., Karen Benson Babri, Mary Joan Roach, & Kathleen S. Placidi. 1989. Adjustment to widowhood and divorce: A review. *Journal of Family Issues* 10:1:5–32.

Kivett, Vira. 1993. Racial comparisons of the grandmother role: Implications for strengthening the family support system of older Black women. *Family Relations* 42:165–178.

Kivnick, Helen Q. 1985. Grandparenthood and mental health: Meaning, behavior, and satisfaction. Pp. 151–158 in Vern L. Bengtson & Joan R. Robertson (Eds.), *Grandparenthood.* Beverly Hills, CA: Sage.

Kohli, Martin. 2005. Generational changes and generational equity. Pp. 518 –526 in Malcolm L. Johnson (Ed.), *The Cambridge handbook of age and ageing.* Cambridge, UK: Cambridge University Press.

Kohli, Martin. 2006. Aging and justice. Pp. 456–478 in Robert H. Binstock & Linda K. George (Eds.), *Handbook of aging and the social sciences,* 6th ed. New York: Academic Press, Elsevier.

Koropeckyj-Cox, Tanya. 1998. Loneliness and depression in middle and old age: Are the childless more vulnerable? *Journal of Gerontology: Social Sciences* 53B:6:S303-S312.

Koropeckyj-Cox, Tanya. 1999. *Distressed parents and happy childless: The conditional link between parental status and subjective well-being.* Paper presented at the American Sociological Association Annual Meetings. August. Chicago.

Koropeckyj-Cox, Tanya. 2002. Beyond parental status: Psychological well-being in middle and old age. *Journal of Marriage and Family* 64:957–971.

Koropeckyj-Cox, Tanya. 2005. Singles, society, and science: Sociological perspectives. *Psychological Inquiry* 16:2&3:91–97.

Koropeckyj-Cox, Tanya, & Gretchen Pendell. 2007. The gender gap in attitudes about childlessness in the United States. *Journal of Marriage and Family* 69:4:899–915.

Koropeckyj-Cox, Tanya, & Vaughn R. A. Call. 2007. Characteristics of older childless persons and parents: Cross-national comparisons. *Journal of Family Issues* 28:10:1362–1414.

Kramer, Betty J. 1997. Differential predictors of strain and gain among husbands caring for wives with dementia. *The Gerontologist* 37:2:239–249.

Kramer, Betty J., & Stuart Kipnis. 1995. Eldercare and work conflict: Toward an understanding of gender differences in caregiver burden. *The Gerontologist* 35:3:340–348.

Krause, N., & Karen S. Rook. 2003. Negative interactions in late life: Issues in the stability and generalizability of conflict across relationships. *Journal of Gerontology: Psychological Sciences* 58B:P88-P99.

Krekula, Clary. 2007. The intersection of age and gender: Reworking gender theory and social gerontology. *Current Sociology* 55:2:155–171.

Kristiansen, Hans W. 2004. Narrating past lives and present concerns: Older gay men in Norway. Pp. 235–261 in Gilbert Herdt & Brian de Vries (Eds.), *Gay and lesbian aging: Research and future directions.* New York: Springer.

Kruk, Edward. 1995. Grandparent-grandchild contact loss: Findings from a study of "Grandparent Rights" members. *Canadian Journal on Aging* 14:4:737–754.

Kruk, Edward, & Barry L. Hall. 1995. The disengagement of paternal grandparents subject to divorce. *Journal of Divorce and Remarriage* 23:1/2:131–147.

Kulik, Liat. 2002. Marital equality and the quality of long-term marriage in later life. *Ageing & Society* 22:4:459–481.

Kurdek, Lawrence A. 1991. The relations between reported well-being and divorce history, availability of a proximate partner, and gender. *Journal of Marriage and Family* 53 (February): 71–78.

Kurdek, Lawrence A. 1992. Relationship stability and relationship satisfaction in cohabiting gay and lesbian couples: A prospective longitudinal test of the contextual and interdependence models. *Journal of Social and Personal Relationships* 9:125–142.

Kurdek, Lawrence A. 1994. Conflict resolution styles in gay, lesbian, heterosexual nonparent, and heterosexual parent couples. *Journal of Marriage and Family* 56 (August): 705–722.

Kurdek, Lawrence A. 1998. Relationship outcomes and their predictors: Longitudinal evidence from heterosexual married, gay cohabiting, and lesbian cohabiting couples. *Journal of Marriage and Family* 60 (August): 553–568.

Kurdek, Lawrence A. 2003. Differences between gay and lesbian cohabiting couples. *Journal of Social and Personal Relationships* 20:4:411–436.

Kurdek, Lawrence A. 2004. Are gay and lesbian cohabiting couples *really* different from heterosexual married couples? *Journal of Marriage and Family* 66:4:880–900.

Kurdek, Lawrence A. 2006. Differences between partners from heterosexual, gay, and lesbian cohabiting couples. *Journal of Marriage and Family* 68:2:509–528.

Kurz, Demie. 2002. Caring for teenage children. *Journal of Family Issues* 23:6:746–767.

Laird, Joan. 1996. Invisible ties: Lesbians and their families of origin. Pp. 89–122 in Joan Laird & Robert-Jay Green (Eds.), *Lesbians and gays in couples and families: A handbook for therapists.* San Francisco: Jossey-Bass.

Lampard, Richard, & Kay Peggs. 2007. *Identity and repartnering after separation.* New York: Pargrave Macmillan.

Landry-Meyer, Laura. 1999. Research into action: Recommended intervention strategies for grandparent caregivers. *Family Relations* 48:4:381–389.

Landry-Meyer, Laura, & Barbara M. Newman. 2004. An exploration of the grandparent caregiver role. *Journal of Family Issues* 25:8:1005–1025.

Lang, Frieder R. 2004. The filial task in midlife: Ambivalence and the quality of adult children's relationships with their older parents. Pp. 183–206 in Karl Pillemer & Kurt Lüscher (Eds.), *Intergenerational ambivalence: new perspectives on parent-child relationships in later life.* New York: Elsevier.

Lang, Frieder R., & Yvonne Schütze. 2002. Adult children's supportive behaviors and older parents' subjective well-being—A developmental perspective on intergenerational relationships. *Journal of Social Issues* 58:4:661–680.

Lansford, Jennifer E., Rosario Ceballo, Antonia Abbey, & Abigail J. Stewart. 2001. Does family structure matter? A comparison of adoptive, two-parent biological, single-mother, stepfather, and stepmother households. *Journal of Marriage and Family* 63:3:840–851.

LaRossa, Ralph. 2005. Grounded theory methods and qualitative family research. *Journal of Marriage and Family* 67:4:837–857.

Larsen, Luke J. 2004. The foreign-born population in the United States: 2003. *Current Population Reports.* (August): 20–551. Washington, DC: U.S. Census Bureau.

Lashewicz, Bonnie, Gerald Manning, Margaret Hall, & Norah Keating. 2007. Equity matters: Doing fairness in the context of family caregiving. *Canadian Journal on Aging* 26 (Suppl. 1): 91–102.

Laslett, Barbara. 1978. Family membership, past and present. *Social Problems* 25:5:476–490.

Lauer, Robert H., Jeanette C. Lauer, & Sarah T. Kerr. 1995. The long-term marriage: Perceptions of stability and satisfaction. Pp. 35–41 in Jon Hendricks (Ed.), *The ties of later life.* Amityville, NY: Baywood.

Law Commission of Canada. 2004. *Does age matter: Law and relationships between generations.* Ottawa, Canada: Author. Catalogue #JL2–23/2003.

Le Bourdais, Celine, Evelyne Lapierre-Adamcyk, & Philippe Pacaut. 2004. Changes in conjugal life in Canada: Is cohabitation progressively replacing marriage? *Journal of Marriage and Family* 66:9:29–42.

Leder, Jan Mersky. 2006. *Thanks for the memories: Love, sex, and World War II.* Westport, CT: Praeger.

Lee, Eunju, Glenna Spitze, & John R. Logan. 2003. Social support to parents-in-law: The interplay of gender and kin hierarchies. *Journal of Marriage and Family* 65:2:396–403.

Lee, Gary R., Jeffrey W. Dwyer, & Raymond T. Coward. 1993. Gender differences in parent care: Demographic factors and same gender preferences. *Journal of Gerontology: Social Sciences* 48:1:S9-S16.

Lee, Gary R., Chuck W. Peek, & Raymond T. Coward. 1998. Race differences in filial responsibility expectations among older parents. *Journal of Marriage and Family* 60:2:404–412.

Lee, Gary R., Marion C. Willetts, & Karen Seccombe. 1998. Widowhood and depression: Gender differences. *Research on Aging* 20:5:611–630.

Lee, John Alan. 1989. Invisible men: Canada's aging homosexuals. Can they be assimilated into Canada's "liberated" gay communities? *Canadian Journal on Aging* 8:1:79–97.

Lee, John Alan. 1990. Can we talk? Can we really talk? Communication as a key factor in the maturing homosexual couple. *Journal of Homosexuality* 20:3–4:143–168.

Lee, Thomas R., Jay A. Mancini, & Joseph W. Maxwell. 1990. Sibling relationships in adulthood: Contact patterns and motivations. *Journal of Marriage and Family* 52 (May): 431–440.

Lerner, Melvin J., Darryl G. Somers, David Reid, David Chiriboga, & Mary Tierney. 1991. Adult children as caregivers: Egocentric biases in judgments of sibling contributions. *The Gerontologist* 31:6:746–755.

Letiecq, Bethany, Sandra J. Bailey, & Marcia A. Kurtz. 2008. Depression among rural Native American and European American grandparents rearing their grandchildren. *Journal of Family Issues* 29:3:334–356.

Letter to the editor. 1999. *Maclean's Magazine.* Aug 23:4.

Lettke, Frank, & David M. Klein. 2004. Methodological issues in assessing ambivalences in intergenerational relations. Pp. 85–113 in Karl Pillemer & Kurt Lüscher (Eds.), *Intergenerational ambivalences: New perspectives on parent-child relations in later life.* New York: Elsevier.

Lieberman, Morton A., & Lawrence Fisher. 1999. The effects of family conflict resolution and decision making on the provision of help for an elder with Alzheimer's disease. *The Gerontologist* 39:2:159–166.

Lin, Ge, & Peter A. Rogerson. 1995. Elderly parents and the geographic availability of their adult children. *Research on Aging* 17:3:303–331.

Linsk, Nathan L., Sharon M., Keigher, Suzanne E. England, & Lori Simon-Rusinowitz. 1995. Compensation of family care for the elderly. Pp. 64–91 in Rosalie A. Kane & Joan D. Penrod (Eds.), *Family caregiving in an aging society: Policy perspectives.* Thousand Oaks, CA: Sage.

Litwak, Eugene. 1985. *Helping the elderly: The complementary roles of informal networks and formal systems.* New York: Guilford.

Logan, John R., & Glenna D. Spitze. 1996. *Family ties: Enduring relations between parents and their grown children.* Philadelphia: Temple University Press.

Loomis, Laura Spencer, & Alan Booth. 1995. Multigenerational caregiving and well-being: The myth of the beleaguered sandwich generation. *Journal of Family Issues* 16:2:131–148.

Lopata, Helena Znaniecka. 1996. *Current widowhood: Myths and realities.* Thousand Oaks, CA: Sage.

Lorenz-Meyer, Dagmar. 2004. The ambivalences of parental care among young German adults. Pp. 225–252 in Karl Pillemer & Kurt Lüscher (Eds.), *Intergenerational ambivalence: New perspectives on parent-child relationships in later life.* New York: Elsevier.

Loseke, Donileen R., Richard J. Gelles, & Mary M. Cavanaugh (Eds.). 2005a. *Current controversies on family violence,* 2nd ed. Thousand Oaks, CA: Sage.

Loseke, Donileen R., Richard J. Gelles, & Mary M. Cavanaugh. 2005b. Introduction: Understanding controversies on family violence. Pp. ix–xxiv in Donileen R. Loseke, Richard J. Gelles, & Mary M. Cavanaugh (Eds.), *Current controversies on family violence,* 2nd ed. Thousand Oaks, CA: Sage.

Lupri, Eugen, & James Frideres. 1981. The quality of marriage and the passage of time: Marital satisfaction over the family life cycle. *Canadian Journal of Sociology* 6:3:282–305.

Lüscher, Kurt. 2002. Intergenerational ambivalence: Further steps in theory and research. *Journal of marriage and family* 64:3:585–593.

Lüscher, Kurt. 2004. Conceptualizing and uncovering intergenerational ambivalence. Pp. 23–62 in Karl Pillemer & Kurt Lüscher (Eds.), *Intergenerational ambivalences: New perspectives on parent-child relations in later life.* New York: Elsevier.

Lüscher, Kurt, & Karl Pillemer. 1998. Intergenerational ambivalence: A new approach to the study of parent-child relations in later life. *Journal of Marriage and Family* 60:2:413–425.

Lynott, Patricia Passuth, & Robert E. L. Roberts. 1997. The developmental stake hypothesis and changing perceptions of intergenerational relations. *The Gerontologist* 37:3:394–405.

Mack, Kristin Y. 2004. The effects of early parental death on sibling relationships in later life. *Omega* 49:2:131–148.

Mackey, Richard A., Matthew A. Diemer, & Bernard A. O'Brien. 2004. Relational factors in understanding satisfaction in the lasting relationships of same-sex and heterosexual couples. *Journal of Homosexuality* 47:1:111–136.

MacRae, Hazel. 1992. Fictive kin as a component of the social networks of older people. *Research on Aging* 14:2:226–247.

MacRae, Hazel. 1998. Managing feelings: Caregiving as emotion work. *Research on Aging* 20:1:137–160.

Mahay, Jenna, & Alisa C. Lewin. 2007. Age and the desire to marry. *Journal of Family Issues* 28:5:706–723.

Mahoney, Sarah. 2003, September 23. Seeking love. *AARP The Magazine Online.* Retrieved October 29, 2008. http://www.aarpmagazine.org/lifestyle/Articles/a2003-09-23-seekinglove

Manalansan, Martin F., IV. 1996. Double minorities: Latino, Black, and Asian men who have sex with men. Pp. 393–415 in Ritch C. Savin-Williams & Kenneth M Cohen (Eds.), *The lives of lesbians, gays, and bisexuals.* FortWorth, TX: Harcourt Brace.

Mann, Robin. 2007. Out of the shadows?: Grandparenthood, age and masculinities. *Journal of Aging Studies* 21:4:281–291.

Mann, Susan A., Michael D. Grimes, Alice Abel Kemp, & Pamela J. Jenkins. 1997. Paradigm shifts in family sociology? Evidence from three decades of family textbooks. *Journal of Family Issues* 18:3:315–349.

Marks, Nadine F. 1996. Flying solo at midlife: Gender, marital status, and psychological well-being. *Journal of Marriage and Family* 58 (Nov): 917–932.

Marks, Nadine F. 1998. Does it hurt to care? Caregiving, work-family conflict, and midlife well-being. *Journal of Marriage and Family* 60:4:951–966.

Marshall, Barbara L., & Stephen Katz. 2006. From androgyny to androgens. Pp. 75–97 in Toni M. Calasanti & Kathleen F. Slevin (Eds.), *Age matters: Realigning feminist thinking.* New York: Routledge.

Marshall, Victor W. 1981. Societal tolerance of aging: Sociological theory and social response to population aging. Pp. 85–104 in *Adaptability and aging 1.* Paris: International Centre of Social Gerontology/Centre International de Gerontologie Sociale.

Marshall, Victor W. 1997. *The generations: Contributions, conflict, equity.* Report prepared for the Division of Aging and Seniors. Ottawa, Canada: Health Canada.

Marshall, Victor W., Fay Lomax Cook, & Joanne Gard Marshall. 1993. Conflict over intergenerational equity: Rhetoric and reality in a comparative context. Pp. 119–140 in Vern L. Bengtson & W. A. Achenbaum (Eds.), *The changing contract across generations.* New York: Aldine de Gruyter.

Marshall, Victor W., Sarah H. Matthews, & Carolyn J. Rosenthal. 1993. Elusiveness of family life: A challenge for the sociology of aging. Pp. 39–72 in G. L. Maddox & M. Powell Lawton (Eds.), *Annual review of gerontology and geriatrics, 13.* New York: Springer.

Marshall, Victor W., & Margaret M. Mueller. 2003. Theoretical roots of the life course perspective. Pp. 3–32 in Walter R. Heinz, & Victor W. Marshall (Eds.), *Social dynamics of the life course.* New York: Aldine de Gruyter.

Marsiglio, William, & Denise Donnelly. 1991. Sexual relations in later life: A national study of married persons. *Journal of Gerontology: Social Sciences* 46:6:S338–344.

Marsiglio, William, Kevin Roy, & Greer Litton Fox (Eds.) 2005. *Situated fathering: A focus on physical and social spaces.* New York: Rowman & Littlefield.

Martin, Terry L. 2002. Disenfranchising the brokenhearted. Pp. 233–250 in Kenneth J. Doka (Ed.). *Disenfranchised grief: New directions, challenges, and strategies for practice.* Champaign, IL: Research Press.

Martin Matthews, Anne. 1991. *Widowhood in later life.* Toronto: Butterworths/Harcourt.

Martin-Matthews, Anne. 1999. Widowhood: Dominant renditions, changing demography, and variable meaning. Pp. 27–46 in Sheila M. Neysmith (Ed.), *Critical issues for future social work practice with aging persons.* New York: Columbia University Press.

Martin-Matthews, Anne. 2000a. Change and diversity in aging families and intergenerational relations. Pp. 323–359 in Nancy Mandell & Ann Duffy (Eds.), *Canadian families: Diversity, conflict, and change,* 2nd ed. Toronto: Harcourt Brace.

Martin-Matthews, Anne. 2000b. Intergenerational caregiving: How apocalyptic and dominant demographies form the questions and shape the answers. Pp. 80–79 in Ellen M. Gee & Gloria M. Guttman (Eds.), *The overselling of population aging: Apocalyptic demography, intergenerational challenges, and social policy.* Don Mills, Ontario, Canada: Oxford University Press.

Martin-Matthews, Anne. 2007. Situating 'home' at the nexus of the public and private spheres: Ageing, gender, and home support work in Canada. *Current Sociology* 55:2:229–249.

Martin Matthews, Anne, & Lori D. Campbell. 1995. Gender roles, employment, and informal care. Pp. 129–143 in Sara Arber & Jay Ginn (Eds.), *Connecting gender and aging: Sociological reflections.* Philadelphia: Open University Press.

Martin Matthews, Anne, & Janice M. Keefe. 1995. Work and care of elderly people: A Canadian perspective. Pp. 116–138 in J. Phillips (Ed.), *Working carers: International perspectives on working and caring for older people.* Aldershot, England: Avebury.

Martin Matthews, Anne, & Carolyn J. Rosenthal. 1993. Balancing work and family in an aging society: The Canadian experience. Pp. 96–122 in George Maddox & M. Powell Lawton (Eds.), *Annual review of gerontology and geriatrics, 13.* New York: Springer.

Masheter, Carol. 1991. Postdivorce relationships between ex-spouses: The roles of attachment and interpersonal conflict. *Journal of Marriage and Family* 53 (Feb): 103–110.

Mason, Mary Ann. 1998. The modern American stepfamily: Problems and possibilities. Pp. 95–115 in Mary Ann Mason, Arlene Skolnick, & Stephen D. Sugarman (Eds.), *All our families: New policies for a new century.* New York: Oxford University Press.

Mason, Mary Ann, & Jane Mauldon. 1999. The new stepfamily requires a new public policy. Pp. 387–394 in Cheryl M. Albers (Ed.), *Sociology of families: Readings.* Thousand Oaks, CA: Pine Forge.

Matthews, Ralph D., & Anne Martin Matthews. 1986. Infertility and involuntary childlessness: The transition to nonparenthood. *Journal of Marriage and Family* 48:641–649.

Matthews, Sarah H. 1994. Men's ties to siblings in old age: Contributing factors in availability and quality. Pp. 178–196 in Edward H. Thompson (Ed.), *Older men's lives.* Thousand Oaks, CA: Sage.

Matthews, Sarah H. 1995. Gender and the division of filial responsibility between lone sisters and their brothers. *Journal of Gerontology: Social Sciences* 50B:5:S312-S320.

Matthews, Sarah H. 2002a. Brothers and parent care: An explanation of son's under-representation. Pp. 234–249 in B. J. Kramer & E. H. Thompson Jr. (Eds.), *Men as caregivers: Theory, research, and service implications.* New York: Springer.

Matthews, Sarah H. 2002b. *Sisters and brothers, daughters and sons: Meeting the needs of old parents.* Bloomington, IN: Unlimited Publishing.

Matthews, Sarah H., & Jenifer Heidorn. 1998. Meeting filial responsibilities in brothers-only sibling groups. *Journal of Gerontology: Social Sciences* 53B:5:S278-S286.

Matthews, Sarah H., & Jetse Sprey. 1985. Adolescents' relationships with grandparents: An empirical contribution to conceptual clarification. *Journal of Gerontology* 40:5:621–626.

Matthews, Sarah H., & Rongjun Sun. 2006. Incidence of four-generation family lineages: Is timing of fertility or mortality a better explanation. *Journal of Gerontology: Social Sciences* 61B:2:S99-S106.

Matthias, Ruth E., James E. Lubben, Kathryn A. Atchison, & Stuart O. Schweitzer. 1997. Sexual activity and satisfaction among very old adults: Results from a community-dwelling Medicare population survey. *The Gerontologist* 37:1:6–14.

Mauthner, Melanie. 2000. Bringing silent voices into a public discourse: Researching accounts of sister relationships. Pp. 78–105 in Jane Catherine Ribbens & Rosalind A. Edwards (Eds.), *Feminist dilemmas in qualitative research: Public knowledge and private lives.* Thousand Oaks, CA: Sage.

McAdoo, Harriette Pipes, Estalla A. Martínez, & Hester Hughes. 2005. Ecological changes in ethnic families of color. Pp. 191–205 in Vern L. Bengtson, Alan C. Acock, Katherine R. Allen, Peggye Dilworth-Anderson, & David M. Klein (Eds.), *Sourcebook of family theory & research.* Thousand Oaks, CA: Sage.

McConville, Brigid. 1985. *Sisters: Love and conflict within the lifelong bond.* London: Pan.

McDaniel, Susan A. 1997. Intergenerational transfers, social solidarity, and social policy: Unanswered questions and policy challenges. *Canadian PUBLIC Policy/Canadian Journal on Aging* (Suppl): 1–21.

McDaniel, Susan A. 2000. What did you ever do for me?: Intergenerational linkages in a restructuring Canada. Pp. 130–152 in Ellen M. Gee & Gloria M. Gutman (Eds.), *The overselling of population aging: Apocalyptic demography, intergenerational challenges, and social policy.* Don Mills, Ontario, Canada: Oxford University Press.

McDill, Tandace, Sharon K. Hall, & Susan C. Turell. 2006. Aging and creating families: Never-married heterosexual women over forty. *Journal of Women & Aging* 18:3:37–50.

McDonald, Lynn. 1997. The invisible poor: Canada's retired widows. *Canadian Journal on Aging* 16:3:553–583.

McGarry, Kathleen, & Robert F. Schoeni. 1997. Transfer behavior within the family: Results from the asset and health dynamics study. *Journal of Gerontology* Series B:52B (Special Issue): 82–92.

McGhee, Jerrie L. 1985. The effects of siblings on the life satisfaction of the rural elderly. *Journal of Marriage and Family* 47 (February): 85–91.

McGraw, Lori A., & Alexis J. Walker. 2007. Meanings of sisterhood and developmental disability: Narratives from white nondisabled sisters. *Journal of Family Issues* 28:4:474–500.

McLaren, Leah. 2000, February 12. The man glut. *The Globe and Mail* R1, R6.

McMullin, Julie. 2004. *Understanding social inequality: Intersections of class, age, gender, ethnicity, and race in Canada*. Don Mills, Ontario: Oxford University Press.

McMullin, Julie Ann, & Ellie D. Berger. 2006. Gendered ageism/Age(ed) sexism: The case of unemployed older workers. Pp. 201–223 in Toni M. Calasanti & Kathleen F. Slevin (Eds.), *Age matters: Realigning feminist thinking*. New York: Routledge.

McMullin, Julie Ann, & Victor W. Marshall. 1996. Family friends, stress, and wellbeing: Does childlessness make a difference? *Canadian Journal on Aging* 15:3:355–373.

McQuillan, Julia, Arther L. Greil, Lynn White, & Mary Casey Jacob. 2003. Frustrated fertility: Infertility and psychological distress among women. *Journal of Marriage and Family* 65:4:1007–1018.

Meadows, Robert, & Kate Davidson. 2006. Maintaining manliness in later life: Hegemonic masculinities and emphasized femininities. Pp. 295–312 in Toni M. Calasanti & Kathleen F. Slevin (Eds.), *Age matters: Realigning feminist thinking*. New York: Routledge.

Medley, Morris L. 1977. Marital adjustment in the post-retirement years. *The Family Coordinator* 26:1:5–11.

Merrill, Deborah M. 1997. *Caring for elderly parents: Juggling work, family, and caregiving in middle and working class families*. Westport, CT: Auburn House.

Merrill, Deborah M. 2007. *Mothers-in-law and daughters-in-law*. Westport, CN: Praeger.

Merton, Robert K. 1968. *Social theory and social structure*. Glencoe, IL: Free Press.

Meyer, Madonna Harrington, & Marcia L. Bellas. 1995. U.S. old-age policy and the family. Pp. 264–283 in Rosemary Blieszner & Victoria Hilkevitch Bedford (Eds.), *Handbook of aging and the family*. Westport, CT: Greenwood.

Michaels, Walter Benn. 2006. *The trouble with diversity: How we learned to love identity and ignore inequality*. New York: Metropolitan Books, Henry Holt.

Milan, Anne. 2000. One hundred years of families. *Canadian Social Trends* (Spring): 4–17. Ottawa, Canada: Statistics Canada.

Milan, Anne, & Brian Hamm. 2003. Across the generations: Grandparents and grandchildren. *Canadian Social Trends* (Winter). Statistics Canada. Cat. No. 11–008.

Milardo, Robert M. 2005. Generative uncle and nephew relationships. *Journal of Marriage and Family* 67:5:1226–1236.

Milevsky, Avidan. 2004. Perceived parental marital satisfaction and divorce: Effects on sibling relations in emerging adults. *Journal of Divorce and Remarriage* 41:1/2:115–128.

Milevsky, Avidan. 2005. Compensatory patterns of sibling support in emerging adulthood: Variations in loneliness, self-esteem, depression and life satisfaction. *Journal of social and personal relationships* 22:743–755.

Millbank, Jenni. 1997. Lesbians, child custody, and the long lingering gaze of the law. Pp. 280–301 in Susan B. Boyd (Ed.), *Challenging the public/private divide: Feminism, law, and public policy*. Toronto: University of Toronto Press.

Miller, Baila. 1998. Family caregiving: Telling it like it is. *The Gerontologist* 38:4:510–513.

Miller, Baila, & Julie E. Kaufman. 1996. Beyond gender stereotypes: Spouse caregivers of persons with dementia. *Journal of Aging Studies* 10:3:189–204.

Miller-Day, Michelle A. 2004. *Communication among grandmothers, mothers, and adult daughters: A qualitative study*. Mahwah, NJ: Lawrence Erlbaum.

Mills, C. Wright. 1959. *The sociological imagination*. New York: Oxford University Press.

Mills, Terry L. 1999. When grandchildren grow up: Role transition and family solidarity among baby boomer grandchildren and their grandparents. *Journal of Aging Studies* 13:2:219–239.

Miner, Sonia, & Peter Uhlenberg. 1997. Intergenerational proximity and the social role of sibling neighbors after midlife. *Family Relations* 46:2:145–153.

Minkler, Meredith. 1999. Intergenerational households headed by grandparents: Contexts, realities, and implications for policy. *Journal of Aging Studies* 13:2:199–218.

Minkler, Meredith, & Esme Fuller-Thompson. 2005. African American grandparents raising grandchildren: A national study using the census 2000 American community survey. *Journal of Gerontology: Social Sciences* 60B:2:S82–S92.

Mitchell, Barbara A. 2000. The refilled "nest": Debunking the myth of families in crisis. Pp. 80–99 in Ellen M. Gee & Gloria M. Guttman (Eds.), *The overselling of population aging: Apocalyptic demography, intergenerational challenges, and social policy*. Don Mills, Ontario: Oxford University Press.

Mitchell, Barbara A. 2006. *The boomerang age: Transitions to adulthood in families*. New Brunswick, NJ: Aldine.

Mitchell, Barbara A., & Ellen M. Gee. 1996. "Boomerang kids" and midlife parental marital satisfaction. *Family Relations* 45 (October): 442–448.

Mitchell, Julia. 2007. Procreative mothers (sexual difference) and child-free sisters (gender). Pp. 163–188 in Jude Browne (Ed.), *The future of gender*. New York: Cambridge University Press.

Mock, Steven. 2002. Retirement intentions in same-sex couples. Pp. 81–86 in Douglas C. Kimmel, & Dawn Lundy Martin (Eds.), *Midlife and aging in gay America*. Binghamton, NY: Haworth.

Moen, Phyllis, & Kelly Chermack. 2005. Gender disparities in health: Strategic selection, careers, and cycles of control. *Journal of Gerontology: Series B.* 60B (Special Issue II): 99–108

Moen, Phyllis, & Scott Coltrane. 2005. Families, theories and social policy. Pp. 543–556 in Vern L. Bengtson, Alan C. Acock, Katherine R. Allen, Peggye Dilworth-Anderson, & David M. Klein (Eds.), *Sourcebook of family theory & research.* Thousand Oaks, CA: Sage.

Moen, Phyllis, & Donna Spencer. 2006. Converging divergences in age, gender, health, and well-being: Strategic selection in the third age. Pp. 127–144 in Robert H. Binstock & Linda K. George (Eds.), *Handbook of aging and the social sciences,* 6th ed. New York: Academic Press, Elsevier.

Moir, Rita. 2006. A small conclave of chairs. Pp. 73–75 in Lynne van Luven (Ed.), *Nobody's mother: Life without kids.* Surrey, British Columbia, Canada: TouchWood.

Monserud, Maria A. 2008. Intergenerational relationships and affectual solidarity between grandparents and young adults. *Journal of Marriage and Family* 70:1:182–195.

Montenegro, Xenia P. 2004. *The divorce experience: A study of divorce at midlife and beyond.* Washington, DC: American Association of Retired Persons. Retrieved October 29, 2008. http://www.aarp.org

Moore, Alinde J., & Dorothy C. Stratton. 2002. *Resilient widowers: Older men speak for themselves.* New York: Springer.

Moore, Alinde J., & Dorothy C. Stratton. 2004. The 'current women' in an older widower's life.' Pp. 121–142 in Kate Davidson and Graham Fennell (Eds.), *Intimacy in Later Life.* London, UK: Transaction Publishers.

Moore, Eric G., & Mark W. Rosenberg. 1997. *Growing old in Canada: Demographic and geographic perspectives.* Ottawa, Canada: Statistics Canada & ITP Nelson.

Morgan, Leslie A. 1992. Marital status and retirement plans: Do widowhood and divorce make a difference? Pp. 114–126 in Maximiliane Szinovacz, David J. Ekerdt, & Barbara H. Vinick (Eds.), *Families and retirement.* Newbury Park, CA: Sage.

Morrison, Peter A. 1990. Demographic factors reshaping ties to family and place. *Research on Aging* 12:4:399–408.

Moss, Barry F., & Andrew I. Schwebel. 1993. Defining intimacy in romantic relationships. *Family Relations* 42:1:31–37.

Moss, Miriam S., & Sidney Z. Moss. 1992. Themes in parent-child relationships when elderly parents move nearby. *Journal of Aging Studies* 6:3:259–271.

Moss, Sydney Z., & Miriam Moss. 1989. The impact of the death of an elderly sibling: Some considerations of a normative loss. *American Behavioral Scientist* 33:1:94–106.

Mouton, Charles P. 2003. Intimate partner violence and health status among older women. *Violence Against Women* 9:12:1465–1477.

Mouton, Charles P., Rebecca J. Rodabough, Susan L. D. Rovi, Julie L. Hurt, Melissa A. Talamantes, Robert G. Brzyski & Sandra K. Burge. 2004. Prevalence and 3-year incidence of abuse among postmenopausal women. *American Journal of Public Health* 94:4:605–612.

Mueller, Margaret M., & Glen H. Elder Jr. 2003. Family contingencies across generations: Grandparent-grandchild relationships in holistic perspective. *Journal of Marriage and Family* 65:2:404–417.

Mugford, Stephen, & Hal L. Kendig.1986. Social relations: Networks and ties. Pp. 38–59 in Hal L. Kendig (Ed.), *Aging and families: Social networks perspectives.* Boston: Allen & Unwin.

Mui, Ada C. 1995. Caring for frail elderly parents: A comparison of adult sons and daughters. *The Gerontologist* 35:1:86–93.

Mui, Ada C., Namkee G. Choi, & Abraham Monk. 1998. *Long-term care and ethnicity* Westport, CT: Auborn House.

Mullan, Joseph T. 1998. Aging and informal caregiving to people with HIV/AIDS. *Research on Aging* 20:6:712–738.

Murphy, Barbara, Hilary Schofield, Julie Nankervis, Sidney Bloch, Helen Herrman, & Bruce Singh. 1997. Women with multiple roles: The emotional impact of caring for ageing parents. *Ageing and Society* 17:277–291.

Murphy, Mike. 2004. Models of kinship from the developed world. Pp. 31–52 in Sarah Harper (Ed.), *Families in ageing societies: A multidisciplinary approach.* New York: Oxford University Press.

Murphy, Mike, Karen Glaser, & Emily Grundy. 1997. Marital status and long-term illness in Great Britain. *Journal of Marriage and Family* 59 (Feb): 156–164.

Mutschler, Phyllis H. 1994. From executive suite to production line: How employees in different occupations manage elder care responsibilities. *Research on Aging* 16:1:7–26.

National Center for Health Statistics. 2007. *Deaths.* Preliminary Data for 2005. Hyattsville, MD. September 12. http://www.cdc.gov/nchs/products/pubs/pubd/hestats/prelimdeaths05/prelimdeaths05.htm

National Economic Council. 1998. *Women and retirement security.* Washington, DC: National Economic Council Interagency Working Group on Social Security.

National Gay and Lesbian Task Force. 2000. *Outing age: Public policy issues affecting gay, lesbian, bisexual and transgender elders.* November. Washington, D.C.

Neal, Margaret B., N. J. Chapman, Berit Ingersoll-Dayton, & A. C. Emlen. 1993. *Balancing work and caregiving for children, adults, and elders.* Newbury Park, CA: Sage.

Neal, Margaret B., & Leslie B. Hammer. 2007. *Working couples caring for children and aging parents: Effects on work and well-being.* Mahwah, NJ: Lawrence Erlbaum.

Neal, Margaret B., Berit Ingersoll-Dayton, & Marjorie E. Starrels. 1997. Gender and relationship differences in caregiving patterns and consequences among employed caregivers. *The Gerontologist* 37:6:804–816.

Neal, Margaret B., Donna L. Wagner, Kathleen J. B. Bonn, & Kelly Niles-Yokum. 2008. Caring from a distance: Contemporary care issues. Pp. 107–128 in Anne Martin-Matthews & Judith E. Phillips (Eds.), *Aging and caring at the intersection of work and home life: Blurring the boundaries.* New York: Lawrence Erlbaum.

Nett, Emily M. 1993. *Canadian families: Past and present,* 2nd ed. Toronto: Butterworths.

Neugebauer-Visano, Robynne. 1995. Seniors and sexuality? Confronting cultural contradictions. Pp. 17–34 in Robynne Neugebauer-Visano (Ed.), *Seniors and sexuality: Experiencing intimacy in later life.* Toronto: Canadian Scholars' Press.

Newman, Jason T., Karen S. Rook, Masami Nishishiba, Dara H. Sorkin, & Tyrae L. Mahan. 2005. Understanding the relative importance of positive and negative social exchanges: Examining specific domains and appraisals. *Journal of Gerontology: Psychological Sciences* 60B:6:P304-P312.

Neysmith, Sheila M. 1991. From community care to a social model of care. Pp. 272–299 in C. T. Baines, P. M. Evans, & S. M. Neysmith (Eds.), *Women's caring: Feminist perspectives on social welfare*. Toronto: McClelland & Stewart.

Neysmith, Sheila M. 1995. Power in relationships of trust: A feminist analysis of elder abuse. Pp. 43–54 in Michael J. MacLean (Ed.), *Abuse & neglect of older Canadians: Strategies for change*. Toronto, Ontario, Canada: Canadian Association on Gerontology.

Norgard, Theresa M., &Willard L. Rodgers. 1997. Patterns of in-home care among elderly black and white Americans. *The Journal of Gerontology* Series B:52B:93–101.

Norris, Joan E. 1980. The social adjustment of single and widowed older women. *Essence* 4:3:135–144.

Nydegger, Corinne N. 1983. Family ties of the aged in cross-cultural perspective. *The Gerontologist* 23:1:26–32.

O'Brien, Carol-Anne, & Aviva Goldberg. 2000. Lesbians and gay men inside and outside families. Pp. 115–145 in Nancy Mandell & Ann Duffy (Eds.), *Canadian families: Diversity, conflict, and change*. Toronto: Harcourt Brace.

O'Brien, Mary. 1991. Never married older women. *Social Indicators Research* 24:301–315.

O'Bryant, Shirley. 1991. Older widows and independent lifestyles. *International Journal on Aging and Human Development* 32:1:41–51.

O'Connor, Deborah. 2006. Self-identifying as a caregiver: Exploring the positioning process. *Journal of Aging Studies* 21:2:165–174.

O'Rand, Angela M. 2003. The future of the life course: Late modernity and life course risks. Pp. 693–701 in Jeylan T. Mortimer & Michael J. Shanahan (Eds.), *Handbook of the life course*. New York: Kluwer Academic/Plenum.

O'Rand, Angela M. 2006. Stratification and the life course: Life course capital, life course risks, and social inequality. Pp. 145–162 in Robert H. Binstock & Linda K. George (Eds.), *Handbook of aging and the social sciences*, 6th ed. New York: Academic Press/Elsevier.

Olson, Laura Katz. 2003. *The not so golden years: Caregiving, the frail elderly, and the long-term care establishment*. New York: Rowman & Littlefield.

Orel, Nancy. 2006. Lesbian and bisexual women as grandparents: The centrality of sexual orientation in the grandparent-grandchild relationship. Pp. 175–194 in Douglas Kimmel, Tara Rose, & Steven David (Eds.), *Lesbian, gay, bisexual, and transgender aging: Research and clinical perspectives*. New York: Columbia University Press.

Ory, Marcia G., Richard R. Hoffman III, Jennifer L. Yee, Sharon Tennstedt, & Richard Schulz. 1999. Prevalence and impact of caregiving: A detailed comparison between dementia and nondementia caregivers. *The Gerontologist* 39:2:177–185.

Ory, Marcia G., Diane L. Zablotsky, & Stephen Crystal. 1998. HIV/AIDS and aging: Identifying a prevention research and care agenda. *Research on Aging* 20:6:637–652.

Parrott, Tonya M., & Vern L. Bengtson. 1999. The effects of earlier intergenerational affection, normative expectations, and family conflict on contemporary exchanges of help and support. *Research on Aging* 21:1:73–105.

Parsons, Jeanette, & Joseph A. Tindale. 2001. Parents who sue their adult children for support: An examination of decisions by Canadian courts. *Canadian Journal on Aging* 20:4:451–470.

Pasupathi, Monisha, & Laura L. Carstensen. 2003. Age and emotional experience during mutual reminiscing. *Psychology and Aging* 18:3:430–442.

Patterson, Charlotte J. 1996. Lesbian and gay parents and their children. Pp. 274–302 in Ritch C. Savin-Williams & Kenneth M. Cohen (Eds.), *The lives of lesbians, gays, and bisexuals: Children to adults*. New York: Harcourt Brace.

Patterson, Charlotte J. 2008. Sexual orientation across the life span: Introduction to the special section. *Developmental Psychology* 44:1:1–4.

Peacock, Molly. 1998. *Paradise, piece by piece*. Toronto: McClelland & Stewart.

Pearson, Jane L. 1993. Parents' reactions to their children's separation and divorce at two and four years: Parent gender and grandparent status. *Journal of Divorce and Remarriage* 20:3/4:25–43.

Pearson, Jane L., Andrea G. Hunter, Joan M. Cook, Nicholas S. Ialongo, & Sheppard G. Kellam. 1997. Grandmother involvement in child caregiving in an urban community. *The Gerontologist* 37:5:650–657.

Peek, Chuck W., John C. Henretta, Raymond T. Coward, R. Paul Duncan, & Molly C. Dougherty. 1997. Race and residence variations in living arrangements among unmarried older adults. *Research on Aging* 19:1:46–68.

Peek, Kristen M., Raymond T. Coward, & Chuck W. Peek. 2000. Race, aging, and care: Can differences in family and household structure account for race variations in informal care. *Research on Aging* 22:2:117–142.

Penning, Margaret J. 1998. In the middle: Parental caregiving in the context of other roles. *Journal of Gerontology: Social Sciences* 53B:4:S188-S197.

Penning, Margaret J., & Norah C. Keating. 2000. Self-, informal and formal care: Partnerships in community-based and residential long-term care settings. *Canadian Journal on Aging* 19 (Suppl.): 75–100.

Penrod, Joan D., Rosalie A. Kane, Robert L. Kane, & Michael D. Finch. 1995. Who cares: The size, scope, and composition of the caregiver support system. *The Gerontologist* 35:4:489–497.

Peplau, Letitia Anne, & Adam W. Fingerhut. 2007. The close relationships of lesbians and gay men. *Annual Review of Psychology* 58:405–424.

Peplau, Letitia Anne, Rosemary C. Veneigas, & Susan Miller Campbell. 1996. Gay and lesbian relationships. Pp. 250–269 in Ritch C. Savin-Williams & Kenneth M. Cohen (Eds.), *The lives of lesbians, gays, and bisexuals*. Fort Worth, TX: Harcourt Brace.

Peters, Arnold, & Aart C. Liefbroer. 1997. Beyond marital status: Partner history and well-being in old age. *Journal of Marriage and Family* 59 (Aug): 687–699.

Peters, Cheryl L., Karen Hooker, & Anisa M. Zvonkovic. 2006. Older parents' perceptions of ambivalence in relationships with their children. *Family Relations* 55:539–551.

Peters-Davis, Norah D., Miriam S. Moss, & Rachel A. Pruchno. 1999. Children-in-law in caregiving families. *The Gerontologist* 39:1:66–75.

Peterson, Candida C. 1995. Husbands' and wives' perceptions of marital fairness across the family life cycle. Pp. 43–53 in Jon Hendricks (Ed.), *The ties of later life*. Amityville, NY: Baywood.

Peterson, Nancy L. 1982. *The ever single woman: Life without marriage*. New York: Quill.

Pfohl, Stephen J. 1985. *Images of deviance and social control: A sociological history*. New York: McGraw-Hill.

Pfohl, Stephen J. 1994. *Images of deviance and social control: A sociological history*, 2nd ed. New York: McGraw-Hill.

Phillips, Judith E., & Miriam Bernard. 2008. Work and care: Blurring the boundaries of space, place, time, and distance. Pp. 85–105 in Anne Martin-Matthews & Judith E. Phillips (Eds.), *Aging and caring at the intersection of work and home life: Blurring the boundaries*. New York: Lawrence Erlbaum.

Phillips, Julie A., & Megan M. Sweeney. 2005. Premarital cohabitation and marital disruption among white, black, and Mexican American women. *Journal of Marriage and Family* 67:2:296–314.

Phillipson, Chris. 2006. Aging and globalization: Issues for critical gerontology and political economy. Pp. 43–58 in Jaan Baars, Dale Dannefer, Chris Phillipson, & Alan Walker (Eds.), *Aging, globalization and inequality: The new critical gerontology*. Amityville, NY: Baywood.

Piercy, Kathleen W. 1998. Theorizing about family caregiving: The role of responsibility. *Journal of Marriage and Family* 60 (Feb): 109–118.

Pillemer, Karl. 1985. The dangers of dependency: New findings on domestic violence against the elderly. *Social Problems* 33:2:146–158.

Pillemer, Karl. 1986. Risk factors in elder abuse: Results from a case-control study. Pp. 239–263 in Karl A. Pillemer & Rosalie Wolf (Eds.), *Elder abuse: Conflict in the family*. Dover, MA: Auburn House.

Pillemer, Karl. 2004. Can't live with 'em, can't live without 'em: Older mothers' ambivalence toward their adult children. Pp. 115–132 in Karl Pillemer & Kurt Lüscher (Eds.), *Intergenerational ambivalences: New perspectives on parent-child relations in later life*. New York: Elsevier.

Pillemer, Karl. 2005. Elder abuse is caused by the deviance and dependence of abusive caregivers. Pp. 207–220 in Donileen R Loseke, Richard J. Gelles, & Mary M. Cavanaugh (Eds.), *Current controversies on family violence*, Thousand Oaks, CA: Sage.

Pillemer, Karl, & Kurt Lüscher. 2004. Introduction: Ambivalence in parent-child relations in later life. Pp. 1–19 in Karl Pillemer & Kurt Lüscher (Eds.), *Intergenerational ambivalences: New perspectives on parent-child relations in later life*. New York: Elsevier.

Pillemer, Karl, & D. Moore. 1990. Highlights from a study of abuse of patients in nursing homes. *Journal of Elder Abuse and Neglect* 2:1/2:5–30.

Pillemer, Karl, & J. Jill Suitor. 1991. "Will I ever escape my child's problems?" Effects of adult children's problems on elderly parents. *Journal of Marriage and Family* 53 (Aug): 585–594.

Pillemer, Karl, & Jill Suitor. 2002. Explaining mothers' ambivalence toward their children. *Journal of Marriage and Family* 64:602–613.

Pillemer, Karl, & J. Jill Suitor. 2006. Making choices: A within-family study of caregiver selection. *The Gerontologist* 46:4:439–448.

Pillemer, Karl, J. Jill Suitor, Steven E. Mock, Tamara B. Pardo, & Jori Sechrist. 2007. Capturing the complexities of intergenerational relations: Exploring ambivalence within later-life families. *Journal of Social Issues* 63:4:775–791.

Pina, Darlene L., & Vern Bengtson. 1995. Division of household labor and the wellbeing of retirement-aged wives. *The Gerontologist* 35:3:308–317.

Pinello, Daniel R. 2006. *America's struggle for same-sex marriage*. New York: Cambridge University Press.

Pinquart, M., & S. Sorensen. 2000. Influences of socioeconomic status, social network, and competence on subjective well-being in later life: A meta-analysis. *Psychology and Aging* 15:187–224.

Pope, Mark, & Richard Schulz. 1990. Sexual attitudes and behavior in mid-life and aging homosexual males. *Journal of Homosexuality* 20:3/4:169–177.

Population Reference Bureau. 2007, March 22. *U.S. birth rate: Still fueling population growth?* Washington, DC: Author. Retrieved October 29, 2008. http://discuss.prb.org/content/ interview/detail/1172/.

Porche, Michelle V., & Diane M. Purvin. 2008. 'Never in our lifetime': Legal marriage for same-sex couples in long-term relationships. *Family Relations* 57:2:144–159.

Potts, Annie, Nicola Gavey, Victoria M. Grace, & Tiina Vares. 2003. The downside of Viagra: Women's experiences and concerns. *Sociology of Health and Illness* 25:7:697–719.

Powell, Jason L. 2006. *Social theory and aging*. Lanham, Maryland: Rowman & Littlefield.

Prager, K. J. 2000. Intimacy in personal relationships. Pp. 229–242 in C. Hendrick & S. Hendrick (Eds.), *Close relationships: A sourcebook*. Thousand Oaks, CA: Sage.

Previti, Denise, & Paul R. Amato. 2003. Why stay married? Rewards, barriers, and marital stability. *Journal of Marriage and Family* 65:3:561–573.

Price, Debora, & Jay Ginn. 2003. Sharing the crust? Gender, partnership status and inequalities in pension accumulation. Pp. 127–147 in Sara Arber, Kate Davidson, & Jay Ginn (Eds.), *Gender and ageing: Changing roles and relationships*. Philadelphia: Open University Press.

Proulx, Christine M., Heather M. Helms, & Cheryl Buehler, 2007. Marital quality and personal well-being: A meta-analysis. *Journal of Marriage and Family* 69:3:576–593.

Pruchno, Rachel A. 1999. Raising grandchildren: The experience of black and white grandmothers. *The Gerontologist* 39:2:209–221.

Pruchno, Rachel A., Christopher Burant, & Norah D. Peters. 1997a. Typologies of caregiving families: Family congruence and individual well-being. *The Gerontologist* 37:2:157–167.

Pruchno, Rachel A., Christopher Burant, & Norah D. Peters. 1997b. Understanding the well-being of care receivers. 1997. *The Gerontologist* 37:1:102–109.

Pruchno, Rachel A., Julie Hicks Patrick, & Christopher J. Burant. 1996. Mental health of aging women with children who are chronically disabled: Examination of a two-factor model. *Journal of Gerontology: Social Sciences* 51B:6:S284-S296.

Pudrovska, Tetyana, Scott Schieman, & Deborah Carr. 2006. Strains of singlehood in later life: Do race and gender matter? *Journal of Gerontology: Social Sciences* 61B:6:S315-S322.

Putney, Norella M., & Vern L. Bengtson. 2003. Intergenerational relations in changing times. Pp. 149–164 in Jeylan T. Mortimer & Michael J. Shanahan (Eds.), *Handbook of the life course.* New York: Klewer Academics/Plenum.

Pyke, Karen. 1999. The micropolitics of care in relationships between aging parents and adult children: Individualism, collectivism, and power. *Journal of Marriage and Family* 61:3:661–672.

Pyper, Wendy. 2006. Balancing career and care. *Perspectives.* 7:11:5–14. Statistics Canada Cat. No. 75-001-XIE.

Quam, Jean K., & Gary S. Whitford. 1992. Adaptation and age-related expectations of older gay and lesbian adults. *The Gerontologist* 32:3:367–374.

Quirouette, Cecile, & Delores Pushkar Gold. 1995. Spousal characteristics as predictors of well-being in older couples. Pp. 21–33 in Jon Hendricks (Ed.), *The ties of later life.* Amityville, NY: Baywood.

Raphael, S. M., & M. K. Meyer. 2000. Family support patterns for midlife lesbians: Recollections of a lesbian couple 1971–1997. Pp. 139–152 in M. R. Adelman (Ed.), *Midlife lesbian relationships: Friends, lovers, children, and parents.* Binghamton, NY: Harrington Park Press.

Ray, Ruth E. 2006. The personal as political: The legacy of Betty Friedan. Pp. 21–45 in Toni M. Calananti, & Kathleen F. Slevin (Eds.), *Aging matters: Realigning feminist thinking.* New York: Routledge.

Reitzes, Donald C., & Elizabeth J. Mutran. 2004. Grandparent identity, intergenerational family identity, and well-being. *The Gerontologist* 59B:4: S213-S219.

Ribeiro, Oscar, Constança Paúl, & Conceição Nogueira, 2007. Real men, real husbands: Caregiving and masculinities in later life. *Journal of Aging Studies* 21:4:302–313.

Richard, Colleen Anne, & Alison Hamilton Brown. 2006. Configuration of informal social support among older lesbians. *Journal of Women and Aging* 18:4:49–65.

Ries, Paula, & Anne J. Stone (Eds.). 1992. *The American woman 1992–93: A status report.* New York: Norton.

Rietschlin, John. 2000. *Parents for life: Negotiating residential arrangements for adults with developmental disabilities.* PhD diss., University of Western Ontario.

Riggio, Heidi R. 2006. Structural features of sibling dyads and attitudes toward sibling relationships in young adulthood. *Journal of Family Issues* 27:9:1233–1254.

Riley, Matilda White, & John W. Riley Jr. 1996. Generational relations: A future perspective. Pp. 283–291 in Tamara K. Hareven (Ed.), *Aging and generational relations: Life-course and cross-cultural perspectives.* New York: Aldine de Gruyter.

Riley, Matilda White, & John W. Riley Jr. 2000. Age integration: Conceptual and historical background. *The Gerontologist* 40:3:266–270.

Roberto, Karen A., Katherine R. Allen, & Rosemary Blieszner. 1999. Older women, their children, and grandchildren: A feminist perspective on family relationships. *Journal of Women and Aging* 11:2/3:67–84.

Roberto, Karen A., Katherine R. Allen, & Rosemary Blieszner. 2001. Grandfathers' perceptions and expectations of relationships with their adult children. *Journal of Family Issues* 22:4:407–425.

Roberto, Karen A., & Johanna Stroes. 1995. Grandchildren and grandparents: Roles, influences, and relationships. Pp. 141–154 in Jon Hendricks (Ed.), *The ties of later life.* Amityville, NY: Baywood.

Roeher Institute. 1996. *Disability, community and society: Exploring the links.* North York, Ontario, Canada: Roeher Institute.

Rogers, Stacy J. 2004. Dollars, dependency, and divorce: Four perspectives on the role of wives' income. *Journal of Marriage and Family* 66:1:59–74.

Roisman, Glenn I., Eric Clausell, Ashley Holland, Karen Fortuna, & Chryle Elieff. 2008. Adult romantic relationships as contexts of human development: A multimethod comparison of same-sex couples with opposite-sex dating, engaged, and married dyads. *Developmental Psychology* 44:1:91–101.

Rook, Karen S. 2003. Exposure and reactivity to negative social exchanges: A preliminary investigation using daily diary data. *Journal of Gerontology: Psychological Sciences* 58B:2:P100-P111.

Rook, Karen S., & Laura A. Zettel. 2005. The purported benefits of marriage viewed through the lens of physical health. *Psychological Inquiry* 16:2&3:116–121.

Rose, Hilary, & Errolyn Bruce. 1995. Mutual care but differential esteem: Caring between older couples. Pp. 114–128 in Sara Arber & Jay Ginn (Eds.), *Connecting gender and ageing: A sociological approach.* Buckingham, UK: Open University Press.

Rosenthal, Carolyn J. 1985. Kinkeeping in the familial division of labor. *Journal of Marriage and Family* 47:4:965–974.

Rosenthal, Carolyn J. 1987. Generational succession: The passing on of family headship. *Journal of Comparative Family Studies* 18:1:61–77.

Rosenthal, Carolyn J. 2000. Aging families: Have current changes and challenges been "oversold?" Pp. 45–63 in Ellen M. Gee & Gloria M. Guttman (Eds.), *The overselling of population aging: Apocalyptic demography, intergenerational challenges, and social policy*. Don Mills, Ontario, Canada: Oxford University Press.

Rosenthal, Carolyn J., Anne Martin-Matthews, & Janice M. Keefe. 2007. Care management and care provision for older relatives amongst employed informal caregivers. *Ageing & Society* 27:755–778.

Rosenthal, Carolyn J., Anne Martin-Matthews, & Sarah Matthews. 1996. Caught in the middle? Occupancy in multiple roles and help to parents in a national probability sample of Canadian adults. *Journal of Gerontology: Social Sciences* 51B:6:S274-S283.

Rose-Rego, Sharon K., Milton E. Strauss, & Kathleen A. Smyth. 1998. Differences in the perceived well-being of wives and husbands caring for persons with Alzheimer's disease. *The Gerontologist* 389:2:224–230.

Ross, Catherine E. 1995. Reconceptualizing marital status as a continuum of social attachment. *Journal of Marriage and Family* 57 (Feb): 129–140.

Ross, Catherine E., & John Mirowsky. 1999. Parental divorce, life-course disruption, and adult depression. *Journal of Marriage and Family* 61:4:1034–1045.

Ross, Helgola G., & Joel I. Milgram. 1982. Important variables in adult sibling relationships: A qualitative study. Pp. 225–249 in Michael E. Lamb and Brian Sutton-Smith (Eds.), *Sibling Relationships: Their nature and significance across the lifespan*. NY: Lawrence Erlbaum.

Ross, Margaret M., Carolyn J. Rosenthal, & Pamela G. Dawson. 1997. Spousal caregiving in the institutional setting: Task performance. *Canadian Journal on Aging* 16:1:51–69.

Rossi, Alice S., & Peter H. Rossi. 1990. *Of human bonding: Parent-child relations across the life course*. New York: Aldine de Gruyter.

Rothblum, Esther D. 2006. Same-sex marriage and legalized relationships: I do, or do I? Pp. 203–214 in Jerry J. Bigner (Ed.), *An introduction to GLBT family studies*. New York: Haworth.

Rothblum, Esther D., Kimberley F. Balsam, & Ruth M. Mickey. 2004. Brothers and sisters of lesbians, gay men, and bisexuals as a demographic comparison group: An innovative research methodology to examine social change. *Journal of Applied Behavioral Science* 40:3:283–301.

Rothblum, Esther D., Kimberley F. Balsam, Sondra E. Solomon, & Rhonda J. Factor. 2006. Siblings and sexual orientation: Products of alternative families or the ones who got away? Pp. 117–133 in Jerry J. Bigner (Ed.), *An introduction to GBLT family studies*. New York: Haworth.

Rothblum, Esther D., & Rhonda Factor. 2001. Lesbians and their sisters as a control group: Demographic and mental health factors. *Psychological Science* 12:1:63–69.

Rowland, Donald T. 2007. Historical trends in childlessness. *Journal of Family Issues* 28:10:1311–1337.

Rubinstein, Robert L. 1987. Never married elderly as a social type: Re-evaluating some images. *The Gerontologist* 27:1:08–113.

Rubinstein, Robert L., Baine B. Alexander, Marcene Goodman, & Mark Luborsky. 1991. Key relationships of never married, childless older women: A cultural analysis. *Journal of Gerontology: Social Sciences* 46:5:S270-S277.

Ruggles, Steven. 1996. Living arrangements of the elderly in America: 1880–1980. Pp. 254–271 in Tamara K. Hareven (Ed.), *Aging and generational relations over the life course*. New York: Walter de Gruyter.

Ruggles, Steven. 2007. The decline of intergenerational coresidence in the United States, 1850 to 2000. *American Sociological Review* 72:6:964–989.

Russell, Graeme. 1986. Grandfathers: Making up for lost opportunities. Pp. 233–259 in Robert A. Lewis & Robert E. Salt (Eds.), *Men in families*. Beverly Hills, CA: Sage.

Ryan, William. 1971. *Blaming the victim*. New York: Vintage.

Ryff, Carol D., Young Hyun Lee, Marilyn J. Essex, & Pamela S. Schmutte. 1994. My children and me: Midlife evaluations of grown children and self. *Psychology and Aging* 9:2:195–205.

Sacks, Oliver. 1993. A neurologist's notebook: To see and not see. *The New Yorker*. May 10: 59–73.

Saluter, Arlene. 1992. Marital status and living arrangements: March 1991. *Current Population Reports, Series P-20, Population Characteristics No. 461*.Washington, DC: Government Printing Office, U.S. Bureau of the Census.

Saluter, Arlene. 1996. Marital status and living arrangements: March 1995. *Current Population Reports, Series P-20, Population Characteristics No. 461*. Washington: Government Printing Office, U.S. Bureau of the Census.

Sands, Roberta, & Robin S. Goldberg-Glen. 2000. Factors associated with stress among grandparents raising their grandchildren. *Family Relations* 49:1:97–105.

Sarkisian, Natalia, Mariana Gerena, & Naomi Gerstel. 2007. Extended family integration among Euro and Mexican Americans: Ethnicity, gender, and class. *Journal of Marriage and Family* 69:1:40–54.

Sarkisian, Natalia, & Naomi Gerstel. 2004. Explaining the gender gap in help to parents: The importance of employment. *Journal of Marriage and Family* 66:331–344.

Sarkisian, Natalia, & Naomi Gerstel. 2008. Till marriage do us part: Adult children's relationships with their parents. *Journal of Marriage and Family* 70:2:360–376.

Savin-Williams, R. C. 1998. Lesbian, gay, and bisexual youths' relationships with their parents. Pp. 75–98 in C. J. Patterson, & A. R. D'Augelli (Eds.), *Lesbian, gay, and bisexual identities and the family: Psychological perspectives*. New York: Oxford University Press.

Sayer, Liana C. 2006. Economic aspects of divorce and relationship dissolution. Pp. 385–406 in Mark A. Fine & John H. Harvey (Eds.), *Handbook of divorce and relationship dissolution*. Mahwah NJ: Lawrence Erlbaum.

Scanzoni, John, & William Marsiglio. 1993. New action theory and contemporary families. *Journal of Family Issues* 14:1:105–132.

Scharlach, Andrew E. 1994. Caregiving and employment: Competing or complementary roles? *The Gerontologist* 34:3:378–385.

Scharlach, Andrew, Wei Li, & Tapashi B. Dalvi. 2006. Family conflict as a mediator of caregiver strain. *Family Relations* 55:5:625–635.

Schiamberg, Lawrence B., & Daphne Gans. 2000. Elder abuse by adult children: An applied ecological framework for understanding contextual risk factors and the intergenerational character of quality of life. *International Journal of Human Development* 50:4:329–359.

Schmeeckle, Maria. 2007. Gender dynamics in stepfamilies: Adult stepchildren's views. *Journal of Marriage and Family* 69:1:174–189.

Schmeeckle, Maria, Roseann Giarrusso, Du Feng, & Vern L. Bengtson. 2006. What makes someone family? Adult children's perceptions of current and former stepparents. *Journal of Marriage and Family* 68:3:595–610.

Schmertmann, Carl P., Monica Boyd, William Serow, & Douglas White. 2000. Elder child coresidence in the United States: Evidence from the 1990 census. *Research on Aging* 22:1:23–42.

Schoen, Robert, & Vladimir Canudas-Romo. 2006. Timing effects on divorce: 20th century experience in the United States. *Journal of Marriage and Family* 68:749–758.

Schone, Barbara Steinberg, & Robin M. Weinick. 1998. Health-related behaviors and the benefits of marriage for elderly persons. *The Gerontologist* 38:5:618–627.

Schooler, Carmi, Andrew J. Revell, & Leslie J. Caplan. 2007. Parental practices and willingness to ask for children's help in later life. *Journal of Gerontology: Psychological Sciences* 62B:3:P165-P170.

Schulz, James H. 1997. The real crisis of the century: Growing inequality, not stealing from our children. Book Review. *The Gerontologist* 37:1:130–131.

Schwartz, Pepper, & Virginia Rutter. 1998. *The gender of sexuality.* Thousand Oaks, CA: Pine Forge.

Schwarz, Beate. 2006. Adult daughters' family structure and the association between reciprocity and relationship quality. *Journal of Family Issues* 27:2:208–228.

Scott, Jean Pearson. 1983. Siblings and other kin. Pp. 47–62 in Timothy H. Brubaker (Ed.), *Family relationships in later life.* Beverly Hills: Sage.

Seccombe, Karen. 1991. Assessing the costs and benefits of children: Gender comparisons among childfree husbands and wives. *Journal of Marriage and Family* 53:1:191–202.

Seccombe, Karen, & Masako Ishii-Kuntz. 1994. Gender and social relationships among the never-married. *Sex Roles* 30:7/8:585–603.

Settersten, Richard A. Jr. 2003. Propositions and controversies in life-course scholarship. Pp. 15–45 in Richard Settersten Jr. (Ed.), *Invitation to the life course: Toward new understandings of later life.* Amityville, NY: Baywood.

Settersten, Richard A. Jr. 2006. Aging and the life course. Pp. 3–19 in Robert H. Binstock & Linda K. George (Eds.), *Handbook of aging and the social sciences.* Burlington, MA: Elsevier.

Settersten, Richard A. Jr., & Karl Ulrich Mayer. 1997. The measurement of age, age structuring, and the life course. *Annual Review of Sociology* 23:233–61.

Sev'er, Aysan. 1992. *Women and divorce in Canada.* Toronto: Canadian Scholars' Press.

Sex and marriage: Can passion survive kids, careers and the vagaries of aging? 1999. *Maclean's* Aug 9:24–29.

Shanas, Ethel. 1979. Social myth as hypothesis: The case of the family relations of old people. *The Gerontologist* 19:1:3–9.

Shapiro, Adam. 2003. Later-life divorce and parent-adult child contact and proximity: A longitudinal analysis. *Journal of Family Issues* 24:2:264–285.

Sharlin, Shlomo A., Florence W. Kaslow, & Helga Hammerschimidt. 2000. *Together through thick and thin: A multinational picture of long-term marriages.* New York: Haworth.

Sharp, Elizabeth A., & Lawrence Ganong. 2007. Living in the gray: Women's experiences of missing the marital transition. *Journal of Marriage and Family* 69:3:831–844.

Sheehan, Nancy W., & Laura M. Donorfio. 1999. Efforts to create meaning in the relationship between aging mothers and their caregiving daughters: A qualitative study of caregiving. *Journal of Aging Studies* 13:2:161–176.

Shernoff, Michael. 1998. Gay widowers: Grieving in relation to trauma and social supports. *Journal of the Gay and Lesbian Medical Association* 2:1:27–33.

Shuey, Kim, & Melissa A. Hardy. 2003. Assistance to aging parents and parents-in-law: Does lineage affect family allocation decisions? *Journal of Marriage and Family* 65:2:418–431.

Siegel, Judith M. 1995. Looking for Mr. Right? Older single women who become mothers. *Journal of Family Issues* 16:2:194–211.

Silverstein, Merril. 2004. Intergenerational relations across time and place. *Annual Review of Gerontology & Geriatrics* 24:xiii-xix.

Silverstein, Merril. 2006. Intergenerational family transfers in social context. Pp. 165–180 in Robert H. Binstock & Linda K. George (Eds.), *Handbook of aging and the social sciences,* 6th ed. San Diego, CA: Academic Press.

Silverstein, Merril, & Joseph J. Angelleli. 1998. Older parents' expectations of moving closer to their children. *Journal of Gerontology: Social Sciences* 53B:3:S153-S163.

Silverstein, Merril, & Vern L. Bengtson. 1997. Intergenerational solidarity and the structure of adult child-parent relationships in American families. *American Journal of Sociology* 103:2:429–460.

Silverstein, Merril, & Xuan Chen, 1999. The impact of acculturation in Mexican American families on the quality of adult grandchild-grandparent relationships. *Journal of Marriage and Family* 61:1:188–198.

Silverstein, Merril, Xuan Chen, & Kenneth Heller. 1996. Too much of a good thing? Integenerational social support and the psychological well-being of older parents. *Journal of Marriage and Family* 58:4:970–982.

Silverstein, Merril, S. Conroy, H. Wang, R. Giarrusso & V. Bengtson. 2002. Reciprocity in parent-child relations over the adult life course. *Journal of Gerontology: Social Sciences* 57:S3-S13.

Silverstein, Merril, & Eugene Litwak. 1993. A task-specific typology of intergenerational family structure in later life. *The Gerontologist* 33:2:258–264.

Silverstein, Merril, & Jeffrey D. Long. 1998. Trajectories of grandparents' perceived solidarity with adult grandchildren: A growth curve analysis over 23 years. *Journal of Marriage and Family* 60 (November): 912–923.

Silverstein, Merril, Tonya M. Parrott, & Vern L. Bengtson. 1995. Factors that predispose middle-aged sons and daughters to provide social support to older parents. *Journal of Marriage and Family* 57 (May): 465–475.

Silverstein, Merril, & Sarah Ruiz. 2006. Breaking the chain: How grandparents moderate the transmission of maternal depression to their grandchildren. *Family Relations* 55:601–612.

Simmons, Tavia, & Jane Lawler Dye. 2003. *Grandparents living with grandchildren.* U.S. Census Bureau, Census 2000 Special Reports, C2KBR-31. Washington, DC: U.S. Government Printing Office.

Simons, Ronald. 1984. Specificity and substitution in the social networks of the elderly. *International Journal of Aging and Human Development* 18:2:121–139.

Sims-Gould, Joanie, & Anne Martin-Matthews. 2007. Family caregiving or caregiving alone: Who helps the helper? *Canadian Journal on Aging* 26 (Suppl. 1): 27–46.

Sims-Gould, Joanie, Anne Martin-Matthews, & Monique A. M. Gignac. 2008. Episodiccrisis in the provision of care to elderly relatives. *Journal of Applied Gerontology* 27:2:123–140.

Sims-Gould, Joanie, Anne Martin-Matthews, & Carolyn J. Rosenthal. 2008. Family caregiving and helping at the intersection of gender and kinship. Pp. 65–83 in Anne Martin-Matthews & Judith E. Phillips (Eds.), *Aging and caring at the intersection of work and home life: Blurring the boundaries.* New York: Lawrence Erlbaum.

Skinner, Denise A., & Julie K. Kohler. 2002. Parental rights in diverse family contexts: Current legal developments. *Family Relations* 51:4:293–300.

Skolnick, Arlene. 1998. Public dreams, private lives. *Contemporary Sociology* 27:3:233–235.

Skultety, Karyn M. 2007. Addressing issues of sexuality with older couples. *Generations* 31:3:31–37.

Slevin, Kathleen F. 2006. The embodied experiences of old lesbians. Pp. 247–268 in Toni M. Calasanti & Kathleen F. Slevin (Eds.), *Age matters: Realigning feminist thinking.* New York: Routledge.

Smerglia, Virginia L., & Gary T. Deimling. 1997. Care-related decision-making satisfaction and caregiver well-being in families caring for older members. *The Gerontologist* 37:5:658–665.

Smith, Deborah, & Phyllis Moen. 1998. Spousal influence on retirement: His, her, and their perceptions. *Journal of Marriage and Family* 60 (August): 734–744.

Snell, James G. 1996. *The citizen's wage: The state and the elderly in Canada, 1900–1951.* Toronto: University of Toronto Press.

Sobolewski, Juliana, & Valarie King. 2005. The importance of the coparental relationship for nonresident fathers' ties to children. *Journal of Marriage and Family* 67:1196–1212.

Soliz, Jordan Eli, Mei-Chen Lin, Karen Anderson, & Jake Harwood. 2006. Friends and allies: Communication in grandparent-grandchild relationships. Pp. 65–79 in Kory Floyd & Mark T. Morman (Eds.), *The family circle: New research in family communication.* Thousand Oaks, CA: Sage.

Solomon, Jennifer Crew, & Jonathan Marx. 1995. "To grandmother's house we go": Health and school adjustment of children raised solely by grandparents. *The Gerontologist* 35:3:386–394.

Somers, Marsha D. 1993. A comparison of voluntarily childfree adults and parents. *Journal of Marriage and Family* 55:3:643–650.

Sotirin, Patricia J., & Laura L. Ellingson. 2006. The 'other' women in family life: Aunt/niece/nephew communication. Pp. 81–99 in Karry Floyd & Mark T. Morman (Eds.), *Widening the family circle: New research on family communication.* Thousand Oaks, CA: Sage.

Spitze, Glenna, & Katherine Trent. 2006. Gender differences in adult sibling relationships in two-child families. *Journal of Marriage and Family* 68:977–992.

Sporakowski, Michael J., & George A. Hughston. 1978. Prescriptions for happy marriage: Adjustments and satisfactions of couples married for 50 or more years. *The Family Coordinator* (October): 27:321–327.

Sprecher, S., & P. C. Regan. 2000. Sexuality in relational context. Pp. 217–227 in C. Hendrick & S. S. Hendrick (Eds.), *Close relationships: A sourcebook.* Thousand Oaks, CA: Sage.

Sprey, Jetse. 1972. On the institutionalization of sexuality. Pp. 80–92 in Joann S. DeLora & Jack R. DeLora (Eds.), *Intimate life styles: Marriage and its alternatives.* Pacific Palisades, CA: Goodyear.

Sprey, Jetse, & Sarah H. Matthews. 1982. Contemporary grandparenthood: A systemic transition. *Annals of the American Academy of Political and Social Science* 464: (November): 91–103.

Sprey, Jetse, & Sarah Matthews. 1989. The perils of drawing policy implications from research. Pp. 51–61 in R. Filinson & S. Ingman (Eds.), *Elder abuse: practice and policy.* New York: Human Sciences Press.

Stacey, Judith. 1998. Gay and lesbian families: Queer like us. Pp. 117–143 in Mary Ann Mason, Arlene Skolnick, & Stephen D. Sugarman (Eds.), *All our families: New policies for a new century.* New York: Oxford University Press.

Stack, Steven, & J. Ross Eshleman. 1998. Marital status and happiness: A 17-nation study. *Journal of Marriage and Family* 60 (May): 527–536.

Stark, Vikki. 2006. *My sister, my self: Understanding the sibling relationship that shapes our lives, our loves, and ourselves.* New York: McGraw-Hill.

Starrels, Marjorie, Berit Ingersoll-Dayton, David W. Dowler, & Margaret B. Neal. 1997. The stress of caring for a parent: Effects of the elder's impairment on an employed adult child. *Journal of Marriage and Family* 59:4:860–872.

Statistics Canada. 2002a. Trends in Canadian and American fertility. *The Daily.* Ottawa. July 3. http://www.statcan.gc.ca/daily-quotidien/020703/tdq020703-eng.htm

Statistics Canada. 2002b. *General social survey—Cycle 15: Family history.* Issued July 2002. Cat. No. 89-575-XIE. Ottawa, Canada: Ministry of Industry.

Statistics Canada. 2005. *General social survey of Canada, 2001—Cycle 15: Family History,* 6th ed. (main file) [machine-readable data file]. Ottawa, Canada: Ministry of Industry.

Statistics Canada. 2006. *Portrait of the Canadian Population in 2006, by age and sex: National portrait.* Ottawa, Canada. Retrieved October 29, 2008.

http://www.12.statcan.ca/english/census06/analysis/ag esex/NatlPortrait8.cfm

Statistics Canada. 2007a, December 4. 2006 census: Immigration, citizenship, language, mobility and migration. *The Daily*. Ottawa, Canada. http://www.statcan.gc.ca/daily-quotidien/071204/tdq071204-eng.htm

Statistics Canada. 2007b, September 21. Births Correction. *The Daily*. Ottawa Canada. http://www.statcan.gc.ca/daily-quotidien/070921/tdq070921-eng.htm

Steelman, Lala Carr, Brian Powell, Regina Werum, & Scott Carter. 2002. Reconsidering the effects of sibling configuration: Recent advances and challenges. *Annual Review of Sociology* 28:243–269.

Stein, Karen F. 2006. What does the elder abuse field need? *The Gerontologist* 46:5:701–704.

Stein, Peter J. 1981. Understanding single adulthood. Pp. 9–21 in Peter J. Stein (Ed.), *Single life: Unmarried adults in social context*. New York: St. Martin's.

Steinmetz, Suzanne K. 2005. Elder abuse is caused by the perception of stress associated with providing care. Pp. 191–205 in Donileen R Loseke, Richard J. Gelles, & Mary M. Cavanaugh (Eds.), *Current Controversies on family violence*. Thousand Oaks, CA: Sage.

Stern, Steven. 1996. Measuring childwork and residence adjustments to parents' long-term care needs. *The Gerontologist* 36:1:76–87.

Stevens, Nan. 1995. Gender and adaptation to widowhood in later life. *Ageing and Society* 15:37–58.

Stevens, Nan. 2004. Re-engaging: New partnerships in late-life widowhood. Pp. 47–64 in Kate Davidson & Graham Fennell (Eds.), *Intimacy in later life*. London, UK: Transaction Publishers.

Stewart, Susan D. 2001. Contemporary American stepparenthood: Integrating cohabiting and nonresident stepparents. *Population Research & Policy Review* 20:345–364.

Stewart, Susan D. 2005. Boundary ambiguity in stepfamilies. *Journal of Family Issues* 26:1002–1029.

Stoller, Eleanor Palo. 1990. Males as helpers: The role of sons, relatives, and friends. *The Gerontologist* 30:2:228–235.

Stoller, Eleanor Palo, & Stephen J. Cutler. 1992. The impact of gender on configurations of care among married elderly couples. *Research on Aging* 14:3:313–330.

Stoller, Eleanor Palo, Lorna Earl Forster, & Tamara Sutin Duniho. 1992. Systems of parent care within sibling networks. *Research on Aging* 14:1:28–49.

Stommel, Manfred, Charles W. Given, & Barbara A. Given. 1998. Racial differences in the division of labor between primary and secondary caregivers. *Research on Aging* 20:2:199–217.

Stone, Leroy O., Carolyn J. Rosenthal, & Ingrid Arnet Connidis. 1998. *Parent-child exchanges of supports and intergenerational equity*. Ottawa, Canada: Statistics Canada.

Stones, M. J., & Michel Bédard. 2002. Higher thresholds for elder abuse with age and rural residence. *Canadian Journal on Aging* 21:4:577–586.

Strain, Laurel, & Barbara J. Payne. 1992. Social networks and patterns of interaction among ever-single and

separated/divorced elderly Canadians. *Canadian Journal on Aging* 11:1:31–53.

Strawbridge,William J., & Margaret I. Wallhagen. 1991. Impact of conflict on adult child caregivers. *The Gerontologist* 31:6:770–777.

Strawbridge, William J., Margaret I. Wallhagen, Sarah J. Shema, & George A. Kaplan. 1997. New burdens or more of the same? Comparing grandparent, spouse, and adult-child caregivers. *The Gerontologist* 37:4:505–510.

Street, Debra, & Ingrid Arnet Connidis. 2001. Creeping selectivity in Canadian women's pensions. Pp. 158–178 in Jay Ginn, Debra Street, & Sara Arber (Eds.), *Women, work and pensions*. Philadelphia: Open University Press.

Strom, Robert, Pat Collinsworth, Shirley Strom, & Diane Griswold. 1995. Strengths and needs of black grandparents. Pp. 195–207 in Jon Hendricks (Ed.), *The ties of later life*. Amityville, NY: Baywood.

Stull, Donald E., & Annemarie Scarisbrick-Hauser. 1989. Never-married elderly: A reassessment with implications for long-term care policy. *Research on Aging* 11:1:124–139.

Stum, M. S. 1999. 'I just want to be fair': Interpersonal justice in intergenerational transfers of nontitled property. *Family Relations* 48:159–166.

Suitor, J. Jill. 1991. Marital quality and satisfaction with the division of household labor across the family life cycle. *Journal of Marriage and Family* 53 (February): 221–230.

Suitor, Jill, & Karl Pillemer. 2006. Choosing daughters: Exploring why mothers favor adult daughters over sons. *Sociological Perspectives* 49:2:139–160.

Suitor, Jill, Karl Pillemer, & Jori Sechrist. 2006. Within family differences in mothers' support to adult children. *Journal of Gerontology: Social Sciences* 16B:S10-S17.

Suitor, Jill, Jori Sechrist, Michael Steinhour, & Karl Pillemer. 2006. 'I'm sure she chose me!' Accuracy of children's reports of mothers' favoritism in later life families. *Family Relations* 55:5:526–538.

Sulloway, Frank J. 1996. *Born to rebel: Birth order, family dynamics, and creative lives*. New York: Pantheon.

Sun, Yongmis, & Yuanzhang Li. 2008. Stable postdivorce family structures during late adolescence and socioeconomic consequences in adulthood. *Journal of Marriage and Family* 70:1:129–143.

Sweeney, Megan M. 1997. Remarriage of women and men after divorce: The role of socioeconomic prospects. *Journal of Family Issues* 18:5:479–502.

Sweeney, Megan M. 2002. Remarriage and the nature of divorce. *Journal of Family Issues* 23:3:410–440.

Sweeney, Megan M., & Julie A. Phillips. 2004. Understanding racial differences in marital disruption: Recent trends and explanations. *Journal of Marriage and Family* 66:3:639–650.

Swicegood, Gary, & S. Phillip Morgan. 2002. Racial and ethnic fertility differentials. Pp. 100-128 in Nancy Denton & Stewart Emory Tolnay (Eds.), *American diversity: A demographic challenge for the 21st Century*. Albany, NY: SUNY Press.

Szinovacz, Maximiliane. 1996. Couples' employment/retirement patterns and perceptions of marital quality. *Research on Aging* 18:2:243–268.

Szinovacz, Maximiliane. 1997. Adult children taking parents into their homes: Effects of childhood living arrangements. *Journal of Marriage and Family* 59:3:700–717.

Szinovacz, Maximiliane E. 1998. Grandparents today: A demographic profile. *The Gerontologist* 38:1:37–52.

Szinovacz, Maximiliane. 2000. Changes in housework after retirement: A panel analysis. *Journal of Marriage and Family* 62 (February): 78–92.

Szinovacz, Maximiliane E., & Adam Davey. 2004. Honeymoons and joint lunches: Effects of retirement and spouse's employment on depressive symptoms. *Journal of Gerontology: Psychological Sciences* 59B:5:P233-P245.

Szinovacz, Maximiliane E., & Adam Davey. 2005. Retirement and marital decision making: Effects on retirement satisfaction. *Journal of Marriage and Family* 67:2:387–398.

Szinovacz, Maximiliane E., & Stanley DeViney. 2000. Marital characteristics and retirement decisions. *Research on Aging* 22:5:470–498.

Talbott, Maria M. 1998. Older widows' attitudes towards men and remarriage. *Journal of Aging Studies* 12:4:429–449.

Taylor, Brent A., Roseann Giarusso, Du Feng, & Vern Leo Bengtson. 2006. Portraits of paternity: Middle-aged and elderly fathers' involvement with adult children. Pp. 127–145 in Victoria Hilkevitch Bedford & Barbara Formaniak Turner (Eds.), *Men in relationships: A new look from a life course perspective.* New York: Springer.

Taylor, Janet E., & Joan E. Norris. 2000. Sibling relationships, fairness, and conflict over transfer of the farm. *Family Relations* 49:277–283.

Teachman, Jay D., Lucky M. Tedrow, and Kyle D. Crowder. 2000. The changing demography of America's families. *Journal of Marriage and Family* 62:4:1234–1246.

Tedebrand, Lars-Goran. 1996. Gender, rural-urban and socio-economic differences in coresidence of the elderly with adult children: The case of Sweden 1860–1940. Pp. 158–190 in Tamara K. Hareven (Ed.), *Aging and generational relations over the life course.* New York: Walter de Gruyter.

The secrets of birth order: New research shows how your family's pecking order really does shape your destiny. October 29, 2007. *Time* 170:18. n.p. Retrieved 9/4/08 from http://www.time.com

Thomas, H. 2005. Web exclusive: Happily ever after. *AARP The Magazine Online.* Retrieved October 29, 2008. http://www.aarpmagazine.org/people/Articles/a2004-11-17-mag-everafter.html

Thomas, Jeanne L. 1995. Gender and perceptions of grandparenthood. Pp. 181–193 in Jon Hendricks (Ed.), *The ties of later life.* Amityville, NY: Baywood.

Thompson Jr., E. H. 2002. What's unique about men's caregiving. Pp. 20–47 in B. J. Kramer & E. H. Thompson Jr. (Eds.), *Men as caregivers: Theory, research, and service implications.* New York: Springer.

Thompson Jr., Edward H. 2006. Being women, then lesbians, then old: Femininities, sexualities, and aging. *The Gerontologist* 46:2:300–305.

Thompson, Elizabeth. 2000. Mothers' experiences of an adult child's HIV/AIDS diagnosis: Maternal responses to and resolution of accountability for AIDS. *Family Relations* 49:2:155–164.

Thompson, Linda. 1993. Conceptualizing gender in marriage: The case of marital care. *Journal of Marriage and Family* 55 (August): 557–569.

Thompson, Linda, & Alexis J. Walker. 1989. Gender in families: Women and men in marriage, work, and parenthood. *Journal of Marriage and Family* 51:845–871.

Thornton, Arland, & Linda Young-DeMarco. 2001. Four decades of trends in attitudes toward family issues in the United States: The 1960s through the 1990s. *Journal of Marriage and Family* 63:4:1009–1037.

Tomassini, Cecilia, Karen Glaser, & Rachel Stuchbury. 2007. Family disruption and support in later life: A comparative study between the United Kingdom and Italy. *Journal of Social Issues* 63:4:845–863.

Too late for Prince Charming? 1986 June 2. *Newsweek*: 54–61.

Tornatore, Jane B., & Leslie A. Grant. 2004. Family caregiver satisfaction with the nursing home after placement of a relative with dementia. *Journal of Gerontology: Social Sciences* 59B:2:S80-S88.

Torres-Gil, Fernando M. 2005. Ageing and public policy in ethnically diverse societies. Pp. 670–681 in Malcolm L. Johnson (Ed.), *The Cambridge handbook of age and ageing.* Cambridge: Cambridge University Press.

Torrey, Barbara Boyle, & Carl Haub. 2003. *Diverging mortality and fertility trends: Canada and the United States..* Washington, DC: Population Reference Bureau. Retrieved October 29, 2008. http://www.prb.org/Articles/2003/DivergingMortalityandFertilityTrendsCanada andtheUnitedStates.aspx

Townson, Monica. 2001. *Pensions under attack: What's behind the push to privatize public pensions.* Ottawa and Toronto: Canadian Centre for Policy Alternatives & James Lorimer.

Traupmann, Jane, & Elaine Hatfield. 1981. Love and its effect on mental and physical health. Pp. 253–274 in James G. March, Robert W. Fogel, Elaine Hatfield, Sara B. Kiesler, & Ethel Shanas (Eds.), *Aging: Stability and change in the family.* Toronto: Academic Press.

Treas, Judith, & Deirdre Giesen. 2000. Sexual infidelity among married and cohabiting Americans. *Journal of Marriage and Family* 62 (February): 48–60.

Treas, Judith, & Anke Van Hilst. 1976. Marriage and remarriage rates among older Americans. *The Gerontologist* 16:2:132–135.

Trimberger, E. Kay. 2005. *The new single woman.* Boston: Beacon.

Troll, Lillian E. 1985. The contingencies of grandparenting. Pp. 63–74 in Vern L. Bengtson & Joan F. Robertson (Eds.), *Grandparenthood.* Beverly Hills, CA: Sage.

Turcotte, Martin. 2006. Parents with adult children living at home. *Canadian Social Trends* 80:2–12. Ottawa, Canada: Statistics Canada.

Turner, Jonathan H. 2005. Is a scientific theory of the family desirable? Pp. 26–29 in Vern L. Bengtson, Alan C. Acock, Katherine R. Allen, Peggye Dilworth-Anderson, &

David M. Klein (Eds.), *Sourcebook of family theory & research*. Thousand Oaks, CA: Sage.

Turner, M. Jean, Carolyn R. Young, & Kelly J. Black. 2006. Daughters-in-law seeking their place within the family: A qualitative study of differing viewpoints. *Family Relations* 55:5:588–600.

Twenge, Jean M., W. Keith Campbell, & Craig A. Foster. 2003. Parenthood and marital satisfaction: A meta-analytic review. *Journal of Marriage and Family* 65:3:574–583.

Twiggs, Julia. 2004. The body, gender, and age: Feminist insights in social gerontology. *Journal of Aging Studies* 18:1:59–73.

U.S. Census Bureau. 2000. *America's families and living arrangements, Table A1: Marital status of people 15 years and over, by age, sex, personal earnings, race, and Hispanic origin*. Retrieved October 29, 2008. http://www.census.gov/population/socdemo/hh-fam/p20–537/2000/tabA1.pdf

U.S. Census Bureau. 2004. *We the people: Aging in the United States*. Census 2000 Special Reports. Washington, DC: U.S. Department of Commerce.

U.S. Census Bureau. 2006. *America's families and living arrangements, Table A1: Marital status of people 15 years and over, by age, sex, personal earnings, race, and Hispanic origin*. http://www.census.gov/population/www/socdemo/hh-fam/cps2006.html

Uhlenberg, Peter. 1990. The role of divorce in men's relations with their adult children after mid-life. *Journal of Marriage and Family* 52 (August): 677–688.

Uhlenberg, Peter. 2000. Introduction: Why study age integration? *The Gerontologist* 40:3:261–266.

Uhlenberg, Peter. 2004. Historical forces shaping grandparent-grandchild relationships: Demography and beyond. *Annual Review of Gerontology and Geriatrics* 24:77–97.

Uhlenberg, Peter, Teresa Cooney, & Robert Boyd. 1990. Divorce for women after midlife. *Journal of Gerontology: Social Sciences* 45:1:S3-S11.

Uhlenberg, Peter, & Bradley G. Hammill. 1998. Frequency of grandparent contact with grandchild sets: Six factors that make a difference. *The Gerontologist* 38:3:276–285.

Umberson, Debra. 1992a. Gender, marital status and the social control of health behavior. *Social Sciences and Medicine* 34:907–917.

Umberson, Debra. 1992b. Relationships between adult children and their parents: Psychological consequences for both generations. *Journal of Marriage and Family* 54:3:664–674.

Umberson, Debra, & Kristi Williams. 2005. Marital quality, health, and aging: Gender equity? *Journals of Gerontology: Series B* 60B (Special Issue): 109–112.

Umberson, Debra, Kristi Williams, Daniel A. Powers, Meichu D. Chen, & Anna M. Campbell. 2005. As good as it gets? A life course perspective on marital quality. *Social Forces* 84:1:493–511.

Uttal, Lynet. 1999. Using kin for child care: Embedment in the socioeconomic networks of extended families. *Journal of Marriage and Family* 61:4:845–857.

Vaillant, Caroline, & George E. Vaillant. 1993. Is the U-curve of marital satisfaction an illusion? A 40-year study of marriage. *Journal of Marriage and Family* 55 (February): 230–239.

Van den Troost, Ann. 2005. *Marriage in motion: A study on the social context and processes of marital satisfaction*. Leuven, Belgium: Leuven University Press.

van Gaalen, Ruben I., & Pearl A. Dykstra. 2006. Solidarity and conflict between adult children and parents: A latent class analysis. *Journal of Marriage and Family* 68:4:947–960.

VanLaningham, Jody, David R. Johnson, & Paul Amato. 2001. Marital happiness, marital duration, and the U-shaped curve: Evidence from a five-wave panel study. *Social Forces* 79:647–666.

Vares, Tina, Annie Potts, Nicola Gavey, & Victoria M. Grace. 2007. Reconceptualizing cultural narratives of mature women's sexuality in the Viagra era. *Journal of Aging Studies* 21:2:153–164.

Verbrugge, Lois M. 1979. Marital status and health. *Journal of Marriage and Family* 41:2:267–285.

Vinick, Barbara H., & David J. Ekerdt. 1992. Couples view retirement activities: Expectation versus experience. Pp. 129–144 in Maximiliane Szinovacz, David J. Ekerdt, & Barbara H. Vinick (Eds.), *Families and retirement*. Newbury Park, CA: Sage.

Voorpostel, Marieke, & Rosmary Blieszner. 2008. Intergenerational solidarity and support between siblings. *Journal of Marriage and Family* 70:1:157–167.

Voorpostel, Marieke, Pearl A. Dykstra, & Henk Flap. 2007. Similar or different?: The importance of similarities and differences for support between siblings. *Journal of Family Issues* 28:8:1026–1053.

Voorpostel, Marieke, & Tanja Van der Lippe. 2007. Support between siblings and between friends: Two worlds apart? *Journal of Marriage and Family* 69:5:1271–1282.

Wacker, Robbyn R. 1995. Legal Issues and family involvement in later-life families. Pp. 284–306 in Rosemary Blieszner & Victoria Hilkevitch Bedford (Eds.), *Handbook of aging and the family*. Westport, CT: Greenwood.

Waehler, Charles A. 1996. *Bachelors: The psychology of men who haven't married*. Westport, CT: Praeger.

Waehrer, Keith, and Stephen Crystal. 1995. The impact of coresidence on economic well-being of elderly widows. *Journal of Gerontology: Social Sciences* 50B:4:S250-S258.

Waite, Linda J. 1995. Does marriage matter? *Demography* 32:483–507.

Waite, Linda J., and Scott C. Harrison. 1992. Keeping in touch: How women in mid-life allocate social contacts among kith and kin. *Social Forces* 70:3:637–655.

Waite, Linda J., & Mary Elizabeth Hughes. 1999. At risk on the cusp of old age: Living arrangements and functional status among Black, White, and Hispanic adults. *Journal of Gerontology: Social Sciences* 54B:3:S136-S144.

Waite, Linda J., & Kara Joyner. 2001. Emotional satisfaction and physical pleasure in sexual unions: Time horizon, sexual behaviour, and sexual exclusivity. *Journal of Marriage and Family* 63:247–264.

Walker, Alan. 1991. The relationship between the family and the state in the care of older people. *Canadian Journal on Aging* 10:2:94–112.

Walker, Alan. 2006. Reexamining the political economy of aging: Understanding the structure/agency tension. Pp. 59–80 in Jan Baars, Dale Dannefer, Chris Phillipson, & Alan Walker (Eds.), *Aging, globalization and inequality: The new critical gerontology.* Amityville, NY: Baywood.

Walker, Alexis J. 1992. Conceptual perspectives on gender and family caregiving. Pp. 34–46 in Jeffrey W. Dwyer & Raymond T. Coward (Eds.), *Gender, families, and elder care.* Newbury Park, CA: Sage.

Walker, Alexis J., Katherine R. Allen, & Ingrid Arnet Connidis. 2005. Theorizing and studying sibling ties in adulthood. Pp. 167–190 in Vern L. Bengtson, Alan C. Acock, Katherine R. Allen, Peggye Dilworth-Anderson, & David M. Klein (Eds.), *Sourcebook of family theory & research.* Thousand Oaks, CA: Sage.

Walker, Alexis J., & Clara C. Pratt. 1991. Daughters' help to mothers: Intergenerational aid versus caregiving. *Journal of Marriage and Family* 53:1:3–12.

Walker, Kenneth N., Arlene MacBride, & Mary L. S. Vachon. 1977. Social support networks and the crisis of bereavement. *Social Science and Medicine* 11:1:35–41.

Wallace, Steven P., Lene Levy-Storms, Raynard S. Kington, & Ronald M. Andersen. 1998. The persistence of race and ethnicity in the use of long-term care. *Journal of Gerontology: Social Sciences* 53B:2:S104-S112.

Wallerstein, Judith. 2007. The transition to adulthood: Children of divorce make their way. *Report* 52:4:F11-F12.

Wallsten, Sharon S. 2000. Effects of caregiving, gender, and race on the health, mutuality, and social supports of older couples. *Journal of Aging and Health* 12:1:90–111.

Walter, Carolyn Ambler. 2003. *The loss of a life partner: Narratives of the bereaved.* New York: Columbia University Press.

Walton, Dawn. 2002. Census reports more Canadians are home alone. *The Globe & Mail,* October 23:A6.

Ward, Russell A. 1993. Marital happiness and household equity in later life. *Journal of Marriage and Family* 55 (May): 427–438.

Ward, Russell A., & Glenna Spitze. 1996. Gender differences in parent-child coresidence experiences. *Journal of Marriage and Family* 58:3:718–725.

Ward, Russell A., & Glenna D. Spitze. 2007. Nest leaving and coresidence among young children. *Research on Aging* 29:3:257–277.

Ward-Griffin, Cathy. 2008. Heath professionals caring for aging relatives: Negotiating the public-private boundary. Pp. 1–20 in Anne Martin-Matthews & Judith E. Phillips (Eds.), *Aging and caring at the intersection of work and home life: Blurring the boundaries.* New York: Lawrence Erlbaum.

Ward-Griffin, Cathy, & Victor W. Marshall. 2003. Reconceptualizing the relationship between 'public' and 'private' eldercare. *Journal of Aging Studies* 17:189–208.

Webster, Pamela S., & A. Regula Herzog. 1995. Effects of parental divorce and memories of family problems on relationships between adult children and their parents. *Journal of Gerontology: Social Sciences* 50B:1:S24-S34.

Weeks, Jeffrey, Brian Heaphy, & Catherine Donovan. 2001. *Same sex intimacies: Families of choice and other life experiments.* New York: Routledge.

Weiss, Robert S. 1973. *Loneliness: The experience of emotional and social isolation.* Cambridge, MA: MIT Press.

Wellman, Barry. 1990. The place of kinfolk in personal community networks. *Marriage and Family Review* 15:1/2:195–228.

Wellman, Barry. 1992. Which types of ties and networks provide what kinds of social support? *Advances in Group Processes* 9:207–235.

Wells, Yvonne D., & Hal L. Kendig. 1997. Health and well-being of spouse caregivers and the widowed. *The Gerontologist* 37:5:666–674.

Wenger, G. Clare, & Vanessa Burholt. 2001. Differences over time in older people's relationships with children, grandchildren, nieces and nephews in rural North Wales. *Ageing and Society* 21:567–590.

Wenger, G. Clare, Pearl A. Dykstra, Tuula Melkas, & Kees C. P. M. Knipscheer. 2007. Social embeddedness and late-life parenthood. *Journal of Family Issues* 28:11:1419–1456.

Wenger, G. Clare, & Dorothy Jerome. 1999. Change and stability in confidant relationships: Findings from the Bangor Longitudinal Study of Ageing. *Journal of Aging Studies* 13:3:269–294.

Wenger, G. Clare, Anne Scott, & Nerys Patterson. 2000. How important is parenthood?: Childlessness and support in old age in England. *Ageing and Society* 20:161–182.

Whipple, Vicky. 2006. *Lesbian widows: Invisible grief.* New York: Harrington.

White, Lynn. 1992. The effect of parental divorce and remarriage on parental support for adult children. *Journal of Family Issues* 13:2:234–250.

White, Lynn. 1998. Who's counting? Quasi-facts and stepfamilies in reports of number of siblings. *Journal of Marriage and Family* 60:3:725–733.

White, Lynn. 2001. Sibling relationships over the life course: A panel analysis. *Journal of Marriage and Family* 63:555–568.

White, Lynn K., & Agnes Riedmann. 1992a. When the Brady Bunch grows up: Step-/ half- and full sibling relations in adulthood. *Journal of Marriage and Family* 54:1:197–208.

White, Lynn K., & Agnes Riedmann. 1992b. Ties among adult siblings. *Social Forces* 7:1:85–102.

White, Lynn K., & Stacy L. Rogers. 1997. Strong support but uneasy relationships: Coresidence and adult children's relationships with their parents. *Journal of Marriage and Family* 59:1:62–76.

Whiteman, Shawn D., Susan M. McHale, & Ann C. Crouter. 2007. Longitudinal changes in marital relationships: The role of offspring's pubertal development. *Journal of Marriage and Family* 69:4:1005–1020.

White-Means, Shelley I., & Rose M. Rubin. 2004. Is there equity in the home health care market? Understanding racial patterns in the use of formal home health care. *Journal of Gerontology: Social Sciences* 59B:4:S220-S229.

Wielink, Gina, Robbert Huijsman, & Joseph McDonnell. 1997. Preferences for care: A study of the elders living independently in the Netherlands. *Research on Aging* 19:2:174–198.

Wierzalis, Edward A., Bob Barrett, Mark Pope, & Michael Rankins. 2006. Gay men and aging: Sex and intimacy. Pp. 91–109 in Douglas Kimmel, Tara Rose, & Steven David (Eds.), *Lesbian, gay, bisexual, and transgender aging: Research and clinical perspectives.* New York: Columbia University Press.

Williams, Beverly Rosa, Patricia Sawyer Baker, Richard M. Allman, & Jeffrey M. Roseman. 2006. The feminization of bereavement among community-dwelling older adults. *Journal of Women & Aging* 18:3:3–18.

Williams, Cara. 2004. The sandwich generation. *Perspectives* 5:9:5–12. Statistics Canada Cat. No. 75-001-XIE.

Williams, Ishan C. 2005. Emotional health of black and white dementia caregivers: A contextual examination. *Journal of Gerontology: Psychological Sciences* 60B:6:P287-P295.

Williams, Kipling, & Steve A. Nida. 2005. Obliviously ostracizing singles. *Psychological Inquiry* 16:2&3:127–131.

Williams, Kristi, & Alexandra Dunne-Bryant. 2006. Divorce and adult psychological well-being: Clarifying the role of gender and child age. *Journal of Marriage and Family* 68:5:1178–1196.

Williams, Kristi, & Debra Umberson. 2004. Marital status, marital transitions, and health: A gendered life course perspective. *Journal of Health and Social Behavior* 48:81–98.

Willson, Andrea E., Kim M. Shuey, & Glen H. Elder Jr. 2003. Ambivalence in the relationship of adult children to aging parents and in-laws. *Journal of Marriage and Family* 65:1055–1072.

Wilmoth, Janet M. 2000. Unbalanced social exchanges and living arrangement transitions among older adults. *The Gerontologist* 40:1:64–74.

Wilmoth, Janet, & Gregor Koso. 2002. Does marital history matter?: Marital status and health outcomes among preretirement adults. *Journal of Marriage and Family* 64:1:254–268.

Wilson, Gail. 1995. "I'm the eyes and she's the arms": Changes in advanced old age. Pp. 98–113 in Sara Arber & Jay Ginn (Eds.), *Connecting gender and ageing: A sociological approach.* Buckingham, UK: Open University Press.

Wineberg, Howard, & James McCarthy. 1998. Living arrangements after divorce. *Journal of Divorce and Remarriage* 29:1/2:131–146.

Winton, Chester A. 2002. *Children as caregivers: Parental & parentified children.* Boston: Allyn & Bacon.

Wiscott, R., & K. Kopera-Frye. 2000. Sharing the culture: Adult grandchildren's perception of intergenerational relations. *International Journal of Aging & Human Development* 51:199–215.

Wisensale, Steven K. 2001. *Family leave policy: The political economy of work and family in America.* Armonk, NY: Sharpe.

Wolf, Douglas A. 1990. Household patterns of older women. *Research on Aging* 12:4:463–486.

Wolf, Douglas A., Vicki Freedman, & Beth J. Soldo. 1997. The division of family labor: Care for elderly parents. *The Journal of Gerontology* Series B:52B (Special Issue): 102–109.

Wolf, Rosalie. 2001. Understanding elder abuse and neglect. Pp. 258–261 in Alexis J. Walker, Margaret Manoogian-I'Dell, Lori A. McGraw, & Diana L. G. White (Eds.), *Families in later life: Connections and transitions.* Thousand Oaks, CA: Pine Forge.

Wolfe, David A. 2001. Elder abuse intervention: Lessons from child abuse and domestic violence initiatives. Pp. 501–525 in Richard J. Bonnie & Robert B. Wallace (Eds.), *Elder mistreatment: Abuse, neglect, and exploitation in an aging America.* Washington, DC: The National Academies Press.

Wolfinger, Nicholas H. 2001. The effects of family structure of origin on offspring cohabitation duration. *Sociological Inquiry* 71:3:293–313.

Wolfinger, Nicholas H. 2005. *Understanding the divorce cycle: The children of divorce in their own marriages.* New York: Cambridge University Press.

Wolfinger, Nicholas H. 2007. Hello and goodbye to divorce reform. *National Council on Family Relations Report* 52:4:F15-F16.

Wolfson, Christina, Richard Handfield-Jones, Kathleen Cranley Glass, Jacqueline McClaran, & Edward Keyserlingk. 1993. Adult children's perceptions of their responsibility to provide care for dependent elderly parents. *The Gerontologist* 33:3:315–323.

Wolinsky, Frederic D., & Robert J. Johnson. 1992. Widowhood, health status, and the use of health services by older adults: A cross-sectional and prospective approach. *Journal of Gerontology: Social Sciences* 47:1:S8–16.

Wong, Rebeca, Chiara Capoferro, & Beth J. Soldo. 1999. Financial assistance from middle-aged couples to parents and children: Racial-ethnic differences. *Journal of Gerontology: Social Sciences* 54B:3:S145-S153.

Worth, Heather, Alison Reid, & Karen McMillan. 2002. Somewhere over the rainbow: Love, trust and monogamy in gay relationships. *Journal of Sociology* 38:3:237–253.

Wright, Carol L., & Joseph W. Maxwell. 1991. Social support during adjustment to later-life divorce: How adult children help their parents. *Journal of Divorce and Remarriage* 15:3/4:21–48.

Wu, Zheng. 1995. Remarriage after widowhood: A marital history study of older Canadians. *Canadian Journal on Aging* 14:4:719–736.

Wu, Zheng, & Margaret Penning. 1997. Marital instability after midlife. *Journal of Family Issues* 18:5:459–478.

Wu, Zheng, & Michael S. Pollard. 1998. Social support among unmarried childless elderly persons. *Journal of Gerontology: Social Sciences* 53B:6:S324-S335.

Wu, Zheng, & Christoph M. Schimmele. 2007. Uncoupling in later life. *Generations* 31:3:41–46.

Yarry, Sarah J., Elizabeth K. Stevens, & T. J. McCallum. 2007. Cultural influences on spousal caregiving. *Generations* 31:3:24–30.

Yee, Jennifer L., & Richard Schulz. 2000. Gender differences in psychiatric morbidity among family caregivers: A review and analysis. *The Gerontologist* 40:2:147–164.

Yorgason, Jeremy B., Fred P. Piercy, & Susan K. Piercy. 2007. Acquired hearing impairment in older couple relationships: An exploration of couple resilience processes. *Journal of Aging Studies* 21:3:215–228.

Young, Rosalie F., & Eva Kahana. 1995. The context of caregiving and well-being outcomes among African and Caucasian Americans. *The Gerontologist* 35:2:225–232.

Zajicek, Anna, Toni Calasanti, Cristie Ginther, & Julie Summers. 2006. Intersectionality and age relations: Unpaid care work and Chicanas. Pp. 175–197 in Toni M. Calasanti & Kathleen F. Slevin (Eds.), *Age matters: Realigning feminist thinking.* New York: Routledge.

Zhang, Zhenmei. 2006. Marital history and the burden of cardiovascular disease in midlife. *The Gerontologist* 46:2:266–270.

Zhang, Zhenmei, & Mark D. Hayward. 2001. Childlessness and the psychological well-being of older persons. *Journal of Gerontology: Social Sciences* 56B:5:S311-S320.

Zhang, Zhenmei, & Mark D. Hayward. 2006. Gender, the marital life course, and cardiovascular disease in late midlife. *Journal of Marriage and Family* 68:3:639–657.

Zick, Cathleen D., & Ken R. Smith. 1991. Marital transitions, poverty, and gender differences in mortality. *Journal of Marriage and Family* 53:327–336.

Zsembik, Barbara A. 1996. Preferences for coresidence among older Latinos. *Journal of Aging Studies* 10:1:69–81.

Index

Aboriginal groups, 277
Adoption, 12, 60, 143, 181, 228, 280
Affectional solidarity, 139
African Americans
  caregivers for intimate partners,
    85, 88–89
  caregivers for older parents, 158,
    159, 166, 168
  childless, 40, 181, 243
  cohabitation by, 128, 173
  co-residence by, 174, 198
  divorced, 32, 35, 118, 120, 209
  egalitarian marital relationships, 66
  fertility rates, 38
  financial abuse of older persons
    among, 285
  gay/lesbian, 76, 170
  geographic location of, 48
  grandparent-grandchild relations, 42,
    193–194, 198–199, 200, 201
  institutionalization of, 43–44, 48,
    158, 273, 278
  interdependence in marital
    relationships, 66
  life expectancy, 26
  living arrangements of, 43–44, 45,
    47, 158
  marital satisfaction among, 57, 68, 111
  marital status, 28, 30 (table), 32
  marital status, by gender, 35,
    36 (table), 37
  remarriage rates of, 124
  same-sex marriage recognition by, 280
  sexuality and, 72
  sibling relationships of, 227, 229, 232,
    243, 250–251
  single, 35, 37, 43, 95, 96, 104
  step relations, 217, 218

  support for adult by, 66, 217, 246
  support for child by, 170
  unemployment and, 197
  widowed, 32, 35, 111–112
  See also Racial and ethnic groups
African American women
  caregivers, 166
  divorce rates, 32
  head of household, 48, 121, 175, 198–199
  poverty of, 121, 174, 198
  single mothers, 100
  support networks, 66
AGE. *See* Americans for Generational
  Equity
Age-condensed family, 25
Age-gapped family, 25
Ageism
  cultural emphasis on youth, 10, 55, 72,
    80, 105, 132
  in employment, 81, 289
  sexism and, 71, 81
  sexuality and, 59–63, 132
Agency within structure, 16
Age-related vulnerability, 282–283
Aging research. *See* Research
AIDS/HIV, 91, 117, 170–171, 199, 249
Alaska Native Americans, grandparents as
  caregivers, 198
Alzheimer's disease, 88, 158, 167, 206
Ambivalence
  in sibling relationships, 255, 231
  intergenerational, 139, 140-141, 156, 160
  psychological, 140-141
  sociological, 141, 142
American Indians, grandparents as
  caregivers, 198
  Americans for Generational Equity
  (AGE), 266

About the Author

Ingrid Arnet Connidis is Professor of Sociology at the University of Western Ontario, London, Canada. In 2001 she spent a stimulating term at Oregon State University researching family gerontology as the recipient of the Petersen Visiting Scholar Award. Her work has been published in a range of journals, including *Journal of Marriage and Family, Journal of Gerontology: Social Sciences, Research on Aging, Journal of Family Studies, Journal of Aging Studies,* and *Canadian Journal on Aging.* She has also contributed chapters to a range of books related to aging, family relations, and feminist scholarship. In 2004 she and Julie McMullin were awarded the Richard Kalish Innovative Publication Award from the Gerontological Society of America for their work on ambivalence ("Sociological Ambivalence and Family Ties: A Critical Perspective." *Journal of Marriage and Family,* 2002:64:3:558–567). In her quantitative and qualitative research, she has explored various facets of aging and family relationships, including work–family balance, sibling ties, family ties across generations, the family ties of gay and lesbian adults, and step relationships.